Masters *of* BEDLAM

Masters *of*

BEDLAM

THE TRANSFORMATION

OF THE

MAD-DOCTORING TRADE

Andrew Scull

Charlotte MacKenzie

Nicholas Hervey

PRINCETON UNIVERSITY PRESS · PRINCETON, NEW JERSEY

Copyright © 1996 by Princeton University Press

Published by Princeton University Press, 41 William Street,

Princeton, New Jersey 08540

In the United Kingdom: Princeton University Press,

Chichester, West Sussex

Library of Congress Cataloging-in-Publication Data

Scull, Andrew T.

Masters of Bedlam : the transformation of the mad-doctoring trade / Andrew Scull,

Charlotte MacKenzie, Nicholas Hervey.

p.   cm.

Includes bibliographical references and index.

ISBN 0-691-03411-7 (CL : alk. paper)

1. Psychiatrists—Great Britian—Biography.   2. Psychiatry—Great Britain—

History—19th century.   I. MacKenzie, Charlotte, 1957– .

II. Hervey, Nicholas, 1952– .   III. Title.

RC450.G7S284   1994

616.89'00941'09034—dc20   96-12051 CIP

This book has been composed in Berkeley Typeface

Princeton University Press books are printed
on acid-free paper and meet the guidelines for
permanence and durability of the Committee on
Production Guidelines for Book Longevity
of the Council on Library Resources

Printed in the United States of America by Princeton Academic Press

10   9   8   7   6   5   4   3   2   1

CONTENTS

ILLUSTRATIONS

ACKNOWLEDGEMENTS

THIS BOOK could not have been written without the generous help and assistance we have received from a multitude of librarians and archivists. We cannot thank them all by name, but it would be remiss of us not to acknowledge those who have been most helpful to us and those who have granted us permission to use and quote from an array of invaluable archival and manuscript materials. These include: the county archivist for Lancashire, and Mrs. Jacqueline Crosby of the Lancashire County Record Office; Patricia Allderidge, archivist at the Royal Bethlem and Maudsley Hospitals; the library staff at the Wellcome Institute for the History of Medicine in London, and at the Royal Colleges of Physicians of London and Edinburgh; the Royal College of Surgeons; the Leicestershire County Record Office; the Warwickshire County Record Office; the librarian at University College London; the National Register of Archives; the Public Record Office; Somerset House; the Greater London Record Office; Dr. F.J.G. Jeffries; the Houghton Library, Harvard University; the Victoria and Albert Museum (materials from the John Forster Papers reprinted with the permission of the Board of Trustees of the Victoria and Albert Museum); the British Library; Bristol University Library; and the staff at the interlibrary loan desk of the Biomedical Library at the University of California, San Diego. It seems invidious to mention individual scholars, when so many have helped to shape our thinking about this subject matter and have contributed generously of their knowledge when we have consulted them, but special thanks are due William F. Bynum, David Gollaher, and Jonathan Andrews. An earlier version of chapter 3 first appeared in W. F. Bynum, R. Porter, and M. Shepherd (eds.), *The Anatomy of Madness* Vol. 1 (1985); and a briefer version of chapter 4 formed the introduction to A. Scull (ed.), *The Asylum as Utopia: W.A.F. Browne and the Mid-Nineteenth Century Consolidation of Psychiatry* (1991). We are grateful to Routledge, the publisher of both books, for permission to draw upon those materials here.

We are most grateful to the Wellcome Institute Library, London, for permission to reprint the pictures of Old Bethlem Hospital, John Conolly as a young and an old man, the Middlesex County Asylum at Hanwell, William Alexander Francis Browne, the Crichton Royal Asylum, Types of Madness, and John Charles Bucknill; to the National Library of Medicine, Bethesda, Maryland, for permission to reproduce the pictures of John Haslam and of Henry Maudsley as a young and an old man (and to Michael Collie for providing us with copies of the Maudsley photographs); to the librarian of the London Borough of Ealing for permission to reproduce the picture of Lawn House; to the Devon County Council for permission to reproduce the picture of Devon County Asylum; to the archivist of the Royal Bethlem and

Maudsley Hospitals for permission to reproduce the pictures of Mary Anne and Sir Alexander Morison and of the third Bethlem Hospital; to the Royal College of Physicians, London, for permission to reproduce the picture of Samuel Gaskell; and to the Scottish National Portrait Gallery, Edinburgh, for permission to reproduce the painting of Sir Alexander Morison by Richard Dadd.

This is perhaps the appropriate place to indicate the nature of the collaboration that has produced this book. The conception of the book as a series of linked biographies of major nineteenth-century alienists and the choice of the individuals we would write about were Andrew Scull's. The basic approach we have taken to the subject is also his, and to ensure stylistic unity, he took responsibility for producing the final draft of the entire manuscript.

Working within that larger framework, Nicholas Hervey wrote chapter 5 on the life and career of Alexander Morison, producing a lengthy first draft that Andrew Scull then rewrote and expanded upon. In the course of planning and writing chapter 6, on Samuel Gaskell, Andrew Scull drew to a significant extent upon materials in Nicholas Hervey's doctoral thesis. Charlotte MacKenzie produced the original drafts of chapter 7 on John Charles Bucknill and chapter 8 on Henry Maudsley. Andrew Scull then revised and amplified the draft chapter on Bucknill and added substantial amounts of new material in the process of reworking and broadening the coverage of the chapter on Henry Maudsley. In the course of our collaboration, as the book took shape, various drafts of the individual chapters circulated among the three of us for comments and suggestions. On two occasions, as well, we were able to meet together in London to coordinate our individual research activities and to reach agreement on various interpretative issues. Working together when separated most of the time by six thousand miles has been a challenge, but an enjoyable and (we hope) a productive one.

Masters of
BEDLAM

Chapter One

THE TRANSFORMATION OF THE

MAD-DOCTORING TRADE

> I am willing to pay Adoration to Virtue wherever I can meet with
> it, with a Proviso, that I shall not be oblig'd to admit any as such
> where I can see no Self-denial, or to judge of Mens Sentiments
> from their Words, where I have their Lives before me.
> (*Bernard Mandeville*, The Fable of the Bees)

> The class of people taking care of lunatics has, within my own
> experience, very much improved, I remember when almost
> every man who kept an asylum was an eccentric, or had
> something peculiar about him, or strange in his appearance,
> and was more calculated to knock a patient down than
> to cure him; that was the general character of them.
> (*John Conolly, testimony before the House of Commons Select
> Committee on the Care and Treatment of Lunatics, 1859*)

> I think it is a very hard case for a man to be locked up in an
> asylum and kept there; you may call it anything you like,
> but it is a prison.
> (*Sir James Coxe, testimony before the House of Commons Select
> Committee on the Operations of the Lunacy Laws, 1877*)

AS IS by now generally acknowledged, in Britain the massive internment of the mad in what were asserted to be therapeutic institutions is essentially a nineteenth-century phenomenon.[1] Though fugitive references to madhouses can be traced back to the seventeenth century, and perhaps before, and though a recognizable "trade in lunacy" clearly became established over the course of the eighteenth century, only after 1800 did systematic provision begin to be made for segregating the insane into specialized institutions. The birth of the asylum in its turn was intimately bound up with the emergence and consolidation of a newly self-conscious group of people laying claim to expertise in the treatment of mental disorder and asserting their right to a monopoly over its identification and treatment. It is with this increasingly organized specialism that this book is concerned. We seek to understand the growth and development of a collective consciousness and organization among a subset of medical men, the ancestors of the modern profession now called psychiatry. And we have chosen to do so through a focus on the interlocking lives and careers of a handful of elite figures whose practices jointly encompass the entire century.

We are aware, of course, that biography has, for the most part, fallen into disfavour in the history of medicine, as in the history of science more generally. Hagiographies of "great men" written by amateurs who lack even the rudiments of historical training have given the whole genre a bad name. Viewed uncritically, and without attention to structures, context, or culture, the lives of a handful of heroes are transmuted into myths bearing no discernable relationship to the complexities of the past—useful ideological constructs for those bent on creating an idealized fiction as a support for their current professional identity, but useless for those seeking a more balanced understanding of the historical record.

Such deficiencies are by no means intrinsic to a biographical approach.[2] In examining the lives of individuals, nothing precludes our attending to these broader structural and contextual concerns—indeed, to do so is essential if we are really to grasp the meaning and significance of their existence and accomplishments. We take seriously the contention that people make their own history, and paying close attention to individual lives obviously provides us with the most vivid sense of just how they accomplish that task. But we are equally aware that human action is always constrained by and responsive to the wider social and cultural context within which it occurs. In examining this constant interplay of structure and agency, we necessarily confront the inherently interactive and collective dimensions of each individual's life. Paradoxically, therefore, the very endeavour to capture what is particular and idiosyncratic about a given actor simultaneously requires us to attend most closely to the realm of the social. Put another way, as we shall seek to demonstrate in the chapters that follow, the more we seek to understand the individual dimensions of someone's life, the more inescapably we find ourselves engaged in an essentially sociological enterprise.[3]

How else, after all, are we to understand lives and careers but by attending to the "particular configuration of social institutional, and intellectual options" available to the protagonists we are interested in?[4] In the process of confronting and coping with a given social reality, even in attempting to modify and transform the options available at a given historical moment, individuals may be making their own place in history. Yet their life courses are also at once constituting and revealing the contours of the culture and social structure within which they exist and struggle, succeed and fail.

Nineteenth-century Britain was the first example of a society turned upside down by the advent of industrial capitalism. The maturing of the Industrial Revolution that had its origins in the second half of the preceding century transformed Britain's politics, culture, social organization, even physical landscape. The revolutionary transformation in people's lives was predicated upon the creation of an urban-industrial civilization of a radically novel sort. It brought in its train a massive rise in human productivity, an expansion of manufacturing and commerce, and a profound alteration even of the agricultural sector of the economy, as the values and disciplines of the marketplace systematically penetrated every corner and cranny of British society.

Not least, the new order witnessed massive upheavals in the social structure associated with the birth of a new class society: the fracturing of old social hierarchies and the creation and expansion of whole new categories of collective actors on the historical scene. Of utmost significance for our present purposes, these included not just an industrial and commercial bourgeoisie (and their counterpart, a burgeoning proletariat) but also an ever-greater enlargement of the knowledge-based professional classes. For the vast increase of wealth that was created in the wake of a mature capitalism created manifold opportunities for the sale of services in the marketplace, with human capital and specialised expertise increasingly the resource from which a growing segment of the middle classes drew their sustenance.

The rise of psychiatry as an organized profession, with which we shall be concerned in the following chapters, is thus but a particular instance of a much broader phenomenon, what Harold Perkin has termed "the rise of professional society."[5] During the nineteenth century, knowledge—particularly but not exclusively scientific knowledge—increasingly became a resource from which a variety of newly consolidating and self-conscious groups sought to extract a living. Mad-doctors, or as they increasingly preferred to call themselves, alienists or medical psychologists,[6] were merely one of a whole array of groups seeking recognition and social status on this basis.

Unlike their entrepreneurial counterparts in the manufacturing sector, the new professionals were in the business of selling something intangible: skill and expertise rather than material goods. Each such group claimed the ability not only to diagnose and understand problems on a more subtle and sophisticated level than was granted to laymen who lacked their specialized knowledge but also to prescribe remedies and solutions on the basis of their greater technical expertise. To the extent that they could persuade others of their talents and capacities and convince relevant audiences that their performances were worthy of hire, professionals were able to transform their standing in the social division of labour. In alchemical fashion, the abstract human capital they claimed to embody could be transubstantiated into real claims on resources: enhanced power, prestige, and influence, to be sure, but also incomes reflective of the scarcity and assumed social value of the services only they were in a position to provide. Professionals sought, as Perkin puts it, to secure "in strict Ricardian terms a rent for the scarce resource of their esoteric skill. The size of the rent, the difference between the professional fee or salary and the price of common labour, was the measure of the success of each profession in claiming that scarcity value and establishing its status. . . . Their rewards were negotiated in the wider societal market of prestige and the social value placed on their service rather than by the sale of their labour in the economic market place."[7]

The professional project, moreover, was still more ambitious and complicated than Perkin here implies. For professionals sought to secure not just an economic but also a social "rent" in return for supplying their services. They were not and could not be satisfied, in other words, with an increase in the financial returns accruing to those who engaged in a particular line of work because they simultaneously coveted a comparable elevation of their standing in the social hierarchy—if possible, public recognition that they belonged among the ranks of "gentlemen." Behaviour that was crassly materialistic and self-interested, or that in too-obvious fashion conjured up the offensive odour of "trade," might serve to advance an occupation's economic interests but threatened to prove fatal to its social aspirations. Likewise, forms of employment that implied a subordinate (and thus servile) status were deeply damaging to the attempt to transform a particular occupation into "a calling by which a gentleman, not born to the inheritance of a gentleman's allowance of good things, might ingeniously obtain the same by some exercise of his abilities."[8]

Like others engaged in this project of collective social mobility,[9] mad-doctors had to seek public approval and trust, and as they struggled to establish control over a particular territory and to define and protect the boundaries of their jurisdiction, they necessarily found themselves engaged in a never-ending campaign of persuasion and propaganda. Trust is vital to the professional because he or she needs to secure assent to claims to possess, not just skills and knowledge that the laity lacks, but skills and knowledge the professional argues the public is not even in a position to assess with any degree of precision.[10] Likewise, the laity must come to trust that members of the profession will exercise their skills in a disinterested fashion and in large degree must be persuaded to rely upon the professionals' own valuation of their knowledge. Yet trust was a particularly difficult commodity for mad-doctors to acquire, not least because their involvement in the trade in lunacy prompted endemic suspicion about their motives,[11] and because their claims to possess expertise in the identification and treatment of madness provoked persistent scepticism even among those laymen most heavily involved in the campaign for lunacy reform.[12] The prominent role played by medical men in the whole series of scandals about treatment in asylums and madhouses that erupted in the first half of the nineteenth century only intensified the difficulty of the task they confronted.

Yet, in the face of these and other obstacles, a recognized specialism did emerge over the course of the nineteenth century and secured some significant measure of public support and patronage. As the number of madmen known to the authorities grew from two or three thousand in 1800 to almost one hundred thousand a century later, their guardians successfully constituted themselves as the public arbiters of mental disorder, the experts in its diagnosis and disposal. They created a professional organization to defend and advance their interests and edited journals and wrote monographs to provide a forum for transmitting (and giving visible evidence of) the body of expert knowledge to which they laid claim. During Victoria's long reign, they increasingly dominated public discourse about insanity, and in the process, they elaborated and refined a set of career structures and opportunities for themselves. Fragile as their public standing might be, marginal and somewhat embarrassing as their medical brethren might find them,[13] psychiatrists nonetheless had secured some accoutrements of professional status, if only as the custodians of a chronically incapacitated and generally economically deprived clientele and as advisers on mental hygiene to a broader population concerned to avoid such a dismal destiny.

Even more than most professions, however, psychiatry was to find that its fate was bound up with the burgeoning growth of an administrative state. At every turn, its practitioners discovered that they were dependent upon state approval, supervision, and sponsorship. The overwhelming majority of their nominal clientele could not afford to pay for the services they offered; the cost of confinement in an asylum was prohibitive for all but the most well-to-do segments of the population so the network of asylums for paupers was necessarily constructed and maintained by taxpayers. A major segment of the profession consequently consisted of salaried employees in the public sector and direct dependents of the state apparatus, broadly defined. The pervasive presence of the state made itself felt in other respects as well. Earlier abuses and the persistence of a private, profit-oriented madhouse sector to which rich lunatics were consigned prompted the creation of a state inspectorate, to whose opinions all segments of the profession were necessarily beholden: the superintendents of the pauper asylums because official criticism could prompt their dismissal; and their private-sector colleagues and rivals because the Lunacy Commission could withdraw their license to operate and thus bring about their professional ruin. More broadly, of course, as with other professions, alienists' professional standing and privileges ultimately required political and legal guarantees only the state could provide.

These circumstances form the broad contours within which the lives and careers of nineteenth-century mad-doctors unfolded. The creation of the profession was, quite naturally, a long and complicated process—just how complex will become apparent in the chapters that follow—and the circumstances and contingencies that confronted those who sought to specialize in the treatment of the mad changed dramatically over the course of the century. In choosing the subjects of our investigation, we have consciously sought to examine those lives that most clearly exhibit the central features and dilemmas that accompanied the development of the profession and that set out, in starkest relief, the enterprise through which these managers of the mad constructed their own peculiar corner of the social universe.

As we have previously indicated, our study encompasses only a handful of figures, all of whom constituted members of the profession's elite. They are not, in any statistical sense, representative figures, and without question a prosopographical study of the still largely anonymous and unheralded rank-and-file members of the fraternity of mad-doctors would provide a great deal of additional and exceedingly welcome knowledge about the structure of psychiatric lives and careers in the nineteenth century. But studying members of the elite has its own rewards, and these extend considerably beyond the more nuanced portraits one can draw because of the richer historical records that tend to survive in such cases.

Almost by definition, the most prominent alienists played leading roles in the emergence and evolution of the profession. It was, after all, precisely their performances on this particular stage that brought them their measure of eminence. Their actions helped to define and to stretch the limits of medical involvement with the mad, and their ideas constituted the platform on which the profession laid claim to its privileged place in the social division of labour. Conolly and Browne, for instance, together did much to create the utopian vision of the curative asylum that lay at the heart of lunacy reformers' attempts to reshape the character of society's provision for the insane. Together with Bucknill and Gaskell, they subsequently helped to define the role of asylum superintendent, the institutional niche occupied by most of the profession. Gaskell and Browne, who went on to occupy the post of Lunacy Commissioner in England and Scotland, respectively, exercised supervisory authority over their separate realms of asylumdom, while Bucknill founded and edited the profession's principal journal, the *Journal of Mental Science* (and was succeeded as editor by Maudsley).

If all these men have traditionally constituted heroes in the profession's pantheon, John Haslam has perhaps occupied a more dubious status: the most prominent of early nineteenth-century mad-doctors, a man of prodigious energies and talents, but the target of some reformers' most biting criticism, and at the very centre of the most notorious asylum scandal of the century in his position as resident apothecary at Bethlem. As we shall see, in the aftermath of this professional disgrace, he nonetheless was to succeed in rebuilding his reputation and practice, all the while taking issue with many orthodox pieties of his day and voicing scepticism about the very technologies and treatments that were to form the foundation for the mainstream practitioners of the emerging profession—a stance in which he was joined by his friend and professional ally, Alexander Morison. Obviously, as their examples demonstrate, professionalization is neither a unidirectional nor a predictable process.

Other dimensions of Morison's career remind us that, despite our retrospective identification of the Victorian era with the striking and sinister asylum buildings that came to contain in ever-larger quantities "the waifs and strays, the weak and wayward of our race,"[14] the profession was never wholly confined within the walls of the institutional sector. Building upon an earlier model of practice, where madness was merely one of a number of disorders a general physician might venture to treat, Morison sought to advance an alternative, for the most part noninstitutionally based, approach to treating the ravages of mental disorder. And if this approach seemed for a time destined to be cast aside into the dustbin of history, it was ironically revived in somewhat different form by Bucknill and Maudsley in the later stages of their careers, as they grew increasingly impatient with and critical of the limitations and drawbacks of institutional psychiatry and looked instead to the lucrative rewards of a private, office-based consulting practice, attending principally to a whole new class of "nervous" patients inhabiting "the borderlands of insanity."[15]

As we trust these preliminary remarks suggest, small though their numbers may be, the overlapping experiences and activities of these seven men thus allow us a peculiarly intimate and revealing set of insights into the place of psychiatry in nineteenth-century society; and they capture many of the most crucial aspects of its development during that formative period. Taken together, they provide us with far-reaching access into the social worlds of the mad-doctors. Likewise, they allow us to watch in a particularly revealing context the transition from a "world of nepotism, privilege, and aristocratic patronage to the more openly competitive, upwardly mobile Victorian society"[16]—a setting in which knowledge, effort, and shrewd exploitation of one's opportunities could be translated into the means of securing one's livelihood and the foundation for newly organised communities of professionals. Of no less importance than these aspects of the transformation of the mad-doctoring trade, the chance to examine the development of these men's ideas about madness in the context of their struggles to build their lives and careers brings home in the most forcible of fashions just how intricate and intimate are the ties that bind together the realms of the cognitive and the social. This reminds us once more of how ultimately untenable is the once-fashionable distinction between the external and internal histories of medicine and science.[17]

Chapter Two

A BETHLEMETICAL MAD-DOCTOR:

JOHN HASLAM (1764–1844)

> But man, proud man,
> Dress'd in a little brief authority,
> Most ignorant of what he's most assur'd
> (*William Shakespeare*,
> Measure for Measure, *act 2, scene 2*)

> But is there so great Merit and Dexterity in
> being a mad Doctor? The common Prescriptions
> of a Bethlemetical Doctor are a Purge and a Vomit, and a
> Vomit and a Purge over again, and sometimes
> a Bleeding, which is no great Mystery.
> (*Alexander Cruden*, The London Citizen
> Exceedingly Injured, *1739*)

JOHN HASLAM'S career began and ended in obscurity. We know very little indeed of the circumstances of his birth and upbringing, and at his death in 1844, his estate amounted to less than £100.[1] His passing merited only a one-paragraph obituary in the *Lancet*—a cursory and misleading eulogy that managed to omit virtually everything of significance about his life and accomplishments.[2] Yet during the first decade and a half of the nineteenth century, Haslam's caustic pen, his skills as an observer and commentator on madness, and his position as the resident apothecary at the most famous English asylum of this or any other age, combined to place him at the very forefront of the mad-doctoring trade: his books were translated into French and German, and his opinions and observations were quoted liberally and with respect by Pinel and Tuke, who were to become the patron saints of lunacy reform throughout Europe and North America. Even his sudden and shocking fall from professional grace, which ironically occurred at the hands of Tuke's most ardent metropolitan followers, initially only thrust him still further into the limelight by connecting him inextricably if unwillingly with the reform movement that created the legal framework of Victorian asylumdom, with its centralized governmental inspectorate, its vast assemblage of "museums for the collection of insanity,"[3] and its newly organized and self-consciously professional managers of the mad.

Entering the Mad-Doctoring Trade

The bald facts of the first three decades of Haslam's life must be pieced together from a handful of sources, and no surviving evidence of a personal sort helps us understand the series of choices he made with respect to his professional education or subsequently in electing to specialize in the treatment of the mad. We know that he was born in London in 1764, the son of another John Haslam.[4] Of his parents' background and financial circumstances we know nothing directly, though their son's educational history and professional training make it certain that they were at least moderately prosperous. From a comparatively early age, the young Haslam prepared himself for a medical career. In itself, this should occasion little surprise, for as Irvine Loudon has recently shown,[5] the second half of the eighteenth century was an "active, busy, and prosperous" period for rank-and-file practitioners of medicine, one marked by an expanding market for medical services with which the supply of doctors had not yet caught up. The massive expansion of the English economy during this period produced that explosion of "getting and spending" which McKendrick, Brewer, and Plumb have termed "the birth of a consumer society,"[6] and such expansion provided a growing proportion of the population with the wherewithal to pay handsomely for a variety of services, including those of medical men. Still not bedevilled by the overcrowding of the profession that was to drive down medical fees in the first third of the nineteenth century and to render precarious the economic and social standing of many a marginal practitioner, medicine had obvious attractions for an intelligent and ambitious young man with the resources to fund his training.

For that training did not come cheap. Haslam himself informs us that his education began, as was typical at the time,[7] with a "period of apprenticeship" (with whom we do not know). This experience alone, which was all the training that many practitioners obtained, could itself be quite costly.[8] Increasingly, however, the more ambitious were seeking the advantages that accrued from a still more expensive period of clinical instruction and/or enrolling in courses of lectures at a London hospital, a developing mode of medical education that formed "a thriving, expanding industry" by the closing decades of the eighteenth century.[9] Following this path, Haslam attached himself to St. Bartholomew's Hospital, first as "a student . . . and afterwards [as] House Surgeon." Here, he attended George Fordyce's lectures on chemistry, materia medica, and the practice of physic (among the most popular lecture series in London) and worked, "as physician's pupil," under David Pitcairn.[10]

Already well trained by the standards of the time, Haslam now embarked on a still more ambitious course of study; he spent the years between 1785 and 1787 at Edinburgh University, clearly at this time the institution that provided the best formal medical instruction in the English-speaking world. "For more than two years" he attended "the medical and chemical Lectures at Edinburgh," while playing an unusually active role in student affairs. (He was, for instance, "elected a president of the Royal Medical, Natural History, and Chemical Societies,"[11] and, together with Thomas Beddoes and James Mackintosh, protested vigorously when the managers of the Royal Infirmary sought to curtail students' opportunities to observe patients in their institution.[12]) For unknown reasons, however, he left without an M.D., proceeding to yet further studies "at Upsal [sic], in Sweden"; before "lastly, [enrolling] at Pembroke Hall, in the University of Cambridge," where, once again, he left before obtaining a degree.[13]

This was a long, expensive, and in many ways an impressive professional pedigree. However, Haslam's curious failure to obtain an M.D. had considerable practical implications. Lacking this formal qualification, he was precluded from practicing at the elite level of London medicine, as a physician, qualifying instead as a member of the Corporation of Surgeons. Perhaps he lacked the social and financial capital essential to building a physician's practice and so elected not to try. Certainly, his subsequent career was to demonstrate no want of ambition or lack of confidence in his own abilities. At all events, within the hierarchical world of English medicine, and particularly in London, the absence of a degree meant that he was inevitably consigned to subordinate status.

Judging from parish records, Haslam moved back to the metropolis in the late 1780s, for we know that he baptized his son at St. Leonard's Church in Shoreditch in June of 1790. With the exception of this fugitive glimpse of him, however, his private life and the nature and extent of his practice in these years remain wholly unknown.[14] Only with his appointment as an apothecary to Bethlem Hospital, in late July 1795, does his career begin to emerge from the shadows.

Haslam's own later writings suggest, though they do not conclusively demonstrate, that prior to his successful application for the vacant post at Bethlem he had somehow been involved in the management of the mad for no more than three or four years, since some time in 1791. To be sure, one of the two papers he had offered to the Royal Medical Society during his student days at Edinburgh had dealt with syphilis and included some limited attention to the brain. But the etiological connection of syphilis with subsequent insanity (in the form of general paresis) was not widely suspected until the late nineteenth century and not definitively demonstrated till early in the twentieth; and Haslam himself specifically denied that "secondary infection" with "venereal pus" extended to the brain, "having examined many venereal heads, without observing any disease in that organ."[15]

Nonetheless, his decision to enter upon a career as a mad-doctor was scarcely idiosyncratic or isolated. On the contrary, one of the most notable features of the last third of the eighteenth century was the rising tide of interest, among medical men and laymen alike, in understanding and treating madness: a development that certainly gained added impetus by the gossip and attention given to George III's recurrent bouts of "mania"[16]—but one with far broader social and cultural roots.[17] Edinburgh was a particularly prolific source of medical men interested in insanity, and among Haslam's contemporaries and near contemporaries, several were prominent in this line of practice: Thomas Arnold,[18] John Ferriar,[19] Joseph Mason Cox,[20] Alexander Crichton,[21] Edward Long Fox,[22] William Hallaran,[23] Alexander Morison,[24] Andrew Halliday,[25] to name just some. William Pargeter, Haslam's fellow student at Barts, likewise began by trying to establish a name for himself in the field,[26] before giving up the practice of medicine to serve as a chaplain in the army; and elsewhere those with Oxbridge pedigrees jostled with a broad spectrum of those with less socially reputable claims to the title of doctor, divines (Anglican and nonconformist alike),[27] and laymen and women from a variety of backgrounds,[28] for some portion of the available clientele.

In substantial measure, of course, this burgeoning interest both reflected and helped foment the growth of a novel market in the management of the mad, a development contemporaries referred to as "the trade in lunacy."[29] The mad and the mopish, the distracted and the deranged, the delusional and the troubled in mind, were (and are) not merely disturbed, but profoundly disturbing: often themselves in great distress and simultaneously the source of great stress on the lives of those forced to interact and to cope with them; a threat, both symbolic and practical, to the integrity of the social fabric; and a profound burden and source of worry to others as they sought to conduct the business of daily life. Whether ranting and raving or melancholy and withdrawn, the insane imposed (as they continue to impose) upheaval and uncertainty at every turn, provoking a kaleidoscope of emotions and a host of practical problems for relatives and the community at large: commotion and disarray in the family; shame and social stigma; fear of violence to people and property; the threat of suicide; and the looming financial disasters that flow from the inability to work or the unwise expenditure of one's material resources. The problems were scarcely novel, but the increased affluence of many segments of Hanoverian England and the entrepreneurial character of a civil society in which people eagerly sought new opportunities to gain a living prompted families with means to be willing to pay others to assume some portion of these troubles for them and provided no shortage of volunteers for the task. Madhouses, as Roy Porter puts it, "arose from the same soil which generated demand for general practitioners, dancing masters, man midwives, face painters, drawing tutors, estate managers, landscape painters, architects, journalists and that host of other white collar, service, and quasi-professional occupations which a society with increased economic surplus and pretensions to civilization first found it could afford, and soon found it could not do without."[30]

For the most part, as this suggests, the earliest establishments catering to the mad tended to concentrate their attentions on the well-to-do, peddling the promise of discreet silence for families anxious to draw a veil over the existence of insanity in their midst. Here was the most lucrative segment of the market, and Haslam himself was among the many who recognized "that considerable fortunes have been accumulated by the proprietors of receptacles for the insane."[31] It was, nonetheless, not this segment of the mad-doctoring trade that he elected to enter, a decision that probably reflected the economic realities of his situation quite as much as any scruples he might have had about a business that already enjoyed a distinctly unsavory reputation.

To be sure, he was well aware that involvement with a private madhouse had potentially negative effects on one's social standing,[32] and one should not underestimate the natural worry this would have provoked in an upwardly mobile man whose claims to gentlemanly status were already precarious. Haslam was subsequently to exhibit an almost obsessive concern with "the honor [sic] and dignity of the healing art,"[33] and he directly acknowledged the stigma that tended to accrue to those identified too closely with a profit-making business: "Whoever may become the proprietor of a house of such description must be regarded as a person deriving his income from trade, and be exposed to all the contingencies of traffic. Like a publican [he must seek] the grant and renewal of his license. . . . This species of farming human beings, these accurate estimates of the sufficiency of aliment, where parsimony and profit are inseparable, appear unsuited to the respectability of a learned profession. . . . This process of amalgamating the dealer and chapman with the physician, appears to be equally incongruous and derogatory."[34]

As Haslam must surely have recognized, however, of far greater moment in view of his personal circumstances was the fact that successful involvement in the upper end of this market required the possession of considerable capital with which to launch the enterprise, and a wide range of social contacts, essential to obtain access to a suitably affluent clientele. Largely for these reasons, the top echelon of the business in the metropolis was for the most part controlled by members of the College of Physicians (a group that Haslam, of course, was ineligible to join). His own niche turned out to be more modest, as a salaried employee in a charity asylum and in a distinctly subordinate position at that.

APOTHECARY AT BETHLEM

The Georgian age had witnessed the foundation of many voluntary general hospitals, and from midcentury on, lunatic asylums were created along parallel lines. Bethlem, to whose staff Haslam was now appointed, was, however, of far more ancient vintage, tracing its origins back to a monastic foundation of the thirteenth century. Since the Renaissance, it had become virtually synonymous with the very idea of Unreason, a symbolic space it would continue to occupy well into the nineteenth century. Consequently, although it was by all accounts "the smallest, most specialized and least affluent of the great London hospitals,"[35] it offered some useful advantages as "a means to success [for someone] early in [his] career."[36]

In theory, election of Bethlem's three medical officers was an annual event, in which the whole assembled General Court of Governors of the charity took part. In practice, until Haslam himself proved an exception to the rule, the incumbents were routinely reelected year after year. Restricting opportunities still further, the post of physician to Bethlem was occupied by a veritable dynasty of Monros, for more than a century,[37] and even the lesser position of surgeon was passed from father to son on at least three occasions in the eighteenth century.[38] Haslam's own opportunity materialized on the death of John Gozna, who had served as Bethlem's resident apothecary from 1772. The post was declared vacant on June 16, 1795, and at the election held a bare two weeks later, Haslam was the Governors' choice, winning by a margin of ninety-two votes to six over his only rival, Christopher Buck.[39] (In the interim, Haslam had taken the precaution of paying the hospital clerk, John Woodhouse, a guinea for a list of the Governors,[40] to facilitate his efforts to intercede with the electors in order to secure the post.)

Initially, his retainer was to be no more than "£100 per annum [plus] a House clear of Taxes repaired and furnished with all necessaries Coals, Candles, Beer and necessary provisions"[41] though his salary was subsequently increased substantially, to £335 a year. He was housed within the Hospital itself, and he was ordered "not to absent himself one day without leave of the Bethlem Committee." Directly subordinate to the visiting physician, who also had at his disposal the services of a part-time surgeon, he was charged with visiting "the patients regularly every morning or oftener if necessary," reporting relevant matters to his superior, carrying out whatever instructions he was given by the physician, directing "the Keepers in the management of the Patients during the absence of the Physician, [and taking] especial care that the Druggs [sic] and Medicines are of the best kind." By contrast, Thomas Monro earned his £100 salary in return for attending the weekly meeting with a subcommittee of the Governors on a Saturday morning and for putting in brief appearances on two other days each week,

Figure 2.1. Old Bethlem Hospital, designed by Robert Hooke and constructed in 1675 and 1676. This view is an engraving by Robert White, and dates from the late seventeenth century. By 1815, when the hospital became the focus of a Parliamentary inquiry, it was on the point of physical collapse.

a requirement he honoured more in the breach than the observance. And while Monro, like physicians at other eighteenth-century hospitals and asylums, was both permitted and expected to treat his hospital duties as incidental to a larger and highly lucrative private practice, the Governors insisted that the apothecary was "to devote the whole of his time to the duties of the Hospital, and not to follow any other business."[42]

Doubtless, Haslam did not expect the Governors to enforce the latter provision too stringently. His hospital duties, while more onerous than Monro's were scarcely such as to occupy his full time and energies, and his predecessors as apothecary had clearly accumulated far more wealth than could be attributed to the relatively meagre sums that accrued to them directly from their official position.[43] And from a variety of sources, he did indeed proceed to find ways to augment his hospital salary. We know, for instance, that he received some income for testifying as an expert witness in trials where the issue of insanity was raised, on occasion travelling as far afield as Devonshire.[44] On a more regular and sustained basis, within a few years of taking office, his growing friendship with Sir John Miles, proprietor of the largest private madhouse in London, led to the payment of a steadily increasing retainer in return for "his recommendation of patients to the house."[45]

A prime source of such patients was readily at hand. The Napoleonic Wars presented the government with the problem of how to handle the inevitable cases of mental disturbance in the armed forces, and as the numbers of lunatic soldiers and sailors threatened to overwhelm the capacity of existing makeshift arrangements, the authorities turned to Bethlem for assistance in housing the overflow.[46] As Bethlem in turn could not cope with their numbers, Haslam succeeded in referring the excess on to Miles.[47] Beyond the surreptitious payments he was already receiving from Miles, he then arranged to visit the madhouse twice a week to inspect the naval patients, pocketing a fee for examining every patient sent by the Transport Office.[48] And he also secured the placement of a sizeable number of private patients, "admitted by my certificates,"[49] undoubtedly a source of still further fees. Such, for the period, were the commonplace actions of a young man attempting to augment his income and improve his professional prospects. The subterranean world of the trade in lunacy was clearly pervaded with arrangements of this sort. Thomas Dunston, the steward and head keeper at the rival establishment of St. Luke's, regularly sent paying patients to Warburton's madhouses at Bethnal Green, establishments that his son John served as surgeon.[50] And at the highest levels of the metropolitan mad-doctoring trade, the close personal and professional ties between the fellows of the College of Physicians who were in charge of inspecting madhouses and the physicians they were supposed to supervise were cemented by extensive cross-referrals and joint consultations about patients, a pattern that helped emasculate an already feeble regulatory apparatus.[51]

In any event, Haslam's private efforts to exploit his position at Bethlem for further financial gain positively paled by comparison with the conduct of his superior. The prestige and notoriety that accrued to the Monros as physicians to Bethlem was sufficient by itself to establish them, in the eyes of both their professional peers and patients' families, as expert mad-doctors—men whose very name rapidly became all but synonymous with the trade and to whom the wealthy and the aristocratic turned for discreet advice and service.[52] Such prominence, when coupled with entrepreneurial instincts, had substantial cash value. Thomas Monro's grandfather had been able to demand a fee of £130 for attendance on a single patient in 1733, and he had a substantial private practice among the aristocracy and gentry.[53] John Monro had built substantially on this foundation, opening private madhouses at Clapham,[54] Hackney, and Clerkenwell and serving as visiting physician to others in Chelsea and Bethnal Green.[55] And even though Thomas Monro's primary avocation in life was water-colour painting,[56] he continued—with the active assistance of his son, Edward Thomas—to make the most of the financial opportunities the madhouse business afforded him.[57]

Within Bethlem itself, Haslam occupied a rather awkward position. In theory, he was wholly subordinate to Monro, and so far as the medical treatment of the inmates was concerned, it appears he was indeed subject to the latter's whims and orders. With Monro rarely deigning to visit the patients in the galleries, however, Haslam clearly played the larger role in day-to-day management of the patients. As he himself subsequently acknowledged, his major duties, besides "precisely ascertaining the state of intellect of the patients," lay in "enforcing the humane treatment of the patients, and endeavouring as much as in my power lies, to diffuse as much good order and decency of manners amongst those unhappy people as possible."[58] In print and in person, Haslam was naturally anxious to suggest that his role was extensive and powerful, a claim he later had occasion to rue. But formally his powers were actually extremely limited, and his own ability to influence the daily conduct of the keepers doubtless diminished sharply after 1803, when he no longer resided at the hospital itself.

Unlike those who assumed the superintendency of Victorian asylums, Haslam had no real authority over the steward, the "basketmen," and the "gallery maids" who had most of the contact with patients. He played no role in hiring them, and he most certainly lacked the authority to fire them.[59] On the contrary, the Governors kept such powers of patronage firmly in their own hands. Haslam made frequent complaints to the steward about drunkenness among the keepers, but these were wholly unavailing and can scarcely have endeared him to his subordinates.[60] (The attempts at discipline may, however, help to explain the keepers' later tendency to try to deflect blame on to Haslam rather than Monro for the mistreatment of patients.)[61]

Nor was his job made any easier by the state of the hospital itself. Originally built in 1675–1676 to a design provided by Robert Hooke, Bethlem had been erected on waste ground that had previously been the city ditch. Constructed primarily as a piece of fund-raising rhetoric, the emphasis was on "the Grace and Ornament of the [exterior portions of the] Building," which were modeled on the Tuileries in Paris. What mattered was its ability to attract the patronage and admiration of the elite, rather than the needs and interests of its inmates. Even in the early eighteenth century, contemporaries had commented on "the ironic antithesis between the hospital's palatial exterior and the impoverishment and chaos that lurked within."[62] By the time Haslam arrived on the scene, however, matters were infinitely worse.

The interior arrangements of space continued to defy any systematic attempt to categorize and classify the patients, even should Haslam have wished to do so.[63] More seriously still, the building was literally collapsing around him. The year before Haslam's appointment, the Governors had authorized as much as £1,483 for repairs to the structure. But the problems ran too deep (or rather too shallow) for such palliative moves to work. By April 1799, the difficulties were so acute that they commissioned a surveyor, James Lewis, with the assistance of "such of the Governors as are of the architectural line," to undertake a thorough physical examination of the building and to prepare an estimate of what it would cost to repair.

Submitted the following year, their report must have made depressing reading.[64] The city ditch had been filled, over the years prior to construction, "with such matter or soil, as was then wished to be got quit of, rather, than for the purpose, of forming a base or platform, whereon any building might be placed with safety." To make matters worse, when the hospital came to be built, "it does not appear, the necessary or even common preparations were made; whereby, a requisite stability might be expected, in and from the foundation. . . . The brickwork was [simply] set down, on the surface of the soil, a few inches below the present floor." Above ground, "want of skill, or attention are obvious in the carpentry of the walls and floors . . . there being no bond, or tyes, between the several parts, which should have been strongly connected. . . . The Roofs of the several buildings, are . . . all of them uncommonly heavy. . . . The Walls are, from all these circumstances combined, neither sound, upright, or level . . . hurried and put together, with inconsiderate zeal. . . . [The result was] numerous, and varied fractures and settlements throughout the whole."

The whole edifice was, in consequence, tumbling down, and to attempt repairs "would be unwise and improvident," not to mention dangerous. The Governors would have to allocate steadily increasing sums just to patch things up, and the situation was only likely to worsen. Accordingly, a search began for a site on which to erect a new building, though evidently it was conducted without much enthusiasm. By 1803, further deterioration of the fabric forced Haslam to move out of his apartment. Because the Drapers Company had just offered a seven-acre site in Islington, he took accommodation in the neighbourhood. But the Governors proved reluctant to lay out the necessary funds, and subsequently, when legal complications arose, the Drapers Company withdrew their offer.

The grant of £10,000 from Parliament in 1806, partly in return for a promise that Bethlem would accommodate insane members of the armed forces, seems to have created no greater sense of urgency, and by now the decayed state of the fabric was forcing closure of whole sections of the hospital and a steady decline in the number of inmates who could be accommodated. From 266 patients on December 31, 1800, the census had fallen to only 135 by the end of 1806; by 1814, it would fall further, to only 119 inmates. Even when the Governors finally did make up their minds, agreeing in 1809 to exchange their site and buildings in Moorfields for land in St. George's Fields,[65] it took six more years before the new hospital was ready for occupancy. In the meantime, part of the building had become so unsafe that it had to be demolished, and "the remainder is obliged to be propped up."[66]

During all this time, Haslam had to cope with what were obviously acute physical problems, and with the additional management problems that flowed from living at a considerable distance from the hospital. Neither he nor Monro was consulted about the site and the design of the new establishment, and when the Governors asked him to testify before the House of Lords about the suitability and salubrity of the land in order to secure passage of the legislation authorizing the exchange of properties, he refused to do so; he subsequently complained that the new hospital was below the level of the river at high tide, damp, and unhealthy.[67] However highly he estimated his own talents, it must have been obvious to him that his employers ignored him whenever it suited them.

As Bethlem's physician, and possessed of large quantities of financial and social capital, Thomas Monro had little occasion to seek further means of embellishing his reputation or raising his professional standing. Like his eighteenth-century counterparts with part-time or honorific appointments at general hospitals, he was perfectly content and at liberty to rely on his affiliation with Bethlem as a source of credentials and social connections and thus as his primary means of securing a lucrative fee-paying clientele. It was quite otherwise, however, with Haslam. As a general rule, in the highly hierarchical world of metropolitan medicine, apothecaries were of little account and less professional moment. It scarcely comes as a surprise under the circumstances that his predecessors in the position at Bethlem had toiled in virtual anonymity. Convinced of his own talents and abilities, however, and ambitious for wider professional fortune and fame, Haslam was not inclined to rest content with an obscure and subordinate, even if moderately lucrative, sinecure.

Madness Anatomised

Characteristically, most of the earliest entrants into the trade in lunacy had sought to advertise their professional services, their discretion, their unusual talents and proclivities for restoring the lunatic to sanity; but they had proved distinctly more disinclined either to spell out the technical basis of their claims to expertise or to let slip the recipes they actually employed in managing and treating the mad. In the family businesses where such knowledge was built up, forming the very foundation of their livelihood, the details of the keeper's practices—so far from being matters for public discussion and dissemination—were more often than not treated as trade secrets. Certainly, in the period between the Restoration and the mid–eighteenth century, a number of theoretical medical disquisitions had appeared, attempting to provide some rational account of the moping, the furious, the seriously mad. But these treatises came from physicians with little or no direct involvement in the mad business, and hence they rested for the most part upon a remarkably restricted clinical acquaintance with insanity, perhaps indicative of distaste on the part of these professional gentlemen for any close or continuing contact with those suffering from the disorder.

In the course of the expansion of the mad-business during the reign of George III, however, a rather different literature began to appear, the product of those directly involved in managing the insane. The growth of a free trade in lunacy was busily creating in its train a social space within which therapeutic experimentation could proceed and a marketplace that would be best exploited by those who could persuade potential customers that they possessed special capacities and knowledge that warranted their fees. Anxious to distance themselves from the imputations of quackery that the notion of secret potions and remedies invited, those who enjoyed a more intimate acquaintance with the raving and the melancholic, both laymen and doctors alike, trumpeted their eagerness to contribute to the advancement of knowledge through the publication of the results of their practice.[68] Like their counterparts in general medicine, who had long sustained their claims to special skills even though the basic logic of the antiphlogistic approach was generally comprehended by most educated folk, many of those treating the mad now substituted for specifics, potions, and miraculous remedies a plausible insistence that mental disorder was not to be cured by a simple cookbook approach. Instead, successful intervention demanded the application of known remedies with discrimination and judgement, due attention to the idiosyncrasies of the individual case, and skills in managing patients that could only be acquired through extensive practical experience.

Three years after his appointment, Haslam produced his own addition to this burgeoning literature. Though beginning with a conventional "apology . . . for the present production," which he acknowledged was far from being "a treatise, or compleat disquisition on the subject," he brashly followed this up with an assault on the credentials of his rivals: while "in our own country more books on insanity have been published than in any other . . . if we except Dr. John Monro's Reply to Dr. Battie's Treatise on Madness, there is no work on the subject of mental alienation which has been delivered on the authority of extensive observation and practice." Here, he asserted, was his own claim to distinction because his observations were derived directly from "the treatment of several hundred patients."[69]

Haslam's claim to uniqueness was, of course, an exaggeration. We cite just a handful of prominent counterexamples: Thomas Arnold's ponderous two-volume *Commentaries on the Nature, Kinds, Causes, and Prevention of Insanity, Lunacy, or Madness* was based upon his experiences as owner of Belle Grove Asylum. William Perfect had produced several shorter books recounting the cases he had treated at his madhouse in West Malling, Kent.[70] And John Ferriar's discussions in his *Medical Histories and Reflections* drew directly on his large experience at the Manchester Lunatic Asylum.

Certainly, then, Haslam was not alone in writing as one experienced in treating insanity, but his efforts to assert his superiority over his rivals were not just the product of the arrogance and self-assurance that were such prominent features of his character: they were also a natural and even necessary response for someone trying to make his way in the highly competitive environment within which he found himself. As a profession attains maturity, its internal organization and dominant position in the marketplace serve to structure a particular segment of the social division of labour: to establish career structures and pathways; to create a sense among its practitioners of a shared knowledge base and of being engaged in a common enterprise; and to discipline and keep in bounds the competition between the individuals who form its constituents. But the mad business in the early nineteenth century conspicuously lacked all these features. Fiercely competitive and highly individualistic, it possessed neither a sense of collective identity nor correspondingly a corporate organization; neither established patterns of recruitment or training nor pathways to a successful career; no consensus even on methods of treatment. Only the feeblest of barriers thus existed to set against the powerful inducements to promote one's own capacities and to denigrate one's competitors.

Haslam, moreover, if he could not sustain his more extreme claims to be uniquely qualified to discuss madness, could more reasonably assert that he had best utilized his experience. At one extreme, Arnold's massive tome relied heavily on compilations of classical authorities and was primarily fixated on drawing up a minutely detailed classification of the varieties of insanity, a nosography that he claimed was "drawn with some care and exactness directly from nature." Even his Edinburgh mentor, William Cullen, himself no mean systematizer, found the results arid and devoid of practical utility. Furthermore, the claim to rely on "nature" and first-hand experience was rhetorically undermined by Arnold's repeated invocation of the ancients and the marginal place he accorded to a discussion of his own practice. At the opposite end of the spectrum, Perfect's volumes, mere compilations of his patients and treatments recited without obvious theme or point, were notable for neither acuteness of clinical observation nor originality of any other sort. Haslam thus had little difficulty in distinguishing himself from Perfect's provincial empiricism while simultaneously distancing himself from the "minute particularities and studied discriminations" of the better known Arnold.[71] More skillfully than any of his competitors, he confidently laid claim to the trust of his audience on the basis of his direct, unmediated encounter with madness.[72]

Haslam was not alone in asserting his superiority over most of his rivals. Within three years of the publication of Haslam's small volume, Philippe Pinel issued his *Traité médico-philosophique sur l'aliénation mentale*,[73] soon to appear in English translation,[74] a book that established his reputation as the leading French alienist of the age and soon secured his recognition as one of the two founders of so-called "moral treatment." Pinel was much concerned with the reputation of the English for some special talent in the treatment of the insane and claimed to have "consulted all the works which have appeared upon it in the English language." For the most part, however, he was scathingly critical of what he had found: Francis Willis had chosen to hide his therapeutics

> under the veil of secrecy . . . [his] general principles of treatment are no where developed, and applied to the character, intensity and varieties of insanity. Dr. Arnold's work upon this subject . . . is principally a compilation from different sources,—scholastic divisions more calculated to retard than to accelerate the progress of science. And as to Dr. Harper, . . . is not his work more of a commentary upon the doctrines of the ancients than an original production upon mental indications? Again, I cannot help admiring the courage of Dr. Crichton . . . [who] has lately published two volumes upon maniacal and melancholic affections, merely upon the basis of some ingenious elucidations of the doctrines of modern physiology, which he extracted from a German journal.

In sharp contrast to this scornful recital, Haslam's work was cited repeatedly and always in tones of admiration and assent. Pinel referred to him, for example, as someone "who is in the habit of discharging the important duties of his office, with integrity, dignity and humanity." And when Pinel sought to demonstrate that "to govern men of great penetration and irascibility, such as maniacs most generally are, will require, on the part of the superintendent, a combination of the rarest talents," he proceeded "to illustrate their importance by an appeal to their successful application at one of the most extensive establishments, in Europe—that of Bethlehem Hospital."[75]

Three years after Pinel's book appeared in English translation, Haslam issued a greatly expanded version of his own volume under a new title. Referring to the first edition (with transparently false modesty) as "a trifle, which the Profession has held in greater estimation than its intrinsic merits could justify," he once more reminded his readers of his particular claims to authority, now strengthened by an additional decade of experience: "The contents of the following pages are . . . to be considered as an abbreviated relation, and condensed display of many years observation and practice, in a situation affording constant opportunities and abundant supplies for such investigations."[76] Though obliged to preface the book with a fawning dedication to Monro, Haslam had clearly understood (as his superior had not) the growing importance of publication as a route to professional prominence and was here staking out his claim to stand at the very summit of English mad-doctoring.

If, in his first book, Haslam had been somewhat cautious about identifying the targets of his professional reproaches, no such reticence was now evident. Contemptuous of the abilities of his fellow practitioners ("If any thing could add to the calamity of mental derangement, it would be the mode which is generally adopted for its cure"), he took a particular delight in quoting Pinel's adverse opinions of the most prominent amongst them, pausing only to add that similar strictures could be applied to his French rival.[77] To this catalogue of criticism, he then added some further stinging remarks of his own.

One particularly dramatic technique that a number of his rivals claimed to employ was the use of "the eye," the ability of the imperious madhouse keeper to reduce the ranting and raving to docility and obedience, simply through the moral force of his gaze. William Pargeter, who had been one of Haslam's fellow students at Barts, had made much of his use of the technique in managing ordinary and anonymous madmen;[78] and Willis had employed it more dramatically in his treatment of the most famous late eighteenth-century lunatic of them all, George III.[79] With malicious glee, Haslam held up such claims to ridicule: "I have . . . heard much of this fascinating power which the mad-doctor is said to possess over the wayward lunatic. . . . It has, on some occasions, occurred to me to meet with gentlemen who have imagined themselves eminently gifted with this awful imposition of the eye, but the result has never been satisfactory; for, although I have entertained the fullest confidence of any relation, which such gentlemen might afterwards communicate concerning the success of the experiment, I have never been able to persuade them to practise this rare talent tête-à-tête with a furious lunatic." The boasts of his rivals notwithstanding, reality "is notoriously otherwise. Whenever the doctor visits a violent or mischievous maniac, however controlling his physiognomy, such patient is always secured by the strait waistcoat; and it is, moreover, thought expedient to afford him the society of one or more keepers."[80]

Haslam was equally scathing about a competitor who had recently acquired a growing measure of prominence in the field. Joseph Mason Cox (1763–1818) was the third member of the Mason-Cox-Bompas family to specialize in the treatment of the mad and the first to qualify medically, training at Edinburgh, Paris, and Leyden, and writing an M.D. thesis, *De Mania* prior to taking on the management of Fishponds madhouse near Bristol. After sixteen years in practice, he published the first edition of his *Practical Observations on Insanity*, and within two years, its favourable reception (and translation into French) had led him to produce a revised and enlarged second edition.[81]

Like Haslam himself, Cox framed his discussion of the disorder and its treatment in the context of his own extensive clinical experience. There was, indeed, substantial overlap between his recommendations and Haslam's own, and it may be precisely because of this overlap, and because of Cox's growing reputation, that Haslam made so much of the differences between them and employed such an ironical, mocking, and dismissive tone in discussing Cox's recommendations. Any difference of opinion—on the value of vomits; on the question of whether it was ever defensible and helpful to employ deceit in an attempt to cure the lunatic; on whether alcohol was therapeutically useful; or on the utility of the swinging chair Cox had introduced into the moral and medical treatment of madness—was the occasion for withering scorn.[82]

Those who lacked Cox's credentials but who dared to question Haslam's judgements could expect rougher treatment still. When Drs. Clutterbuck and Birkbeck attempted, a year later, to dispute the (in)sanity of a Bethlem inmate, he turned the full force of his sarcasm against them: these "two learned and conscientious Physicians" were *of course* "gentlemen deeply conversant with this disease, and doubtless instructed by copious experience to detect the finer shades and more delicate hues of intellectual disorder."[83] It was unfortunate, then, that their testimony in this case demonstrated that they were unable to detect even the most obvious of cases. But then, "every person who takes the degree of Doctor becomes, in consequence of taking such degree, a learned man; and it is libellous to pronounce him ignorant. It is true, a Doctor may be blind, deaf and dumb, stupid or mad, but still his Diploma shields him from the imputation of ignorance."[84]

Convinced of his own intellectual superiority, Haslam was but seldom inclined to accord a hearing to those who dissented from his judgements. Quite typically, for instance, when he was questioned a few years later about whether a professional consensus existed on the value of vomiting insane patients, he professed himself uninterested in the matter: "I am so much regulated by my own experience, that I have not been disposed to listen to those who have less experience than myself. I hope you will excuse the appearance of vanity in that answer." It was ironic, then, that in his own practice he had been forced to suppress his own inclinations on the use of emetics because his conclusion that vomiting was useless conflicted with Monro's opinion, and "I submit my judgment to the physician."[85]

Haslam was insistent that insanity was a unitary disease rooted in a real physical disorder of the body. Some might suppose that "a scientific mode of treating . . . Madness" would require close attention to "the powers and operations of the human mind: but the various and discordant opinions, which have prevailed in this department of knowledge, have led me to disentangle myself as quickly as possible from the perplexity of metaphysical mazes." Perhaps "from the limited nature of my powers," he added acidly, "I have never been able to conceive . . . *a disease of the mind.*" Besides, "if insanity be a disease of ideas, we possess no corporeal remedies for it: and . . . to endeavour to convince madmen of their errors, by reasoning, is folly in those who attempt it, since there is always in madness the firmest conviction of the truth of what is false, and which the clearest and most circumstantial evidence cannot remove."

To clinch the issue (and in the process, of course, to decisively reinforce the conclusion that the mad-business ought to be uniquely the province of doctors), he then proceeded to review the macroscopic appearance of the brains of some twenty-nine inmates of Bethlem who had died since his appointment, "not . . . selected from a variety of others, but compriz[ing] the entire number which have fallen under my observation." Disingenuously insisting that he had "no particular theory to build up" and that the cases "have been related purely for the advancement of science and truth" he insisted that all the brains showed evidence of pathology—though the changes were very varied, and uncorrelated with the mental symptoms, and he accepted that "we are not likely soon to attain" knowledge of "how far disease, attacking any of these parts [of the brain], may increase, diminish, or otherwise alter its functions." Still, "when we find insanity . . . uniformly accompanied with disease of the brain, is it not more just to conclude, that such organic affection has produced this incorrect association of ideas, than that a being, which is immaterial, incorruptible and immortal, should be subject to the gross and subordinate changes which matter necessarily undergoes?"[86]

THE THERAPEUTICS OF INSANITY

One might expect that such an insistence on the centrality of the body would have been associated with a purely medical therapeutics. In fact, however, Haslam devoted relatively little space to the topic, and such remarks as he did offer on the subject were prefaced by the disclaimer that he would "only . . . speak of those medicines which I have administered, by the direction of Dr. Monro, the present celebrated and judicious physician to Bethlem Hospital." Here were no opportunities to claim originality, for his subordinate position left him subject to the whims and opinions of a "superior" who remained wedded to the conservative antiphlogistic regime he had unthinkingly inherited from his father and grandfather: bleedings, purges, vomits, cold baths, and a handful of pharmaceuticals, including camphor and opium. At best, Haslam could mark his distance from some of these techniques by delicately suggesting that *his* experience cast doubt on the utility of vomits, recommending cupping rather than venesection as the preferable means of drawing blood, and suggesting that neither camphor nor opium was of much evident use.[87]

It was rather the *management* of patients to which he elected to give his primary attention. For a half century and more, this approach had been propounded as the key to treating the insane, by James Monro and John

Monro quite as emphatically as by their chief critic, William Battie. But earlier in the century, the term largely retained the cluster of meanings associated with its French and Italian origins, where it referred to the handling or training of animals, especially horses, and referred in particular to the disciplinary methods by which horses were accustomed to the bit and bridle, brought under control, and induced to submit to the rule and authority of their human masters. Analogously, when management was recommended as the royal road to the control of madness, it was originally associated with the use of techniques of intimidation and coercion and ways of exciting fear as means of taming the insane.[88]

Now Haslam and others were beginning to use the term in the quite different sense of using tact, care, or skill to manipulate the behaviour of others, and these techniques, permitting this very different form of intervention, he and others now began to expound upon. Like many of his counterparts, Haslam stressed the charismatic authority of the mad-doctor, the centrality of his skill at managing his presentation of self. Removal of patients from their homes and confinement in an asylum "should be enforced as early in the complaint as possible," and the superintendent "must first obtain an ascendancy over them" and thereafter "should never threaten, but execute." Still, "coercion should only be considered as a protecting and salutary restraint," and older methods of "impressing terror" and inflicting "corporal punishment upon maniacs" were dismissed as "disgraceful and inhuman" and "setting aside [their] cruelty, . . . manifestly absurd." Seclusion in a dark room might prove necessary in "the most violent state of the disease," and such restraint should be employed as was necessary to "prevent [them] from committing any violence." But in general, "madmen . . . are rendered much more tractable by wounding their pride, than by severity of discipline." In consequence, Haslam asserted, "I can truly declare, that by gentleness of manner, and kindness of treatment, I have never failed to obtain the confidence, and conciliate the esteem of insane persons, and have succeeded by these means in procuring from them respect and obedience."[89]

Here was a regime that, superficially at least, appeared to bear a number of similarities to the approach known as "moral treatment," which was being developed by the Tukes at the Retreat, near York. A Quaker establishment opened the year after Haslam took up his post at Bethlem, the Retreat attracted increasing attention from the philanthropically inclined from the turn of the century onwards. On a broader scale, however, the publication of a narrative by Samuel Tuke, the grandson of its founder, brought it national attention, served to identify it with a novel approach to the management of the mad widely perceived as more humane than any heretofore, and made this hitherto obscure provincial asylum the focus of a movement for reform in the treatment of the insane.[90]

Implicitly critical of the practice of most mad-doctors, Tuke's book, like

Pinel's before it, singled out Haslam for repeated praise. Like Haslam, Tuke claimed that those running the Retreat were ruled by induction from experience, and he endorsed Haslam's complaints that "those who have devoted their whole attention to [insanity's] treatment, have been either negligent, or cautious of giving information respecting it." To this generalization, "the apothecary at Bethlem" constituted a notable exception, and Tuke acknowledged that "the Retreat, at an early period, derived advantage" from his first book. Haslam's opinions on the value of secluding violent maniacs in a quiet and darkened room, for instance, his view of coercion as "only a protecting and salutary restraint," and his instructions on how to force-feed with a minimum of violence patients attempting to starve themselves—all were endorsed as corresponding to the experience at the Retreat. Likewise, "the superintendents of the Retreat give precisely the same evidence" about the value of gentleness and kindness in securing the respect and obedience of the insane as "the ingenious author of 'Observations on Madness'"; and "the apothecary of Bethlem" could thus be considered as a prime example of one of "those who have care of [the insane], and who treat them with judgment and humanity."[91]

SCANDAL

Within a year of the publication of these encomiums, however, Haslam's career had begun to unravel, and within three years, he stood on the brink of professional and financial ruin. Moreover, one of Tuke's most avid followers, Edward Wakefield, secured Haslam's downfall by pursuing the medical staff at Bethlem with a relentlessness that allowed of no escape. One great pitfall that has bedevilled much of the history of psychiatry has been a tendency to assume a correspondence between someone's published work and their clinical practice. Precisely the gulf that stood between the two now threatened Haslam with a total loss of reputation and livelihood, as the contrast between his rhetoric and the realities of life in Bethlem began to come to light.

Wakefield was a London-based Quaker land agent who had long professed a philanthropic interest in the welfare of the insane. In 1812, he had published a brief article endorsing the idea of adapting Jeremy Bentham's Panopticon scheme to accommodate the mad,[92] and his fellow Quakers' institution now provided him with a still more appealing model of what an asylum could be. In April 1814, he announced in the *Medical and Physical Journal* that an attempt would be made to set up a "London Asylum" run on the lines of the York Retreat. A committee was formed to raise funds for the project, and, as part of its work, the group undertook an investigation of the existing provisions for London's insane, at Guy's Hospital, at St. Luke's, and at Bethlem.

Figure 2.2. John Haslam, apothecary at Bedlam, at once, perhaps, the most famous and infamous mad-doctor of his generation.

The committee of reformers first sought to visit Bethlem on April 25, 1814.[93] The rules of the hospital required that they be accompanied by a Governor,[94] and to satisfy the regulations, Alderman Cox had agreed to accompany them. Not for long, however: the Alderman's "feelings being overpowered before we had gone over the men's side, [he] was under the necessity of retiring to the Steward's office." In his absence, the steward refused to allow Wakefield's party to continue their visit and ushered them out of the hospital. On May 2, though, Wakefield and four other gentlemen again appeared at the gates, this time accompanied by Charles Callis Western, M.P. for Essex, and by a Governor less susceptible to episodes of nausea, Robert Calvert.[95]

Tuke's *Description of the Retreat* had portrayed an asylum as a purpose-built refuge from the pressures of the world, a regime of "judicious kindness" where the mad were treated as fellow creatures still possessed of their essential humanity. In this ideal world, whips and chains were banished; brutality on the part of the keepers unknown; fear used sparingly, and only "when a *necessary* object cannot be otherwise obtained"; the patients induced to control themselves and collaborate peaceably in their own recapture by the forces of reason, in an atmosphere designed in every way for their comfort. Given individual attention in a harmonious and orderly domestic environment (symbolized most strikingly by the image of madmen and women sitting sipping tea and exchanging social pleasantries with the superintendent), Tuke asserted that recovery ensued for many, and a comfortable shelter was provided for all.

Armed with images like these, and recalling Samuel Tuke's tributes to Haslam's talents, the visitors now encountered a starkly different reality: an establishment that conjured up the ancient associations of madness with coercion, nudity, and bestiality. Here, as Wakefield was subsequently to testify, were patients treated like animals or "vermin." The inspection party proceeded first to an examination of the female galleries: "One of the side rooms contained about ten [female] patients, each chained by one arm to the wall; the chain allowing them merely to stand up by the bench or form fixed to the wall, or sit down on it. The nakedness of each patient was covered by a blanket gown only . . . with nothing to fasten it in front. . . . Many other unfortunate women were locked up in their cells, naked, and chained on straw. . . . In the men's wing, in the side room, six patients were chained close to the wall by the right arm as well as by the right leg. . . . Their nakedness and their mode of confinement gave this room the complete appearance of a dog kennel."[96]

Crammed together in a decaying structure that was literally crumbling to bits around them, the furious, the violent, and the frenetic were distributed indiscriminately among the mild and the convalescent, managed by five keepers of a ruffianly sort: "Whilst [we were] looking at some of the bed-lying patients, a man arose naked from his bed, and had deliberately and quietly walked a few paces from his cell door along the gallery; he was instantly seized by the keepers, thrown into his bed, and leg-locked, without enquiry or observation: chains were universally substituted for the strait-waistcoat." "About a third . . . [were] considered as dirty patients" (i.e., had lost control of their bladders and bowels) and these, together with those prone to destroy or tear their clothing, were dubbed "blanket patients" and confined without clothes.[97] "One female," in particular, "was an object remarkably striking; she mentioned her maiden and married names, and stated that she had been a teacher of languages; the keepers described her as a very accomplished lady, mistress of many languages, and corroborated her account of herself. [One] can scarcely imagine a human being in a more degraded and brutalizing situation than that in which I found this female, who held a coherent conversation with us, and was of course fully sensible of the mental and bodily condition of those wretched beings, who, equally without clothing, were closely chained to the same wall with herself."[98]

But there was one: most dramatically of all, the inspecting party now came upon James Norris, an incurable patient confined in his own cell. An American seaman, Norris had been admitted to Bethlem on February 1, 1800, and transferred to the incurable wing on February 14 of the following year. Questioned by his visitors, he

> stated himself to be 55 years of age, and that he had been confined about 14 years; that in consequence of attempting to defend himself from what he conceived the improper treatment of his keeper, he was fastened by a long chain, which passing through the partition, enabled the keeper by going into the next cell, to draw him close to the wall at pleasure; that to prevent this, Norris muffled the chain with straw, so as to hinder its passing through the wall; that he afterwards was confined in the manner we saw him, namely a stout iron ring was rivetted around his neck, from which a short chain passed to a ring made to slide upwards downwards on an upright massive iron bar, more than six feet high, inserted into the wall. Round his body a strong iron bar about two inches wide was riveted; on each side of the bar was a circular projection, which being fashioned to and enclosing each of his arms, pinioned them close to his sides. This waist bar was secured by two similar bars which, passing over his shoulders, were riveted to the waist both before and behind. The iron ring round his neck was connected to the bars on his shoulders, by a double link. From each of these bars another short chain passed to the ring on the upright iron bar. . . . He had remained thus encaged and chained more than twelve years.[99]

Intent on gathering still more evidence, Wakefield and his party returned to Bethlem for a third visit, on June 7, discovering that "all the male patients who were then naked and chained to the beds in their cells, were in that situation by way of punishment for misbehaviour, and not from disease." Norris, however, had finally been freed from the bulk of his restraints, "and the chain around his neck lengthened from 12 to 24 inches."[100] By now, the Governors can hardly have been unaware that problems were looming. Over the next two weeks, Wakefield's allegations of the "cruelties" at Bethlem surfaced "in the public papers," and questions were raised in the House of Commons. When the Governors assembled on June 23, the stories that had appeared in *The Times* and the *Morning Chronicle* were read out, and a decision was quickly reached to form a subcommittee from among their number to inquire into the allegations.[101]

Marshalling the hospital's reserves of social capital, the subcommittee included three peers (including the sixth Earl of Shaftesbury), and three M.P.s (two of whom were baronets), as well as eleven other Governors. It proceeded with great dispatch, meeting at Bethlem on Saturday, June 25, to interview Haslam and Monro, the steward and attendants, and those Governors who, over the years, had served on the weekly subcommittee that met to conduct the business of the hospital. Three days later, the committee of inquiry reported back to the General Court.

Having examined the "general charge of cruelty and mismanagement . . . and also the particular charge of one of such patients [Norris] having been for many years confined in Irons in a manner repugnant to humanity and not warranted by the necessity of the case," they declared themselves convinced that "no foundation whatever exists for such a charge." Those voicing complaints had evidently overlooked the fact that the incurables kept at Bethlem were confined precisely because they were "absolutely mischievous and dangerous to others." As for the general administration of the hospital, "every attention has on the contrary been paid . . . to the cleanliness and health and the comfort of the patients . . . and . . . every degree of indulgence consistent with the security of the Patients, and the safety of those employed has been observed." Bethlem was "equal if not superior" to any asylum in the country, "creditable to the Governors and others concerned in its administration."[102]

What of Norris? He was, they averred, an unusually dangerous and malignant madman. His initial confinement had taken place after he had stabbed William Hawkins, a keeper, with a knife, had attacked a patient who came to Hawkins's rescue, and had subsequently tried to murder a third person. On still another occasion, he had bitten off a patient's finger. Because of the peculiar confirmation of his hands and wrists, ordinary handcuffs turned out to be useless to restrain him: having slipped them off, these "instruments were then converted by him into dangerous weapons and thrown at others." Haslam had proposed, they acknowledged, dealing with problem by confining Norris in two rooms, herding him from one to the other as the occasion demanded; but with the crowding of the hospital with Army and Navy patients, the Governors had rejected that solution; they chose instead, in consultation with Monro, to create his unusual restraint. The subcommittee had now reexamined this apparatus and declared themselves satisfied that "no better mode could have been devised for securing a Patient of so dangerous a description." "However unsightly . . . it appears to have been on the whole rather a merciful and humane, than a rigorous and severe imposition."[103]

Haslam and Monro could scarcely have asked for a more ringing endorsement of their actions and must have considered their jobs secure, even though, with the public airing of the allegations, their reputations (Haslam's in particular) had obviously suffered a body blow in some circles. If such was their judgement, however, they had badly underestimated their adversary. Wakefield now approached George Rose, an old friend of George III's and an M.P. who had a long-standing interest in lunacy questions,[104] and by the following year, they had secured the appointment of a Select Committee to inquire into the state of madhouses. Among its members were a number of M.P.s who had visited Bethlem with Wakefield, and, unsurprisingly, the hospital was among the first and the most sustained targets of its investigation.

On April 25, 1815, a week before the Select Committee opened its hearings, in what both of them must have seen as a further vote of confidence, Haslam and Monro were once again routinely reelected to their posts by the assembled Court of Governors.[105] On May 1, however, after opening testimony about abuses at the York Asylum, directly uncovered by the Tukes and their allies, Edward Wakefield took the witness stand and before an obviously sympathetic audience laid out a lengthy and detailed indictment of conditions in Bethlem.[106] Over the next twelve months, many others were to testify, several on more than one occasion, about all aspects of the hospital's administration and its treatment of patients. Collectively, their evidence built up a portrait of systematic neglect and malfeasance—an institution in which many inmates were largely abandoned to their fate and subjected to a therapeutic regime the reformers clearly regarded as indiscriminate and ineffectual.

Thomas Monro appeared before the Committee only once, on May 19, facing a generally hostile cross-examination in which he sought, so far as possible, to deflect blame for the hospital's state on to Haslam, as the medical officer who had day-to-day charge of the institution. He conceded, however, his own responsibility for the medical treatment of the curable patients and under increasingly sharp questioning provided details of his therapeutics: "In the months of May, June, July, August and September, we generally administer medicines; we do not do so in the winter season, because the house is so excessively cold that it is not thought proper. . . . We apply generally bleeding, purging, and vomit; those are the general remedies we apply. . . . All the patients who require bleeding are generally bled on a particular day . . . and after they have been bled they take vomits once a week for a certain number of weeks, after that we purge the patients. . . . That has been the practice invariably for years, long before my time; it was handed down to me by my father, and I do not know any better practice."[107] Such uniformity was regarded with grave suspicion by those newly converted to Tuke's stress on the importance of individualizing treatment, and the bad impression Monro had already created was made worse later in his testimony, when he conceded that "I really do not depend a vast deal upon medicine; I do not think medicine is the sheet anchor; it is more by management that those patients are cured than by medicine; . . . if I am obliged to make that public I must do so."[108]

Nor can his defence of Norris's confinement have endeared him to the Committee. He asserted that Norris was "the most mischievous person I ever saw in my life . . . the most determined ferocious madman I ever saw." Several members of the Committee had personally seen and spoken with

Norris, finding him capable of conversing on a variety of topics. Yet Monro insisted his coercion was of little moment because "he seemed to me to be a most insensible man, little better than a brute, he had not the least feeling whatsoever." As for Bethlem's more general reliance on fetters and chains, he conceded that "if a gentleman was put into irons, he would not like it" and that such coercion was never employed at his private madhouse. For paupers, however, chains were all but indispensable: "there are so few servants kept for the purpose, that it is the only mode of restraining them."[109]

On Haslam's shoulders, however, the main burden of defending Bethlem fell. Summoned before the Committee on five separate occasions,[110] his performance unquestionably made a bad situation worse. He knew, of course, that Wakefield's visits would prompt a severe interrogation, but he can scarcely have anticipated the depth and the scope of the cross-examination he would face or the precise details about individual cases and hospital personnel that his inquisitors would turn out to have at their disposal.

For a ghost from Haslam's past now rose up to haunt him. James Tilly Matthews had been admitted to Bethlem on January 28, 1797, only eighteen months after Haslam had taken up his appointment. From the outset, Matthews and his family proved to be a thorough nuisance to the Governors. For more than a decade, they were bombarded with petitions from relatives seeking his release, repeated efforts to secure his freedom through legal proceedings, letters to and from the Home Secretary, and affidavits of Matthews' sanity from physicians the family had brought into the case.[111] But the Governors stood firm, presumably fortified by Haslam's and Monro's assurances that Matthews was as unbalanced as ever and most certainly responding to political pressure to keep him incarcerated.[112]

Haslam had clearly been incensed by these repeated challenges to the hospital's and his own authority, neither of which he took lightly. Ultimately, he had been provoked to publishing a whole volume devoted to Matthews' case, holding both the man and his supporters up to ridicule.[113] And if the testimony of Matthews' relatives, and of the Bethlem staff, is to be believed, he had over the years taken a violent dislike to the patient himself.

Matthews harboured identical feelings about the man he believed his tormentor, and now, from beyond the grave, he managed to take his revenge. How long his delusions had persisted following his admission to Bethlem is unknown, but he was unquestionably a man of considerable talents and accomplishments, much of whose intellect remained intact—someone who, from an early period in his stay at Bethlem, became a favourite of the keepers and his fellow patients. Rather like Little Dorrit's father in the Marshalsea,[114] "for the whole time of his being there, the man, so far from interrupting the peace of the house or creating a disturbance, was the man to whom all parties, whether patients or servants of the house, if there were any grievances, made their reference for redress."[115]

Matthews had kept detailed notes of the scenes he observed and the events he was told about and openly used them to prepare an indictment of the hospital. As Haslam was later ruefully to recall, Matthews often threatened to make this manuscript public, and "pluming himself on the retaliation he could make for the supposed injuries he had received, he read to me the greater part of it."[116] It was a threat Haslam took extremely lightly: "I conceived that its circulation ought not to be prevented, on the presumption, that there existed in the judgement of those who passed for persons of sound mind, a sufficient disrelish for absurdity, to enable them to discriminate the transactions of daylight, from the materials of a dream."[117] In the event, this decision—the product of his overweening self-confidence and his assumption that any future audience would share his own view that the writings of a madman were mere symptoms of a disordered brain—[118] proved a disastrous mistake.

Dismissal and Disgrace

When his time came to testify before the Parliamentary Select Committee, to whom the document in question had been passed, Haslam found himself facing a barrage of remarkably detailed and hostile questions, many of which were based in substantial measure on Matthews' indictment.[119] Haslam was by turns truculent and evasive. He did little to disguise his contempt for criticisms emanating from those whose knowledge of madness was so clearly inferior to his own. He insisted, in the face of obvious scepticism from his listeners, that chains and handcuffs were distinctly preferable to other modes of restraint.[120] And when forced to concede instances of ill-treatment and neglect, he absolved himself of any responsibility. Much of the fault lay at the feet of the Governors, who had continued to employ a superannuated steward and matron to supervise the servants. Meanwhile, he alleged, the surgeon, Bryan Crowther, had spent much of the preceding decade "generally insane and mostly drunk. He was so insane as to have a strait-waistcoat." As for Norris, the design and employment of his unique restraint device must be laid at the feet of the Governors and of Monro, as, indeed, the hospital records demonstrated. But his alternative solution of housing him in two rooms having been rejected, Haslam defended the Governors' orders as essential in view of the peculiarities of Norris's anatomy and the malignity of his disposition.[121]

However accurate these claims were, none of them put Haslam's employers in a very favourable light. Nor can his reiterated criticisms about the deficiencies of the new Bethlem buildings have endeared him to the Governors.[122] Nonetheless, the hearings had revealed nothing of which the Governors were previously unaware. Having received several previous votes of confidence from his employers, Haslam, like Monro, presumably thought the whole matter would now blow over, these feelings must have been strengthened when the Governors, assembled for their annual feast on St. Matthew's day, September 21, 1815—"*after* my examination before the Committee of the House of Commons, and the circulation of their printed report"—proceeded to drink a toast to his health and to congratulate him on the vigour and effectiveness of his parliamentary testimony.[123]

Wakefield, though, was relentless. In letters to the *Examiner* and *The Times* on March 31, 1816, he insisted that "the fact is sufficiently obvious; the Governors and the Public have been deceived" by their medical officers. Privately, he informed the new steward at Bethlem "that so long as your Physician [and Apothecary] are permitted to hold their situations, he will continue his . . . attacks against [Bethlem] and its Medical Officers, through the medium of the daily newspapers and other periodical publications.[124] And at his instigation, the Select Committee, "having been informed that the Annual Election of Officers of Bethlem Hospital is about to take place on the 5th of this month," sent a copy of its printed report to each governor. At that meeting, the Court of Governors voted in turn "to postpone the election of the Medical Officers" to allow "an opportunity of investigating the subject." In the meantime, copies of the evidence were forwarded to the medical officers for their comments.[125]

Haslam and Monro now found themselves in a very difficult position. Both informed the Governors at a meeting on April 17 that they wished to keep their posts and would supply explanations of their conduct that would satisfy the Court. But when they came to write their defences, both men complained that they were forced into the invidious position of offering "reasons in my justification without precisely knowing against what charges I am to justify myself, and am compelled to frame my own accusation in order to enter upon my defence."[126] Confronting "the painful humiliation of an abrupt suspension," neither proved up to the task. In all probability, the political pressures now operative rendered it a hopeless prospect. Both men reminded the Governors of their own prior report exonerating their officers of all malfeasance; and they rehearsed the by now well-worn defence of the necessity of Norris's confinement. Monro reminded the Governors of the limited role the visiting physician was supposed to play; and Haslam pointed out that the two of them "have never had the command nor supervision of the servants; such responsibility has always attached to the steward."[127] But neither these defences nor reminders of their long years of service were of any avail.

On May 16, 1816, the General Court met to debate the issue. Their numbers now augmented by one member of the Select Committee, Lord Robert Seymour (who had made the customary donation and become a Governor), they first voted on a motion to reelect Monro and then on a parallel motion to reelect Haslam. Both motions lost heavily, and the two offices were declared vacant.[128]

At age fifty-two, Haslam now found himself cut completely adrift from what had been his major source of a livelihood, his reputation in tatters, and his prospects bleak. His sense of injustice can only have intensified when, less than a month later, Monro's son was elected as one of the replacement physicians.[129] (Monro senior, of course, could fall back on his lucrative private madhouse, always his primary source of income.) In desperation, Haslam wrote to the Governors requesting a pension, such as they had previously awarded the steward and matron. But the Treasurer's motion to award him an annual salary of £200 was "negatived," and the Governors then proceeded to appoint the new steward, George Wallett, as apothecary.[130] As a feeble gesture towards his claims, at their next meeting, "this Court, taking into consideration the distressed state of Mr. Haslam and his family earnestly recommends to the Governors . . . to enter into an immediate subscription for their relief."[131] But there is no evidence that such funds were ever forthcoming, and in any event, a one-time gratuity provided no solution to his long-term problems.

REBUILDING A CAREER

Haslam's name had now become anathema to the reformers, and the regime at Bethlem was emblematic of everything they promised to sweep away. Unable to afford to retire and bemoan his fate, however, he resolutely sought to rebuild his career. Over the years, he had accumulated a substantial library of more than a thousand volumes—some of it medical books, others rarities dating to 1482. On July 5, 1816, all were auctioned by Leigh and Southeby to raise some initial capital.[132] By September 17, 1816, he had purchased an M.D. from Marischal College, Aberdeen, and had set about creating a new career as a physician in London (though he did not become a Licentiate of the Royal College until 1824).[133]

Symptomatic of the arrogance and self-belief that presumably enabled him to bear up under all these trials, his first publication after his disgrace was a brief volume on *Considerations on the Moral Management of Insane Persons*.[134] Moral treatment as developed at the York Retreat had been very much a lay initiative, and Tuke had been highly sceptical of the value of medicine in the treatment of insanity.[135] Haslam's bête noir, Edward Wakefield, had expressed even greater hostility to medicine's claims before the

1815–1816 Select Committee,[136] as had a number of other witnesses,[137] and in these circles, moral treatment was clearly seen as an alternative to largely useless medical interventions.

Haslam would have none of it. "There is something so interesting, and to appearance so dignified, in the contemplation of the human mind, and its disorders, that most persons, who have not received a medical education, have been fully persuaded, they could arrange and compose it in its utmost state of distraction." Unfortunately, "it is a still more lamentable truth that many of these pretenders possess a sturdiness which never shrinks at error, and disdains to be corrected by the disasters of experiment." Insanity was a "corporeal disease," and experience demonstrated that it was rightly "the peculiar and exclusive province of the *medical* practitioner." Those anxious "to transfer this important and responsible department of medicine into the hands of magistrates and senators" were ignorant "zealots of reformation, [whose] powerful and adventurous spirits have the magnanimity to depreciate experience; flushed with hope, and confident of untried speculation, they nobly press forward to surmount the obstacles of nature." Sadly, however, their "bold and costly projects" were instead likely to produce "a dreary waste—a desolate monument of folly and expense."[138]

Wholly uncontrite, Haslam made a particular point of insisting that restraint was an essential element in managing the insane: not just a means of preventing the madman from acting on "the immediate impulse of his will, uncontrolled by reason . . . but a mean[s] of cure." He continued to maintain, moreover, that handcuffs and "manacles" were preferable to the straitjacket, a position that put him sharply at odds with Tuke's followers but one supported by other mad-doctors. For him, the choice was clear: the patient in a straitjacket "is unable to feed himself. . . . He cannot assist himself in his necessary evacuations, and thereby is induced to acquire uncleanly habits. He is incapable of scratching to appease any irritation . . . [and] the friction of the skin against a polished metallic substance does not produce excoriation, which shortly takes place when it is rubbed against any linen or cotton materials."[139]

In the wake of the 1815–1816 parliamentary inquiry, legislation was introduced in 1816 and again in 1817 to set up a Board of Inspection for the madhouses of each county; board membership would be drawn from among the county magistrates. Reflective of the reformers' antagonism towards the medical profession, both bills empowered boards of laymen to inquire into the treatment and management of patients, to direct discontinuance of any practices they considered cruel or unnecessarily harsh, and to order the discharge of any patient they considered restored to sanity.[140] They constituted, in the process, a stern challenge to mad-doctors' claims to the status of experts in the control and treatment of insanity.

In December 1817, Haslam renewed his assault on these proposals. Unblushingly, he granted the need "for a *bill* to protect the insane, and regulate the receptacles wherein they may be confined. . . . Those who will probably attempt to frame this measure, have much to learn, and more to dismiss." Beyond argument, "the production of a wise and salutary bill requires ample research and temperate reflection." By contrast, the current proposals were "the offspring of minds void of information, and saturated with prejudice. As insanity is a disease, . . . it ought to be a leading object with those who possess the power to legislate, to afford every facility to the medical attendant. . . . But if the practitioner is to be pinioned by threats, or deterred by obloquy—if his skill is to be circumscribed by ignorance, and his experience subjected to wild hypothesis, and baseless conjecture; then, the enactment will be oppressive in its operation, and incompetent to meet the exigencies of intellectual calamity—a bill calculated to confirm and aggravate the horrors of madness—to invite suicide, and multiply murder."[141]

After his treatment at the hands of the gentlemen who proposed these legislative changes, for personal reasons Haslam was obviously but little inclined to see their schemes realized, and the animus that lay behind these passages is entirely transparent. One suspects, however, that more than personal pique was at work. In rallying to the defence of medical prerogatives, he was unquestionably also building up credit with his professional colleagues, many of whom deeply resented the reformers' meddling as an attack on their property, their integrity, and their livelihood.[142] His dedication of his work on moral management to John Latham, president of the College of Physicians, surely reflects the hope that public abuse from lay reformers would not be translated into professional ostracism—a hope that, it was soon apparent, was not wholly misplaced.

In the interim, as he sought to retrieve his reputation and build his practice, Haslam produced a veritable blizzard of publications. In December 1817, still another small volume appeared, this time on *Medical Jurisprudence as it Relates to Insanity*[143] In it, Haslam announced that he would "speedily" publish a thorough account of events at Bethlem, including "authentic letters and original documents" and commentary on the parliamentary inquiry, as well as a new treatise on *The Natural History and Physiology of the Human Intellect*. Both publications materialized over the next eighteen months.[144] More ambitiously still, he also promised a third edition of his *Observations on Madness and Melancholy*—a promise he failed to fulfill.

The sheer volume of Haslam's publications in this period suggests that his practice initially developed somewhat slowly. But they served a vital function: in a world where any form of advertising was frowned upon as a species of quackery, books and pamphlets constituted a very effective way of keeping his name before his professional peers and the public, as well as constituting a practical exemplification of his claims to expertise.[145] His discussion of medical jurisprudence was, he asserted, unique,[146] and it was clearly designed to stake his claims in what was becoming an increasingly lucrative field. Both testimony in criminal trials where the insanity defence was raised and medical evidence in lunacy inquisitions, where the sanity of Chancery patients was determined,[147] were obvious sources of income for the entrepreneurially inclined and professionally visible. Simultaneously, though, they were of great symbolic importance to those claiming expertise in the diagnosis of insanity, for they constituted a very public forum in which those claims to expertise (quite as much as the mental status of the nominal subject of the inquiry) were on trial.

Both were almost necessarily fraught occasions. The invocation of the insanity defence in criminal cases was only too readily seen as a ruse to escape just punishment—a threat to the concept of responsibility and thus to the very foundations of the criminal justice system.[148] In parallel fashion, lunacy inquisitions, where control over large amounts of property was commonly at stake, raised in peculiarly acute form public fears of the improper confinement of the sane for corrupt motives—a spectre that was to inspire periodic moral panics throughout the nineteenth century. With respect to the insanity defence, Haslam himself acknowledged the doctor's obligation "not to palm on the court the trash of medical hypothesis as the apology for crime"; but he immediately reminded his readers of the opposite danger: "neither should the lunatic receive his cure at the gallows by the infirmity of [the doctor's] evidence."[149] Here was the social space within which there was room for the expert on madness to make manifest distinctions that would otherwise escape a lay audience. As to the question of when there existed "that morbid condition of intellect which requires the interposition of the law to protect the person and property of the party so affected"—a conclusion that Haslam acknowledged had been likened to "signing the death-warrant of an individual"; "in many instances, the insanity of the person is so clear, so evident and demonstrable, that it is immediately acknowledged by the commissioners and jury." Here quite obviously the medical practitioner's role was almost superfluous. But there were, he insisted "occasions where the state of the persons's [sic] mind involves considerable doubt . . . ; and in these equivocal and embarrassing circumstances, the skill and experience of the physician must furnish the documents and reasons for the decision of the jury."[150]

One should not minimize the difficulty of the task: "The members of the medical profession have long and anxiously endeavoured to frame a definition of insanity, which is an attempt in a few words to exhibit the essential character of this disorder; so that it may be recognized when it exists;— these efforts have been hitherto fruitless, nor is there any rational expectation that this desideratum will be speedily accomplished." One awkward consequence of this situation was that "on many occasions where several medical practitioners have deposed, there has been a direct opposition of opinion." But here surely was a decisive argument in favour of "the most experienced physician who has seen insanity in all its forms, and viewed its more delicate shades"—provided only that he "should not come into court merely to give his opinion—he should be prepared to explain it, and able to afford the reasons which influenced his decision:—without such elucidation, Opinion becomes a bare Dictum, and endeavours to claim precedence, without courtesy or obligation to science."[151]

The scanty materials that have survived on the nature of Haslam's practice in the 1820s and 1830s do not allow us to estimate how much of his income derived from testimony in legal forums. It is evident, however, that his short temper and self-assurance did not always permit him to follow his own advice or to serve as the most effective witness before a jury. For instance, at an inquisition on the sanity of a Miss Bagster held in 1832, his insistence that insanity was always a matter of degree came under sharp cross-examination. Pressed to draw the boundary between sound and unsound mind, Haslam lost patience with his interlocutor and replied, "I never saw any human being who was of sound mind." And when questioned about whether he really meant this literally, he responded acidly, "I presume the Deity is of sound mind, and *he* alone."[152]

Statements like these invited ridicule and cannot have helped his practice.[153] But such evidence as we have suggests that, at least during the first decade and a half after his dismissal, Haslam prospered.[154] His wit, cutting as it might be, provided him with a wide circle of friends within and beyond the medical profession. His acquaintance with William Jerdan, editor of the *London Literary Gazette and Journal of Belles Lettres*, allowed him another forum for his literary talents, and its policy of publishing contributions anonymously allowed him to indulge in some biting satirical jabs at the medical profession and at humbug and pretence wherever he saw it.[155] The wealthy gourmand and gourmet, Dr. William Kitchiner (1775?–1827) counted Haslam among his very closest friends and made him his constant companion—a founding member of the "Committee of Taste," the six or eight men who assembled weekly to indulge themselves at his lavish dinner parties.[156] (Presumably the starving, no matter how pungent their wit, would not have maintained a place at this particular table.) Meanwhile, among fellow members of the mad-doctoring trade, he assumed a leading place, counting two of the most prominent and respectable, Alexander Morison and Alexander Robert Sutherland, as his most intimate friends.

REPUTATION RE-ESTABLISHED

The highly ambitious and well-connected Morison, who ironically was to be appointed visiting physician to Bethlem in 1835 and to have his appointment terminated following still another official inquiry into what were alleged to be scandalous conditions at that establishment,[157] was but little inclined to befriend a poor professional outcast. But Haslam was fast becoming a prominent member of the medical establishment.[158] Increasingly active at the College of Physicians after his admission in 1824, by May of that year, he was also sufficiently affluent to donate the fifty guineas it took to become a governor of St. Bartholomew's Hospital.[159] At the suggestion of Sutherland, who served as the physician to St. Luke's, Bethlem's traditional rival, Haslam was elected a governor there, too, an irony he must have appreciated.

During the 1820s, he gave a series of extremely well-received public lectures before the London Medical Society; a single lecture in 1826 "On the Study of the Human Mind,"[160] was followed by a far more ambitious series of six the next year on "The Intellectual Composition of Man."[161] By then, the repair of his reputation largely complete,[162] he was elected president of the Society, and he presided over most of its regular weekly and biweekly meetings until 1829.[163] Of his private practice in these years, we know almost nothing, though returns in the Public Record Office suggest he sent perhaps a dozen patients to private madhouses in 1830–1831.[164]

His ascension to the presidency of the London Medical Society, however, coincided with a renewal of parliamentary interest in madhouses. A new Select Committee, this time focusing its attention more narrowly on the condition of pauper lunatics in Middlesex, was established in 1827. Its findings, on many points closely resembling those of its predecessor, constituted a further critique of the supine role of the College of Physicians in inspecting madhouses and led to renewed proposals for legislation. Pulling back from earlier proposals for a national inspectorate, which had attracted intense opposition from those opposed to administrative centralization, lunacy reformers now sought (and ultimately obtained) a more limited system, which left inspection in the provinces to the local magistrates, while establishing a new Metropolitan Commission in Lunacy to oversee asylums in the capital.

The inquiry itself and the subsequent legislation were the subjects of much anxious comment and criticism from the medical profession. Well-known mad-doctors attacked the proposed bills in testimony to the House of Lords,[165] and they privately lobbied hard against many of its provisions.[166] The College of Physicians assailed it as an attack on the profession's prerogatives. And the *London Medical Gazette* complained bitterly that the proposed legislation "proceeds upon the somewhat ungracious assumption that all proprietors and medical superintendents of lunatic asylums are rogues," its provisions being such as to "render it doubtful whether respectable medical men will be able, with safety to themselves, to continue" in this line of work.[167] The reformers, the editor sniffed, "are in too great a ferment on the subject to judge coolly and dispassionately about it; . . . they know so little of the disease as to expect things which are utterly impractical; and that they estimate too lightly the tasks of those who are entrusted with the care of the insane."[168] Notwithstanding the medical profession's opposition, however, the bills passed into law.

Two years later, at the risk of reviving memories of his own prior involvement with the reformers and their parliamentary allies, Haslam could not refrain from entering the fray. His entirely characteristic performance addressed directly to the Commissioners themselves, savage and sarcastic by turns, amounted to a full-blown assault on the new system as the product of prejudice and ignorance and as introducing changes liable to damage rather than assist those it purported to help. His targets were both the legislation itself and the commission's role in attempting to implement it.

Evangelicals, forming the core of the 1827 Select Committee, had played the leading role in framing the legislation that resulted from its deliberations. At their insistence a central role was reserved in the inspectorate for laymen, and they took pains to ensure that a majority of the nonmedical appointments to the Metropolitan Commission had Evangelical sympathies. Both the predominance of the lay element and the specific policies the Commission sought to implement were anathema, not just to Haslam, but to the more conservative elements in the College of Physicians and in the medical profession more generally.[169] And the Commission's power to interfere in the conduct of the mad-business continued to be bitterly resented by mad-doctors, even though its powers were much less extensive than those proposed in the reformers' earlier bills.

Haslam's central objections were thus representative of widespread sentiment among his professional colleagues. The Act "degraded" the medical profession and ignored the fact that its central goals of promoting the comfort and cure of the insane "are to be accomplished solely by MEDICAL science and experience. The prominent defect in the Parliamentary Bill under which you [the Commissioners] act, consists in appointing to the treatment of a disease gentlemen who are altogether ignorant of medical knowledge: because the detection of existing insanity, and the decision of the patient's recovery are submitted to your determination."[170]

Haslam's language, however, was scarcely such as to make converts among those he addressed. The Commission, "this hybridous compound of gentleman and physician can never assimilate for any public benefit." Of course, "if in parliamentary metaphysics Insanity be considered other than a disease, then you and the elderly ladies in the metropolis are competent to treat it in all its presentations, and the remedial aid of the physician becomes unnecessary."[171] But the reality as he saw it was quite obviously otherwise: "it has uniformly occurred, that when persons not medically educated have attempted to meddle with the regulation and care of lunatic persons, their interference has always been detrimental. Their career has usually commenced by deploring the imperfection of the prevailing system, complaining of undue restraint, and when they have discovered the in tractable nature of Madness, a disease that yields not to persuasion, and despises the terrors of the law, they have had recourse to those unjustifiable severities that science has proscribed, and at which humanity revolts."[172] Medicine was on the brink of major advances in the understanding and treatment of insanity, "and when the seeds of knowledge have taken root, and the germs of future promise are expanding, it is to be hoped that the strides of mischievous authority will not trample on the expected harvest."[173]

The Commission's first report was ominous, however; its text suggested that "the usurpation of unqualified persons" was proceeding apace. Perhaps this should come as no surprise, given the increased intrusion of politicians into what was properly a professional sphere. After all, in direct contrast to the physician—whose education and moral character, he claimed, were the object of great labour and searching inquiry—there were no qualifications of intelligence or learning requisite for becoming an M.P.: "If he has attained the state of manhood, and possesses property of a certain description, to a definite amount, his qualifications are complete. There is no previous survey of his intellectual capacities, nor any valuation of his learning."[174]

Having informed his professed audience that they were grossly ignorant and quite possibly stupid, Haslam had not quite exhausted his invective. The full measure of his scorn was reserved for the Evangelicals. The whole tone of the Commission's report, he noted, "displays more of the confident and didactic tone of St. Stephen's Chapel than of the accurate and unassuming phraseology of Pall-Mall-East." "Against all reasoning and experience" these religious enthusiasts had insisted, to quote the 1828 Act, "on bringing the hopes and consolations of religion" in the form of divine service to those afflicted with madness. Mockingly, Haslam pointed out the moral: "if these religious opiates and demulcents could soothe a raving paroxysm, or compose the distractions of mind that are indicated by delusions, morbid hostilities, and a propensity to suicide:—could they confer an atom of intellect on existing imbecility, or rouse Idiotism into comprehension, the cure of this malady, ought to be exclusively confided to the clergy. . . . [Moreover,] if the minds of lunatics can be *soothed* and *composed*, by the *hopes* and *consolations* of religion, and if such administrations actually tended to *subdue* the malady under which they are suffering, they cannot be too frequently performed."[175]

Of course, such expectations were delusory, and at least the Commission had been honest enough to confess that "very few, if any, [lunatics] derive real benefit from the celebration of Divine Service."[176] But such was the Evangelicals' obsession with religious consolation that this dismal outcome led them to insist that the charade must be continued, if only because it might possibly benefit the keepers.[177] They should rather, Haslam argued, draw the more logical conclusion from their folly: "if these ghostly thera-peutics have failed in subduing the malady of insanity, it is presumed that you can have no rational objection to confide the entire treatment of this disease to the medical practitioner."[178]

FINAL YEARS

Given his lingering personal bitterness towards the reformers and his strongly held views about the impropriety of lay interference in medical matters, Haslam must have obtained considerable emotional satisfaction from the publication of this verbal assault. It was, of course, hardly the most politically effective of interventions, however much it expressed widely held opinions among the mad-doctoring fraternity. But, as we have seen, the dis-position to ridicule those who disagreed with him had always formed a prominent part of his character. Besides, he was sixty-six by now and in the twilight of his career. The mad-doctoring trade as a whole would have to develop a modus vivendi with the new inspectorate, for the latter's powers would be strengthened and extended over time until they virtually defined the contours within which alienists created and practiced their profes-sion.[179] By contrast, the aging Haslam could afford to adopt a more intransi-gent and principled position, articulating resentments his successors would have to learn to swallow or subdue.

On May 28, 1830, Haslam informed his friend Morison that his daughter, Henrietta Hunter, had herself decided to enter the mad-business and "was applying to be Matron of the Dundee Asylum!"[180] "The experience which she has had in all the detail and minutiae of lunatic institutions from her very infancy," did much to secure her the post,[181] where she was to remain for the next decade. In 1840, however, just four years before her elderly father's death, she returned to London to take up the position of matron at Bethlem. Here, she worked alongside E. T. Monro, one of the two visiting physicians to the hospital, until a further scandal ended the association of the two families with the hospital.[182]

Haslam himself played little further role on the public stage. To his dis-tress, his fellow alienists were increasingly adopting the tenets of Tuke's moral treatment as their own. Following the lead of Gardiner Hill and then Conolly, by the end of the 1830s, a number of them had even announced the possibility and desirability of managing the insane wholly without recourse to any form of mechanical restraint.[183] As the parliamentary re-formers, now led by Anthony Ashley Cooper (the future seventh Earl of Shaftesbury) campaigned ever more openly for a national inspectorate and a compulsory system of public asylums, so most medical men interested in insanity adopted views these laymen found congenial.

In other quarters, however, these claims about therapeutics were heresies, "pseudo-philanthropic gestures" for which Haslam (like a number of more traditionally oriented mad-doctors) had nothing but contempt. In 1842, Alexander Morison founded the Society for Improving the Condition of the Insane to serve as a rallying point for those committed to more traditional views, under the presidency of the sixth Earl of Shaftesbury (Ashley's father and a Bethlem governor). One of the first to join and to read a paper to the assembled membership was Morison's old friend Haslam. Now approaching eighty years of age, the former apothecary was as unrepentant as ever: his speech directly attacked the fallacies and foolishness of the nonrestraint movement and truculently reasserted the essential role played by restraint in the medical treatment of insanity.

Others might bend in the face of uninformed assaults on their skill and humanity. Haslam would have none of it. Defiantly, if ultimately in vain, he insisted that the reformers were ignorant and misguided and their proposed remedies a sure recipe for making things worse.[184] Certainly, they had succeeded in attracting public support: "it would seem that the inhabitants of county towns do not consider them sufficiently complete and embellished without the ostensible erection of a Lunatic Hospital, and such abundant provision can only be paralleled by the pious zeal for building new churches. [But] if the philanthropic promoters of this scheme for multiplying madhouses had foreseen the result of their contrivance, they would probably have reflected before it was precipitated into action."[185] As it was, for all the sanctimonious talk about the virtues of the reformed asylum, in reality "confinement, in its mildest acceptation, amounts to incarceration, and the patients in a public hospital or private receptacle are equally prisoners with the inhabitants of the Queen's Bench or Newgate." Nor should one be taken in by the extravagant claims to have dispensed with other dimensions of the apparatus of coercion: "The pretension to effect impossibilities," he commented acidly, "is readily believed by the weak and unreflecting portion of mankind, and they are always prepared to vituperate the necessary precautions that have wisely and humanely been adopted."[186] Yet despite all "the pretense and imposture of non-restraint," for violent and suicidal patients, for "insane persons mischievously disposed," and for those who would otherwise engage in "self-pollution," few forms of intervention were more useful—indeed indispensable—than "mild and efficient restraint."[187]

On July 14, 1844, Morison "called [for the last time] on Dr. Haslam who had his shoulder dislocated and is in a declining state of health."[188] Whatever passed between them was left unrecorded. Six days later Haslam was dead; his death certificate recorded the cause as "Debility." Within less than twelve months, the lunacy reformers of whom he had been so bitterly critical finally passed a version of the legislation that had been introduced shortly after his dismissal from Bethlem: all counties were henceforth required to build asylums for the pauper insane; and a national Lunacy Commission acquired broad powers over public and private asylums and all those engaged in the mad-doctoring trade.

Chapter Three

A BRILLIANT CAREER? JOHN CONOLLY (1794–1866)

> We have in this asylum, Sir,
> Some doctors of renown
> With a plan of non-restraint
> Which they seem to think their own.
> All well-meaning men, Sir,
> But troubled with a complaint
> Called the monomania
> Of total non-restraint.
> (*Epistle to Mr. Ewart, M.P., by a Reverend*
> *Gentleman, Lately a Patient in the*
> *Middlesex Asylum, 1841*)

JOHN CONOLLY'S place in the pantheon of heroes of English psychiatric history seems secure. Contemporaries likened his achievement in introducing nonrestraint in the treatment of the insane paupers at Hanwell Lunatic Asylum to Howard's labours in the cause of penal reform and Clarkson's role in the abolition of slavery.[1] Lord Shaftesbury, for forty years the chairman of the English Lunacy Commissioners and chief spokesman for the lunacy reform movement, referred to Conolly's work as "the greatest triumph of skill and humanity that the world ever knew."[2] And the doyens of late nineteenth-century medicine were only marginally less hyperbolic: for Sir James Crichton-Browne, "no member of his profession—except Jenner and Lister—has done a tithe as much as he to ward off and alleviate human suffering."[3] "It is to Conolly," said Sir Benjamin Ward Richardson, "that we really owe the modern humane treatment of the insane as it exists today in all its beneficent ramifications . . . the abolition of restraint . . . has placed us first among all the nations as physicians of medical disease."[4] These are judgements, which historians have for the most part been content to echo, crediting Conolly with completing the work begun by Pinel and Tuke, by introducing "reforms which simultaneously gave freedom to the mentally ill and psychiatry to medicine." [5]

But Conolly's medical career is too long and varied to be reduced to a simple tale of his triumph as the author of "nonrestraint." Quite apart from any other considerations, the system he is popularly assumed to have initiated was, as he periodically acknowledged, not his invention at all. Moreover, he was well into middle age before he became the resident physician at Hanwell, and he occupied that post for less than four years. A more extended look at his professional life provides valuable insight into some of the vicissitudes attending the choice of a medical career in Victorian England; and the sharp transformations that mark his thinking on psychiatric matters, closely paralleling the twists and turns of his own career, point up the intimate relationship that often exists between developments in disinterested medical "knowledge" and the varying social interests of those propounding it.

YEARS OF STRUGGLE

John Conolly was born at his grandmother's house in the small town of Market Rasen in Lincolnshire, in 1794. His father, "a younger son of a good Irish family, . . . had been brought up to no profession; had no pursuits; died young," leaving his wife with three young children to raise. The three boys were soon separated, and John, at the age of five, found himself boarded out, like "an inconvenient superfluity," with an elderly widow, a distant relative of the family, in the decaying Borough of Hedon. Here he spent a "barren" and "wretched" boyhood, receiving a "dull, mechanical," and, as he later confessed, grossly inadequate education at the local grammar school. The descent from even a shabby gentility "to the commoner arrangements inseparable from school, and to a society of the lower kind, where nothing was tasteful, and nothing was beautiful, and nothing was cheerful"[6] made a profound impression on Conolly. The experience may well have contributed to the insistent concern he displayed in his later years that others acknowledge his gentlemanly status; and they certainly must have intensified the pressures engendered by the uncertain course that marked his professional and financial life until the age of forty-five.

Conolly's mother had moved to Hull in 1803 and supported herself by opening a boarding school for "young ladies." Within a few years she remarried a Mr. Stirling, an émigré Scot from Paris who taught languages, and in 1807, she brought her son John home to live with them. Despite the further decline in social status that these domestic arrangements implied, Conolly seems to have enjoyed the next five years. With his step-father's encouragement, he became fluent in French, dabbled in Enlightenment philosophy, and obtained a rudimentary general and literary education. In 1812, at the age of eighteen, he procured a commission as an ensign in the Cambridgeshire militia and spent the closing years of the Napoleonic Wars in Scotland and Ireland.[7] Apparently he found military life to his taste, for Henry Maudsley reports enduring (a half century later) many conversations filled with "lively and pleasant recollections" of his service.[8] Napoleon's defeat and exile, however, foreclosed the possibility of a military career, and by 1816 Conolly had resigned his commission and returned to Hull. With the death of his mother and step-father he received a small inheritance, and in March 1817 he married Eliza Collins, daughter of the recently deceased Sir John Collins (himself the illegitimate son of the second Earl of Abermarle). Such an early marriage, with very little capital and no real prospects, would by itself have struck most Victorians as foolhardy, and the couple quickly compounded their difficulties by the sort of financial ineptitude Conolly was to exhibit throughout his life. After the marriage, they left immediately for France and spent an idyllic year in a cottage near Tours, on the banks of the Loire. At the end of this period, with the arrival of his first child and the rapid shrinking of his capital, it seems finally to have dawned on Conolly that he had to develop some stable source of income.

For those in early Victorian England lacking independent means but aspiring to gentlemanly status, the choice of careers was meagre indeed.[9] Anything connected with "trade" was out of the question, leaving only law, the Church, and perhaps medicine as ways of gaining a livelihood without irrevocable loss of caste. Medicine, in fact, was not an unambiguously acceptable choice: as Trollope observed (in the person of Miss Marable), "She would not absolutely say that a physician was not a gentleman, or even a surgeon; but she would not allow to physic the absolute privilege which, in her eyes, belonged to the law and the church."[10] Still, Conolly settled on medicine, based in part on the advice of his older brother William, who was already medically qualified; and like many an ill-connected and impecunious provincial, he elected to obtain his training in Scotland, first at Glasgow and then for two years at Edinburgh.

Possessed of a talent for making friends and moving easily in society, Conolly enjoyed a moderately successful student career, becoming one of the four annual presidents of the Royal Medical Society in his second year. He was strongly influenced by Dugald Stewart, the professor of moral philosophy, and like a number of Edinburgh students of this period, he developed a special interest in the problem of insanity. Reflecting this, his M.D. dissertation of 1821 was devoted to a brief discussion of *De statu mentis in insania et melancholia*.

He now had to earn his living and faced immediately the dilemma of where to set up his practice. Lacking the means to buy into an established practice, and without any family ties he could call on to help obtain a clientele, Conolly faced an uphill battle.[11] His difficulties were further compounded by the fact that he already had a wife and child to support. And because his Scottish training left him without any institutional or personal linkages to the London hospitals and medical elites, he had perforce to begin his career in a provincial setting. Inevitably, this meant engaging in general practice in an isolated and highly competitive environment, in which it generally took several years before one began to earn even a modest competence and where one was highly dependent on somehow securing the approval and patronage of the well-to-do.[12] To make matters worse, medical men working in such settings were regarded with ill-concealed contempt by the professional elites of Edinburgh and London, reflecting their marginal status in the larger social world. They were, sniffed the *Edinburgh Medical and Surgical Journal*, "engaged in the trading, money-making parts of the profession, and not one in a hundred of them distinguished by anything like science or liberality of mind."[13]

Conolly's first efforts to make his way in this difficult environment met with abject failure. After a three-month stay in Lewes, he abandoned the attempt to build a practice there and removed his family to Chichester to try again. Here, however, he had to compete with another young practitioner, John Forbes.[14] Though the two were to become lifelong friends, there was insufficient work to support them both, and within a year it had become apparent that Conolly would have to leave. Of the two, he was undoubtedly "the greater favourite in society, his courteous manner, his vivacity of character, and his general accomplishments, rendered him an agreeable companion."[15] But however enjoyable the local notables found his company, when they required professional medical services, they turned instead to Forbes. Conolly, as his son-in-law Henry Maudsley later remarked, was a poor "practical physician," with little talent or ability to inspire confidence in "the exact investigation of disease, or in its treatment; he had little faith in medicines, and hardly more faith in pathology, while the actual practice of his profession was not agreeable to him."[16]

Now blessed (or burdened) with a second child, his son Edward Tennyson, Conolly once more uprooted his family and moved, this time to Stratford on Avon, then a small town of some four thousand inhabitants. Here he at last began to prosper, albeit in a very modest way. He was elected to the Town Council and twice served as mayor, the £80 salary serving as a useful supplement to his still slender professional income. He took a leading role in establishing a dispensary for the treatment of the sick poor and was active in civic affairs more generally, the well-worn path for a young practitioner trying to make his way. Perhaps because of the interest he had developed in the subject while in Edinburgh, and no doubt because the honorarium attached supplemented his inadequate income, he also secured an appointment as "Inspecting Physician to the Lunatic Houses for the County of Warwick," a position that required only that he accompany two local justices of the peace on their annual inspection of the county's half-dozen mad houses. In his best year at Stratford, though, Conolly's income is reported "not to have exceeded £400," an amount barely sufficient to maintain a suitable lifestyle for a professional man with a growing family.[17]

A METROPOLITAN MIRAGE

Quite suddenly, however, the prospect arose of substituting the rewards of a London teaching and consulting practice for the dull routines of general practice in a provincial backwater. The founders of the new University of London had decided to include a medical school in the new foundation. Somewhat to his surprise, Conolly managed to obtain an appointment as professor of the nature and treatment of diseases; he was helped in part by being previously known to Dr. George Birkbeck and Lord Brougham, two prime movers in the project. While the University had "sought to engage men of high standing, . . . it could offer but small emoluments and a precarious future" in its early years.[18] And accordingly, a number of the early appointments were of young or relatively unknown men.[19]

In general, however, "assured income and national visibility . . . went with status as full physician or surgeon at a hospital and as teacher at a medical school" in London,[20] and Conolly undoubtedly thought that he was about to cross successfully the great divide that marked off the social and financial world of elite London physicians from the humble surroundings of the rest of the profession. He instantly wrote back accepting: "Gratified, as I cannot but be, by the confidence which has been placed in me, an untried person, I know that it only remains for me to justify it by my services."[21] Though the first scheduled teaching session was not to begin until October 1828, some fourteen months hence, he at once refused offers to write and edit for London publishers on the grounds that "the attention and care required by the lectures of so inexperienced a teacher as I am . . . occupy almost every hour of my time."[22] And towards the end of 1827, he announced plans to travel to Paris for three months to obtain materials that would assist him in preparing his lectures.[23]

On October 2, 1828, Conolly gave his inaugural lecture, the second at the new medical school.[24] It was apparently quite successful,[25] although largely given over to some rather platitudinous advice to his students. His lecture's one departure from the expected was his announcement: "It is my intention to dwell somewhat more fully on Mental Disorders, or to speak more correctly, of disorders affecting the manifestations of the mind than has, I believe, been usual in lectures on the practice of medicine."[26] Conolly's attempts, over the next two years, to get permission to give students clinical instruction in mental disorders at a London asylum proved unavailing. After initially encouraging him, the University Council rejected the idea.[27] Thwarted in this direction, he decided instead to publish a book on the subject, not least because "I disapprove entirely of some part of the usual management of lunatics."[28]

An Inquiry Concerning the Indications of Insanity, published in 1830, is, in many respects, a rather conventional treatise, "investigating the mind's history, from its most perfect state, through all its modifications of strength and through all its varieties of disease, until it becomes affected with confirmed madness."[29] But Conolly broke sharply with contemporary orthodoxy over the key issue of how and where the lunatic ought to be treated. His book appeared in the midst of the early nineteenth-century campaign for "reform" in the treatment of lunatics—a movement that took some thirty years to achieve its goals, and one whose proponents were absolutely convinced that asylum care was the only appropriate form of treatment for the insane. The heightened public attention to the problems posed by the mentally disturbed stimulated a large number of medical men to produce books and pamphlets on insanity; running through this literature, and repeated with growing emphasis and conviction, were the assertions that all forms of madness required institutional care and treatment and that the sooner those displaying signs of mental imbalance were removed from domestic to asylum care, the greater their chances of ultimate recovery.

From this almost universal consensus about "the improbability (I had almost said moral impossibility) of an insane person's regaining the use of his reason, except by removing him early to some Institution for that purpose,"[30] Conolly issued a lengthy and closely argued dissent. Seeking to offer "no opinions which have not received some confirmation from observation and experience," he asserted that the emphasis on the centrality of the asylum "originated in erroneous views of mental disorders, and has been perpetuated with such views." Existing authorities argued that any and all forms of mental unsoundness warranted—indeed required—confinement. If this doctrine of "indiscriminate treatment, including deprivation of property and personal liberty" were to prevail, then, said Conolly, "no man can be sure that he may not, with a full consciousness of his sufferings and wrongs, be one day treated as if all sense and feeling were in him destroyed and lost; torn from his family, from his home, from his innocent and eccentric pursuits, and condemned, for an indefinite period, to pass his melancholy days among the idiotic and the mad."[31]

It was precisely the expert's task, not just to distinguish the mad from the sane, but "to point out those circumstances which, even in persons decidedly insane, can alone justify various degrees of restraint," and the latter was clearly the more difficult accomplishment. At present, "certificates of insanity" were heedlessly and ignorantly . . . signed," with the result that "the crowd of most of our asylums is made up of odd but harmless individuals, not much more absurd than numbers who are at large." Moreover, "once confined, the very confinement is admitted as the strongest of all proofs that a man must be mad . . . It matters not that the certificate is probably signed by those who know very little of madness or of the necessity of confinement; or by those who have not carefully examined the patient; a visitor hesitates to avow, in the face of such a document, what may be set down as a mere want of penetration in a matter wherein nobody seems in doubt but himself; or he may be tempted to affect to perceive those signs of madness that do not exist."[32] Hence the central importance of clinical instruction of medical students in the recognition and treatment of insanity.

Perhaps a trifle disingenuously, Conolly announced that he had "no wish to exaggerate the disadvantages of lunatic asylums." There were, after all, certain classes of patients for whom public asylums were "unavoidable evils." "For a hopeless lunatic, a raving madman, for a melancholy wretch who seems neither to see nor to hear, or for an utter idiot, a lunatic asylum is a place which affords all the comforts of which unfortunate persons are capable." But their regrettable necessity as places of last resort must not be allowed to obscure the fact that "it is a far different place for two-thirds of those who are confined there. . . . To all these patients confinement is the very reverse of beneficial. It fixes and renders permanent what might have passed away and ripens eccentricity or temporary excitement or depression, into actual insanity."[33]

The first principle of asylum treatment was the isolation of the mad from the sane. This sequestration from the world was alleged to be therapeutic, a notion Conolly scathingly attacked: "whatever may be said, no one in his senses will believe, that a man whose mind is disordered is likely in any stage of his disorder to derive benefit from being surrounded by men whose mental faculties are obscured, whose passions and affections are perverted, and who present to him, in place of models of sound mind, in place of rational and kind associates, in place of reasonable and judicious conversation, every specimen of folly, of melancholy, and of extravagant madness."[34] People's mental and moral capacities varied markedly according to the circumstances in which they were placed, and their thoughts and actions were, in large degree, the product of an interaction between habits, situational pressures, and the influence and reactions of their associates. The capacity to control one's wayward passions and imagination and to avoid the perils of morbid introspection was thus essentially dependent upon social reinforcement and support.[35] Granting these realities of our mental life, "who can fail to perceive that in such an unhappy situation [as asylum life provided] the most constant and vigorous assertion of his self-command would be required to resist the horrible influences of the place;—a place in which a thousand fantasies, that are swept away almost as soon as formed in the healthy atmosphere of our diversified society, would assume shapes more distinct; a place in which the intellectual operations could not but become, from mere want of exercise, more and more inert; and the domination of wayward feelings more and more powerful." Taking even "the most favourable case for the asylum," its effects were likely to be harmful.[36]

The defect was, as Conolly saw it, structural and consequently not removable by any conceivable reform. Confinement in an institution acted like a self-fulfilling prophecy, intensifying and even creating the very behaviours that were its alleged justification and bringing about a steady and insidious atrophy of patients' social capacities: "the effect of living constantly among mad men and women is a loss of all sensibility and self-respect or care; or not infrequently, a perverse pleasure in adding to the confusion and diversifying the eccentricity of those about them . . . in both cases the disease grows inveterate. Paroxysms of violence alternate with fits of sullenness; both are considered further proofs of the hopelessness of the case. . . . [Eventually,] after many hopeless years, [they] become so accustomed to the routine of the house, as to be mere children; and are content to remain there, as they commonly do, until they die."[37]

For whole classes of lunatics, therefore, asylum treatment was grossly inappropriate. If social practices could be brought to reflect these realities, "the patients *out* of the asylum being the majority, and consisting of all whose circumstances would insure them proper attendance—better arrangements might be made for the smaller number of public asylums, or central houses of reception." Such asylums must, first, be public, that is, state supported; for only by removing the distorting effects of the profit motive could one avoid the problems created by a system in which "the patients are transmitted, like stock-in-trade, from one member of a family to another, and from one generation to another": a free trade in lunacy attracts, besides a handful of "respectable, well-educated, and humane individuals," the "ignorant and ill-educated" and those "capable of no feeling but a desire for wealth." Second, each asylum should become a center in which aspiring medical men could be taught to recognize and treat mental disorder.[38] The possession of such clinically derived skills and knowledge—the fruit of the sort of arrangement he had unsuccessfully urged on the university—would give the average medical practitioner both the competence and the confidence to treat most cases of insanity on a domiciliary basis.

If Conolly hoped that the publication of *An Inquiry Concerning the Indications of Insanity* would serve to advance his reputation and enlarge his private practice, he was soon disabused. Still smarting from their earlier exchange, Thomas Wakley characteristically seized the opportunity to pour scorn on the book: it was, he asserted, "infinitely more ample than the occasion demands," full of "carelessness and confusion," and contributed nothing "to the stores of science."[39] Another reviewer, in the *Medical-Chirurgical Review*, did praise Conolly for performing "a very important service to the profession, in calling their attention to the construction and properties of the mind," and expressing himself in superior "language and style."[40] But for the most part, his suggestions were not even debated,[41] but simply ignored. By now the overwhelming weight of opinion among both the profession itself and those laymen interested in lunacy reform was that in cases of insanity, asylum treatment was indispensable and could not be embarked upon too quickly for the patient's own good—a position Conolly himself was to embrace less than a decade later.

In the meantime, he was involved in a series of controversies at the medical school, which, within six months, were to prompt his resignation. The early years of the University were stormy. The Council, chosen from among the University's Proprietors, exhibited a constant disposition to interfere with the conduct of the institution, threatening to send inspectors to check on the quality of lectures given, to exercise the power to censor the books used in teaching, and "to regulate minutely not only the number, length, and hours, but also the scope and content of the various courses." In general, "it regarded the professors in the same light as any other of its employees, and all its employees with suspicion."[42] The frictions such conduct was sure to arouse were exacerbated by the activities of Warden Leonard Horner, the salaried officer to whom the Council had delegated day-to-day supervision of University affairs. For Horner, too, had an exalted view of his position, and his arrogant and autocratic manner, his constant petty interference and intrigue aroused widespread discontent among the professoriate—an antipathy strengthened by the fact that the warden, though paid four or five times as much as those he supervised, was an erstwhile linen manufacturer possessed of limited education and no scholarly qualifications.

The medical faculty considered that "a Hospital is absolutely necessary for the prosperity of the Medical School,"[43] since only by providing clinical instruction could they hope to compete effectively with rival London institutions for students. For a time it appeared that a suitable arrangement could be reached with the nearby London Fever Hospital, but when the council insisted on being given complete control, its intransigence led to the collapse of the negotiations. As a temporary, if inadequate, substitute, Conolly and his colleagues proposed the establishment of a university dispensary, which they would attend "without compensation . . . as a help to a rising school"[44]—a plan to which the parsimonious council quickly agreed.[45] But the dispensary soon became a new source of friction. It was to have a resident apothecary, and Conolly and his colleague Anthony Todd Thomson immediately expressed concern that the appointee be someone who aspired "solely to being efficient in that useful but still subordinate capacity."[46] Their concern to protect their status soon proved prescient, for Horner began to use John Hogg, who had secured the position, to check on the professors' performance of their duties. Conolly viewed such "very offensive" machinations as an intolerable affront to his dignity: "you have constituted the Apothecary, who ought to be under the orders of the physicians and surgeons, a kind of spy over those physicians and surgeons, and have thereby completely subverted the discipline of the establishment. Among respectable men of my own rank in the medical profession, I find but one opinion concerning this matter; and that opinion makes it impossible for me to continue my attendance at the Dispensary. . . . The Council have no right to impose a degradation on me, and I cannot submit to it."[47]

Two months later, Horner informed him that "the Council considered it a part of the duty of the Professor of the Practice of Medicine to attend as Physician at the Dispensary."[48] But Conolly stood his ground: "No opinion of the Council, or of any body of men, can, or ever shall, induce me to act inconsistently to my character as a physician and a gentleman." Only a change in the lines of authority at the dispensary would induce him to return.[49] Eventually a meeting with the Council itself led to the quarrel being patched up, though not until Conolly had incurred further slights from the warden.[50]

On other fronts, too, the relationship between the university and its professors grew strained. The proprietors wished to move to a system in which a professor's pay was directly proportional to the income he generated from his lectures. Initially, forced to modify this plan in order to attract faculty to a new and untried enterprise, they had offered salary guarantees for the first three years of the university's existence. By the spring of 1830, however, financial difficulties were increasing as student numbers declined, and "the University was eating up its capital at a rate of £1,000 a year."[51] Rumours began to circulate that the Council was contemplating an early end to the system of guaranteed salaries. A number of professors, Conolly among them, responded by laying out an alternative plan to rescue the institution's finances. They insisted that "a salary should be secured for every professor in the event of his fees from pupils not attaining a certain amount" and argued that the institution was still too new for payment by results to work and that the failure to provide such a guarantee would inhibit the professors' study of their subjects, since such activities would be "unproductive of immediate pecuniary advantage." Some professors' lecture fees amounted to less than £100, of which the University proposed to take a third, and yet "it is expected that the professor will subsist in the rank of a gentleman upon the balance." To balance the budget, they proposed tailoring the length of courses to the convenience of students because the University could not expect, "for many years to come, to draw any considerable number of students from the upper ranks [of society]";[52] and *reducing* fees so as to attract additional students who would otherwise attend the cheaper courses given by such places as the Royal Institution and the London Institute. Finally, much money could be saved by abolishing the office of warden, with his salary of £1,200 a year, a suggestion scarcely inclined to endear its authors to Horner. These proposals were leaked to the press and met by anonymous responses from the warden, a war of words that continued until April 21, 1830, when the *Sun* reported that with some lecture rooms all but empty, the proprietors had decided to reduce the salary guarantees to the least successful professors.[53]

This news must have been a considerable blow to Conolly, for his financial situation had been precarious since his arrival in London. On the same day that the new salary policy was announced, he wrote to Horner declining to repeat the summer session lectures he had given the year before, partly because the number of students was likely to be small, rendering the course unremunerative, and also because "I am under the necessity of employing some of the year in occupations unconnected, or not immediately connected, with my Professorship, which I could not possibly do if I were to lecture ten months out of twelve."[54] During the 1829–1830 session, his University salary declined from £300 to £272 15s, and before the year was out, he was forced to request an advance of "£100 on account" from the warden he detested,[55] a humiliation he was compelled to undergo twice more before he finally left London the following spring.[56]

Conolly could scarcely have viewed the prospect of a further decline in his guaranteed salary with equanimity, for, notwithstanding all his laborious preparation and his personal charm, his lectures "were not great successes, if they were not in truth failures, [being] somewhat vague and diffuse, wanting in exact facts and practical information."[57] Here, as elsewhere, in the judgement of one of his friends, "the aid which Dr. Conolly rendered to the diffusion of knowledge was not special or professional."[58] Unfortunately, his efforts to augment his income from private practice were likewise unsuccessful. Conolly was blessed with considerable advantages that ought to have brought him patients: Lords Russell, Auckland, and Brougham provided aristocratic sponsorship; his University affiliation ought for once to have been an advantage; and he was amply provided with the necessary social graces. "Though by nature passionate and impetuous, he had great command over his manner which was courteous in the extreme. Indeed he never failed to produce, by the suavity of his manner and the grace and ease of his address, the impression of great amiability, kindness, and unaffected simplicity; while his cheerful and vivacious disposition and his lively conversational powers rendered him an excellent social companion."[59]

He sought to capitalize on these advantages, following the well-worn path of the aspiring London practitioner. He joined the Medical and Chirurgical Society of London and became an active member of the Society for the Diffusion of Useful Knowledge. He took the examination of the Royal College of Physicians and became a licentiate; and he secured election to the staff of the London Fever Hospital. Notwithstanding all his efforts, however, "practice did not come sufficiently quickly."[60] On a larger stage, he enjoyed a repetition of his failures at Lewes and Chichester and almost certainly for the same reasons: his own deficiencies in the investigation of disease, his evident lack of faith in the medicine he prescribed, and his dislike of the tasks medical practice imposed, coupled with his settled disposition "to shrink from the disagreeable occasions of life, if it were possible, rather than encounter them with deliberate and settled resolution."[61]

Unlike the deficiencies of some of his colleagues, at least Conolly's failures were not the focus of public attention. Granville Sharp Pattison, the professor of anatomy, was not so fortunate. Having been one of Conolly's teachers at Glasgow (where he had successively been indicted for body-snatching, accused of malpractice, infected with syphilis, and forced from his post following an affair with Andrew Ure's wife), he had subsequently emigrated to the United States to take up an appointment at the University of Maryland. Apparently his tenure there was less than an overwhelming success (he was attacked in a pamphlet published in Philadelphia as "an adventurer with a tainted reputation"),[62] but he succeeded in securing one of the first chairs at the University of London, with Conolly providing a testimonial in his behalf. The appointment proved to be a mistake. He neglected his work or performed it incompetently, giving superficial and perfunctory lectures when he bothered to attend. By contrast, J. R. Bennett, who had been appointed demonstrator in anatomy and had previously taught in Paris, "was a competent and popular teacher, and came to feel a contempt for Pattison as an anatomist which he was at no pains to conceal."[63] Conflict flared in the very first session and continued intermittently for more than two years. Pattison at first secured the support of many of his colleagues by alleging that Horner, whom they detested, was plotting his removal. But by the spring of 1830, student complaints about his performance grew more insistent, and the scandal surfaced in the medical press. A student memorial published in the *London Medical and Surgical Journal* "charge[d] him with *unusual ignorance* of old notions, and *total ignorance of* and *disgusting indifference* to new anatomical views and researches. . . . He is ignorant, or, if not ignorant, indolent, careless, and slovenly, and above all, indifferent to the interest of science."[64] Conolly remained one of Pattison's staunchest supporters (as Wakley was one of his fiercest critics).[65] He complained to the Council that "the most heartless and iniquitous persecution has been carried on against the Professor of Anatomy . . . because his ruin would be convenient to the Warden's friends."[66] And for a few months, Pattison managed to cling to his position. But when the new session opened in October 1830, student discontent grew increasingly unmanageable. Pattison's classes were periodically boycotted and routinely disorderly. By February 1831, the students had opted for open rebellion, and "for over a month it was impossible to lecture. The scenes in the anatomy theatre reminded a contemporary reporter of Covent Garden during O.P.[Old Price] riots."[67] Conolly, too, began to lose control of some of his students, and on at least one occasion, nearly half of his class failed to attend his lecture.[68] Ultimately, the tumult subsided only after Horner abruptly relinquished his post and when Pattison was forced to resign. By then Conolly, too, had left the University.[69]

Pattison was not the only colleague of doubtful competence whom Conolly sought to defend. His intervention on behalf of John Gordon Smith proved similarly unavailing, perhaps not surprisingly in view of its maladroitness. Smith, a former army surgeon, had secured an appointment as professor of medical jurisprudence. A knowledge of forensic medicine conferred few obvious advantages on those seeking to practice medicine, and Smith's prospects of attracting a sufficient number of students to his classes were not aided by his rambling and disjointed lecture style. "Condensation . . . is not a virtue of Dr. Smith's," the *Morning Chronicle* commented on the occasion of his inaugural lecture,[70] and students voted with their feet not to listen to interminable stories of his wartime exploits. In early December 1830, while depressed and in his cups, he offered the Council his resignation; then on sobering up, sought to withdraw it. Conolly's intervention can only have sealed his fate. He had been treating Smith, he informed them, for a periodic "severe affection of the stomach," most probably this was a side effect of Smith's heavy drinking. These episodes lasted for only a few days at a time, but "on the decline of each attack, he is subject to a peculiar, but temporary, excitement of the nervous system which has once or twice, I believe, led to the interference of his friends. It was during one of these afflicting accessions that he lately conveyed to you his determination not to lecture in the University unless certain concessions were made to which he has ceased to attach any importance; and I know that he unfeignedly and extremely laments that he made such a communication to you."[71] Lament he might, for the Council, notwithstanding Conolly's warning that the loss of Smith's chair would be "an irretrievable, perhaps a ruinous calamity to him,"[72] gratefully accepted the opportunity to be rid of him. (Conolly, incidentally, proved a better prophet than advocate: within three years, Smith was dead, dying of alcoholism in a debtor's prison.)[73]

Exile to the Provinces

Conolly's manifold failures and disappointments made his resignation from the University not unexpected, but its manner and timing were nevertheless distinctly odd, lending weight to Maudsley's observation that he was "apt to do serious things in an impulsive way."[74] Only a few hours after sending a letter to the Council begging them to ignore Smith's resignation, Conolly submitted his own. Bellot comments that "the reasons for Conolly's resignation are obscure,"[75] and Conolly himself, in requesting Horner "to lay my resignation before the Council" added: "I have not troubled them with a useless detail of all my motives, but I am anxious that they should not think that I resigned from any want of interest in the university."[76] The penultimate paragraph of the same letter suggests that the Council's refusal to heed his pleas on Smith's behalf may have constituted the final straw. ("I am sorry to have to trouble the Council with a second communication on the same day, but Dr. Smith is so deeply concerned in my doing so that I hope it will be excused"); and there are hints that some of his colleagues may have been glad to see him go ("I cannot doubt that Dr. Thomson and Mr. Amos will approve of what I have done in this matter");[77] but finally, Conolly is content to express no more than a veiled hope that his successor will have "a more favourable combination of circumstances than those in which I have endeavoured to perform [my duties]."[78]

Characteristically, his valedictory address, given at the end of the academic year, offers little substance at great length. He acknowledges that others may be puzzled by his decision: "Retiring as I do, from a station, none of the prospective advantages of which have altogether escaped my attention—from a station which I was, four years ago, ambitious to obtain, and to which I felt it a great honour to be appointed—retiring, too, without the excuse of years, or any consciousness of a growing incapacity for exertion— I feel that a few words of explanation may be thought necessary, addressed to those who have interested themselves in my success." Many words but no explanation then follow. He grants that "it will be believed that powerful motives must exist which induce me to resign all these expectations, and when every previous hope has been sacrificed, to retire from a scene of public activity in which I might at least have continued without discredit." He then adds, "I think I could show that circumstances exist—have for some time existed—which so limit my usefulness here as to make it no less my duty, than it is my inclination, to withdraw from this institution." But the nature of those "circumstances" he glides over in silence, not wishing "to carry with me any unpleasant recollections."[79]

Whatever the precise reasons for his departure, the blow it constituted to his pride, to say nothing of his prospects, must have been staggering.[80] Victorian medicine was marked by an enormous "division between the prestigious and influential men at the top of the profession and the ordinary practitioners [beneath]."[81] Having once had hopes of belonging to the elite, Conolly now appeared to be thrust back, all but irretrievably, into the ranks of provincial obscurity. As one who later confessed "that he did not care for money, but that he very much liked the comfort and elegancies which money brings,"[82] the prospect was scarcely inviting.

Placing his furniture in storage (where it was to remain for eighteen months until he could afford to rent a house large enough to contain it), he gathered his wife and four children (a third daughter, Anne Caroline, had

Figure 3.1. John Conolly in his forties, an impecunious but ambitious provincial physician with uncertain prospects. A likeness drawn in 1837, during the period when he lived on Theatre Street in Warwick, from a painting by Kirby.

been born in 1830) and removed once more to Stratford. But the attempt to pick up the threads of his old practice was a failure, and within a few weeks he felt compelled to uproot them all again and move to the nearby town of Warwick. His one remaining tie to the metropolis was Thomas Coates, the secretary of the Society for the Diffusion of Useful Knowledge, now Horner's replacement at the University (though at a salary of £200 rather than

£1,200); and the correspondence between them gives us what little insight we have into Conolly's existence over the next seven years.

Conolly at first feigned optimism. While complaining that the demands of practice, being "unsettled as to house, and distracted at times with the noise of children," were interfering with his book on Ardent Spirits for the society, he boasted that "my practice [at Warwick] began at once, and the average thus far has equalled that of my best year before I left Warwickshire to be tormented 'for some sin' in the University." As for the future of "that Institution . . . , much may be hoped from the timely (or untimely) death of some of the Council and Professors."[83] Two weeks later, the attractions of the provincial backwater had begun to diminish. Conolly had begun a second book for the Society, a popularization for the lower classes of medical ideas about cholera, only to discover that "this is a land where no books are to be borrowed or even stolen. The latest publication in the hands of any of my medical neighbours is a dissertation on the diseases which followed the Great Flood." Perforce he had to order three or four from London, "very unwillingly," because he could scarcely afford to purchase them. "Since these are for a piece on Cholera for the Society," he wondered whether "the publishers for the Society have the means of getting them more advantageously than I can do." In the future, he assured Coates, his financial position was bound to improve: "I really begin to think that at last I shall become a prosperous man, for I find myself getting Jewish."[84]

Such expectations were doomed to disappointment. In late December, he wrote an answer to Coates's "kind inquiry about my proceedings here. I think I am getting on so as to have a hope in time, of struggling through many difficulties."[85] But the difficulties were formidable. He finished the manuscript on cholera just before Christmas, 1831,[86] but the small sum it earned him was swallowed up in the attempt to satisfy some of the creditors he had left behind in London: "after the 15th, Mr. Denies of 27 Princes Street Bank who is occasionally 'paying off' things for me will call to receive the £50—to save you any trouble." The companion volume on Ardent Spirits, first promised for December, then for January,[87] remained unwritten, though Conolly in each letter promised its imminent dispatch.[88] Meanwhile, he proposed that he write other titles for the Society, only to have Coates decline them.[89]

By May of 1832, the burden of his past failures and the struggle to scratch an inadequate living from his practice began to show in his letters: "I have been very busy lately, both in practice, and in lecturing to the Mechanics' Institution here, and in commemorating Shakespeare's birthday at Stratford. But I require constant task work to overcome a restlessness which what I suffered latterly in London has left in my brain and nervous system, which I sometimes fear will never leave me."[90] And his protestations that, except for the SDUK, "I hardly regret having lost anything else that London contains" sound increasingly hollow.[91] After a long silence, he wrote plaintively to Coates, "Once upon a time there was a professor of my name, where is he now? May I flatter myself that you sometimes wonderingly ask that question?" If Coates were to visit him in Warwick, "You will find me a very rustic physician with some provincial fame, no doubt, but as my foolish friends say, buried." Revealingly, he continued, "I often wish I really were. . . . The London University has provided me for life with incurable care—but 'what's that'!—I have learned that resignation is the best philosophy."[92]

The "incurable care" was not to be vanquished so easily, however. Less than two years later, Conolly wrote to Coates again begging for a commission to write a series of popular treatises for working men on diseases of the chest, stomach, brain, and so on, to appear in the *Working Man's Companion*. "It is but candid to say that I am in some degree driven to the idea of this industry by necessity. . . . I have long been trying[?] to extricate myself from the ruin [*sic*] which London brought me. . . . I am looking out for work. I am convinced I could prepare the little volumes of the Physician *one every three months*. Please think about it, and drop me a line soon—something I must set about and nothing takes my fancy more."[93]

But nothing came of this proposal, and in 1838, still drowning in debt, Conolly embarked on a desperate attempt to escape from his provincial exile. "Not much encouraged thereto by his friends, who regarded such a step as the suicide of reputation and the confession of complete failure in life,"[94] he applied for the vacant position of superintendent of the Middlesex County Lunatic Asylum at Hanwell. At least this offered the security of a salary of £500 per annum, together with free room and board for his family in the asylum; and he had, after all, a long-standing interest in the treatment of the insane, had written on insanity and served as inspector of the Warwickshire madhouses. To his dismay, however, his application was rejected, and in his stead the magistrates appointed J. R. Millingen, a retired army surgeon with no discernible background in the treatment of insanity.[95]

Conolly's humiliation was now complete. "The outlook into the future as black as ever, family cares increasing," he once more uprooted his household and moved to Birmingham, to see whether, in a different setting, his luck would change.[96] At forty-four, this latest failure appeared to have permanently dashed all the hopes he had once nurtured "of obtaining, through my exertions . . . , that reputation and those advantages of fortune, about which no reasonable man can, or ought to be indifferent."[97] His fixed disposition to refuse "to recognize or accept the painful necessities of life" meant that throughout his life, "troubles, shirked at the time, were gathered up in the future, so as to demand at last some convulsive act of energy, in order to disperse them."[98] But by this time, it must have seemed that even convulsive efforts would not suffice.

FAME, IF NOT FORTUNE

Ironically enough, Conolly was to be rescued from this depressing prospect by someone else's failures. The superintendency at Hanwell had originally fallen vacant when the Middlesex magistrates decided to experiment with a system of divided authority, allowing the superintendent to continue as the final arbiter of medical matters, but handing over administrative chores to a lay steward.[99] The arrangement proved unworkable, and exacerbated by Millingen's inexperience and quarrelsome disposition, conditions in the asylum degenerated until they verged upon anarchy. Finally the magistrates were forced to intervene; they dismissed the steward, Mr. Hunt, and accepted Millingen's resignation.[100] This time Conolly's application was successful. Less than a year after his initial rejection, a few lines appeared in *The Times* announcing that "Dr. Conolly, late of [Warwick], is appointed to the very important office of Resident Physician at the Hanwell Lunatic Asylum, Middlesex."[101]

Quite unexpectedly, the stern critic of asylum treatment, a man apparently incapable of managing his own affairs with even a modest degree of success, turned out to be an able and effective administrator of what was already the largest and—because of its metropolitan location—the most visible English asylum. Within a few weeks, the magistrates cheerfully announced that a remarkable change for the better had already taken place in the discipline and order of the establishment.[102] Conolly had at last found something he could do well, and to his final days was to insist "that if his life were to come over again, he should like nothing better than to be at the head of a large public asylum, in order to superintend its administration."[103] All the doubts he had once expressed about the appropriateness of the asylum solution, all questions about the deleterious effects of institutional existence, were at once suppressed in his enthusiasm for his new task.[104]

Thomas Bakewell, not many years before, had commented that "the regular [medical] practitioner has little advantage either of reputation or profit to expect from the treatment of [insanity]."[105] But whatever the general merits of this proposition, in Conolly's case it was emphatically disconfirmed. His achievements at Hanwell brought him, in rapid succession, national attention, royal notice and favour, election to a fellowship of the Royal College of Physicians, and ultimately recognition as "the most valuable consulting physician in mental disorders in Great Britain, and I suppose, in the world."[106] In Maudsley's words, "On the crest of the wave which he raised and rode he was carried to great fame and moderate prosperity."[107]

The first half of the nineteenth century witnessed a long struggle to "reform" the treatment of the mentally ill. Indeed, Hanwell, like all other

"County Asylums," was one product of this movement. It was the proud boast of the reformers that the adoption of their program, based on the new system of moral treatment pioneered by the Tukes at the York Retreat, did away with the cruelties previously visited upon the insane and replaced them with a regime based on kindness and forbearance. Whips and chains, those traditional accoutrements of the madhouse, were, like the straw and stench that were their inevitable accompaniment, to be banished from the modern asylum. The most sanguine hopes of the reformers had their limits, though. In Samuel Tuke's own words, "With regard to . . . the necessity of coercion, I have no hesitation in saying, that it will diminish or increase, as the moral treatment of the patient is more or less judicious. We cannot, however, anticipate that the most enlightened and ingenious humanity, will ever be able entirely to supercede the necessity of personal restraint."[108]

Yet it was precisely this extraordinary feat that Conolly claimed to have accomplished. Beginning with his very first report of Hanwell, he boldly asserted "that the management of a large asylum is not only practicable without the application of bodily coercion to the patient, but that, after the total disuse of such a method of control, the whole character of the asylum undergoes a gradual and beneficial change."[109] So far from being a regrettable necessity, or even a means of cure, restraint "was in fact creative of many of the outrages and disorders to repress which its application was commonly deemed indispensable;"[110] and to that extent "restraints and neglect, may be considered as synonymous."[111] In their place, "we rely wholly upon constant superintendence, constant kindness, and firmness when required. . . . Insanity, thus treated, undergoes great, if not unexpected modifications; and the wards of lunatic asylums no longer illustrate the harrowing description of their former state. Mania, not exasperated by severity, and melancholia, not deepened by the want of all ordinary consolations, lose the exaggerated character in which they were formerly beheld."[112]

These were large and astonishing claims, and they were greeted in many quarters with scepticism, if not outright hostility. They were, sniffed "Medicus" in the correspondence columns of *The Times*, "a piece of contemptible quackery and a mere bait for the public ear."[113] Millingen seized the opportunity to denounce his successor: "Nothing can be more absurd, speculative, or peculative than the attempts of theoretic visionaries, or candidates for popular praise, to do away with all restraint. Desirable as such a management might be, it can never prevail without much danger to personal security, and a useless waste and dilapidation of property."[114] Others went further still and reiterated the traditional medical claim that restraint was a form of therapy. Dr. Samuel Hadwin, former house surgeon at the Lincoln Lunatic Asylum, wrote, "Restraint forms the very basis and principle on which the sound treatment of lunatics is founded. The judicious and appropriate adaptation of the various modifications of this powerful means to the

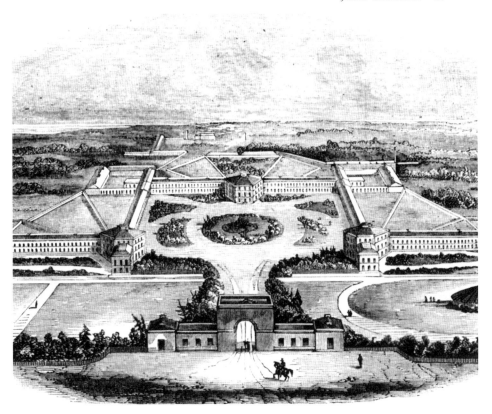

Figure 3.2. Middlesex County Asylum, Hanwell: the site of Conolly's triumph with nonrestraint and the largest asylum of the early Victorian age.

peculiarities of each case of insanity, comprises a large portion of the curative regimen of the scientific and rational practitioner; in his hands it is a remedial agent of the first importance, and it appears to me that it is about as likely to be dispensed with, in the cure of mental diseases, as that the various articles of the materia medica will altogether be dispensed with in the cure of the bodily."[115]

But while many medical men viewed nonrestraint with extreme suspicion, the new system quickly attracted powerful support in other quarters. During the first month of 1840, the correspondence columns of the *Lancet* were opened impartially to both proponents and opponents of the new system, in an effort "to contribute, in any way, to the solution of a question of so much importance."[116] However, the strain of such uncharacteristic even-handedness eventually told on its editor, Thomas Wakley. Never one to abide by his own admonition to the disputants that "angry recrimination can do no good, and may do much evil,"[117] he soon switched to a fervent advocacy of the cause of reform, couched in his inimitable mixture of panegyric and vituperation. More respectable opinion also rallied to Conolly's support. The venerable Samuel Tuke visited and bestowed his benediction ("Who can visit or contemplate the establishment of Hanwell, containing 800 insane persons, governed without any personal restraint, without gratitude or surprise?").[118] Lord Anthony Ashley Cooper, by now leader of the parliamentary forces seeking "lunacy reform," saw nonrestraint as the vindication and epitome of reform: he "could not speak too highly either of the system itself, or of the manner in which it was carried out by the talented Superintendent, Dr. Conolly."[119] Meanwhile, the *Illustrated London News* brought Conolly's achievements to the notice of a still wider audience, by extolling still another British contribution to the triumph of humanity.[120]

Perhaps the most important force in transforming Conolly into a national celebrity was, however, *The Times.* Beginning in late 1840, it devoted close and sympathetic attention to the progress of his experiment for a period of some four years.[121] Commenting on the "very considerable opposition . . . the attempt to obtain so desirable an object" had stirred up, it noted that such resistance had also surfaced within the institution, "not simply on the part of several of the county magistrates, but even from many of the servants and officers of the asylum." Fortunately, "that humane gentleman," Dr. Conolly, had, with the staunch support of another faction among the magistrates, vanquished the peculiar notion that there was "more actual cruelty hidden under the show of humanity in the system of non-coercion than was openly displayed in muffs, strait-waistcoats, leg-locks, and coercion chairs"; and had successfully brought to fruition "one of the greatest works that the dictates of the humane mind could suggest."[122] Three weeks later, a report on the celebration of "Old Year's Night" at Hanwell demonstrated for the paper's readers the happy effects of the salutary system of nonrestraint. The furies of madness were thoroughly domesticated, and "the utmost tranquillity prevailed." Indeed, when the four hundred patients assembled for the commencement of the merriment, "scarcely a word was to be heard and the effect produced was most striking and pleasing."[123] Soon afterward, nonrestraint received the royal imprimatur: the Duke of Cambridge arrived and spent two and a half hours at "this admirable institution," lunched with Conolly (presumably not on ordinary asylum fare), and left proclaiming himself "highly delighted" with all he had seen.[124]

Basking in this unexpected praise and attention to one of their pauper institutions, the Middlesex magistrates at once issued Conolly's first four annual reports bound together in a single new edition. Professional recognition of his achievement also grew apace. At the third annual meeting of the new Association of Medical Officers of Asylums and Hospitals for the Insane, Conolly was asked to take the chair. In 1844, he was elected a fellow of the Royal College of Physicians. The 1844 Report of the Metropolitan

Commissioners in Lunacy, it is true, exhibited rather more ambivalence about the value of nonrestraint, but two years later, the new national Lunacy Commission had thrown aside such doubts, and nonrestraint became the ruling orthodoxy of British asylumdom.

Conolly had thus become, in the eyes of his admirers, "one of the most distinguished men of the age, and one whose name will pass down to posterity with those of the Howards, the Clarksons, the Father Matthews, and other great redressers of the wrongs, crimes, and miseries of mankind."[125] Oxford University awarded him an honorary DCL; and his marble bust was executed by Benzoni.[126] In 1850, the Provincial Medical and Surgical Association fêted Conolly at their annual meeting at Hull.[127] And two years later, with Lord Shaftesbury presiding, Conolly's achievements were again celebrated, and he was presented with a gift of a three-quarter-length portrait by Sir John Watson Gordon, R.A., and an allegorical piece of silver plate standing two feet high and valued at £500, which illustrated mental patients with and without restraint, all surmounted by the god of healing.[128]

Such extraordinary praise and recognition suggests that Conolly's achievement had a symbolic significance for the Victorian bourgeoisie that extended far beyond its contribution to the welfare of the mad. Confronted by the threats of Chartism and a militant working class; surrounded by the all-but-inescapable evidence of the devastating impact of industrial capitalism on the social and physical landscape; and themselves the authors of a New Poor Law assailed by its critics (most memorably in Dickens's *Oliver Twist*) as the very embodiment of inhumanity and meanness of spirit, the Victorian governing classes could at least find a source of pride in the generous and kindly treatment now accorded to the mad. In a wholly practical way, the work of the lunacy reformers constituted a proof of their society's progressive and humane character. (Hence the curious claim made by Sir George Paget, that the Victorian asylum was "the most blessed manifestation of true civilization the world can present.")[129]

As the man who epitomized and had brought the new approach to perfection, John Conolly had thus richly earned his audience's applause. The paternal order he had established demonstrated that even the irrational and raving could be reduced to docility, by moral suasion and self-sacrifice rather than force. Here, as he put it in the concluding lines of his panegyric on the new asylum, "Calmness will come; hope will revive; satisfaction will prevail. Some unmanageable tempers, some violent or sullen patients, there must always be; but much of the violence, much of the ill-humour, almost all the disposition to meditate mischievous or fatal revenge, or self-destruction will disappear. . . . Cleanliness and decency will be maintained or restored; and despair itself will sometimes be found to give place to cheerfulness or secure tranquillity. . . . [The asylum is the place] where humanity, if anywhere on earth, shall reign supreme." A Potemkin village characterized

by an absence of conflict and strife, it constituted a veritable utopia wherein
the lower orders of society could coexist in harmony and tranquillity with
their betters, personified by the figure of a superintendent devoted to their
welfare and content to "sacrifice . . . the ordinary comforts and convention-
alities of life" for their sake.[130]

A Rival Claimant

In celebrating Conolly's accomplishment, Victorians were thus simultaneously affirming the moral validity of their social order itself; and his powerful friends, while acknowledging that he "no doubt received important
assistance from fellow-labourers in the same field," now closed ranks
around the proposition that "Dr. Conolly himself put an end to the use of all
forms of mechanical restraint in our asylums."[131] But such claims were, as
Conolly himself periodically acknowledged,[132] at best a serious distortion.
Nonrestraint was introduced, not by him, but by Robert Gardiner Hill, then
a twenty-four-year-old house surgeon at the provincial subscription asylum
at Lincoln. Hill had announced the system in a public lecture to the Lincoln
Mechanics Institute in 1838: "I wish to complete that which Pinel began. I
assert then in plain and distinct terms, that in a properly constructed building, with a sufficient number of suitable attendants, restraint is never necessary, never justifiable, and always injurious, in all cases of lunacy whatever."[133] For almost two years before Conolly assumed his duties at
Hanwell, Hill had demonstrated in practice the feasibility of such an approach. And it was, in fact, a visit to Lincoln that prompted Conolly to try
the new system.[134]

Yet Hill's obvious claims as the originator of nonrestraint brought him
little honour and scant reward of any other sort. Though bearing the brunt
of the early assaults on the system as speculative and wildly misguided,[135]
he was granted none of the subsequent recognition and social lionization so
readily accorded to Conolly. On the contrary, machinations among the staff
and governors at the Lincoln Asylum forced his resignation there,[136] and he
found himself unable to obtain another asylum post. Ironically, a failure
that must have been especially galling, he was even rejected when he sought
the position of medical officer under Conolly at Hanwell,[137] and so he was
forced by default to enter general practice. Though a decade later, he became the proprietor of a private licensed house, he never managed to obtain
an appointment at another public asylum.

One can readily imagine the effects of this on someone as sensitive to
questioning of his own merits as Hill was. The last straw seems to have been
when he was present at the 1850 meeting of the Provincial Medical Surgical

Association and heard Conolly praised as the author of his system. Though Conolly graciously indicated that the merit was not his alone but was shared with Dr. Charlesworth, the visiting physician at Lincoln, and though Charlesworth then indicated that "the real honour belonged to Mr. Hill,"[138] he was not satisfied, not least, perhaps, because it was forcibly brought home to him how soon his claim to priority had been forgotten.

He promptly sought to reassert his claims by writing to the medical press, only to be met by an attempt by his former enemies at Lincoln to claim the merit for Charlesworth. And when Hill's supporters took up a collection for a testimonial to rival Conolly's, his opponents promptly erected a statue of Charlesworth, with a plaque on the base describing him as the originator of nonrestraint, on the grounds of the Lincoln Asylum.[139] More seriously, Hill fell afoul of Thomas Wakley's pen and found himself traduced in the *Lancet's* columns in the latter's typically unscrupulous fashion.[140]

Conolly's role in all of this was hardly innocent. With whatever motives, he consistently declined to give Hill his due. That he had borrowed the idea of nonrestraint from Lincoln he could not deny; that the discovery was Hill's he sought constantly to obscure; and when Hill in exasperation at length lashed out at his now deceased rival,[141] he succeeded only in alienating his audience and further tarnishing his own reputation. His shrill and strident claims of priority, his wearisome marshalling of minutiae to prove his own originality, were "not only boring, but repellent."[142] As he proved chronically unable to grasp, one who exhibited such boorish and ungentlemanly qualities could never hope to be accorded a place of honour in a profession desperate to dissociate itself from all that smacked of lower class, tradesmanlike behaviour.

The elegant and socially graceful Conolly inflicted no such handicaps on himself, displaying "a certain humility of manner, a degree of self-deprecation . . . which failed not to attract men; it was nonetheless captivating because it might seem the form in which a considerable dash of self-consciousness declared itself."[143] On the public stage that he had secured for himself at Hanwell, he took delight in the opportunity to display the liberal and paternalistic instincts of the gentleman:

> His interest in the patients never seemed to flag. Even cases beyond all hope of recovery were still objects of his attention. He was always pleased to see them happy, and had a kind word for each. Simple things which vainer men with less wisdom would have disregarded or looked upon as too insignificant for their notice, arrested Dr. Conolly's attention, and supplied matter for remark and commendation—e.g., a face cleaner than usual, hair more carefully arranged, a neater cap, a new riband, clothes put on with greater neatness, and numerous little things of a like kind, enabled him to address his poor illiterate patients in gentle and loving accents, and thus woke up their feeble minds, caused sad faces to

gleam with a smile, even though transient, and made his visits to the wards to be longed for and appreciated. Dr. Conolly rejoiced in acts of beneficence. To be poor and to be insane were conditions which at once endeared the sufferers to him; and when the insanity was removed, and when the patient left the asylum, he generally strove to obtain some pecuniary aid for her from the "Adelaide Fund" (a fund originated for the relief of discharged patients), and supplemented this very often indeed with liberal donations from his own purse.[144]

DEPARTURE FROM HANWELL

Despite a patient population nearing a thousand, a "monstrous multitude of diseased humanity" crammed into buildings originally designed for half that number,[145] and notwithstanding a dismally low cure rate, Conolly's Hanwell was widely regarded as a splendid advertisement for the merits of reform and nonrestraint.[146] From time to time, protesting mildly that the asylum was too big,[147] he objected to the Middlesex magistrates' propensity to seek cheeseparing economies. But for the most part, he sought to exploit Hanwell's fame to persuade others of the advantages, indeed the necessity, of expanding the numbers of county asylums. Such endeavours acquired a new urgency in the wake of the passage of the 1845 Lunatic Asylums Act, for although public provision for the pauper insane was now made compulsory, magistrates in many parts of the country sought to delay or evade building asylums of their own. Accordingly, Conolly wrote a series of articles for the *Lancet* (republished the following year as a monograph) extolling the humanity and economy of asylums devoted to the cure of the lunatic and urging their rapid construction. Ironically, enough, his own role at Hanwell was by this time much diminished and soon to end. His disengagement was not provoked by any disenchantment with administering an ever-larger warehouse for the unwanted; nor did it constitute a protest at the deficiencies of an overcrowded establishment later described as "a vast and straggling building, in which the characteristics of a prison, a self-advertising charitable institution, and some ambitious piece of Poor Law architecture struggle for prominence."[148] Instead, it derived from administrative changes that threatened his own authority and status.

The Middlesex magistrates had long exhibited a much greater disposition to interfere in the daily running of "their" asylum than was to be found elsewhere. Their evident belief that nonmedical administration could affect significant economies had already led them to a proposed reorganization of Hanwell that had provoked their first superintendent, Sir William Ellis, to resign. And they were apparently not dissuaded by the fact that their subsequent experiment with a system of divided authority had dismally failed, forcing the resignation of the physician and the dismissal of the steward and thus indirectly bringing about Conolly's appointment. For when the Metropolitan Commissioners in Lunacy insisted that Hanwell's "extreme magnitude" required more extensive supervision, the justices once more developed a scheme to place daily administration in lay hands.[149] Conolly did not wait for the plan's implementation but promptly offered his resignation; in later years, he spoke of "the absurdity—I could almost say the criminality,—of committing one of the most serious of human maladies to the charge of anyone uninstructed in medicine."[150]

This time, as had not been the case with Ellis, a compromise was arranged. Anxious to retain the connection with Conolly that had brought them so much favourable publicity, the magistrates offered him the post of "visiting and consulting physician" at a reduced salary of £350, and he accepted. His duties now became "to give his attendance for two days a week, and for six hours at every attendance." At other times, medical matters were to be dealt with by the House Surgeons who had formerly acted as his assistants.[151] Convinced that it was imperative to have a single resident officer exercising ultimate control over the asylum and its staff, and equally certain that medical men were fit neither by temperament nor by training to assume such a role, the magistrates announced the appointment of John Godwin, a retired army officer, to fill the position.[152]

Under the terms of the appointment, it was specified that "the Governor has the power of suspending not only the servants but even the Medical Officers and Matron of the Asylum. He has, also, the entire control over the classification, employment, amusements, instruction, and general management of the patient . . . subject only to the general control of the Visiting Justices."[153] His superiority was reflected in the higher salary paid him; while the two resident medical officers received £200 each, the Governor was paid £350 a year. In view of the range and scope of affairs in which his lay judgment was supposedly given precedence, there was a disingenuousness about the claim that "in regulating his particular duties . . . the Visiting Justices have endeavoured to reconcile his position as their officer whom they will vest with paramount authority to enforce all their orders and regulations, with the distinct responsibility of the Medical Officers in all that concerns the moral management as well as the strictly medical treatment of the Patients."[154] For, in practice, to concede the doctors' right to direct the moral treatment of the patients would involve taking away from the governor the very areas of supervision where his authority was supposed to be paramount; while to refuse to concede it was to reduce the asylum physicians to mere decorative appendages. Conflict was thus unavoidable, though the ensuing struggle reached a swift conclusion.

In August 1844, just four months after his initial appointment, the justices cryptically announced, in two lines buried at the end of their report that Godwin's resignation had been tendered and accepted.[155] In their next report, they indicated that "after the retirement of the late Governor, the Visiting Justices resolved to defer filling up the vacancy for awhile, and to entrust the management of the Asylum to the ability and experience of the principal [i.e., medical] officers until they could determine what course for its future government it would be most advisable to adopt."[156] Already, however, they were noting "the progressive improvement in the order and discipline of the Establishment" since Godwin's departure. Six months later, they conceded that under medical supervision, "good management and order prevail . . . [and] that they have every reason to be satisfied with the way in which the Asylum continues to be conducted."[157]

The idea of employing a lay administrator to direct the asylum's affairs was now quietly buried; but the attempt to implement it had already served to all but sever Conolly's connection with Hanwell, after less than four years on the job. "Mutual trust between himself and the Justices was lost. He felt that they preferred the opinion of others and that his authority and system were eroded."[158] He hung on to his visiting appointment until 1852 when he finally resigned, to the relief of the magistrates, to whom his departure now meant little more than saving the ratepayers some money.[159]

The Pursuit of Private Practice

Even before this final rupture, Conolly's situation was such that he was forced to seek some alternative means of earning his livelihood. At £500 per annum, his salary as resident officer at Hanwell had scarcely been munificent, but at least he was also provided with room and board, a not inconsiderable benefit. His visiting appointment, however, entailed not just a reduced salary, but also the loss of this hidden subsidy. His new-found eminence ought presumably to have allowed him to escape the penury he had endured until middle age, but the difficulty was to know how to earn a living given that there were no defined alternative careers for alienists outside the burgeoning asylum system.

Almost fifty, Conolly had never possessed the qualities to succeed in single-handedly defining and developing a new form of specialist practice. Not until much later in the century, with the careers of men like his son-in-law, Henry Maudsley,[160] or Sir George Savage,[161] did the alternative of a practice based almost exclusively on the consulting room become possible. Conolly's fame did lead to his being called in as a consultant in difficult cases,[162] and he was also a frequently called expert witness in criminal cases where the insanity defence was raised.[163] But as in his earlier efforts at private practice, he scarcely distinguished himself in these spheres. His forensic testimony in the Pate case, for example, prompted the *Morning Chronicle* to complain that

"Dr. Conolly appears to have devoted his attention so exclusively to . . . mental disease that . . . he can apparently no longer distinguish where absolute madness begins and moral and legal responsibility ceases. There are very few of our fellow subjects, we suspect, who could get from Dr. Conolly a certificate of perfect sanity."[164]

Both lunacy inquisitions and criminal trials in which the insanity defense was invoked were highly charged occasions. While the latter was widely seen as a ruse to escape just punishment, a threat to the concept of responsibility and, thus, to the very foundation of criminal justice, the former raised the spectre of wrongful confinement of the sane in asylums, "a living death" that inspired periodic moral panics throughout the nineteenth century. Large segments of the Victorian public seem to have questioned both the motives and the competence of alienists who claimed expertise in assessing madness, and Conolly's published opinions and his actions both helped to feed these suspicions. Before entering upon a career as an asylum doctor, he had insisted that not every case of unsound mind required incarceration in an asylum. Rather, there was a need for a careful assessment of each case to determine *whether or not the departure from sound mind be of a nature to justify the confinement of the individual*"; and such inquiries were likely to disclose that "complete restraint is very rarely required." A less discriminating approach posed a serious threat to individual freedom and peace of mind.[165]

Two decades later, these were almost precisely the fears his clear repudiation of his earlier views seemed calculated to arouse. In 1849, in the case of *Nottidge v. Ripley*, Lord Chief Baron of the Court of the Exchequer Sir Frederick Pollock declared that, in his opinion, "no lunatic should be confined in an asylum unless dangerous to himself or others."[166] Notwithstanding the fact that Conolly's own earlier opinions were the expressed authority for this decision,[167] he at once issued a lengthy remonstrance declaring Pollock's dictum "both mistaken and mischievous." It transpired that he now believed an extraordinary range of behaviours qualified one for the madhouse: "excessive eccentricity," "utter disregard of cleanliness and decency," "perversions of the moral feelings and passions," a disposition "to give away sums of money which they cannot afford to lose," indeed all cases where people's "being at large is inconsistent with the comfort of society and their own welfare." Particularly in the young, incipient madness took on protean forms, and its cure required active and early intervention. Suitable cases for treatment included:

Young men, whose grossness of habits, immoderate love of drink, disregard of honesty, or general irregularity of conduct, bring disgrace and wretchedness on their relatives; and whose unsound state of mind, unless met by prompt and proper treatment, precedes the utter subversion of reason;—young women of ungovernable temper, subject, in fact, to paroxysms of real insanity; and at other times sullen, wayward, malicious, defying all domestic control; or who want that restraint over the passions without which the female character is lost. For these also such protection, seclusion, and order, and systematic treatment as can only be afforded in an asylum, are often indispensable. Without early attention and more careful superintendence than can be exercised at home, or in any private family, . . . [many] will become ungovernably mad, and remain so for life.[168]

Conolly's eagerness to consign the morally perverse and socially inadequate to the asylum was widely shared by his colleagues but seen in other quarters as a dangerous blurring of immorality and insanity.[169] In addition, many of the public were inclined to believe that alienists' willingness to define others as mad on such slender pretext reflected their financial interests in expanding their pool of patients. Conolly's actions in the Ruck case served only to reinforce these suspicions. Ruck was an alcoholic whose wife had secured his commitment to a private asylum on certificates issued by Conolly and Dr. Richard Barnett. Enforced abstinence brought about a rapid recovery, but several months passed before Ruck, at a cost of £1,100, secured an inquisition in lunacy, at which a jury found him sane by majority vote. He then sued Conolly and others for false imprisonment. At the trial that followed, Conolly was forced to make a series of damaging admissions. He had issued his certificate of Ruck's lunacy after a joint examination with Barnett, a clear violation of the law; and, more seriously, he had received a fee from Moorcroft House, where he was the consulting physician, for referring Ruck. The jury was obviously not impressed with Conolly's disingenuous defense: "I know the act says that a certificate should not be signed by any medical man connected with the establishment. I do not consider myself connected with the establishment, as I only send male patients to it"![170] As a result, he faced swingeing judgement against him for £500 damages.

Subsequently, too, his transparent rationalizations and the convenient congruence between his beliefs and his self-interest was savagely burlesqued in Charles Reade's scandalous best-seller, *Hard Cash*, where Conolly appears in thinly disguised form as the bumbling Dr. Wycherly.[171] Wycherly, in the sardonic words of Reade's hero, Alfred Hardie, "is the very soul of humanity," in whose asylum there are "no tortures, no handcuffs, nor leg-locks, no brutality."[172] But his "vast benevolence of manner" and the "oleaginous periphrasis" of his conversation concealed a second-rate mind "blinded by self interest" and apt to perceive insanity wherever he looked. In Reade's savage caricature, Conolly/Wycherly's pretensions to gentlemanly status are mocked, and his vaunted psychological acumen exposed as a pious fraud. "Bland and bald," this psychocerebral expert was "a voluminous writer on certain medical subjects . . . a man of large reading and the tact to make it subserve his interests," a task in which he was greatly aided by his settled disposition "to found facts on theories instead of theories on facts." As "a collector of mad people . . . whose turn in mind, cooperating with his instincts, led him to put down any man a lunatic, whose intellect was manifestly superior to his own," he is easily duped into diagnosing a sane man as lunatic, and thereafter persists stubbornly in his opinion till the unfortunate inmate is willing to grant that "Hamlet was mad."[173] In the climactic courtroom scene that brings the melodrama to a close, Reade puts Wycherly on the witness stand and gives him for his lines Conolly's most damaging admissions in the Ruck case. Wycherly, like his alter ego, tries to bluster his way through by protesting that counsel's questions are an affront to his professional dignity, but to no avail. When questioned, " 'Is it consistent with your dignity to tell us whether the keepers of private asylums pay you a commission for all the patients you consign to durance vile by your certificates?' Dr. Wycherly fenced with the question, but the remorseless Colt only kept him longer under torture, and dragged out of him that he received fifteen per cent from the asylum keepers for every patient he wrote insane; and that he had an income of £800 a year from that source alone."[174]

Along with his sometimes embarrassing forays into the courtroom and his moderately rewarding practice as a consultant,[175] Conolly was forced to turn to the private "trade in lunacy" as an additional source of income. His private residence, Lawn House, only a stone's throw from Hanwell, was adapted to take a handful of female patients.[176] Subsequently, he acquired an interest in another small asylum at Wood End and opened a third house, Hayes Park, in partnership with his brother, William.[177] In 1853 he became consulting physician to Moorcroft House Asylum from which he received both a salary and a percentage of the patients' fees.[178]

"A man," said Conolly a few years later, "must live by his profession, and a physician who devotes himself to mental disorders has to deal with a very small portion of the population, and he generally adds to his consulting practice, the plan of having a place where the treatment of patients can be conducted entirely under his own observation."[179] There can be no doubt, however, that trading in lunacy was at first distasteful to him. He had long argued that "every lunatic asylum should be the property of the State, and should be controlled by public officers,"[180] and during his time at Hanwell had become the leading spokesman for the new county asylums. Moreover, with its obvious overtones of "trade" and its long established unsavoury reputation (to which the writings of reformers like himself had in no small measure contributed), the business of running a private asylum was widely regarded as one of the most déclassé forms of medical practice, potentially lucrative, to be sure, but abhorrent to those of gentlemanly sensibilities.

But however repugnant, it was unavoidable. Conolly's income at Hanwell had been "barely sufficient to maintain his family," even with accommodation and food provided. Thrown back entirely on his own resources, his difficulties were compounded by the fact that he was once more "very lib-eral-minded in practice and otherwise, and gave little attention to financial matters."[181] More seriously, however, his household remained a large, even a growing burden. His eldest daughter soon married a Chinese missionary; but Sophia Jane did not marry until 1852, at the age of twenty-six,[182] and Anne Caroline not until 1866, at the age of thirty-five.[183]

Much the greatest source of concern, though, was his son, Edward Ten-nyson, who far exceeded even his father's youthful fecklessness and dis-played a remarkable inability to find any settled pursuit. When he was eighteen, his father's connections had secured him a position as part-time secretary to the Society for the Diffusion of Useful Knowledge. But in 1846, with the disbanding of the society, this came to an end, and the elder Con-olly's appeal to Lord Brougham for another patronage appointment for his son met with no response.[184] Five months later, Edward himself renewed the petition, asking specifically for an appointment with the new Railways Commission.[185] Spurned, he was not discouraged. Five years later, he sought Brougham's assistance to obtain a position as "a Poor Law Inspector," urging his experience as "one of the Guardians of the Poor for Brentford Union, [undertaken] in the absence of any more remunerative employ-ment," as a qualification for the job.[186] He was no more successful on this occasion, and because he had now reached his late twenties, it seems at last to have occurred to him that further efforts of his own were required. An attempt to practice as a barrister brought no improvement: "prospects of . . . business are anything but encouraging, and I am every year more desirous of doing something profitable in the world." The upshot was still another appeal to Brougham: "I venture to apply to your lordship to know whether there is likely to be any appointment connected with the new Charities Commission which I have any chance of obtaining."[187] There was not.

Now married, he still remained almost entirely dependent on his father's largesse, a burden that was further augmented with the arrival of the first of a series of children. At thirty-three, he had "been four years at the bar; . . . had hardly any practice" and decided to renew his entreaties: "My Lord, I have been so often troublesome with applications that I am ashamed to make another." Nevertheless, he did not let a little embarrassment stand in his way; this time he sought the vacant post of secretary to the Lunacy Com-mission.[188] But even the Conolly name could not secure this appointment, or a similar post with the Scottish Lunacy Commission, for which he ap-plied some two years later.[189] As late as 1864, his father still did not know what was to become of him: "Past forty—seven or eight children [sic]—no present means of educating them, nor of emigration where they might pros-per—no friends whom he has continued to see—no prospects at the Bar, etc., etc."[190] (In 1865, however, a year before his father's death, he finally adopted the favorite strategy for failed scions of the Victorian middle classes

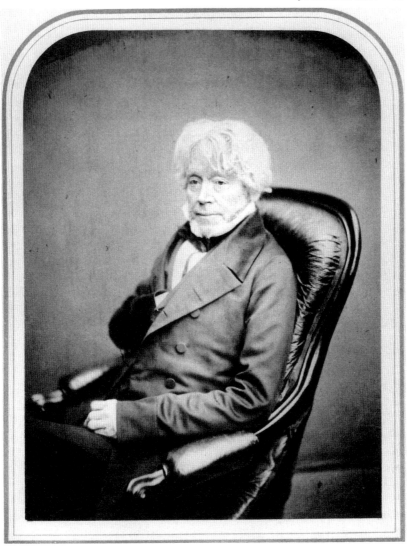

Figure 3.3. John Conolly as an old man: a photograph taken in his study at Lawn House, Hanwell, in February 1866, only days before his death.

and emigrated to New Zealand, where he became successively a member of Parliament, minister of justice, and a Supreme Court judge.)[191]

Faced with these demands on his income, it is not surprising that John Conolly had to swallow his pride and seek financial reward where he could find it. But just as he had earlier turned from a sceptic about asylum treatment into an advocate of a greatly expanded asylum system, so he now publicly defended the private institutions he once anathematized. Repudiating his prior stance on domestic treatment, he contended that "the management essential to recovery is impracticable in [the lunatic's] own house, or in any private family."[192] Yet out of the strong desire to conceal the presence of insanity, the wealthy attempted to resort to these expedients, with the result that "the whole house becomes a kind of asylum, but without the advantages of an asylum."[193] The consequences were necessarily antitherapeutic: "the alarm and even the affection of surrounding friends lead to hurtful concessions and indulgences, and to the withdrawal of all wholesome control; until the bodily disorder present in the first stages is increased, and the mind is much more irritated, thus making eventual recovery more difficult, and often altogether doubtful or impossible."[194] Still less enviable was the situation of those placed "in detached residences, where no other patient is received." Gloom, solitude, and neglect, both physical and moral, were their lot, "such, indeed, as to make the position of lunatics of wealthy families inferior to that of the lunatic pauper."[195] Private asylums had once been notorious for similar abuse and neglect. But their current proprietors were, with few exceptions, men "of high character and education"; and the institutions themselves "are now so well conducted as to present every advantage adapted to the richer patients, and to secure all the care and comfort which the poorer patient enjoys in our admirable county asylums"; with the result that the patient's reception into the asylum "is usually followed by an immediate alleviation of his malady, and he becomes at once surrounded by every circumstance and means favourable to cure."[196]

This Panglossian portrait was far from universally admired. Bucknill dismissed private asylums as "institutions for private imprisonment";[197] and the success of Reade's *Hard Cash* suggests that this opinion reflected a widespread public suspicion. But Conolly's views certainly corresponded closely with the official mythology of the Victorian asylum system and were fitting for one who now ranked as the doyen of his profession.

The publication of his defence of private asylums represented Conolly's last significant public activity. By 1860, he lived "in an elegant retirement" at Lawn House,[198] consulting occasionally in difficult cases, but for the most part concentrating upon *A Study of Hamlet*, an essay designed to show that the prince was indeed mad.[199] His health steadily worsened until, on March 4, 1866, he suffered a massive stroke. By the following day, he was dead. "His name," as the *Journal of Mental Science* puts it, "liveth forevermore."[200]

IDEAS AND INTERESTS

John Conolly not only played a central role in the success of the Victorian lunacy reform movement, but the vicissitudes of his individual biography also nicely illustrate some general sociological features that attended the constitution of Victorian alienism as a specialism. His widely publicized work at Hanwell contributed significantly to the creation of a marketplace for the alienists' services and helped to legitimize medical monopolization of the treatment of lunacy. Both ideologically and practically, his activities consolidated the Victorian commitment to institutional "solutions" to the problems posed by the deviant and the dependent. Furthermore, notwithstanding his scepticism about the value of most medical remedies for madness and his own overt reliance upon and preference for moral suasion and management in the treatment of his charges, he was most insistent on the crucial importance of medical control over the treatment of the insane. Any alternative to this professional monopoly he stigmatized as fatally misguided, almost "criminal." In this he echoed and lent the considerable weight of his prestige to the opinions of his colleagues.

As was generally true of Victorian alienists, his prerogatives as a professional Conolly defended most fiercely against outside threats. Thus, a proposal to limit the authority of the medical superintendent, not such critical issues as the unwieldy size and organized monotony of the Victorian asylum, provoked his resignation from Hanwell, though size and routine undoubtedly contributed the more powerfully to the transformation of the ideal of curative institutions into the reality of museums for the collection of the unwanted.[201] So far from acquiescing in the dilution of his authority, Conolly was among the first to insist that, for the alienist, everything that occurred within the institution was relevant to cure, and in consequence nothing could be safely delegated into lay hands. This claim, widely shared in the profession at this time, reflected the importance of monopolistic control of asylum administration as support for an otherwise shaky professional authority; hence the urgency with which alienists sought to persuade their employers that they alone should have authority over the most minute details of day-to-day activity in this "special apparatus for the cure of lunacy."[202]

As we have seen, Conolly's major concern, in the course of his writings on insanity, was with the administrative aspects of the treatment of insanity, and over the course of his career he evinced a declining interest in contributing to the scientific understanding of the condition itself. Almost certainly, this hierarchy of concerns accounts for a good measure of the hostility that lurked only just beneath the surface of Henry Maudsley's strikingly ambivalent "Memoir" of his late father-in-law. The markedly different—almost diametrically opposed—priorities of these two men, probably the leading figures of their respective generations of British alienists, in turn, mirror the sharp alteration of the context within which the profession operated in the two periods: the movement from what came to be seen as the naive optimism of the first half of the century, that medicine possessed the means to diagnose and successfully treat insanity, to the deepening pessimism of the late Victorian psychiatry, with its sense that insanity was all-but-incurable, the product of defective heredity and Morelian degeneration.

For those adhering to the latter orthodoxy, the issue of improving the treatment of the insane naturally lost some of its urgency, to be replaced by the need to explain (or explain away) the profession's apparent therapeutic impotence.

But even Conolly's own position underwent dramatic internal evolution in the course of his career. In his earliest writings on insanity, the product of a period in which he was very much the outside critic of existing practices, he assailed the indiscriminate confinement of the insane, urged the elimination of the private, profit-making "madhouses," and touted the merits of domiciliary care. A decade later, on his appointment as superintendent of one of the largest of the existing county asylums, he became a most important and effective proselyte of the expansion of the asylum system, and before long he was railing against those who wanted to confine asylum admissions to lunatics dangerous to themselves or others. Towards the close of his career, at a period in which he had become a leading private specialist in the treatment of insanity, he exhibited yet another volte-face by using the occasion of his second presidential address to the Medico-Psychological Association to issue a lengthy defense of the social utility—indeed indispensability—of the private asylum system.

It is possible, if one is charitably inclined, to view the evolution of his views as the product of greater experience and maturity. The inexperienced observer of his earlier years was disposed to promote impractical, if superficially attractive, visionary schemes of nonasylum treatment. Later acquaintance with the realities of treating insanity and the therapeutic possibilities of asylum treatment forced him to revise his ideas, as did his subsequent experience of running a private asylum. Equally, of course, one may opt for a cynical interpretation of his intellectual "progress." As Conolly himself remarked, early on in his career, "When men's interests depend upon an opinion, it is too much to expect that opinion always to be cautiously formed, or even in all cases honestly given."[203] The close correspondence between the evolution of his ideas and the unfolding of his career is too marked to escape comment. And even in the nineteenth century, some saw the parallels as more than coincidental. Sir John Charles Bucknill, whose own intellectual development, as we shall see, was in precisely the opposite direction to Conolly's—from an enthusiastic advocate to a scathing critic of the asylum system, both public and private—was convinced that Conolly's judgement had been subverted by self-interest. Praising the positions Conolly had adopted in *The Indications of Insanity* ("Nothing which Dr. Conolly ever wrote does more credit to his head and heart than these opinions"), he noted with sorrow his later repudiation of them. One could only regret that "advancing years and personal interests had made him indulgent to the evils he had denounced."[204]

The less moralistically inclined may prefer to adopt a rather different perspective on the internal evolution of Conolly's ideas. It is instructive to note how difficult it is for modern readers to portray his intellectual journey as "progress." For our generation has learned to view the asylum as an almost unmitigated disaster, a fatally mistaken approach to the problems of managing the mad and one that cannot be too swiftly consigned to the dustbin of history. Viewed from this perspective, Conolly's changing views appear to mark an almost perverse shift from enlightenment to error. To his earliest work our contemporaries turn, when they count him the author "of principles of treatment that have scarcely been improved in all the succeeding epochs of vanguard practice."[205] But for the Victorians, it was precisely this early critique of the asylum and advocacy of domiciliary care that was anomalous; and the abandonment of such aberrant opinions in favour of an elaborate defence of asylum treatment required no special explanation: it simply represented an acknowledgement of the findings of modern medical science. Here, as elsewhere, we observe how slippery the concept of "scientific knowledge" is in the human sciences and how profoundly dependent the content of that "knowledge" is upon the nature of the larger social order.

Chapter Four

THE ALIENIST AS PROPAGANDIST:

W.A.F. BROWNE (1805–1885)

> You may as well
> Forbid the sea for to obey the moon,
> As or by an oath remove, or counsel shake
> The fabric of his folly, whose foundation
> Is pyld upon his faith.
> (*William Shakespeare*, The Winter's Tale,
> *act I, scene 2*)

THE EDUCATION OF AN ALIENIST

BETWEEN THE publication of his first and only book in 1837 and his retirement from his post as the first Scottish Lunacy Commissioner in 1870, William Alexander Francis Browne occupied a position among Scottish alienists that was every bit as dominant as that of his English counterpart, John Conolly, and the parallels between the two men's lives and careers present some intriguing points of comparison. In the middle years of the nineteenth century, Browne's reputation extended south of the border, to the Continent, and even to North America, and derived principally, though not exclusively, from the impact of his book—a course of lectures he delivered when only thirty-two years of age to the managers of the obscure provincial asylum at Montrose. Much of Conolly's fame and influence, as we have seen, may be traced to his successful adoption of Robert Gardiner Hill's policy of running an asylum without any resort to what was termed "mechanical restraint"—strait-jackets, muffs, and the like—an innovation for which he managed to appropriate almost all the credit and to make the ruling orthodoxy of British asylumdom. More broadly, however, Conolly's stature derived from his role as the foremost English spokesman in behalf of the new system of reformed asylums and the most eloquent and effective exponent of the expropriation of the new system of moral treatment by medical men. His contributions in precisely these directions account for Browne's prominence among Scottish alienists and for the extension of his fame and influence beyond his native land.

We should not be surprised by this state of affairs. Notwithstanding the long history of medical speculations about the causes and cure of insanity, and the involvement of some segments of the medical profession in the eighteenth-century "trade in lunacy," only during the first half of the nineteenth century, with the emergence of state regulation of the mad business and the rise of a publicly funded asylum system, did medicine seek a cognitive and practical monopoly of the treatment of insanity. In this project, the reformed asylum, its image distanced as far as possible from the stereotyped portrait of the eighteenth-century madhouse, was pictured as the indispensable apparatus for the remanufacture of sanity from madness. Equally important, it constituted the built form whose replication and control would give medical men an unchallengeable physical and institutional foundation on which to erect exclusive and exclusionary claims to jurisdiction over insanity. In parallel fashion, moral treatment, while in its origins a lay discovery that threatened to undermine medical claims to special expertise or competence in the therapeutics of madness, was inescapably linked in the public mind with the new humane system of treatment for insanity and provided the essential technical means for administering the reformed asylum. Thus, those who most effectively persuaded the public of the virtues of an asylum-based response to madness and who simultaneously managed to secure the unambiguous assimilation of moral treatment into the medical armamentarium, had richly earned the gratitude of their alienist contemporaries and quite properly are accorded a central place of honour by those historians who equate the rise of psychiatry with the advance of science and humanity.

The striking similarities in the underlying sources of the prominence achieved by Browne and Conolly in their mature years find a curious echo in the circumstances of their early biographies. Browne was born into a precariously genteel family in Stirling, central Scotland, on June 24, 1805. Within a few weeks of his birth, his father, an army officer en route to join Wellington's troops in fighting the Peninsular War, was drowned when his troop transport was wrecked and sank on the Goodwin Sands. William was thus left to be brought up in his maternal grandparents' house, receiving a meagre education at the local high school and facing uncertain prospects for retaining his middle-class status. Conolly, some eleven years his senior, came from a not dissimilar social background (his father being the younger son of an impecunious minor branch of the Irish gentry), and he, too, was orphaned at a very early age, farmed out to relatives, and burdened with an inadequate childhood eduation.

The "choice" Browne and Conolly made of a career in medicine was in many respects scarcely a choice at all, given that the socially acceptable alternative professional careers of the Church and the military remained heavily dependent on the possession of quantities of social connections and capital, which both conspicuously lacked. Their prospects of making a decent living at their chosen profession were inevitably clouded, however, by the large numbers of middle-class boys who had reached identical conclusions. The remarkable expansion and reconstitution of the traditional professions in the nineteenth century may have comprised, as Magali Larson has argued,[1] an attempt at collective social mobility on the part of an expanding middle class, but the market for professionals' services failed to expand (early in the century, at least), as fast as the supply of eager recruits. The consequence, as Irvine Loudon's meticulous study of general practice has shown,[2] was that the 1820s were an extraordinarily inhospitable period in which to attempt to launch a medical career, a time of unparalleled intraprofessional rivalry in a grossly overcrowded professional marketplace.

Nonetheless, such was the prospect facing Browne and Conolly, both of whom elected to seek their training at Edinburgh University. For the provincial Scot as for the provincial Englishman, this decision must have seemed equally obvious. Medical training was then at its nadir at Oxford and Cambridge, the only sources of university credentials south of the border. Besides, a career as a physician to the upper classes, the only prospect for which the desultory classical instruction at Oxbridge might prove suitable, demanded social capital, connections, and advantages neither man possessed. Edinburgh, by contrast, was in a flourishing state, providing unquestionably the finest clinical training in the English-speaking world, even if the snobbery and reactionary politics of the English Royal College of Physicians still largely barred its graduates from the richest rewards open to a medical man, which were confined to elite practice in London.[3]

Conolly's arrival at Edinburgh in 1819 just antedated Browne's. The former proceeded to acquire the M.D. degree, the prerequisite to practice in the elite branch of the profession as a physician, rather than the surgical licentiate leading to general practice, with which Browne was forced to content himself. In other respects, their student careers were almost carbon copies of one another's: both served a term as president of the Royal Medical Society; and both acquired an interest in insanity that was to prefigure their later specialisation. Conolly's M.D. dissertation of 1821 was devoted to a brief discussion of *De statu mentis in insania et melancholia*; and as Browne boasted some years later, when applying for the vacant superintendency of the Montrose Lunatic Asylum, he, too, throughout his undergraduate training and even after his qualification as LRCSE in 1826, "made the human mind, both in its healthy and diseased condition, an especial subject of investigation."[4] Both men also acquired an acquaintance with the doctrines of phrenology—something they could scarcely avoid, given its prominent presence on the Edinburgh intellectual scene—[5] and adopted its major tenets; in common with most other prominent alienists of their generation,[6] each man incorporated the new "science of mind" into their understanding of the roots of insanity.

The two men's embrace of phrenological doctrine, and Browne's subsequent dedication of *What Asylums Were, Are, and Ought to Be* to Andrew Combe, M.D. (with his brother George the most prominent figure in British phrenological circles), may strike the modern reader as somewhat odd. After all, phrenology was for many years "an approved object of laughter for . . . intellectual historians."[7] One had simply to recall its association with carnival sideshows offering character readings to the credulous and could safely dismiss it as a pseudoscience of the lumps and bumps on the cranium, a doctrine whose proper place in the scheme of things was neatly encapsulated in the name of one of its most successful itinerant practitioners, J. Q. Rumball. Recent historiography, however, has demonstrated the foolishness of such judgements. Phrenology, in Ackerknecht's words, was "at least as influential in the first half of the nineteenth century as psychoanalysis in the first half of the twentieth."[8] Gall and Spurzheim's researches into the anatomical structure of the brain were anything but the work of charlatans; and socially, phrenological ideas were of the utmost significance, linked closely to campaigns "for penal reform, more enlightened treatment of the insane, the provision of scientific education for the working classes, the education of women, the modification of capital punishment laws, and the re-thinking of British colonial policy."[9]

In the local Edinburgh context, the conversion of Browne and Conolly is still more readily understandable. Among the established Edinburgh cultural elite—the traditional upper estates of law, landed property, and established learning—phrenology was always viewed with hostility and disdain. From the appearance of John Gordon's critical article on phrenology in its July 1815 issue, the *Edinburgh Review* never passed up an opportunity to scorn the science's adherents or to treat its doctrines with contempt, and throughout the 1820s phrenology remained "under almost continuous siege from Edinburgh intellectuals."[10] But the obverse of this fierce rejection in elite circles was an equally passionate attachment to the new science on the part of bourgeois and petit-bourgeois elements, particularly the commercial and mercantile classes and those ambitious younger professionals with weak or deficient kinship ties or other social linkages to traditional landed interests—precisely the social background from which Browne and Conolly came. Phrenology's association with "a far-reaching programme of social and cultural reform"[11] and its intellectual challenge to the Scottish Common-Sense philosophy that was the ruling orthodoxy in traditional elite circles, brought it a steady stream of adherents from amongst those "young middle-class liberals who resented the political, social, and cultural restrictions still imposed upon them by the ancien regime."[12]

As a medical student, Browne struck up a close personal friendship with both Combes, assisting George with his phrenological studies and soon establishing himself as one of the more popular phrenological lecturers in the city. But in 1828, he left Edinburgh for the Continent, having been entrusted with the care of a well-to-do lunatic who was to be treated through travel and changes of scene. During the two years that followed, as he travelled through Belgium, France, and Italy, Browne "attentively examined the arrangements and mode of treatment in some of the most celebrated asylums in the different countries through which I passed."[13] Having been particularly impressed by the Parisian asylums, he returned to Paris during the summer and autumn of 1832, studying under Esquirol at Charenton and Pariset at the Salpêtrière before returning to Stirling in early 1833 to try to establish himself as a general practitioner.

Barely a year later, the March 22, 1834, issue of the *North British Advertiser* carried a notice of an opening as superintendent of the Royal Lunatic Asylum at Montrose (the oldest charity asylum in Scotland), with what was promised to be "a liberal salary" attached. Andrew Combe himself was tempted to apply, writing to his brother George that "I have a hankering after some such charge, as better suited to my present condition of body and mind than general practice, for which I do not feel I have adequate stamina." The next post, however, brought a letter from Browne, soliciting the support of both brothers for *his* application, at which Andrew "immediately gave up all idea of himself applying for the situation, and cordially supported the pretensions of his young friend," (support that proved weighty because of the Combes's high "standing with the Sheriff and some of the resident gentry of Forfarshire").[14]

As Browne and Conolly's biographies remind us, in the early part of the nineteenth century, recruitment into the ranks of asylum superintendents was largely, and necessarily, an unstructured process. Even among the medical men entering the field, few could claim to have had any formal training or practical experience in the care and cure of the insane. Indeed, with jurisdiction over the treatment of madness anything but the monopoly of a particular group, the issue of what kind of background, personal and intellectual qualities, and experience qualified an individual to run an asylum was unavoidably uncertain and potentially contentious. Stable and formalized patterns of recruitment and training would only emerge once doctors had acquired sole jurisdiction over the rapidly burgeoning network of institutions that were to make up Victorian asylumdom, for until this task was accomplished, it was "always possible that people outside the [proto] occupation [could] claim equal or greater skill"[15] in the management of the mad.

Browne's application for the vacancy at Montrose sought to put the best possible face on his qualifications. He stressed his long-standing interest in insanity, dating back to his student days, and pointed to his extensive acquaintance with some of the best European institutions. Together with his powerful outside support, this sufficed to gain him the position by a majority vote—though he was to confess, some thirty years after the fact, that "so exclusive and mysterious were these abodes, that the first time I entered, or could enter, an asylum in this country, was to take possession as a superintendent."[16] In consequence, once installed as head of the asylum, it was "with fear and trembling" that he advanced "the simplest and most innocent innovations—such as that airing yards should be planted with shrubs, that Divine service should be performed on Sunday,—I saw expressive looks, and shrank from significant whispers, that the doctor was as wild and visionary as his charges." But Browne persisted, even insisting upon "the first lighting [of] the Montrose Asylum with gas in 1836," an event that prompted the assembly of a crowd "at the gate to witness and perhaps to enjoy the conflagration, which was expected inevitably to follow so daring and desperate an experiment."[17]

The asylum did not burn down. On the contrary, it flourished in Browne's hands as never before. The principles of the new moral treatment, which he had observed at first hand in Paris, were imported for the first time into a Scottish establishment and made the foundation of its institutional routines. What the asylum had been was increasingly overtaken by Browne's vision of what it could and ought to be: an ideal environment in which to provide for the moral and physical management of the insane and to work towards their restoration to sanity.

In the autumn of 1836, emboldened by his success, Browne, seeking a wider audience, announced a course of public lectures to be given before the managers of the asylum and assorted local notables. Intending in these talks "to condense, in a plain, practical, and still popular form, the results of observation in the treatment of insanity, for the specific and avowed purpose of demanding from the public an amelioration of the condition of the insane,"[18] Browne succeeded in producing an extraordinarily effective piece of propaganda. Published in May 1837, *What Asylums Were, Are, and Ought to Be* contains perhaps the single most influential portrait by a medical writer of the horrors of the traditional madhouse system; and its powerful and ideologically resonant description of the contrasting virtues of the reformed asylum, a hive of therapeutic activity under the benevolent autocratic guidance and control of its medical superintendent, provided within a brief compass a strikingly attractive alternative vision of an apparently attainable utopia. Small wonder, then, that Browne's modest volume rapidly received a string of favourable notices in the medical press,[19] propelled its author to the forefront of the newly consolidating profession of alienism, and secured for him a new job as head of the most richly endowed new asylum in the British Isles. For almost twenty years, Browne was to serve as superintendent of the new Crichton Royal Asylum in Dumfries, turning down lucrative offers to head the Edinburgh Royal Asylum and even Bethlem itself before resigning in 1857 to become the first Scottish Commissioner in Lunacy. And despite his long self-imposed exile in the provinces, he remained during all this time among the four or five most prominent British alienists of his generation.

Figure 4.1. William Alexander Francis Browne, the doyen of Scottish alienists and the foremost propagandist in behalf of the reformed asylum.

THE MOVEMENT FOR LUNACY REFORM

One does not have to search very far afield to discern some of the more important factors that prompted Browne's (and Conolly's) initial interest in insanity. By the late eighteenth century, general medical interest in the subject was clearly on the upswing, a development given further impetus by George III's recurrent bouts of "mania." The Hellenic tradition of a humoural physiology, pathology, and therapeutics provided a recognizably medical account of mental disorder; though such traditional claims to jurisdiction over the insane had hitherto been neglected by the bulk of the profession, within an increasingly naturalistic and secularized cultural universe, they provided perhaps the most intellectually coherent available explanation of the etiology of insanity—an explanation that possessed the not inconsiderable advantage of offering ready-made the means "to classify [insanity], to reason about it, and to take action on it: in more formal terms, to diagnose, to infer, and to treat."[20] In the context of a growing interest in madness and an expanding market for those "trading in lunacy," William Cullen had begun offering lectures on the subject at Edinburgh as early as the 1770s. Most of the prominent mad-doctors of the late eighteenth and early nineteenth century—such figures as Thomas Arnold, Alexander Crichton, William Hallaran, John Ferriar, Thomas Trotter, and John Haslam—had preceded Browne and Conolly at the University, and contemporaneously with the latter's matriculation, Alexander Morison was busily (if unsuccessfully) lobbying for the establishment at the medical school of a chair for the study and treatment of mental diseases, with himself as its first occupant.

More immediately, the English parliamentary inquiries of 1807 and 1815–1816, had alerted a larger public to the issue of the treatment of the insane. The generalized portrait of inhumanity and neglect, and the lurid revelations of medical malfeasance, maltreatment, and even murder that had punctuated the latter inquiry had placed lunacy reform at the center of philanthropic attention; the *Edinburgh Review* took a major role in retailing the Select Committee's findings to a wider audience.[21] Moreover, unlike the situation in 1807, when the absence of a clear alternative conception of how to cope with madness had checked reformers' ambitions and limited the scope of the legislation they proposed, the new-found prominence of the York Retreat in the following decade, with its practical demonstration of a therapeutic regime founded on the principles of what William Tuke called "moral treatment," provoked the introduction of far more ambitious and wide-ranging legislative proposals.

For medical men, neither the founding of the York Retreat nor the findings of the House of Commons investigation constituted an unmixed blessing. Though even in an English context moral treatment was not solely Tuke's invention,[22] it had now been firmly identified in the collective consciousness with him and with his institution. In sharp contrast with more traditional practices, Tuke had insisted upon "the superior efficacy . . . of a mild system of treatment." External, physical coercion was minimized, and, in its most blatant forms—"gyves, chains, and manacles"—done away with entirely. In its place came an emphasis on "treating the patient as much in the manner of a rational being as the state of mind will possibly allow" and on carefully designed measures to induce inmates to collaborate in their own recapture by the forces of reason.[23] From the reformers' perspective,

Tuke had successfully established that the supposedly continuous danger and frenzy to be anticipated by maniacs were the *consequence* of rather than the occasion for harsh and misguided methods of management and restraint; indeed, he argued that this reputation was in great measure the self-serving creation of the madhouse keepers. More promisingly still, he had apparently demonstrated that the asylum could provide a comfortable and forgiving environment that not only spared the insane the neglect which would otherwise have been their lot but also played a vital role in restoring a substantial proportion of them to sanity. At the same time, however, as Samuel Tuke had boldly announced, "the experience of the Retreat . . . will not add much to the honour or extent of medical science. I regret . . . to relate the pharmaceutical means which have failed, rather than record those which have succeeded." All the enthusiastic efforts of the medical men working at the Retreat had led to failure, demonstrating only, as one of them conceded, "that medicine, as yet, possesses very inadequate means to relieve the most grievous of human diseases" and prompting a rueful acknowledgement of "how much was to be done by moral, and how little by any known medical means."[24]

To make matters worse, many of the most serious abuses exposed by the 1815–1816 Committee had occurred at medically run institutions, and medical men were deeply implicated in the beatings and maltreatment of patients, even in their deaths. Nor was the performance of the medical witnesses called before the Committee—whether of those implicated in the scandals or those representing and trying to rescue the interests of the profession at large—such as to salvage their collective reputation,[25] or to quell what taken together amounted to "a rather damning attack on the medical profession's capacity to deal with mental illness."[26] If madness was now the subject of potential legislative intervention, and of ever greater public interest and concern, it was by no means clear that the outcome of such interventions would prove favourable to medical interests.

The 1815–1816 inquiry had been almost entirely the product of lay initiative: the investigations of provincial figures like the Yorkshire magistrate Godfrey Higgins[27] and his allies, Jonathan Gray[28] and Samuel Nicoll,[29] and of their metropolitan counterparts, Henry Alexander, and the prominent Quaker philanthropists, Edward Wakefield[30] and Thomas Hancock.[31] Higgins and Wakefield, the most active in the cause, had developed a thorough-going scepticism, even a hostility to medical claims to jurisdiction over insanity and did not hesitate to make their feelings known. Wakefield denounced doctors as "the most unfit of any class of persons" to serve as "Inspectors and Controllers of Madhouses" because "medicine has little or no effect on the disease" and medical men had shown themselves amply inclined to engage in ruthless profiteering at the expense of the mad.[32] And Higgins, his pen dripping sarcasm, noted that "among much medical nonsense, published by physicians interested to conceal their neglect, and the abuses of their establishments, it has been said, that persons afflicted with insanity are more liable than others to mortification of their extremities. . . . If members of the royal and learned College of Physicians were chained, or shut up naked, on straw saturated with urine and excrement, with a scanty allowance of food—exposed to the indecency of a northern climate, in cells having windows unglazed—I have no doubt that they would soon exhibit as strong a tendency to mortified extremities, as any of their patients." He had found, he confidently proclaimed, a "medicine" far superior to the bleedings, purges, and powders prescribed by these mountebanks, a rigorous system of inspection and supervision by lay "visitors and committees."[33] Echoing these sentiments, the reformers' parliamentary allies endorsed schemes that not only gave no recognition to medicine's claims to a privileged position in the treatment of the insane, but even threatened to subordinate those medical men already engaged in the madhouse trade to supervision and direction from outside committees of laymen.

To a large extent, the 1815–1816 Select Committee confined its attention to an examination of the treatment of the insane in England. It examined a parade of witnesses and undertook direct inquiries into conditions in a variety of asylums and madhouses. By contrast, it did not turn its attention to Scotland until making the last of its three 1816 reports. Even then, the Committee simply summarized uncritically the results of written queries to five Scottish sheriffs, supplemented by token testimony about conditions in the Glasgow Lunatic Asylum. This virtual neglect of conditions there was significant because, even after the Union in 1707, Scotland had remained legislatively separate from the remainder of the united kingdoms; its poor law arrangements, in particular, differed quite markedly from those operating south of the border. The Scots, indeed, recoiled with horror from the English use of the compulsory poor rate, retained a Calvinist distrust of relief for the able-bodied unemployed, viewed the effects of Speenhamland as confirmation of the evils of the English approach, and continued to rely on a parish-based system of "voluntary contributions . . . [as] the prime method of financing poor relief expenditure."[34] No legislation to alter this religiously based system was passed until 1845,[35] with the legal basis of the system continuing to rest on an act of 1574 designed to secure "the punishment of strong and idle beggars and provision for the sustenation of the Poor and Impotent."

The upshot of the 1815–1816 reports of the Select Committee on Madhouses was nonetheless separate legislative proposals for both England and Scotland which shared a number of common features: the compulsory provision of systems of asylums built at public expense and designed to accommodate at least all pauper lunatics (so as to eliminate the inducements to maltreatment that the reformers were convinced were inherent in allowing lunatics to be kept for profit); and the introduction of a vigorous national system of inspection by outsiders with no ties to the asylum administration (designed to provide a check against the tendency of all institutions to fall away from their initial ideals and the temptations for the madhouse keepers to neglect and maltreat their helpless charges, the mad).

Even for the English, these proposals were too much to swallow. The essential difficulty was that such measures threatened a transformation in political relationships whose importance extended far beyond the narrow sphere of lunacy reform. If enacted, they would have set the precedent for a notable expansion of the central coercive machinery at the disposal of the state. Opposition to such a concentration of power at the national level remained extraordinarily widespread and well entrenched at both the structural and ideological levels;[36] it was some thirty years before the lunacy reformers were to secure legislative enactment of their plans in England and Wales, and it took even longer for Scotland to fall into line. Only after the obstacles to central administration had been confronted and dealt a decisive defeat, not over the marginal issue of the treatment of lunatics, but over the critically important issue of Poor Law reform, was there a serious possibility of passing such far-reaching legislation.

For the Scots, the proposals were if anything still more pernicious, for they constituted a serious and threatening attempt to breach the foundational principles of their own poor law system (and system of governance more generally), by replacing voluntary, religiously motivated charity with state-financed relief and compulsory taxation. The precedent was too awful to contemplate, and the 1818 Scottish Lunacy Bill, introduced in February by Lord Binning, was rapidly and decisively sent down to defeat. Till the arrival in 1855 of the formidable American lunacy reformer, Dorothea Dix, the Scots continued to insist that a combination of family care, the boarding of harmless lunatics with strangers, and the limited accommodation provided by a handful of charity asylums (the so-called "Royal Asylums")[37] was superior to English asylumdom, compromised and contaminated as that system inevitably was by the morally corrupting effects of compulsory taxation.

Lunacy reform was thus an extremely protracted affair on both sides of the border. To resistance founded on opposition to increased political centralisation were superadded worries about the exposure of shameful and stigmatising family secrets if asylums were efficiently inspected and regulated and apathy and parsimony that blocked the expenditure of the capital sums a system of reformed public asylums would require. Necessarily, therefore, those committed to the restructuring of existing arrangements found themselves embarked upon a complex task of political persuasion, one which required that they develop a convincing ideological account of the superiority of their chosen solution.

Much of the reformers' moral fervour came from their acquaintance with the worst features of the "trade in lunacy," and one of their most effective weapons in the thirty-year struggle to implement their plans was the periodic exposure of "the crimes and horrors" endemic in existing madhouses. The difficulty with this tactic, of course, was that it threatened to undermine their simultaneous attempt to persuade the public of the virtues of a reformed "madhouse" or asylum as the preferred solution to the problem of managing the mad. Thus, quite central to their efforts was an attempt to develop both an elaborate account of the *differences* between the places they planned to erect and institutions of a more traditional sort and a vision of the asylum as the place of first rather than last resort, preferable to even the best and most solicitous domestic arrangements.

The task was the more difficult because institutional responses to all forms of dependence and debility still lacked social legitimacy. Even the poorest families among the working classes made strenuous efforts to avoid the disgrace of confinement in a workhouse. Similarly, hospitals for the physically sick, their enormous mortality rates uncompensated for by greatly improved chances of recovery, enjoyed a public reputation of being little better than charnel houses, vectors of disease and death to be avoided by all who had the means to do so. As for the deranged, an audience periodically regaled with evidence that appeared to confirm their worst gothic nightmares about what transpired behind the high walls and barred windows of the madhouse had somehow to be brought to embrace the need for a network of purpose-built asylums and to be convinced, should the occasion arise, that they should send their own loved ones into the institution for treatment.

For the reformers sought not merely to transform existing asylums for the benefit of those already immured in them, but to expand the system greatly, to embrace many more of the insane than had hitherto been thought to require institutionalization. The burgeoning literature on insanity in the 1820s and 1830s contended that madness was an ever more prevalent and deeply threatening problem, the dark side—indeed the product—of the growth of civilization, and an expanding threat to the social order and to civil and domestic peace. At the same time, those laying claim to jurisdiction over the insane insisted that with proper treatment, which necessitated early removal to a properly constituted asylum, this disorder was one of the most readily cured of the afflictions to which human flesh was heir. Expenditures on asylums were thus justified by an increasingly elaborate claim that there existed an "economics of compassion"—that the higher initial costs of a properly constituted asylum system would be rapidly offset by the high proportion of cures that would result, with the return of the dependent to the ranks of the productive citizenry.[38]

The Defence of Medical Prerogatives

Thus, the construction of a more benign and salubrious image for the asylum and the insistence on the potential curability of insanity when properly treated were vital components of the reformers' efforts to reshape attitudes towards madness and the mad. The contrast between what asylums were, and what they ought to be, lay at the heart of their attempts to overcome the political and economic obstacles to lunacy reform. Perhaps unsurprisingly, however, those medical men who interested themselves in the subject exhibited an equally central concern with the question of how to establish an exclusively *medical* jurisdiction over the treatment of insanity.

In the aftermath of the 1815–1816 inquiry, medical men clearly found themselves on the defensive, their claims to jurisdiction (as one of them fearfully, if exaggeratedly, noted) "almost . . . wrestled by the philosopher out of the hands of the physician."[39] Francis Willis, grandson of the Lincolnshire physician-cum-divine who had treated George III's madness, complained that "derangement has been considered by some to be merely and exclusively a mental disease, curable without the aid of medicine, by what are termed moral remedies; such as travelling and various kinds of amusements."[40] His insistence on the value of medical treatment was reiterated in more truculent form by William Lawrence, the newly appointed surgeon at Bethlem: "Arguments, syllogisms, discourses, sermons, have never yet restored any patient; the moral pharmacopoeia is quite inefficient, and no real benefit can be conferred without vigorous medical treatment, which is as efficacious in these affections, as in the disease of any other organ."[41] Others, however, while insisting that medical men remained the most qualified to administer asylums, drew a rather different picture, conceding that "the powers of medicine, merely upon mental hallucinations are exceedingly circumscribed and feeble. . . . We want principles on which to form any satisfactory indications of treatment. . . . Almost the whole of . . . what may be called the strict medical treatment of madness must be regarded, at present, at least, as empirical, and the most extensive experience proves that very little is to be done."[42]

As we have seen, outside the ranks of the medical profession, and especially among those writing the first bills to implement the reformers' plans, an even more sceptical position appeared to hold sway. Hence the introduction of legislation in which, as an alarmed John Haslam noted, "it has been seriously proposed, in a great deal to remove both the medical treatment and the moral treatment of insane persons from the care of physicians, and to transfer this important and responsible department of medicine into the hands of magistrates and senators. For the welfare of these afflicted persons, and for the security of the public," he insisted, "it is to be hoped that such a transfer may never be established; but that the medical and moral treatment of the insane may continue to be directed by the medical practitioner."[43]

Haslam's alarm was widely shared, and the medical men interested in insanity mobilized to help to defeat the reformers' initial proposals. George Man Burrows, having recently played a major role in securing the passage of the Apothecaries Act of 1815, led the lobbying,[44] and other prominent mad-doctors engaged in a similar campaign in 1828, when a renewed attempt was made to legislate some control of the mad business.[45] Despite some temporary successes, however, the attempt "to vindicate the rights of [the medical] profession over Insanity"[46] clearly required a less reactive strategy, one that offered a realistic prospect of pushing the reform movement in directions more congenial to medical interests. Crucial to any long-term success in these respects was the development of a firmer and more fully articulated intellectual rationale for granting exclusive jurisdiction over insanity to the medically qualified, a task to which much effort was devoted over the course of the next two decades.

On all these fronts—persuading those with power in the political arena of the horrors of the traditional and still flourishing madhouse system and thus of the urgency of reform; establishing asylums run on the new system of moral treatment as the solution to the problem of providing care and treatment for the insane; and reasserting and establishing on a more secure foundation medicine's threatened jurisdiction over madness—*What Asylums Were, Are, and Ought to Be* was to prove enormously influential. Browne's genius did not lie in his diligence in investigating and exposing the realities of the trade in lunacy, an area where he depended almost wholly on the labours of others; in the novelty of the ideas he put forward, for it is difficult to discern wherein this might consist; or in his own special talents in the treatment and cure of the mad, although it must be said that his years at the Crichton Royal were subsequently to demonstrate his devotion and skill as asylum administrator. His recognition that "I have no claim to originality, either in the design or the execution of the present production" represents,[47] from these points of view, no false or feigned modesty. But if his lectures comprise, from this limited perspective, no more than a combination of the findings of investigations conducted and reported by others, together with an expropriation of Tuke's and Pinel's ideas about the moral treatment of insanity and a derivative defence of medicine's claims to exclusive jurisdiction over the mad, then one must simultaneously recognize that they also constitute, in a wider view, the single most skilled and forceful synthesis of these various elements produced between 1815 and 1840—a powerful piece of propaganda that proved of major value in both advancing the plans put forth by the lunacy reform movement and securing medical men's prerogatives in the administration of the emerging Victorian empire of asylumdom.

In Browne's own words, he sought to use his lectures to launch "a crusade."[48] Endeavouring to secure an audience among the politically influential, he aimed "to condense, in a plain, practical, and still popular form, the results of observation in the treatment of insanity, for the specific and avowed purpose of demanding from the public an amelioration of the condition of the insane." The consequence, he hoped, would be to raise "the cry for improvement ... where hitherto the silence of indifference has reigned."[49]

For several weighty reasons, one might have expected that this "cry for improvement" would be couched in the rhetoric of phrenology. Among George Combe's earliest arguments for "the utility of ... phrenology" had been the claim that "it is peculiarly fitted to throw a powerful light [on] Education, Genius, the Philosophy of Criticism, Criminal Legislation, and Insanity,"[50] and a number of scholars have noted the doctrine's "pronounced association with movements for social reform."[51] Of even more direct and immediate relevance to those concerned with reforming the treatment of the insane, the appearance in 1831 of Andrew Combe's *Observations on Mental Derangement* had (briefly and temporarily) reinforced the sense among medical men that phrenology had taken a decisive step towards resolving the enigma of mind, an advance the younger Combe had insisted was of direct and immediate *practical* significance. After all, "if Phrenology is any thing, it is an exposition of the functions of the brain; and if insanity is any thing, it is disease of the brain, which implicates the integrity of the mental functions."[52] And from the insights it provided into the structure and functioning of the brain, "phrenology gives us a power of acting, and of adapting external circumstances to the exigencies of the case, with a precision, confidence, and consistency, which it is impossible to obtain in any other way."[53]

Given their role in affording a clear physiological explanation of the operations of the brain, one that permitted a parsimonious account of abnormal as well as normal mental functioning while advancing a coherent rationale for the application of *both* medical and moral treatment in cases of insanity, one would be astonished if phrenological ideas had failed to exert a considerable fascination for the emerging profession of alienism. In fact, a large proportion of the most prominent figures among this generation of asylum superintendents—John Conolly, Sir William Ellis, Disney Alexander, Richard Poole, David Uwins, and Forbes Winslow, to name but a few—professed themselves converts to the doctrine during the 1820s and 1830s.[54] And at this crucial period in medical men's efforts to monopolize the treatment of madness, phrenology clearly played a vital role in physicians' attempts to assimilate moral treatment into the medical armamentarium.[55]

If there appear at first glance to be strong general grounds for expecting that phrenological ideas would occupy a prominent place in Browne's text, then his own experience and allegiances seem to make this still more likely. We have seen that as a student Browne was an early convert to phrenology and developed close ties to both George Combe and Andrew Combe. In the early 1830s, he had established himself as "one of the most popular lecturers on phrenology to middle- and working-class audiences throughout Scotland,"[56] and his earliest published writings on insanity, appearing in the *Phrenological Journal*, exhibited a close embrace of phrenological thinking.[57] Moreover, the sponsorship of the Combe brothers had played a vital role in his obtaining the superintendency of the Montrose Asylum. Intellectually and personally, few were more firmly a part of the phrenological camp.

Yet in late January 1837, when Browne forwarded the page proofs of his lectures to Andrew Combe for comment, they contained not a single reference to phrenology. This apostasy prompted a swift response from Combe: "I am not aware whether you intend to introduce Phrenology openly as your guide in the investigation and treatment of insanity. In the first sheet there is no allusion to it, and it therefore seems *possible* that you do not mean to notice it. If you really do not, I would strongly advise a contrary course, as due both to the cause of truth and to yourself. . . . It is true, present popularity is gained; but my conviction is, that truth is retarded in the long run."[58] Somewhat shamefaced, Browne proceeded to dedicate the published text to his mentor, "as an acknowledgement of the benefits conferred on society, by his exposition of the application of phrenology in the treatment of insanity and nervous diseases";[59] and to add a preface acknowledging that "insanity can neither be understood, nor described, nor treated by the aid of any other philosophy."[60] With these exceptions, however, his private convictions about phrenology's value were set to one side and lacked any discernible influence on his discussion of insanity and its treatment.

As Combe acknowledged,[61] Browne was scarcely the only alienist who by this time exhibited considerable circumspection about publicly owning up to his phrenological convictions. However useful phrenological accounts of insanity had previously proved to be, and notwithstanding Browne's still powerful private conviction that "whatever success may have attended my efforts to ameliorate the condition of those confided to my charge, . . . I am inclined to attribute . . . to [phrenology],"[62] the fact was that by the late 1830s, Gall's system had lost credibility among serious intellectuals and had been "effectively rejected as a scientific system."[63] Increasingly the province of itinerant head-readers and mountebanks, at whose hands it was being transformed into "a form of entertainment,"[64] phrenology had become far too dangerous a doctrine to be openly embraced by a profession as marginal as alienism. In 1837, notwithstanding his tactical silence, Browne and his alienist colleagues may yet have hoped for a reversal of phrenology's fortunes, for its doctrines were of potentially great utility in anchoring the treatment of madness in medicine. Instead, however, its reputation declined further still, until it was little more than "the object of popular ridicule"; this decline prompted him to confess to George Combe some two decades later "that if he were to state his views on the dependence of mental disorder in explicitly phrenological language, he would provoke incredulity."[65]

Subsequent events thus vindicated Browne's tactical choice to "avoid . . . the phraseology of the science" and to pursue "the noble cause which I have undertaken" by different means.[66] His discussion opens with two chapters only tangentially related either to his avowed goal of transforming the treatment of the insane or to the subject matter announced in his title: a lengthy examination of the definition and classification of the varieties of madness; and another concerned with what epidemiologists would now call its incidence and prevalence. In many respects, these most tedious, least successful portions of his polemic lack much interest for the lay audience he claims to be courting and function quite poorly as a call to action, particularly in comparison with the vivid contrast he subsequently draws between the gothic horrors of the traditional madhouse and the utopian idyll of the asylum as it ought to be. John Conolly saw this as symptomatic of "a defective arrangement very prevalent in his lectures" and suggested that "the real commencement of the book" was its third chapter, on "What Asylums Were."[67]

Understandable as this view is, to accede to the suggestion that one can safely ignore these first two chapters would be to commit a serious historiographic error. Retrospectively, of course, they are of considerable interest to those attempting to reconstruct and understand the beliefs held about the nature and incidence of madness by early Victorian alienists. But, more than this, embedded in these passages are arguments and assumptions of great contemporary significance.

Of utmost importance, the definition and aetiology of insanity were obviously subjects of enormous moment when it came to deciding who should have jurisdiction over the treatment of the insane. Recognizing "how momentous the interests are which hinge upon a clear comprehension of what insanity is,"[68] this was the first topic on which Browne focused attention. Here there was no room for argument or ambiguity: Insanity, in his view, "is inordinate or irregular, or impaired action of the mind, of the instincts, sentiments, intellectual or perceptive powers, depending upon and produced by an organic change in the brain. . . . In all cases where disorder of the mind is detectable, from the faintest peculiarity to the widest deviation from health, it must and can only be traced directly or indirectly to the brain."[69] As a phenomenon that was "strictly a bodily disease,"[70] it was therefore a condition medical men were uniquely qualified to treat.[71]

Moreover, provided only that relatives, "from mistaken kindness or an erroneous estimate of the soothing and curative powers of friendship and affection,"[72] did not attempt to treat the case at home, but promptly forwarded the patient for treatment in a properly conducted asylum, Browne insisted that the happiest results could be anticipated. "Medical men [themselves had] long acted as if nothing could be done with any chance of success in insanity," but recent experience had demonstrated how misplaced such pessimism was. An array of British and American mad-doctors—Monro, Burrows, Ellis, Todd—utilising the combined resources of medical and moral treatment, had been able to "cure ninety out of every hundred cases. Such a result," Browne commented, "proves . . . that instead of being the most intractable it is the most curable of all diseases."[73]

In making claims for the somatic origins of all cases of mental disorder and for the medical profession's ability to cure an extraordinarily high proportion of the mad, Browne is echoing the consensus of his professional colleagues. Indeed, he relies heavily on their assertions to lend authority to his own statements. It was, he scornfully commented, "A want of power or inclination to discriminate between the inutility of medicine from its being inapplicable, and from its being injudiciously applied, [which] has led to the adoption of the absurd opinion that the insane ought not to be committed to the charge of a medical man."[74] Likewise, talk of "functional" cases of mental disorder simply reflected ignorance or incompetence. In all cases of insanity where a careful post-mortem examination could be conducted, "In, or around the brain will be detected some obvious alteration of structure, with the existence of which health was incompatible."[75]

Notwithstanding his recital of medical authorities, Browne's claims that the theoretical commitment to physicalism had an unimpeachable empirical basis were simply false and hence vulnerable to contradiction. The many assertions he cites that death made the physical basis of the disease transparent were not matched by any consensus about what was visible, and many medical men confessed that, though they were convinced that insanity was brain disease, they could not detect any form of pathology however hard they looked. As Nisbet summarised the evidence, "In three fourths of the cases of insanity, where they have been subjected to dissection after death, the knife of the anatomist has not been able, with the most scrutinizing care, to trace any organic change to which the cause of the disease could be traced."[76]

Nor did Browne provide any satisfactory resolution to a related problem, "the connection of the faculties of the mind with the brain."[77] As a student, with the rashness typical of the young, he had not hesitated to address the issue head-on and in straightforwardly reductionist terms. Speaking before the Plinian Society at Edinburgh University, he had boldly asserted that "mind, as far as one individual's sense and consciousness are concerned, is material."[78] Predictably, this unabashed materialism had been greeted with uproar, for views of this sort were widely held to verge on atheism. In the eyes of many, they called into question the existence of an immaterial soul and threatened thereby to demolish the essential moral foundations on which the stability of the social order rested.[79] So sensitive was the issue, indeed, that the Society subsequently took the extraordinary step, not just of striking Browne's paper from the record, but of going back to the minutes of the previous meeting to expunge the announcement that he *intended* to give such a paper.

Returning to this fraught territory a decade later, Browne had clearly learned his lesson. No longer the impolitic young man, he elected to circumvent the whole question. Like Burrows before him (for whom, "to discuss the validity of this or that hypothesis would be plunging into an inextricable labyrinth"),[80] he now found a way to dismiss the issue: "In what manner this connexion between mind and matter is effected, is not here inquired into. The link will, perhaps, ever escape human research." It was, quite simply, a divine mystery and, as such, beyond man's power to solve. The physical basis of insanity remained, however, "the foundation of all inquiries into the nature of mental alienation, and of all attempts to improve the condition of the insane"[81] (to say nothing of medicine's jurisdictional claims).

And yet, if, in Roger Smith's words, "medical aetiology was strikingly incoherent in its language of mind and body,"[82] and rested on a distinctly murky empirical foundation, it nevertheless was tied to metaphysical underpinnings of great weight and power. Overwhelmingly, in the 1820s and 1830s, medical men writing on insanity had pictured the mind as immaterial, an entity corresponding to the immortal soul of the human organism, forced in this world to operate through the medium of a material instrument, the brain.[83] Disease, debility, and death, therefore, could not afflict the mind itself, on pain of calling into question the very foundation of Christian belief. By contrast, a physicalist account created no such dilemma: "From the admission of this principle, derangement is no longer considered a disease of the understanding, but of the centre of the nervous system, upon the unimpaired condition of which the exercise of the understanding depends. The brain is at fault and not the mind."[84] The brain, as a material organ, was liable to irritation and inflammation, and it was this which produced insanity.[85] Consequently, "but let this oppression [of the brain] be relieved, this irritation removed, and the mind rises in its native strength, clear and calm, uninjured, immutable, immortal"[86]—a conclusion that made it abundantly clear why the treatment of madness necessarily involved attention to the body and unambiguously belonged within medicine's recognized sphere of competence.

Madness and Civilisation

Establishing that insanity was a physical disorder settled one crucial issue, but it left a number of related questions unresolved: how much insanity existed in the community; what caused people to go mad; and the differential social incidence of mental alienation—these were all matters of the most significant import. The more extensive the legions of the mad, the more urgent the question of lunacy reform became. The more closely insanity was bound up with the conditions of modern civilized existence, the more threatening the future prospects for society at large and the more crucial the necessity for expert and effective intervention to mitigate the problem. And the more susceptible the rich and powerful to the ravages of mental disorder, the more urgently their own self-interest commanded them to adopt the reformers' prescriptions, lest they wake some morning to find themselves incarcerated in one of those "wild and secluded abodes of human misery" to which the mad were traditionally consigned.

Browne's conclusions on all these points were scarcely reassuring. Conceding the defects of existing statistics, he nonetheless concurred with Halliday and Esquirol, "that a much greater number of cases is known to exist, and to require treatment, than formerly" and that the numbers of the insane appeared to be increasing at a far more rapid rate than the population in general. Nor should one be surprised to find "the poisoned stream larger, and wider, and deeper" given "the too palpable multiplication of the causes which produce mania." Wherever "the sources of moral agitation and excitement are most abundant," there, he confidently asserted, "will the proportion of insanity be the highest"[87]—grim news indeed for a social order characterized by wrenching social change and upheaval, and for the commercial, manufacturing, and professional elites who so relentlessly sought to exploit the resulting opportunities for social and material advancement.

The Rousseauan myth that the noble savage was somehow immune from the ravages of insanity was quite widely canvassed by Regency and early Victorian writers on the subject.[88] In Browne's formulation, "as we recede, step by step, from the simple, that is, the savage manners of our ancestors, and advance in industry and knowledge and happiness, this malignant persecutor strides onward, signalizing every era in the social progress by an increase, a new hecatomb of victims." Here was a paradox, particularly for an audience which as a matter of course equated a "higher" civilization with progress in almost all spheres of existence. Moreover, if the connection were to prove inseparable and inevitable, it was a peculiarly discomforting paradox, for it implied that one could look forward to a rapid and persistent rise in the numbers of mad folk. In the face of this troubling prospect, Browne offered both warning and consolation: it was true that "the barbarian escapes this scourge" while "the members of civilized communities are subjected to it." Yet this occurs, not inevitably, but

> because the enjoyments and blessings of augmented power are abused; because the mind is roused to exertion without being disciplined, it is stimulated without being strengthened; because our selfish propensities are cultivated while our moral nature is left barren, our pleasures becoming poisonous; and because in the midst of a blaze of scientific light, and in the presence of a thousand temptations to multiply our immediate by a sacrifice of our ultimate gratifications, we remain in the darkest ignorance of our own mind. . . . With civilization then come sudden and agitating changes and vicissitudes of fortune; vicious effeminacy of manners; complicated transactions; misdirected views of the objects of life; ambition, and hopes, and fears, which man in his primitive state does not and cannot know. But these neither constitute, nor are they necessarily connected with, civilization. They are defects, obstacles which retard the advancement of that amelioration of condition towards which every discovery in art, or ethics, must ultimately tend.[89]

If society could but be brought to listen to those who were lifting the veil of "ignorance of our own mind" (and who were simultaneously developing expertise in restoring the mad to sanity), the worst might be averted. But, unavoidably, insanity would remain a major social issue because "the occupations, amusements, follies, and above all, the vices of the present race, are infinitely more favourable for the development of the disease than at any previous period. We live under the dominion of the propensities and we must pay the penalty for so doing: and madness is one of these."[90]

Neither wealth nor social position could provide any security against its inroads. While he conceded that "we do not possess sufficient data to determine the relative proportions of the insane rich and the insane poor [nonetheless], the information which has been obtained tends to show that the former are most numerous." Such was the opinion of no less an authority than Esquirol, and Browne found further confirmation in the growth of the trade in lunacy, the "very great number of Retreats, etc., in this country, which are mere speculations, and have been intended for the reception of those who can afford to pay for such an investment of capital." Circular reasoning from the postulated causes of insanity provided the final "proof" that not only do "rank, riches, and education, afford no protection against this disease as they do against others"; but they give "rise to hopes and fears, and exertions and vicissitudes which the humble and illiterate escape." While the agricultural population, and particularly the rural poor, "is to a great degree exempt from insanity," the bourgeoisie and the plutocracy remain especially susceptible to its ravages, exposed as they are "to excitement . . . and . . . to the formation of habits of thought and action inimical to the preservation of mental serenity and health."[91]

To the extent that such assertions secured a measure of public credibility and acceptance, they provided a powerful motive among the well-to-do to embrace Browne's suggested reforms. Once a network of reformed asylums was constructed, it was from the ranks of the poor and disenfranchised that the overwhelming bulk of the patient population was to be drawn; and within a generation or so, alienists would respond with a very different portrait of the aetiology and social distribution of insanity—one that emphasised the role of physical degeneration and hereditary taint and portrayed the insane as "morbid varieties or degenerates of the human kind," a horde of antisocial beings who "will, if not rendered innocuous by sequestration . . . , or if not extruded violently from [society], give rise to disorder incompatible with its stability."[92] With pauper asylums bulging at the seams, the notion of who was susceptible to madness would undergo rapid revision, and in place of assertions that the rich were at least as liable to mental disturbance as the poor, alienists would proclaim the mad "an infirm type of humanity largely met with in the lower classes," a pauper residuum that bore plainly visible stigmata of its moral and mental depravity.[93]

In the 1830s, however, the asylum was still far from constituting a legitimate feature of the social landscape, and the question of who would constitute the inhabitants of an enlarged and reformed madhouse system remained the subject of speculation and uncertainty. For those in a position to exercise some choice in the matter, institutionalization remained very much a last resort. As Browne's first professional employment had ironically confirmed, "So indifferent is even now the repute of public asylums, that the physician in many instances recommends change of scene or of occupation, travelling, anything in fact rather than mere incarceration." And in the light of recent developments, no informed observer could doubt that "it will long be difficult to convince the rich, who can purchase other, and, as they imagine, better modes of isolation, that the vicious condition brought home to certain asylums no longer continues, or to allay the horror inspired by the prospect of being exposed to the system supposed to be prevalent in all, because certainly prevailing in many."[94]

THE MADHOUSE AND THE ASYLUM: DYSTOPIA AND UTOPIA

Browne's own description of what asylums "were and are" is drawn directly from the findings of the parliamentary inquiries of 1815–1816 and 1827–1828 (supplemented by some European materials). A carefully orchestrated denunciation of the evils of the ancien régime and the defects that characterised the traditional "trade in lunacy," his account simultaneously makes plain what "everyone knew" about asylums and just why the informed public should have learned to view them with "horror." Sex, madness, maltreatment, and murder are repeatedly linked in a series of exemplary tales designed at once to titillate and to repel, while illustrating "the errors, absurdities, and atrocities of the old system," a system pictured as little more than a protracted "reign of terror."[95]

The audience is invited to contemplate, for instance, the effects of the indiscriminate mingling of male and female, flung together without the pretence of classification or supervision. The "decorum and purity of the intercourse which ensued" can be imagined, bearing in mind "that the beings thus having uninterrupted access to each other were irrational, acting under the impulse of ungovernable passions, and unrestrained, perhaps by the sacred obligations of religion, and certainly unmindful of the conventional check of public opinion." Meanwhile, even those madwomen who retained some remnants of innate feminine purity and modesty were not safe; their bodies were at the disposal of the ruthless and lascivious ruffians who served as madhouse attendants. The lurid consequences of a system in which the mad were "regarded as wild beasts, [and] all maniacs were indiscriminately treated as such" extended in every direction: public inquiries provided graphic descriptions of patients dying in the act of force-feeding; the indiscriminate bleeding and drugging of patients into insensibility; the array of "bolts, bars, chains, muffs, collars, and strait-jackets" employed to coerce a measure of order; the public display of inmates, like "the animals in a menagerie"; the corrupt confinement of the sane, "guiltless, not even guilty of being diseased" amidst the shrieks and ravings of the mad; the mysterious deaths and disappearance of more than 140 inmates at the York Asylum; the notorious case of James Norris, confined in Bedlam with a purpose-built iron cage round his body for some fourteen years. All these and more were "but a fraction of the evils which have been brought home to asylums as they were," giving asylums the reputation "rather as places for the concentration and aggravation, than for the relief of disease."[96]

Having portrayed the past in the bleakest of hues, Browne now hastens to offer a vivid contrast. From Pinel's liberation of the insane, at the height of the bloodiest excesses of the French Revolution, "may be dated a total revolution in the opinions of medical men and legislators, respecting the insane, and in the principles upon which houses of detention are professed to be conducted."[97] Henceforth, "from darkness [the mad] passed into light—from savage ferocity into Christian benevolence." But not completely: more precisely, the "promised land was [merely] in sight; it was not reached . . . it has succeeded at certain points only, in shaking the strongholds of prejudice and ignorance."[98] The principles of a rational, humane, and curative treatment of the insane were to hand: it remained only to implement them to transform asylums as they are into asylums as they ought to be.

The most striking images in Browne's book occur in its final chapter, where he sketches for his audience the characteristics of an ideal asylum, the moral qualities of its physician-superintendent, and the therapeutic regime that promises to restore the vast majority of the mad to sanity and back to society. As other scholars have noted, a strong utopian strand runs through early nineteenth-century discussions of the asylum, and this is nowhere more manifest than in Browne's discussion of what asylums ought to be. Indeed, he begins his concluding lecture by acknowledging that "a perfect asylum may appear to be a Utopia; 'a sight to dream of, not to see.'"[99]

The contrast with the images of the traditional madhouse—the shit, straw, and stench, the beatings, intimidation, and rapes—could scarcely be more marked. So far from being "a moral lazar house" wherein the deranged were hidden and hope and humanity abandoned, the asylum is now transmuted into the "moral machinery" through which the mind is strengthened and reason is restored. Indeed, properly organized and managed, like the Invisible Hand now regulating civil society, "the system is at once beautiful and self-operating. [The] presence [of keepers] is required to regulate the machine, but its motions are spontaneous," serving all but imperceptibly to secure "the regulation and tranquillization of the unhealthy mind."[100]

How is such a miraculous transformation to be accomplished? By careful attention to the location and construction of the asylum buildings; by insisting upon the moral and intellectual character of the medical superintendent who serves as the autocratic guiding spirit of the whole apparatus; and by the introduction of active moral treatment, requiring a constant insistence on kindness and the steady occupation of the inmates. Physically, the reformed asylum could scarcely be more remote from the old madhouse. Designed from the outset to facilitate "the comfort and the cure of the inmates," and providing spacious and aesthetically pleasing accommodations, it made its own vital contributions to their "moral training" and to replacing "their morbid feelings . . . [with] healthy trains of thought."[101] Browne emphasized how even its siting could influence both patients' thoughts and behaviour; its architecture, the possibility of classification and separation (both central to the implementation of moral treatment); its grounds, the availability of exercise and the possibility of employment in farming and similar healthy activities.

Organizationally, Browne acknowledged, the "association of lunatics requires to be skillfully managed."[102] Here, he touched on dangerous ground, for many people, including some of his medical brethren,[103] questioned the logic of gathering the insane together under one roof, fearing emulation and imitation, to say nothing of isolation from sane influences, would only serve to deepen their alienation. Classification was in any event a vital component of moral treatment, but it here acquired a double significance by allowing Browne to stress the careful separation of the tranquil and the raving, the convalescent and the incurable, while emphasizing the advantages to be derived from interaction among inmates in carefully constructed communities of the mad. Such segregation was also vital to allow treatment to be individualized, adapted to "the idiosyncracies of the patients, . . . the symptoms, the duration and the complications of the disease"[104]—an implicit and telling contrast with the indiscriminate mass-medication of the ancien régime.

Classification also allowed asylum keepers to offer another kind of reassurance: no improper mingling of the social classes would be permitted. One might well imagine the "unhappiness which would flow from bringing the ignorant and brutal into constant and compulsory contact with the enlightened and refined." Besides, "the pauper could not appreciate, nor prize, nor derive benefit from the refinement and delicacies essential to the comfort, and instrumental in the recovery of the affluent. Most fortunately, [therefore,] this arrangement, which is called for by the usages of society, is found to correspond with those higher and less artificial distinctions which are dictated by philosophy." Class distinctions finding support in Nature itself, the asylum superintendent could proceed with a clear conscience to make "fitting preparations" with which to "tempt the rich to have recourse to those measures from choice, which the poor have long pursued from necessity."[105]

Internally, the structural differentiation of space corresponded not only to social boundaries, but to moral ones as well, providing the asylum's guiding spirit with the means to "watch, analyze, grapple with insanity among the insane, and seek for his weapons of aggression in the constitution and dispositions of each individual, and not in general rules or universal specifics."[106] In particular, linking classification to amenities and rewards allowed one "to offer temptations to the lunatic to cooperate in his own restoration" through active employment;[107] and facilitated the use of every aspect of the environment as "a more powerful lever in acting upon the intractable."[108]

Crucial in this whole process, of course, were the abilities, character, and discrimination of the asylum's director, someone who must be able to exploit the "slightest differences of disposition, and sympathies in pursuit or taste" to induce his patients to exercise self-control and advance towards mastery over their madness. Previously, "the care of the insane was monopolized by medical and other adventurers [creating] a ridiculous stigma [which] deterred regular and well-educated practitioners from attempting to compete, and even from qualifying to do so." Finally, however, the quack and "mere drug exhibiter" were giving way to the professional man of "high integrity and honour," possessed of "that moral and physical courage which confer calmness and decision in the midst of danger . . . and imbues the whole character with that controlling influence, which . . . governs the turbulent while it appears to guide, and commands the most wild and ferocious by the sternness and at the same time by the serenity of its orders."[109] In such hands, humanity and cures were all but assured.

Browne's concluding paragraphs conjure up a quite extravagant portrait of ideal asylums as "miniature worlds, whence all the disagreeable alloys of modern life are as much as possible excluded, and the more pleasing portions carefully cultivated."[110] Here the social universe constitutes an organic, harmonious whole—a hierarchical order arrayed under its benevolent philosopher-king,[111] in which everyone knows and respects his or her place; where even the rage of madness is reined in without whips, chains, or corporal chastisement, amidst the comforts of domesticity and the invisible yet infinitely potent fetters of the "desire for esteem"; a community whose inhabitants "literally work in order to please themselves," virtually without recompense, but so readily that "a difficulty is found in restraining their eagerness, and moderating their exertions"; a setting in which, amongst the higher ranks, the most elevated cultural and intellectual pursuits find their place—a utopia in which "all are so busy as to overlook, or all are so contented as to forget their misery." "Such," he grandly concludes, "is a faithful picture of what may be seen in many institutions, and of what might be seen in all, were asylums conducted as they ought to be."[112]

Ideologically, of course, this was a vision of extraordinary resonance and attractiveness, particularly for a ruling class surrounded by alarming signs of increasing social friction and political discontent and forced to confront the discord, disruptions, and divisiveness so central to the Great Transformation.[113] Browne's stress on social harmony and tranquillity; his claim to replace violent repression, conflict, and strife by moral suasion, docility, and willing submission to authority, even among the depraved and unruly; his practical demonstration of the powers of "reason and morality" when allied to a new kind of "moral machinery"—these constituted a potent advertisement for the merits of reformed asylums run by practitioners initiated into the mysteries of moral treatment and medical psychology. Accepting these claims as the "description, . . . not . . . of a theorist, or of an enthusiast, but of a practical man long accustomed to the management of lunatics,"[114] the Victorian governing classes were provided with powerful incentives to embrace the lunacy reformers' schemes and to construct the new realm of asylumdom. And in England and Wales, at least, there was rapid progress over the next few years towards both making the provision of county asylums compulsory and instituting a national system of asylum inspection and supervision.

The Asylum as It Turned Out to Be

The publication of Browne's lectures had a dramatic effect on his own career, prompting a brief visit to Montrose by Elizabeth Crichton, during which she offered him the superintendency of the new Crichton Royal Asylum at Dumfries, at an annual salary of £350.[115] Doubtless attracted by the

Figure 4.2. Crichton Royal Asylum, Dumfries: the original design for one of the most opulent and best-endowed asylums in Europe.

new institution's generous endowment and by the prospect of implementing his ideas in a more favourable environment, Browne accepted the offer just as promptly. The next year was spent in fitting up and furnishing the building and in organizing the staff; the asylum finally opened to receive patients on June 3, 1839. For almost twenty years, Browne remained its superintendent,[116] resigning with apparent reluctance in 1857 to become the first Scottish lunacy commissioner, when the Scots finally succumbed to pressures to build a network of publicly funded asylums on the English model.

Browne's long tenure as superintendent of a richly endowed asylum designed as it "ought to be," as a vehicle for implementing moral treatment, provides us with an almost irresistible temptation to compare the ideal and the real, the theory and the practice of asylum administration in the moral treatment era. It is a temptation worth succumbing to, though it is as well to note at the outset that the surviving source materials do not allow us to probe very deeply into these antimonies. Not the least of the drawbacks is that our primary data for investigating Browne's practice turn out to be his own annual reports, documents obviously written to put the best possible front on the asylum's achievements, to attract potential patrons and patients' families, to forward the cause of lunacy reform, and to persuade a broader public of the legitimacy of psychiatric expertise.

With all their limitations and partiality, however, Browne's lengthy reports, viewed over the entire span of his superintendency, turn out to be remarkably revealing documents. Regardless of their propagandistic intent, they disclose someone who devoted enormous energy and ingenuity to the moral discipline and treatment of his charges, with little or no respite or relief from the strains this entailed.[117] Browne was unquestionably a very talented administrator, and he took advantage of the considerable resources at his disposal in a variety of imaginative ways. A wide range of activities was made available in an effort to restore the patients to sanity (and, as he later confessed, as ways of "combatting monotony, the giant evil of even well regulated seclusion"):[118] within the asylum walls, "concerts, public readings, evening parties, dances, games at bowls, billiards, summer ice, cards, chess, backgammon, have afforded means of diversifying the dull routine of discipline; although, perhaps, the exhibition of the magic lantern yielded the most unalloyed pleasure, and to the greatest number"; and, notwithstanding initial trepidation and complaints from the town-folk, escorted outside, "the patients have participated in every public amusement which combined present gratification with prospective benefit, and in which they could mingle without excitement or injury to themselves, or offense or disturbance to others"—races, regattas, art and natural history exhibits, fishing, walks, concerts, circus, outings to the theatre.[119]

In the face of considerable disapproval in some local Calvinist circles, the theatre was next brought within the walls, the patients themselves presenting (and forming the audience for) a performance "on Twelfth Night, 1843, . . . of James Kenney's farce, 'Raising the Wind,' all the parts in which being sustained by the patients, who also contributed musical selections."[120] By the following year, Browne confidently announced that "the attempt is no longer an experiment. It is a great fact of moral science, and must be accepted and acted upon."[121] And in December 1844, the patients began publication of their own monthly journal, *The New Moon, or Crichton Royal Institution Literary Register.* An omnibus was procured to make outside activities "more agreeable and accessible to a greater number."[122] Gymnastics, hymn writing, instrumental music and singing, drawing and painting, language lessons in Arabic, Greek, Hebrew, French, and Latin, and the keeping of animals as pets, all were introduced to create "a healthy tone and an invigorating moral climate."[123] And (though not among the patients of the higher ranks, for whom labour was socially stigmatising), patients were routinely pressed to employ themselves in a variety of useful ways.[124]

All these activities took place within a minutely organised, rigidly structured routine. Patients outside the highest classes were to rise at six in the summer, seven in the winter; to breakfast at eight; take dinner at one, after two and a half hours of walking and an hour of rest; tea came at four; exercise was resumed at six, and supper and bed followed by eight. As a general rule, "the patients are left less to their own discretion . . . the distribution of their time and occupations, and so far of their very thoughts, is taken into the hands of their governors. Every hour has its appropriate object and occupation; and they become more the creatures of a system, and less the sport of their own distempered inclinations."[125]

Nor was the possible utility of medical treatment neglected. In keeping with his continued insistence on the "incontrovertible proposition, that derangement never occurs in a healthy body,"[126] Browne made sure that "medical are associated with moral means in the efforts to re-establish health." From the outset, opiates were employed freely, as a narcotic and tranquillizer, "to such an extent as would startle those who repose confidence in the time-honoured doses of days gone by. The quantities even alarmed those who were accustomed to deal with the singular power of resistance to medicine, which is often a characteristic of insanity . . . although triple, quadruple, in some cases six times, the amount of the ordinary doze [sic], neither drowsiness nor sleep have been observed." Convinced that "the narcots used [must] have a special, and it may be unobserved effect on the nervous system, apart from, and altogether independent of the production of sleep," Browne nonetheless persisted with them, while acknowledging that "further investigation and experiment are required as to the assistance to be derived from particular drugs."[127] In later years, he displayed equally aggressive tendencies, trying inhalation of ether, perchloride of formyle, and chloroform, and even experimenting with animal and electro-magnetism—and justifying his behaviour with the argument that it was "a duty that all new and powerful agents should be tried in the treatment of a disease which so often defies the ordinary resources of medicine."[128]

The dismal clinical outcomes of these somatic interventions failed, even momentarily, to shake his confidence that only to a "well-educated physician" was the "sacred and momentous trust" of treating the insane to be consigned.[129] Still, they could not but confirm his conviction that "moral means . . . unquestionably constitute the most powerful class of remedies that has yet been discovered"[130]—and it was therefore to the various forms of moral treatment that he principally gave his attention. Through careful planning, he insisted that these various elements were to be brought to act in concert, so as to constitute an extraordinarily powerful mechanism for remoralizing the mad and restoring "that respect for order and tranquility which is the basis of all sanity and serenity of mind."[131]

Reflecting the professional consensus of his peers, Browne viewed the exercise of self-control and the ability to repress one's morbid propensities as the defining characteristics of sanity, and he saw the asylum regime and its "curative discipline"[132] as contributing in multiple ways to the achievement of these ends:

> In order to obtain [various] gratifications [for instance], in anticipation of them, and from the conviction that propriety of demeanour will alone entitle to indulgence, the insane exercise control over their minds; secondly, during enjoyment they control their minds, or rather their minds are controlled, as they become engrossed, as the happiness of others spreads to them, and as the memory of the past is shut out by the agreeable feelings of the present; and thirdly, they control their minds under the fear of compromising their right and expectation of a repe-

tition of the indulgence. This power of control, or of concealment of predominating and morbid feelings is an indication of health, a beneficial exercise of the will,
which may be trained, strengthened, and established.[133]

Browne insisted that towards accomplishing these ends the asylum's
"moral governor" must devote his energies, presiding over the whole establishment, witnessing and regulating "the most minute working of the great
moral machine" and making "discriminate use of ordinary circumstances
and trifles in depressing, elevating, tranquilising, rousing, persuading, or
governing the insane." Within the tightly controlled asylum environment,
he could thereby ensure that "the impress of authority is never withdrawn,
but is stamped upon every transaction."[134]

Such passages make quite transparent, as Browne himself insisted, that
"there is a fallacy even in conceiving that Moral Treatment consists in being
kind and humane to the insane."[135] While marking a clear rupture with the
more directly brutal coercion, fear, and constraint that characterized an
older asylum regime, the new approach constituted a prodigiously effective
set of techniques for imposing and inducing conformity and incorporated a
latent (and rapidly realized) potential for deterioration into a repressive
form of moral management. And even in Browne's generously endowed and
imaginatively run establishment, this darker side soon came to dominate.

Within five years of receiving the first patients at the Crichton Royal,
Browne begins to sound a distinctly more cautious note about the likely
outcome of asylum treatment. His own statistics reveal that only a little
more than a third of those admitted are being cured, and even this figure, he
suggests, may give the wrong impression: "It is a question of some importance," he informs his readers, "whether the human mind be ever restored
to its original health and strength after an attack of insanity." Certainly, expert intervention can restore a measure of "calmness and composure . . .
and that self-possession and correctness of external deportment which are
regarded as indices of health." Patients may even regain "the capacity to
engage in complicated matters of business or abstruse studies . . . ; but is
there not generally retained some peculiarity or perversity, some tendency
to excitement or extravagance, some infirmity or unsteadiness which require shelter or sympathy?" Were one to ignore this difficulty, it would be
"easy to augment the apparent curability of derangement," but to do so
would be to "usher . . . into the world persons of odd and eccentric dispositions, disturbers of families and of society, who are tolerated, but not
trusted; who perpetrate crimes and outrages under the protection of their
infirmity."[136] The asylum, he starts to hint, can fail to deliver on the extravagant promises of its early promoters and yet continue to fulfill vital social
functions, remaining therefore, in some larger sense, a successful enterprise.

A year later, in a letter to the Royal Commission investigating the Scottish

Poor Laws, he more bluntly articulates this very different rationale for maintaining and expanding the asylum system. As one might expect, the prospects of curing a certain fraction of cases and the potential savings this would represent are still presented as one argument for preferring treatment to neglect. But Browne no longer urges the likelihood of curing 80 or 90 percent of those afflicted; he now opts for the far more modest claim that "if the recognised and approved medical and moral expedients be resorted to, there is almost a certainty that one-third of them will recover."[137] There is still a nod, too, towards an earlier emphasis on the need to rescue the insane from the neglect and hardships too often their lot in the community. But the urgent necessity to ensure that "the gaps, and gashes, and leprosy of the mind . . . be withdrawn from the public eye" has a very different source, the threat their continued presence poses to morality and social order: "It is not calculated to improve morals, that half-naked maniacs should haunt our paths, with the tendencies, as well as the aspect of satyrs. . . . They have appetites as well as we. Unchecked, uncontrolled, they obey the injunction to multiply; and, undoubtedly, multiply their *own kind*. They commit murder; they commit suicide . . . while they are inaccessible to the shame, the sorrow, or the punishment; presenting the humiliating spectacle of drunken, ribald, rebellious maniacs. Reason or religion cannot reach them, and they are abandoned to the dominion of sin."[138]

The turn away from an emphasis on the asylum as a reliable mechanism for manufacturing sane citizens from mad raw materials appears to have had little discernible impact on its growing popularity with the families of potential patients. Certainly, Browne's own establishment suffered from no lack of recruits. Each year, his reports recorded a large excess of applications for admission, both private and pauper, over those for whom there was room, and the Crichton Royal attracted moneyed patients from considerable distances, many of them from England. But Browne was losing his illusions about why they were sent and about what could be accomplished once they had been admitted:

> patients are constantly sent to asylums because they have become burdens; and not merely because they have exhausted the pecuniary resources, but the tender mercies, the sympathy, the love of their friends. They are exiled from the home of their youth, because their presence is incompatible with the interests or comforts of other members of the family. . . . Patients are secluded as public nuisances; they are cast off from the community as offending members, and are consigned to the asylum on similar grounds to those that consign a robber or a rioter to a prison. Retained among their relatives so long as they are calm and manageable, so long as they are robust; whenever affected with bodily ailment or infirmity, they are sent to asylums to die.[139]

Clearly the campaign to persuade the public of the near-certain curability of insanity, with prompt treatment of recent cases in a properly run asylum, had been lost.[140] Worse yet, the widespread refusal to accept the alienists' optimistic claims came to seem increasingly well-founded. As Browne himself was to concede before the decade was out, "all men entrusted with the care of the insane must be conscious how infinitely inferior the actual benefit conferred is to the standard originally formed of the efficacy of medicine, or of the powers of the calm and healthy over the agitated and perverted mind . . . how intractable nervous disease is found to be and how indelible its ravages are even where reason appears to be restored."[141]

But from some points of view, it turned out not to matter. Cures might prove evanescent, but the asylum retained its utility as a convenient depository for inconvenient people, a valued and valuable way "of secluding the insane, and of protecting the public from the evils which arise from contact with debased appetites, violent passions, and excited imaginations."[142] Therapeutically successful or not, there remained ample demand for them as places "to receive and reduce to subordination, and symmetry, and peace, all the degraded appetites, ungovernable passions, the wild and erratic imaginations, and blinded judgments, which have been cast out as inconsistent with the order and well being of society."[143]

"Success," it now transpired, "may be estimated in various ways." Every bit as important as the cures one promoted "is the development of sources of calm and contentment, where restoration cannot be effected . . . the general amount of mental health and happiness secured to all residing in the Institution, and especially those whose calamities must render them permanent inhabitants . . . [the creation of] a new and artificial modification of society adapted to the altered dispositions and circumstances of the insane."[144] And fortunately, moral and medical treatment, though nowhere near as effective in producing cures as once advertised, remained rather more efficacious "in establishing tranquillity, and in suggesting a deportment which closely resembles, if it do [sic] not entirely realise, that of sanity and serenity."[145] The accumulation of chronic patients was of great assistance here, for a large fraction of this group could be exploited to form "a permanent and stationary basis or stock which is of great utility in manipulating the details of classification. It forms a sort of conservative body, whose tendency is, on the whole, to support constituted authority and regular government."[146] The goal of tranquillity and good order, at least, was thus within reach: "The effect of long-continued discipline is to remove all salient parts of the character, all obtrusive and irregular propensities and peculiarities. . . . The majority [of asylum inmates], enfeebled by monotony, by the absence of strong impulses and new impressions, tamed, and stilled, and frozen, by the very means to which they may owe life, and some re-

mains of reason, exhibit a stolidity and torpor which are obviously superadded to their original malady"[147]—but which are equally obviously of great
utility to those charged with managing and supervising such dead souls.

Self-evidently, such sharply diminished ambitions, acceptable though
they may have proved to patients' families and to the public at large, carried
highly damaging implications for alienists' social standing, and constituted
a bitter pill for Browne to swallow. For all his attempts to reassure his audience (and himself) that "the progress is in the right direction, and that the
efforts and aspirations of so many ardent and powerful, and pure minds, as
are now devoted to the amelioration of the insane, must ultimately and
speedily elicit the truth and the whole truth . . . ,"[148] reality on a daily basis
remained recalcitrant and bleak. A note of quiet desperation about "the intrinsic repulsiveness of the records of sorrow and suffering,"[149] which he
must constantly encounter now entered his reports, and he conceded that
"there are no more painful convictions in the mind of those engaged in the
care and cure of the insane than that so little can be done to restore health,
to re-establish order and tranquillity, than that, after the best application of
the most sagacious and ingenious measures, the results are so barren and
incommensurate, that in defiance of sympathy and solicitude, misery and
violence, and vindictiveness should predominate."[150] Astonishingly, given
his own role in creating the image of the asylum as utopia, he subsequently
complained of those who foster "the erroneous impression that alienation is
scarcely a privation, and the restraints which it entails may be converted
into golden bonds. It has become a fashion to paint Asylum interiors in
brilliant and attractive colours. This error, as it is, may be the natural tendency of generous and sanguine minds to describe that which is hoped and
expected and might be, as objects already accomplished—to present a
course which it may be a duty to tread as a goal which has been reached."[151]

His final report as superintendent at Dumfries was written in 1857. Producing it was, he acknowledged, "a difficult and painful duty"[152]—partly
because of his imminent departure from the scene of his lifetime's labours,
but surely also because of the depressing contrast between the high hopes
he had entertained on assuming his post and the grim realities that now
confronted him. The Crichton Royal was as popular as ever with its clientele: in the preceding twelve months, of 100 applicants for admission from
the affluent classes, he had been able to admit but 26; and from the 122
pauper applicants, but 51. Moral treatment was pursued as vigorously as
before, and on an experimental basis convalescent patients were now spending some time at a neighbouring country house. Still, in ministering to "the
waifs and strays, the weak and wayward of our race," Browne could find
many reasons for disquiet. The overcrowded state of the asylum could perhaps be a source of some pride, as a sign of people's confidence in the estab-

lishment. "It may even be argued that the physical and moral evils created by the crowded state of a moral hospital are infinitely less than the miseries and misfortunes which follow refusal of admission." But such attempts to find consolation were in some larger sense misplaced. For, inescapably, "the moral evils of a vast assemblage of incurable cases in one building, are greater still. The community becomes unwieldy; the cares are beyond the capacity of the medical officers; personal intimacy is impossible; recent cases are lost, and overlooked in the mass; and patients are treated in groups and classes. An unhealthy moral atmosphere is created; a mental epidemic arises, where delusion, and debility, and extravagance are propagated from individual to individual, and the intellect is dwarfed and enfeebled by monotony, routine, and subjection."[153]

His own asylum's cure rate compared favourably with its competitors, but even this could not be a source of pride because "it is incumbent to confess, that the nature of what there is a disposition to describe as cures, is not satisfactory." One must recognize a bitter truth: "The subversion of reason involves not only present incompetency, but a prospective susceptibility of disease, a proclivity to relapse. . . . The mind does not pass out of the ordeal unchanged. . . . Recovery . . . may be little more than the exercise of great cunning, or self-control, in concealing the signs of error and extravagance. The intellect that recovers its balance may not always recover its strength."[154] Nor could Browne find solace in the romanticized portraits of the amusements and attractions of asylum life that were so prominent a feature of his early reports. Alongside the usual recital of plays and concerts given, activities and occupations engaged in, a strikingly different picture now appears:

It has been customary to draw a veil over the degradation of nature, which is so often a symptom of insanity. But it is right that the real difficulties of the management of large bodies of the insane should be disclosed; it is salutary that the involuntary debasement, the animalism, the horrors, which so many voluntary acts tend to, should be laid bare. No representation of blind frenzy, or of vindictive ferocity, so perfectly realises, so apparently justifies, the ancient theory of metempsychosis, or the belief in demoniacal possession, as the maniac glorying in obscenity and filth; devouring garbage or ordure, surpassing those brutalities which may to the savage be a heritage and a superstition. . . . These practices are not engrafted upon disease by vulgar customs, by vicious or neglected training, or by original elements of character. They are encountered in victims from the refined and polished portions of society, of the purest life, the most exquisite sensibility. Females of birth drink their urine. . . . Outlines of high artistic pretensions have been painted in excrement; poetry has been written in blood, or more revolting media. . . . Patients are met with . . . who daub and drench the walls as hideously as their disturbed fancy suggests; who wash or plaster their bodies, fill every crevice in the room, their ears, noses, hair, with ordure; who conceal these precious pigments in their mattresses, gloves, shoes, and who will wage battle to defend their property.[155]

In the face of these realities, the optimistic might still choose to speak (as some now did) of asylums as mental hospitals. But those who set aside their rose-tinted spectacles must face a grimmer truth: "An Asylum is only in one sense an hospital. They both receive and relieve the suffering. But in an hospital the patients enter, depart, die. In an Asylum, the inmates, or about one-half of them, remain for life."[156] Institutional care was still preferable, in Browne's view, to the alternatives—a position he would subsequently defend at greater length;[157] yet what asylums had become—reasonably well-tended cemeteries for the still breathing—constituted a system almost startlingly remote from his earlier visions of what they ought to be.

THE ELDER STATESMAN

Browne's departure from his position as superintendent of the Crichton Royal was the direct consequence of the passage of the 1857 Scottish Lunacy Act (20 and 21 Vict., cap. 71) The act in its turn was the product of Dorothea Dix's brief visit to Scotland in 1855 and of her subsequent complaints to the British government about the neglected condition of Scottish lunatics. Acting with characteristic vigour and determination, and employing to great effect the tactics she had repeatedly used to force change on reluctant state legislatures in the United States, Dix had brushed aside dissent from her views as misguided or venal, personally lobbied members of the government and of both Houses of Parliament, and forced the establishment of a Royal Commission to examine Scottish asylums and lunacy law.[158]

James Coxe, one of the most active members of the Commission of Inquiry, was one of a number of correspondents who had kept in close touch with Dix during the more than two years it took to gather evidence and issue its report.[159] Having repeatedly expressed his impatience with the slow pace with which evidence was gathered,[160] and the delays in producing its findings,[161] it was with evident relief that he reported in 1857 that at long last the Report "has broken its shell and seen the light." On its appearance, he had initially been concerned lest the Commission's efforts should prove to have been in vain, and so "at first I took what steps I could to direct the public attention to the results of our labours, but soon my only fear was that the general clamour would pass beyond just bounds." Unprepared "for the popular outcry that has ensued," he acknowledged that "we are quite surprised by the sensation the Report has produced."[162] Parliament, he thought, would strike while the iron was hot and quickly enact remedial measures.

Less than three weeks later, doubts had set in. The proposed legislation was encountering grave difficulties, and in his view was certain to "encounter the strongest opposition from Scotch members. . . . Already on every side is heard the din of preparation for resistance. Town councils, county meetings, parochial boards, and the existing . . . asylums, are banding together for this object, all animated with the desire to avoid legal interference." Hence the bill's "only chance of becoming law will depend upon the support it receives from England."[163]

In the event, the opposition's attempts to maintain the status quo failed. Despite fierce resistance, motivated in part by self-interest and Calvinist frugality, but also by a horror of the English system of tax-supported poor relief, the new legislation was modelled quite directly on the precedents established south of the border. It established a new General Board of Commissioners in Lunacy for Scotland, charged with the supervision of all asylums and lunatics in the country; and it required the construction of District Asylums at taxpayers' expense throughout Scotland.

In view of his standing as the most eminent Scottish alienist of his era, it may seem unsurprising that Browne was subsequently chosen as one of the first two medical commissioners and directly placed in charge of enforcing the new legislation. In fact, the choice was fraught with irony, and can scarcely have met with Dix's approbation. Indeed, had she not been three thousand miles from the scene, there is little reason to doubt that she would have moved to block his appointment.[164]

Long one of the most vocal proponents of the superiority of the Scottish approach to the problem of poverty, with its reliance on private charity, Browne had from the outset fiercely resented Dix's meddlesome interventions in his country's affairs. Soon after the establishment of the Royal Commission was announced, he wrote directly to Dix to express "my great and deep regret that your sense of duty has led you to induce Government" to proceed in this fashion. The consequences of her actions were likely to prove "most discouraging" and were the source of "what is to me a distressing contemplation." In part, he informed her, his dismay reflected the fact that "in this country such a proceeding indicates the existence or the suspicion of abuse or maladministration; and if the public Asylums be included—as from a trustworthy source I believe they are—these Institutions must be involved in the suspicion or accusation. . . . Personally and selfishly it is natural that I should regret to be placed among my fellow labourers at the bar of public opinion as a culprit after Twenty five years of humble toil!!" But on other grounds as well, "I deplore the measure: and my anticipation of the legislation which will, or may be founded upon the results of such an inquisition. . . . For, while I ever bear in mind the claims of 'those fastbound in misery' I cannot forget that the interests of general humanity and of my country are larger and broader."[165] With his active encouragement, the trustees of the Crichton Royal had consistently opposed compulsory, tax-financed asylums and a system of central inspection,[166] and when the Dix-inspired Royal Commission visited the asylum in 1856, Browne proceeded to remind them "that in Scotland hitherto the charity of the affluent has supplied spontaneously what in other countries is exacted by law from the whole community; and that he hopes that this peculiarity will continue to distinguish our national policy."[167]

From first to last, then, Browne had proved one of the most formidable and implacable opponents of the policies embodied in the new legislation. Once the new system was announced, however, and the lucrative position of Commissioner in Lunacy on offer, he exhibited a remarkable volte-face: insisting that his actions were motivated "rather by a desire for rest and for change in the exercise of my faculties than from any vain aspiration after either rank or riches" and contending that "I see clearly vast opportunities of being useful and of exercising benevolence and gathering knowledge on a wider range," he devoted all his resources to securing the prize. "I have," he confided to none other than Dix herself, after the appointment was safely in the bag, for some months "been engaged in carrying out an ambitious project which engrossed every moment which was not claimed by professional pursuits. My object was an appointment as Commissioner under a new Lunacy Act for Scotland. . . . I know not what candidature for such an office in your country may suppose; but here the correspondence with friends and antagonists was overwhelming and I was often about to recoil from the labor [sic] of ascent even when the top of the ladder was in sight. Perseverance and the support of friends . . . have, however, secured the coveted position and I am now contemplating a great extension of my usefulness."[168] With some public display of reluctance to leave the Crichton Royal, and with the approbation of his colleagues, he accepted the proffered position and was promptly launched on a new and more financially rewarding career.

Browne spent a good portion of the next thirteen years on the official circuit, visiting the existing Royal Lunatic Asylums and workhouses and advising on the construction and organization of the new District Asylums. In the event, the task suited him less well than the day-to-day challenge of running an asylum, and he seized such opportunities as came his way to broaden the range of his responsibilities. He seems to have particularly enjoyed the opportunity of combining, from time to time, his official visit to some provincial asylum with a clinical lecture on some aspect of insanity and its treatment, usually delivered by pre-arrangement to Thomas Laycock's Edinburgh students in medical psychology.[169]

In both these lectures and his presidential address to the Medico-Psychological Association, delivered in 1866,[170] Browne devoted much of his attention to a further defence of medical prerogatives and jurisdiction over the insane, a choice perhaps prompted by the sobering realization of just how tenuous the foundations of alienism's privileged status still remained. The vaunted utopia of asylums run as they ought to be had failed to produce results commensurate with the profession's promises. Indeed, in private moments, even Browne had come close to confessing therapeutic bankruptcy. Surely, one had to fear the consequences of this situation: "If therapeutical agents are cast aside or degraded from their legitimate rank, it will become the duty of the physician to give place to the divine or moralist, whose chosen mission it is to minister to the mind diseased; and of the heads of an establishment like [the Crichton Royal] to depute their authority to the well-educated man of the world, who could, I feel assured, conduct an asylum fiscally, and as an intellectual boarding-house, a great deal better than any of us."[171]

Browne's response to the implicit threat, like that adopted by most of his colleagues, was to insist on "the absurdity of a pure metaphysician being entrusted with the study of the mind diseased":[172] "We know it as a physiological truth that we cannot reach the mind even when employing purely *psychical* means, when bringing mind to act on mind, except through material organs. It may be that even moral means exercise *their* influence by stimulating or producing changes in organization. It is *certain* that all we know of mental disease is as a symptom, an *expression*, of morbid changes in our bodies."[173]

In language all-too-revelatory of the political issues at stake, he denounced "he who refuses the aid of medicine [as being] as much a heretic to the true faith as he who doubts the efficacy of moral agents"[174]—a conclusion that prompted a rueful retrospective glance at the very book that had brought him fame and professional prominence: "Benevolence and sympathy suggested and developed, and, in my opinion, unfortunately enhanced the employment of moral means, either to the exclusion, or to the undue disparagement of physical means, of cure and alleviation. I confess to have aided at one time in this revolution; which cannot be regarded in any better light than as treason to the principles of our profession."[175] In the final analysis, one might abandon the millenarian expectations on which the edifice that was Victorian asylumdom had been mistakenly constructed but not betray one's commitment to the medical monopolization of the treatment of the mad.

Browne's election as the first president of the newly named Medico-Psychological Association capped a long career as one of the most prominent of British alienists. Soon thereafter, however, an accident brought an abrupt and unexpected end to his service as a Lunacy Commissioner and to his active involvement in the administration of Victorian asylumdom. While inspecting the condition of lunatics in Haddingtonshire in the winter of 1870, he was thrown from his carriage, suffering serious head injuries that within six months left him blind. For the last fifteen years of his life he was thus forced into an unwanted retirement, cared for by his two unmarried daughters at his Dumfries home, till his sudden death from a heart attack on March 2, 1885, just three months short of his eightieth birthday.

Chapter Five

TREATING THE MAD OUTSIDE ASYLUM WALLS:

SIR ALEXANDER MORISON (1779–1866)

> Beyond all *darkness*, *chains*, and *keepers* blows,
> Sir *Madquack*, is the *Physick* you impose;
> Threatning, because my *Satyres* frisk & dance,
> With *Purge* and *Vomit* them to tame and Lance.
> (*James Carkess, "The Patient's Advice to the Doctor,"*
> *in* Lucida Intervalla: Containing Divers
> Miscellaneous Poems)

IF ALEXANDER MORISON is remembered at all, it is usually as the author of *The Physiognomy of the Insane* and as the man who first delivered a coherent series of lectures on mental diseases to doctors.[1] However, in the same breath, this achievement is generally bracketed with John Conolly's more "successful" lectures at Hanwell. The fact that Conolly delivered a very ordinary course of lectures at London University is conveniently forgotten. Similarly Conolly's series of articles on "The Physiognomy of the Insane" in the *Medical Times and Gazette* during 1858 have created a comparison that has proved unfavourable to Morison, whose practice for much of the 1840s and 1850s stood across the Thames in direct contrast to Conolly's.[2]

A close examination of Morison's career tends to reinforce the view of many contemporaries that he did not provide any great intellectual impetus to the profession. His obituary in the *Journal of Mental Science* was damning in its faint praise, remarking that he was, "tall and thin, with features rather expressive of kindness and benevolence than of great mental power, but was beloved of his patients." And yet his early mentors at Edinburgh had held out high hopes for his career,[3] he accumulated a number of prestigious hospital affiliations during his time in London, had a substantial practice among the upper classes, and, unusually for an alienist in this or any other age, he obtained a knighthood. What accounts for the discrepancy between his apparent success as a practicing physician and the marginal place he was accorded, by both his contemporaries in the newly organizing psychiatric profession and generations of historians?

We suggest that a range of factors were involved. It is clear that Morison was extremely well read, but his large private practice, multiple asylum attachments, and huge familial responsibilities militated against writing the kinds of weighty publications that might have brought him recognition as a major contributor to the developing professional literature on madness.[4] More important, though, the nature of his professional activities and success—while providing us with, among other things, a striking measure of the demand in some quarters for nonasylum based treatment of insanity and an important corrective to the temptation to produce an oversimplified historiography of alienism that attends *only* to its ties to asylumdom—depended upon a strategy for career building and a therapeutics that proved ill-adapted to the shifting legal, cultural, and social context within which the professionalization of the treatment of the mad was to develop. Morison's career reminds us that alternative models of professional practice and different means of coping with the ravages of mental disturbance existed in the first half of the nineteenth century, even as the utopian visions of proponents of the reformed asylum came to dominate public discourse about madness. But the fate of his style of practice ultimately reemphasizes how powerful the attachment to the asylum proved to be in the Victorian era. Simultaneously, it provides us with a range of fascinating insights into the development of early nineteenth-century psychiatric practice and into the consolidation of the emerging specialism.

A Scottish Childhood

Alexander Morison was born in Bailie Fyfe's Close, Edinburgh High Street on Saturday May 1, 1779. On his father's side he came from a family of small tenant farmers and property owners, at Troup in Banffshire. His grandfather John Morison was the tenant of Home Farm at Troup, and there had been several generations of Morisons, variously spelt, living in the Aberdeen area since 1700. Alexander's father, Andrew Murison, was the eleventh of twelve sons, but despite this potentially disadvantageous position, had received a reasonable education thanks to the local Laird, Francis Garden.

Francis Garden, a member of the Scottish bar, was the second son of Gardenstone of Troup and succeeded to the family estates in 1785. He employed Andrew Murison as a clerk, in which position the latter learned his profession as a Writer to the Signet. Andrew evidently possessed independent initiative, and from the security of his legal post developed an involvement in the wine trade with France and Portugal, which counted Leith as an important entrepôt at this time. As a result of his dealings he was able to buy a nearby property overlooking the Firth, called Anchorfield, which became the family home.

It was also through Lord Gardenstone that Alexander's parents had met. Alexander's mother, Mary Herdman, was a ward of Gardenstone's. Both her parents had been tainted by their adherence to the Stuart cause, and she had been left destitute. Lord Gardenstone had her educated and apprenticed her to Miss Wilson, an Edinburgh milliner. Subsequently he also arranged her marriage to Andrew Murison.[5] Andrew and Mary had five children, Francis (1765–1795), John (1766–1837), Margaret (1770–1840), Andrew (1772–1786), and lastly Alexander (1779–1866). There is no record of Alexander's very earliest years at Anchorfield, but in July 1784 he was sent to school at a Mr. Dunsmure's. He also had a private tutor, Mr. Gladstanes from Leith.

In 1787 Alexander joined the High School in Edinburgh, and it is clear that he did not enjoy his time there. A mild natured man all his life he rebelled against the prevailing culture of the place. Henry Cockburn, the memorialist, who was a year Morison's junior at the school, recorded that it was notorious for the severity of its masters and the riotous behaviour of the boys, amongst whom coarseness of language and manners were the fashion. Nevertheless Morison shared lessons with some illustrious classmates, including Henry Cockburn, Francis Horner, John Murray, and most famous of all the future Lord Brougham.

Three years later, in 1790, both Brougham and Morison were in the rector's class. Dr. Adam, a learned man, had introduced Greek to the school curriculum. He was also a Whig and admirer of the French Revolution, using events across the channel to illustrate his discussion of classical texts. The cosmopolitan and continental flavour of this education undoubtedly had its effect on Morison, who later travelled widely in Europe during the first three decades of the nineteenth century. Although the main focus of his attention during these travels was on contemporary developments in psychiatric, medical, and social care, he also spent a great deal of time sampling the cultural life of these countries.[6]

Throughout late 1790 and early 1791 Alexander truanted from the High School. During these absences he went for long walks in the surrounding countryside, which fuelled what became a lifelong love of agriculture and rural life. He also developed an abiding interest in walking, a feature of his future professional career when he covered vast distances on foot. Sandy's illicit excursions included trips as far abroad as Arbroath, and on one occasion he was, according to his father's day book, "catched at Leith," on the eve of a similar escapade.

As he was approaching the end of his time at the High School, Morison became increasingly unsettled. The constant panorama of the Firth of Forth, with its masted ships and flow of river traffic must have exerted a powerful influence towards a life at sea. This combined with the slightly stifling atmosphere of an Evangelical household, encouraged Alexander to ask his father's permission to go to sea. (His older brother Andrew had already done so at the age of fourteen and had drowned off the coast of France.) Though Alexander was only eleven, his father agreed to a trial voyage. Once was clearly enough: the young Morison promptly abandoned his seafaring ambitions, and on his return from Portugal in October 1790, was packed off to a Reverend Sewell at Ousebridge, in Cumberland. He remained there for a year receiving private tuition, before returning once more to Scotland.

MEDICAL TRAINING AT EDINBURGH

In 1792, now all of thirteen, Alexander went up to Edinburgh University, where he spent the first two years of his education studying astronomy, dancing, fencing, French, geography, Greek, mathematics, and music.[7] Thereafter, he turned to the serious pursuit of training in medicine. Lisa Rosner has shown that a medical education in Edinburgh could vary enormously. Students were able to purchase tickets for a range of courses and not all who enrolled wished to qualify as M.D.s. Many, like W.A.F. Browne some three decades later, went on to practice with no formal qualification.[8] Morison, however, took the most comprehensive course of medical education available at that period, and, like many other students, he also took tickets for John Walker's course on natural history, which was popular across the student body and noted for its excellence.

These studies were combined with extensive private practice under a surgeon. Two years after matriculating at the university, in November 1794, Alexander had been apprenticed for five years to Messrs. Alexander and George Wood, Surgeons. At the age of fifteen, after an exhange of £60, he began a training that, was to prove a seminal experience and exert a consistent influence on his subsequent career. At a time when a surgeon's training was still far from respectable, associated as it was with the activities of "resurrection men" and the barely tolerated dissection of corpses, Alexander was lucky to have been apprenticed to one of the more respectable figures in the field. Alexander Wood, better known as "lang Sandy Wood," was an eminent and notably skilful Edinburgh surgeon, and he directed Morison's studies.[9] At the same time, Wood provided him with first-hand and extensive training in anatomy, knowledge he was to draw upon in later years when attempting to determine a pathological basis for insanity. More generally, contemporary accounts make clear that he was a diligent and attentive student who had a lively interest in all aspects of medicine.

In his choice of a medical career Alexander was once again following in the footsteps of an older brother whose life had ended in tragic circumstances. Francis Morison, born in 1765, became a doctor of medicine in 1787 and had also received a surgical training with Alexander Wood. By 1795, Alexander had started his own surgeon's apprenticeship, rubbing shoulders occasionally with his older brother, who was living and working in the Edinburgh Infirmary. It was a terrible shock for the aspiring doctor when Francis suddenly died of typhus fever in December that year, and there seems every likelihood that Alexander's subsequent career was initially blighted by unspoken family expectations that he somehow replace Francis.

It is probable that the greatest influence his older brother had on Alexander came through his friendship with Alexander Crichton, which started when both were apprentices of Sandy Wood's. The two older boys had studied together under Cullen, and Crichton subsequently got to know Alexander. After qualifying in 1799, the younger Morison went to London for two years to continue his studies at the London Hospitals and whilst there renewed contact with Crichton, by now established as a physician at Westminster Hospital.[10] Five years later he was to visit him in Russia, when Crichton was Physician-in-Ordinary to Tsar Alexander I. They became good friends and remained so until Crichton's death in 1856.

If Morison did study under Crichton, then it might help to explain his later specialised interest in mental medicine. Crichton, who had disliked surgery, obtained a disfranchisement from the College of Surgeons in 1791, and after his appointment to Westminster Hospital in 1794 he lectured on chemistry, materia medica, and the practice of physic. Four years later just as Morison was nearing the end of his formal medical training Crichton produced, *An Inquiry into the Nature and Origin of Mental Derangement*, the first treatise on insanity published by a teaching hospital physician since the sixteenth century. Crichton's approach had two notable features: a tendency to downplay nosology in favour of a focus on the possible causes of insanity; and the adoption of Thomas Reid's schema for analysis of the human mind—an introspective approach in which the investigator was directed back to his own childhood to explore how his mind had been modelled by instruction. Morison, too, was to favour this strategy, often focussing heavily in his analysis of cases on the dysfunctional upbringing of patients, while his own version of moral treatment favoured resocialization techniques. Similarly, Crichton voiced the opinion that even lunatics' actions had motives and were therefore potentially intelligible, and, in parallel fashion, Morison often proved much slower than some of his colleagues to label behaviour as pathological and requiring restraint.

The five years of Morison's apprenticeship were a time of significant personal development in other respects. He himself remarked in a retrospective account written in 1865 that in the early part of his apprenticeship he was "like other boys diligent enough at his business and studies but without a proper sense of religion." At some time in 1796, however, an important change took place in Alexander's views of religion. Reading Fletcher's *Appeal to Common Sense* and Philip Doddridge's *Rise and Progress of Religion in the Soul of Man*, together with the conversion of Mr. McCrae, his brother-in-law, led him to a conviction "of his sinful state and of his need of his Blessed Saviour."[11] He therefore decided to make a solemn covenant of dedication between himself and the Supreme Being. This dedication to serve God was one he took seriously and was the start of an Evangelical life, which although constant also contained some puzzling contradictions.

Signs of Evangelical activity abound in Morison's diaries. The latter represent a personal account of his stewardship, and in them he refers approvingly to various Evangelical devices for personal stock taking. In 1817 for example while reading William Sherlock's *A Practical Discourse on Death*, he noted the latter's useful method of reminding us of the certain passing away of our lives, by observing daily the diminution of our days, using the life expectancy yardstick of three score years and ten. Morison then in his thirty-eighth year calculated he wanted 11,732 days of seventy years and continued, "tomorrow I shall want 11,731. May God enable me to improve my time so that I may apply myself to wisdom."[12]

For many this intense and urgent faith, with its anti-intellectual bias, led to self-obsessive concerns and anxieties. This was not the case with Morison. His religion although important did not lead to extreme sabbatarian views or prevent him from enjoying a wide range of worldly pleasures, including playing cards, attending the theatre, and dining out in company, although it is true that some of these activities diminished as he became older.[13] It is also true that his faith provided an enormous comfort in the face of regular adversities, not the least of which was the early death of six children. Family letters, including his own to his wife, illustrate the comfort derived from the family's religious beliefs. In later life, too, his appreciation of the uses of "consolation" among Parisian alienists was heightened by his own sympathies, and his religious convictions thus helped to inform his use of moral treatment.

An Advantageous Match

Following upon his religious conversion came another dramatic change in Morison's life. In March 1799, although still aged only nineteen, he was released from his apprenticeship eight months early so that he could get married. His bride-to-be was Mary Anne Cushnie, a first cousin once removed. Like Alexander's mother, Mary Anne and her immediate family had been tainted by association with the Jacobite cause. Seven of her relatives had gone to Jamaica in 1745, and there they had built up a successful sugar plantation. The youngest of these, Thomas Stratton, was eventually left in sole possession of the estate, which by now had realized a considerable fortune, and on his death the property passed finally to his three sisters, one of whom was Mary Anne's grandmother. Mary Anne thus inherited a one-third share of the plantation.[14]

Figure 5.1. Mary Anne Morison and Alexander Morison, aged thirty-four and thirty-seven, respectively, as painted by Milburn. As these portraits were completed, the income from Mary Anne's Jamaican plantation was about to disappear, prompting Alexander to seek to establish himself as a specialist in the mad-doctoring trade.

Mary Anne, clearly a beauty, was referred to as "a perfect Venus" by Alexander's grand-aunt Barbara Forbes. Perhaps of greater moment, as Forbes noted when she wrote to congratulate him on the match, was that he was marrying someone who was "not only beautiful, but rich."[15] Apparently, the couple had met in early 1798, the date of their earliest surviving correspondence. At the time Mary Anne was sixteen years old, and her father Alexander was already terminally ill. Her mother had died in 1784 when she was just two and a half years old, and she was therefore in an extremely vulnerable situation. Alexander looked after Mary's father in the last weeks of his life, during which time he obtained the paternal blessing on the marriage.[16]

His wife's handsome legacy transformed Alexander's prospects by providing him with an apparently secure financial foundation on which to launch his career. But he proved chronically unable to take full advantage of his good fortune, vacillating endlessly between Edinburgh and London, unable to settle on a definite career or to establish a settled home life. Within six months of his marriage, in October 1799, he had secured his Edinburgh M.D., and he promptly set out for London to pursue two more years of medical study. His new wife, meanwhile, was left behind with her in-laws, where she was to remain, save for brief intervals, for most of the next five years. Making matters worse, Alexander left her perpetually short of money, and the heiress thus found herself in the embarrassing position of periodi-cally having to borrow from his brother John.

It was a suitable introduction to what was to prove by most measures a very strange marriage, characterized by prolonged periods of separation over a period of more than twenty-five years, as Morison migrated back and forth trying to establish his career. Each time he arrived on the scene, he appears to have stayed just long enough to father a child (she endured six-teen pregnancies in the course of her marriage), before once again leaving to pursue his vaguely defined ambitions. Rarely was he present to support her, and for his children, he was, of course, an absentee parent for much of their lives.[17] Her letters to him during the first part of their marriage are nonethe-less filled with affection, on one occasion, for instance, she wrote that she had just kissed his picture and that she prayed for him night and morning. His letters back are more restrained, but early on, they are at least filled with interesting news and details of his activities. Later, though, they become more formal, conveying homilies on how Mary should behave as a wife and mother and sending instructions about family business.

Alexander had travelled south in 1799 as a licentiate of both Colleges in Edinburgh (1798 and 1799) and with his sociable character soon made sev-eral friendships that provided him with the essential stability he needed to operate so far from home. As soon as he reached the capital, he became involved in a social whirl amongst the large expatriate Scottish community, many of whom were relatives.[18] He also found his way by October 1801 into lodgings with a Mr. and Mrs. Foy in Walworth. The Foys and their daughters were to become lifelong family friends.[19] At the end of the month, Mary Anne joined him, in the first of many abortive attempts to settle in London.[20]

Between 1802 when he left London and 1807 there is no evidence of Morison's professional activities, except for his visit to Russia. It is likely that most of this period was spent in and around Edinburgh, and we know that he received various proposals to set up as a general practitioner, either there or in Aberdeen. But with his wife's legacy in hand, and no pressing need to seek a regular income, these opportunities evidently did not seem sufficiently attractive to him. At least his wife was able to move into her own house in this period. In 1803, using some of her money, he acquired the lands of Bankhead and some nearby acreage in the parish of Currie, near Edinburgh, and the following year Larchgrove, the family house, was built.[21]

After several years without making much discernible progress towards establishing himself in a career, an opening that more nearly matched his own estimate of his abilities finally materialized. In October 1807 Morison was offered the chance to become personal physician to a Scottish peer Lord

Somerville who was going to England.[22] Over the next decade, Somerville became a powerful patron who opened up numerous social contacts, many of whom became his patients, as a physician and later as an alienist. Among these were Lord and Lady Manvers, the Earl and Countess of Carhampton, Miss Boyd (Lady Carhampton's sister), Miss Canning (aunt of the Prime Minister), Lady Portarlington, Lady Ilchester, Colonel and Mrs. Alcock, several members of the dispossessed French aristocracy, and Sir Joseph and Lady Mawbey.[23] Somerville likewise offered to try to obtain a Lord Lieutenancy for Morison in Surrey, and through his contact with Sir Lucas Pepys, president of the Royal College of Physicians, obtained him the post of Visiting Physician to the Surrey madhouses.[24]

Somerville's health problems did not justify a full-time medical attendant, although he did periodically need urgent medical attention and was to die when quite young. To compensate for this lack of employment, he gradually extended Morison's role to include acting as a general factotum and advisor in his agricultural and fishery interests. Morison proved receptive to these overtures, not least because of the bleak prospects of developing a viable medical practice in the Guildford, Cobham, and Esher area of Surrey where he was living.[25] In return, he received a very generous retainer of £200 p.a., which must surely have been welcome as the financial burden of a large and growing family began to make itself felt.

Alexander was clearly tempted by a life in agriculture and always spent a large portion of his time in Scotland working on his own estate at Larchgrove. He also devoted a great deal of time to protracted and increasingly urgent negotiations concerning his wife's plantation, Windsor Castle, in Jamaica. From 1815 onwards, the returns on the estate diminished markedly, and his financial prospects, which had already taken a turn for the worse as his family grew steadily larger, became an increasing source of worry. In the end, all efforts to improve the estate's management failed, and in 1822, it finally had to be sold off.

A CAREER AS A MAD-DOCTOR?

From about 1815 or 1816 onwards, therefore, the need to establish his medical career on a more reliable and financially dependable basis increasingly weighed on Morison. Almost immediately, and quite possibly in response to the publicity attending the hearings of the 1815–1816 Select Committee on Madhouses, he seems to have conceived the idea of developing a more specialised practice in mental diseases. He had, as we have seen, a long-standing intellectual interest in this area, and the ferment surrounding the parliamentary inquiry made madness seem a likely source of future income. Soon, in characteristic fashion, he was seeking to make use of his contacts to obtain a patronage appointment and, with a new sense of urgency, to establish himself in professional and lay circles as an expert on the subject.

In 1817, he informed Dr. Maton he was thinking of publishing a book on Cases of Diseases of the Head, some of which he had collected. At the same time, he was also hoping to obtain one of the well-paid Lunacy Commissioner posts proposed in the Lunacy Bills being put before Parliament by George Rose. When this legislation fell by the wayside he was forced, however, to consider other options.

He set his friends and patrons to work on a variety of fronts. Henry Halford was trying to get him employment as a travelling physician with a nobleman, as was Lord Somerville.[26] By this time he had also developed a small but dedicated following of patients from the local aristocracy and gentry in Surrey which had brought him into contact with noted society physicians such as Sir William Knighton, Henry Halford, Matthew Baillie, and Dr. Maton. These patients included a number of Surrey and Middlesex magistrates who would prove influential patrons later on in his career, but at this stage, nothing suitable materialised. Seeking to strengthen his credentials, he therefore arranged to go to Paris in March 1818 to visit its asylums and hospitals.

As was the custom, Morison travelled to Paris with letters of introduction, addressed to le Comte Anglais, Préfet de Police, and also Dr. Esquirol at the Salpêtrière. This was the first of five visits to Esquirol, which had a profound influence on Morison. They continued to correspond for many years, and Esquirol sent his students over with letters of introduction to Morison.[27] The trip was intended to be a broad educative experience, medically and culturally. Morison toured not just places dealing with the insane, but most of the major institutions of the Hôpital Général—Le Charité, Hôtel Dieu, Hospice des Hommes Incurables, Hôpital St Louis, La Pitié, La Grand Force, La Conciergerie, Le Petit Force, St. Lazare, Madelonettes, Hôpital Val de Grâce, the venereal hospital at Capuchin, Hôpital des Invalides, Hospital for Lying-in Women, Hôpital des Enfants Malades, St. Pélasgie, and the Hospice des Orphélins—and he recorded details of treatments for a range of complaints.[28] He noted with interest the price of corpses: 20 francs at La Charité and almost nothing at the Hôpital St. Louis. He also visited the morgue, but nowhere did he comment on the vastness of this apparatus of civil administration, although he did differentiate between those institutions he thought well run and those he thought not.[29] The other main concept Morison was introduced to in these hospitals and prisons was the use of work as both occupation and punishment. This was something later reinforced by his contact with Sir William Ellis at Hanwell and a feature he introduced at Springfield Asylum and Bethlem, to provide patients with a sum of money to take home on their discharge.[30]

Morison, already thirty-nine when he made this trip, was keen to soak up every opportunity for broadening his knowledge. He attended lectures by the catastrophist Cuvier on the history of seventeenth-century mineralogy and geology and by Dr Vaugelins on surgical practice in Paris. A private tutor was engaged to improve his French. Also attending the opera and theatre regularly,[31] he toured various medical and natural history museums. We can picture him, for example, at Cuvier's museum of comparative anatomy poring over the pickled privates of Sarah Bartmann, the Hottentot Venus, or the cranium of Kleber's assassin. His love of painting also drew him to David's inspirational paintings, echoes of an earlier Republican culture. He also visited other sites on the tourist trail, icons of the Revolutionary period: the cells of Marie Antoinette and Madame Elizabeth at La Conciergerie, the Elysée Palace, Versailles, the Palais de Justice, the Chamber of Deputies, the Tuileries and Buonaparte's Elephant on the site of the Bastille. All testify to his earnest desire for self-improvement.[32]

Morison's central purpose, though, was to observe practice in the Paris asylums. His first contact with Esquirol was significant, as the latter immediately launched into an account of his two hundred plaster of paris casts of the faces of the insane and his collection of six hundred skulls. After a later visit to Paris in 1825 Morison acquired a similar set of plaster casts that he used for demonstration purposes during his lectures. Both these and the drawings Esquirol commissioned from Gericault provided the germ from which Morison elaborated his ideas on physiognomy. Esquirol's enthusiasm for work with the insane was infectious. In discussion, Esquirol elaborated the fairly standard theory that insanity was in general the effect of other bodily disease to which attention should be addressed. In particular he advised Morison to look for suppressed discharges and derangement of the abdominal viscera. As in the London asylums that took poor patients, Morison saw a high incidence of skin diseases in the Paris asylums, and there were two wards set aside for patients with these disorders.

Esquirol afforded Morison every facility on his visit and generously gave of his own time. He read aloud parts of a planned book on asylums throughout the world, took him around the wards, showed him a brain he had dissected, and gave him further letters of introduction. Morison was less complimentary about conditions at the Bicêtre, but noted with interest the bath treatment with water on the head. He also visited other private asylums, Charenton, St. Lazare, and M. Belhomme's. At the Bicêtre and Salpêtrière, though, Morison was to imbibe the whole culture of French alienists' practice in the wake of Pinel. The trip also provided his first introduction to craniology, as he attended Gall's lecture vindicating his doctrine from the charge of materialism and fatalism. Later he attended Spurzheim's course of lectures twice in London when pursuing his own interest in the outward appearances of mental disease.

On his return to England Morison began to extend his new-found interest. He visited the Quaker Retreat and called on the architect of the new Wakefield asylum. In June 1818, he got an introduction to Dr. Sutherland and visited St. Luke's. He also toured Wakefield accompanied by William Ellis, with whom he later formed a close friendship, and in July he visited Glasgow asylum, then being run by a Mr. Doury, who had previously worked at St. Luke's.[33] Although these activities clearly signalled his interest in developing a more specialized practice, his source of professional income still remained that of a physician working through a network of family and friends.

An Uncertain Future

In December 1818 the Alcocks wrote from Tonbridge Wells that there was an opening for a physician there with the prospects of £800 to £1,000 p.a. Obviously tempted, Morison nonetheless hesitated to pursue the opening because he was once again hoping for a national post as an inspector for the insane under the proposed Lunacy Act (he had a battery of people applying for him—Miss Canning, Lady Manvers, Lady Blackwood, Mr. Grenfell) and because his wife opposed the idea.[34] This uncertainty about his future and multiple applications for posts were typical of his career. It was a measure of his desperation that he cast his net so wide.

In June 1819 the last Madhouse Bill finally failed, and two months later he again went over to Paris after being sent for by Lord Somerville who was ill.[35] Whilst there he was introduced to the *Cercle Médicale* and presented a paper on want of Iris in the Eye, based on a case he had been seeing in Surrey three years earlier. After returning he sent Esquirol copies of asylum pamphlets by Tuke and Duncan, and one from Glasgow initiating a correspondence of many years. He also continued his asylum-visiting programme, going to Nottingham, and William Finch's new licensed house at Mitcham, Surrey.[36]

In October 1819 Morison again asked Halford and Alcock to try to find him a post as a travelling physician, and in December 1819 he put in a canvass for Rutherford's post as professor of botany at Edinburgh; but he was unsuccessful on both fronts. In August of the following year, however, he contracted to accompany two of Thomas Coutts's daughters, Lady Bute and Lady Guildford, together with their entourage of children and tutor, on a European sojourn.[37] This expedition was typical of its type, a medical version of the Grand Tour made by invalids—in this case Lady Bute—who travelled the continent searching for better climes and improved health. In later years Morison recommended to many patients, insane and otherwise, that they should travel abroad in this way.

The initial journey took the party to Paris and then down through France to Nice where they settled for nearly six months, with further lengthy stays in Switzerland, Rome, and Naples, before he finally escaped back to England in June 1822. Morison clearly found the enforced company and empty days irksome at times. His medical duties were light and to fill the time he gave lectures on chemistry and other subjects to the ladies and their children, sought to improve his French and Italian, tried to learn German, and—ever the earnest self-improver—re-read the Bible.[38] In Nice he was able to develop a limited medical practice amongst the expatriate community. He did not however share the ladies' interest in poetry, Scott's Marmion, or German poetry, which he remarked was "rather a bore." The costume balls and dinner parties also lost some of their appeal without his wife's company, and he found Lady Bute's dithering about travel arrangements intensely frustrating.[39]

On his return to England, still without more stable long-term prospects, Morison was offered a similar post as in-house physician to Thomas Coutts's widow, the *ci-devant* actress Harriet Mellon.[40] That Morison took this post reflected how straitened his personal situation was becoming. His wife's West Indian estate had ceased to be financially viable, and his application for various professional posts had failed. The position with Lady Coutts lasted until December 1823, but their relationship was subsequently to be marred by a double falling out. Harriet Mellon was known as a generous soul, but ostentatious and fiery in temper. However, initially, she and Morison got on well, and she agreed to fund Morison's proposal for a lectureship in mental diseases, as a suitable memorial to her late husband.

LECTURES ON MENTAL DISEASES

Here was still another token of Morison's interest in developing a more specialized practice in what he had recognized as an increasingly promising new avenue for medical careers. Over the next few years, he made protracted efforts to attach the lectureship to an established institution of some sort, in an obvious attempt to bolster his own credentials and to lend weight to the novel venture. In Edinburgh he approached the University, Town Council, Morningside Asylum, and Royal College of Physicians in turn, but various vested interests were opposed to approving his plans.[41] Morison had close links with several private anatomy lecturers in Edinburgh—Lizars, Barclay, and Abercromby among them—but was unable to capitalize on his ties to them. These men had the advantage that students wanted to take private lectures in anatomy make up for deficiencies in the official curriculum at the University. But there was much less enthusiasm for lectures on mental medicine. As Lisa Rosner has shown, students only tended to take those lectures that they could see as directly relevant to their future careers,[42] and while Morison was astute enough to identify (and help to create) a growing market for doctors claiming expertise in the management of lunacy, the opportunities still seemed limited to most of his colleagues, and student interest in preparing for such a career was generally low. With Mrs. Coutts's money, Morison was nonetheless able to establish an annual series of between eleven and eighteen lectures in Edinburgh, generally commencing in November and finishing the following month; and in 1826, he began giving a similar course in March each year in London.[43]

The territory Morison sought to stake out is apparent from his *Outlines of Lectures on Mental Diseases*, which went through four editions between 1825 and 1848.[44] When the book first came out, Wakley defied anyone to review it, stating that it was impossible to disentangle what was borrowed from what was original, but he had revised his views by April 1827, when the *Lancet* noted "this work forms an extremely useful text book for its author's pupils and for medical inceptors generally." In fact, the book (like the lectures) *was* an unoriginal melange of ideas, uncritically assembled from existing works in the field. The lectures were, moreover, quite poorly attended, certainly when compared with the huge university classes in Edinburgh. (Morison's best attended lecture attracted only forty, and on occasions, when his advertising had been last minute, no-one turned up at all.)[45]

But to focus on these deficiencies is in many ways to miss the point. Beyond their value as an exercise in self-promotion, Morison's lectures and their associated textbook had a larger political and cultural significance. The courses were given over a seventeen-year period when nothing similar existed, and during this period the composition of the 140 or 150 people who attended changed, as did the content of the lectures themselves. Some came to the course over a period of several years, and Morison's friends made numerous attempts to persuade students from other institutions to attend. Sir Patrick MacGregor, a distant relative, encouraged Army and Navy personnel to take the course, and John Thornhill, an East India Company director, did the same in that service.[46] Further symbolizing the growth of medical interest in insanity in the first half of the nineteenth century, and providing visible testimony to the asserted growth of medical knowledge of this territory, Morison's textbook expanded from a mere 72 pages in 1825 to 495 pages by 1848.

For many of those who attended, Morison's course was probably the only teaching they received directly related to the clinical practice of mental medicine. Most university lectures that touched on insanity treated the subject in a very theoretical manner. Morison, by contrast, attempted to provide his students with a practical guide to the various forms of mental disorder, their management and treatment. Not surprisingly, therefore, the most important part of his audience were those medical men who sought visible testimony that there existed "a body of knowledge and skill necessary for the occupation" of mad-doctor,[47] and that they had received training in its mysteries.[48]

Most of those in attendance in the early years were London physicians who had private practices incorporating a good deal of contact with the insane. For Morison, whose psychiatric experience in the 1820s (aside from his impressive-sounding but largely exiguous official role as visitor of the Surrey madhouses) was wholly with private patients in the community; this group was made of mostly peers from the Royal College of Physicians. Men like Sir Henry Halford, Matthew Baillie, and Sir Matthew Tierney, who had large and successful society practices, had as a matter of routine long obtained some of their fees for providing discreet advice and treatment for mad folk related to their upper-class clientele.[49] The well-to-do shunned hospitals for the treatment of their physical ailments, and they were even less inclined to resort to madhouses when coping with mental disorder. Beyond the stigma that attached to such establishments and reputation they had acquired for man-handling their charges, asylum care threatened one of the most dearly held preferences of aristocratic families with a lunatic in their midst: the desire, at almost all costs, to avoid gossip and publicity about the existence of the object of their shame.

Such families possessed the financial wherewithal to employ relays of private attendants to cope with lunatics' eccentricities and disruptions or even to send those who threatened to embarrass the family name abroad. And their medical men had long found ways to adapt the standard therapeutics of the age—with its emphasis on bleeding and purges, diet and regimen, and the mutual interpenetration of mind and body—to the treatment of the mad. Morison's own previous clinical experience with the insane, as we have indicated, had come about in just such ways, and the extent of his innovation lay largely in realizing that the growing attention now being paid to the problem of lunacy signalled the emergence of an opportunity to build upon what had traditionally formed a *part* of many physicians' practice, and to transform his involvement into a full-time specialized career.

Clearly, his peers thought he had something to offer in this regard,[50] and Morison went to considerable lengths to fulfill their expectations. He had, for example, discussed the content of his lectures at length with Crichton and Haslam, who gave him case material from their own experience to use.[51] And in 1825, after another visit to France and the Low Countries, he began to include other media to enliven the lectures: plaster casts bought in Paris to illustrate his physiognomical ideas, a phrenological head for a while, and plates of the brain that he obtained from Lizars in Edinburgh.

For a small number of students, these formal lectures were supplemented by the opportunity of clinical demonstrations. In 1827, the surgeon Thomas Copeland suggested to Morison that his lectures' defect "is want of shewing practice on patients." Morison had already discussed this problem with Haslam who had suggested demonstrations using workhouse patients as one possible solution. Eventually, though, Morison approached Wastell at the Hoxton Madhouse and was given leave to bring students at any time between 11:00 a.m. and 4:00 p.m. This was on top of the permission he had received to take portraits at St Lukes, Hoxton, Miles House, and Aberdeen for his physiognomical plates. Almost immediately he took Gordon Smith, an army officer who was attending his lectures, to visit the patients there.[52]

His recognition of the importance of these arrangements for the marketability and value of his teaching is further evidenced by the fact that he sought permission in October 1835 to have his pupils admitted to Hanwell. He discussed this idea with the superintendent, William Ellis, suggesting that "it would be an inducement to [give] my pupils the opportunity of examining the brain etc. which we do in almost every case before the bodies could be taken away." Ellis was generally supportive (since 1832 Morison had been the Visiting Physician and a close colleague at Hanwell), but he felt Alexander had proceeded in an unnecessarily heavy-handed fashion, almost jeopardizing the necessary approval by the Middlesex magistrates.

The text of Morison's petition to admit them mentions the fact that medical students were starved of opportunities for becoming familiar with mental diseases and that this inexperience was often acutely felt when being asked to sign an opinion of the mental state of a patient or to give evidence in court. Ellis felt that even here Morison had been somewhat clumsy and suggested he would have done better to make "a much lighter matter of it." A much more serious tactical mistake, in his view, was Morison's mention of the need to provide for observation of post mortems. Only five years earlier, an inquiry at Bethlem had elicited the information that Dr. Wright had been involved in various dissections of patients whilst drunk, and as Morison must have known from the Burke and Hare murders in Edinburgh, dissection of dead bodies was in any case a highly sensitive issue. On November 14, Sir Peter Laurie told him that his petition to take two pupils was granted, but that the post mortem clause was omitted. The following day Ellis told him that the post mortem clause "had almost thrown [the whole proposal] overboard as some of the Magistrates said they would be tasked with giving liberty to cut up the patients. Sir William said that was done already and would still be done." The chair of magistrates, Colonel Clitherow, had expressed other fears, namely "that the *Lancet* might interfere in some way as it had about Bransby Cooper." But in the end the opposition gave way.[53]

The permission Morison obtained is interesting in view of Conolly's experience a few years later. In June 1828, Morison recorded that Sutherland had put forward his name to Leonard Horner, at University College London, as a fit person to give lectures on mental diseases. Horner had approached Sutherland initially, as the physician to St. Luke's, but the latter had declined the offer. Having attended Morison's lectures himself, and knowing of his colleague's struggle to establish these lectures in an academic setting, Sutherland presumably thought Morison was better qualified for whatever Horner had in mind.[54]

Much as he would have welcomed the opportunity to obtain such official sanction, however, Morison was never asked. Instead, in his inaugural lecture, delivered in 1828, John Conolly, the new professor of the practice of medicine, announced that *he* was going to "dwell somewhat more fully on mental disorders, or to speak more correctly, of disorders affecting the manifestations of the mind than has, I believe, been usual in lectures on the practice of medicine." It is at least possible that Conolly made this proposal to preempt the hiving off of separate lectures on mental diseases, and this manoeuvre perhaps marks the genesis of Morison's long-standing antipathy to his rival.[55]

Morison's efforts to establish a professorship in mental diseases (with himself as its first incumbent) included an extensive canvass of the Commissioners appointed to examine the Scottish universities (1826–1827). Professor Alison in his evidence to the Commission suggested just such a post, as an adjunct to the medical school, and with a clinical ward attached. He cited the example of the Salpêtrière, where he had attended Esquirol's lectures. Morison's friend, Dr. J. Abercrombie, did not go quite so far, but felt a lectureship might be attached to the university with advantage.[56] Unfortunately for Morison this Commission's work was never taken up, and his efforts to secure the additional legitimacy an appointment at Edinburgh University might have conferred thus came to naught. Many doctors nonetheless continued to attend the lectures, as a certificate of attendance from Morison was considered a passport to other opportunities in connection with the expanding number of posts for alienists.

Despite all these strenuous and creative efforts at self-promotion and at establishing the lecture series on a firm foundation, after four annual series of lectures, Lady Coutts abruptly withdrew the promised funding. Apparently, she had increasingly felt that Morison's labours failed to achieve the status she had envisaged as a testament of her husband's good works. Morison was furious at this setback, and at one point contemplated legal action against his patroness, but in the end, took his friends' advice and decided not to proceed.[57] Once again, however, he faced the problem of how to secure a stable source of income and a secure foundation for his practice.

Within a matter of months, in December 1827, Morison was elected president of the Royal College of Physicians in Edinburgh.[58] As usual he took every opportunity to puff this achievement, although as Halford acidly pointed out, he had been elected in rotation, rather than through any intrinsic merit of his own. He proved a competent president, but his presidential term speaks volumes about his personal style. He generally eschewed anything which smelled of "party" and was antipathetic to "unnecessary innovation."[59]

Whatever his personal inclinations, Morison was almost immediately plunged into a conflict over the Infirmary's appointment of a surgeon, William Cullen, as one of its physicians, and he played a central role in smoothing over relations between the College and Infirmary. The animosity created by Cullen's appointment was part of a much wider debate about the relative status of medical men in different branches of the profession. On this issue, Morison had no doubts where his own allegiances lay. Although he made use of the surgical and botanical skills he had acquired in his medical training throughout his professional life, he was very single minded in his adherence to the primacy of the physician. As a member of the most prestigious branch of the profession, Morison saw surgeons, and later the house surgeons of asylums, as very much his inferiors, an attitude that later inevitably caused a parting of the ways with colleagues in the Association of Medical Officers of Asylums and Hospitals for the Insane.

Despite having struggled for some thirty years now to find a niche for his talents, even at this stage he continued to turn down opportunities for jobs he felt were beneath him. In Edinburgh Dr. Stewart suggested partnership in a lunatic establishment, and in Surrey the magistrates Briscoe and Lawson explored the idea of a joint stock lunatic asylum with him.[60] He also received further appeals to move to Kent and Aberdeen as a general practitioner, but in every case he replied that he did not wish to be encumbered with a post that required his residence in a particular place. Meanwhile, as president, Morison gained, ex officio, further experience of visiting madhouses, two of which contained his own private patients, and he wrote detailed case histories of the patients he saw, with various suggestions for their treatment.[61]

A FLIRTATION WITH PHRENOLOGY

During the 1820s, like many of the emerging group of professional maddoctors, Morison had engaged in a serious flirtation with phrenology. His first contact with this doctrine had been on his initial visit to Paris, when he attended one of Gall's lectures. In 1823 Crichton recommended that he read Gall's book, and he obtained an introduction to Edward Wright, the surgeon at Bethlem, whom he now started to visit. Wright was a "disciple of Spurzheim" and very involved in the London Phrenological Society. In May 1823 Alexander attended a course of lectures by Gall at Bossanger, the booksellers, and met Crichton there at the opening talk. A day after the last lecture he watched Gall dissect a brain at Carpue's and demonstrate the decussation of the pyramids.[62]

By 1825 he was more actively interested, visiting Spurzheim and his wife in London during April and purchasing casts from Deville in the Strand.[63] Morison had his own head taken. In May he attended a Phrenological Society Meeting on the Diversity of the Forms of the Head by Allen of Wakefield, and he was still visiting Wright at Bethlem. Wright was experimenting with taking casts of the convolutions of the brain after removing the membranes, in an effort to confirm phrenological accounts of insanity, and he had destroyed several specimens in the process. He also showed Morison how he applied leeches to the affected parts of the head to treat insanity of various types.[64] In May, Alexander was back in Paris again, calling on Spurzheim and Esquirol and attending a dissection performed by Foville, in which he demonstrated the triae of the corpus callosa and challenged Gall's ideas on the distribution of the medullary fibres.

During the same visit, he called on Spurzheim, who expressed his disagreement with Esquirol's divisions of mania and monomania, which Morison himself had adopted. Spurzheim told him the diseased state in insanity was to be found in disease of the brain's organs affecting its functions. Privately, Morison was already beginning to review his interest in phrenology, although he still believed that hallucinations of the senses were related to the disordered state of the brain,[65] and he continued for some time to treat Gall's and Spurzheim's theories with respect.

Morison's ideas on physiognomy, for instance, were clearly linked to his exploration of phrenology, and on this visit to Paris, he paid an artist, Theodore Susemichl, to do some portraits of the insane from Esquirol's heads. In his discussions with Esquirol, the latter told him that the casts he had taken of the skull were done to discover whether there was any connection between the fixed physiognomy (form and position of the bones of the face) of the insane and their insanity. As he indicated in his *Outlines*, however, Morison suspected still another connection might exist, between the moveable physiognomy and insanity.

Hence his use of an artist's impression, which gave more scope for capturing the appearance of a lunatic during the paroxysms of their illness than a cast could do.[66] Morison never attempted to elaborate a detailed theoretical basis for this idea.[67] His interest was rather in the potential clinical applications of such observations. Like Esquirol, he contended that a skilled alienist using physiognomical assessments could distinguish the subtle features of different illnesses and even give warning of the onset of illness in those with a predisposition.[68] Morison asserted that a full history of the patient's life was essential, "especially the chief mental cause of the illness, i.e., study, business, political anxieties, religious doubts, disappointed love and remorse." Armed with this information and a study of the physiognomy, he believed it was possible to understand the association and likely direction of the patient's ideas better, thus forestalling mental irritation and lessening fits of fury. In particular, he thought that in monomania, where patients were thought to have only one delusive object, it was possible to see erroneous ideas about religion, love, fear, and grief etched on their faces,[69] and to use a study of their expressions as an aid in diagnosis and treatment. After all, "the appearance of the face, it is well known, is intimately connected with and dependent upon, the state of the mind. The repetition of the same ideas and emotions, and the consequent repetition of the same movements of the muscles of the eyes, and of the face, give a peculiar expression, which, in the insane state, is a combination of wildness, abstraction, or vacancy, and of those predominating ideas and emotions which characterise the different species of mental disorder."[70]

His initial interest in phrenology likewise derived from his belief that it could provide useful clues about the differential treatment of individual cases.[71] On his return to Scotland at the end of 1825, Morison accordingly began lecturing using the casts he had bought in Paris, and later that winter, in February, he started to attend still another course of Spurzheim's lectures, whilst delivering his own first course in London. There is little doubt that material from Spurzheim's talks found its way into his own lectures at this time, along with information he had gleaned in conversation with Deville.

During the same month, however, Morison recorded his difficulties with phrenology's materialist assumptions,[72] and gradually over the course of the next weeks and months, his doubts intensified. At one level, his growing scepticism reflected an accumulation of physiological evidence that cast doubt on phrenological claims and the critical attitudes of a number of his acquaintances.[73] Study of his diary makes clear how closely he attended to the debate on these issues and documents his disenchantment with phrenology's claims to be based in physiological reality. But the same body of evidence left many of his fellow alienists, including Conolly, Browne, and Ellis, unmoved. What accounts for these variant reactions?

One is sorely tempted to attribute them to social factors. As Cooter has argued, most supporters of phrenology were younger men who came, by and large, from relatively deprived social backgrounds, had had to struggle for their medical educations and were linked to strains of antireligious materialism and political radicalism.[74] Conolly and Elliotson were among these, working at the "godless" University College, and in Conolly's case the radicalism extended to an interest in Chartism and workers' education. Browne and Ellis shared broadly similar backgrounds and outlooks, politically and professionally. Phrenology's association with radicalism, in religion and politics, would not have endeared it to Morison, however, given his own Evangelical beliefs, his innate conservatism, and his strong ties to an aristocratic clientele. His initial flirtation with a doctrine that had such unpalatable associations in fact provides another measure of just how strong phrenology's appeal was to this generation of alienists. Seen in this context, his tendency subsequently to read the accumulating evidence in a negative light and to abandon phrenology a decade and more before many other mad-doctors did so, surely depends as much on the personal circumstances of his own background and career as on the determinative force of a still ambiguous set of observations.

A BURGEONING PRIVATE PRACTICE

While Morison had acted as a general physician into the 1820s, his diaries reveal that from 1824, as he began to direct more of his attention to lunacy, he had started to take on private insane patients, and as with other physicians who cared for the mentally ill, the therapeutic optimism already engendered in his work with general patients migrated to his care of the insane. Starting with a relative in need of care, he gradually expanded his network of patients through his friends and medical contacts. Once his two-year term as president of the Edinburgh College of Physicians was over, it was to this type of practice that Morison increasingly turned his attention, finally achieving a substantial measure of professional and financial success.

The system of lodgings or "single" care that Morison and others now began to develop on a more systematic basis grew, as we have already suggested, out of an older tradition of home care, in which general physicians like Halford, Baillie, Hue, and Tierney had provided care for the upper- and middle-class insane. That approach was propelled by strong consumer demand, but it now faced increasing official disapproval and legal constraints. Ideologically, during the 1820s and 1830s, the public debates over the treatment of insanity were dominated by the evermore elaborate arguments put forward in favour of asylum treatment, and as lay reformers increasingly rewrote the statute book, most of the more prominent and vocal doctors carving out careers in the treatment of the mad added their own arguments in behalf of institutional care.

There were, of course, some exceptions to this apparent public consensus in favour of the asylum. We have seen, for example, that in the late 1820s, before he embarked on a career in asylumdom, John Conolly strongly advocated the private care of the insane in their own homes or under supervision in lodgings in the community, in preference to asylum admission. Such proposals, one may add, were not dissimilar from what increasingly characterized Morison's practice and that of most of the London physicians who privately cared for insane patients.

In fact, Morison's *Outlines*, published in 1825, although a mere sketch in comparison with Conolly's prolix prose, had previously made many of the same points about the treatment of insanity. Morison believed that patients generally could not be nursed successfully at home owing to their aversion to being restrained in any way by relatives. However, he was clearly in favour of lodgings care wherever possible. In his view, it avoided the stigma of an asylum and afforded the patient a doctor's undivided attention, while also allowing better access for relatives. The only drawback lodgings possessed, from his perspective, was their high cost. Given the latter problem, and the existence of many poor patients, Morison depicted Hospitals for the Insane as a necessary evil, which should be made as comfortable as possible. He made the obligatory comments on asylum design, much of which he had picked up from Esquirol, and although espousing a greater level of restraint than Conolly, he clearly believed this should be carefully monitored. Simultaneously (and presciently), his lectures also warned against overly large institutions, as leading to more disturbed wards.[75]

Such dissenting views were ignored as the consensus in favour of asylum care began to harden.[76] Publicly, leading reformers argued that private care, by definition hidden from public scrutiny and difficult or impossible to police, invited abuse and mistreatment (to say nothing of the corrupt confinement of inconvenient people who were nonetheless not mad). Furthermore, only the well-ordered asylum, in their view, allowed for the employment of the powerful new therapeutic techniques of moral treatment, and they contrasted an idealized portrait of asylum existence with the situation of lunatics in single care, who often spent weeks and months alone in the company of an attendant who provided little intellectual stimulation. In keeping with these convictions, they actively sought through legislation, and through the activities of both the Metropolitan and national Lunacy Commissions, to curtail, if not eliminate, the practice of single care.

In 1828, the Madhouse Act required certification for single patients by two doctors (copies of the certificates to be forwarded to London within five days), together with making provision for central notification of deaths, discharges, and removals, and an annual return describing the patient's state of health. Passive resistance rendered the legislation almost a dead letter, prompting Brougham to offer a less stringent amendment in 1832, under which central notification of the existence of single patients was not mandatory until twelve months after they had been certified. Once again, these regulations were widely avoided: sometimes by the simple expedient of moving the patient to a different house before twelve months were up; more often, by merely ignoring them.

With the passage of the far-reaching lunacy legislation of 1845, which culminated a thirty-year campaign to implement the reformers' chosen nostrums, provision of public asylums for paupers was made compulsory and a national inspectorate finally established. Unsurprisingly, given this resounding official endorsement of asylums and of the principle of inspection, renewed efforts were also made to restrict and control the system of single patient care: such lunatics were supposed to receive fortnightly medical attendance from a doctor who did not directly or indirectly derive any profit from the case; single patients had to be centrally registered; without certification and notification to the commission, it became illegal to take on even a single patient for profit; and the commission was given the power to visit and inspect the conditions under which such lunatics were being kept.[77]

Necessarily, therefore, Morison's practice, and the practices of those who followed his lead, operated in a shadowy netherworld, sometimes on the borders of legality, often transgressing them. Although working in an apparently hostile ideological and legal environment, Morison and others nonetheless found an ample market for their services. Paradoxical as it may seem, and for all the authorities' overt disapproval, they did little to curtail the activities of those profiting from this sector during the following two decades.

DEMAND FOR EXTRA-INSTITUTIONAL CARE

In fact, the very strength of the demand for such services from the moneyed classes constrained all efforts to impose the formal regulations, which were in principle quite adequate. Victorian letters, diaries, and autobiographies provide ample evidence that, despite all the propaganda in favour of reformed asylums, upper- and middle-class families feared them and had low expectations about the kind of care their relatives would receive in confinement.[78] And certainly only a handful of private asylums, such as Ticehurst and Brislington House, could offer a regime remotely approximating the upper-class mode of life, meaning that institutionalization necessarily constituted a degrading experience for those exposed to it.[79] Single lodgings, perhaps most important of all, avoided the damaging labelling process (and possible publicity) associated with private asylums; and they approximated more closely to the aristocracy's preference for treating illness at home, where they could maintain some semblance of control over the proceedings. When even a former member of the Metropolitan Lunacy Commission, E. J. Seymour, was privately caring for Sir Robert Peel's mad brother in this fashion, those nominally charged with enforcing the statutes could not help being aware that public opinion among the governing classes would not condone an abrupt intrusion into such cases.[80]

Within the social space which thus continued to exist, men like Morison were free to take advantage of the demand for their services, subject only to the requirement that they behave discreetly. Like others with similar practices, Morison endorsed from ten to twenty lodgings at a time, while supplying many more with patients.[81] Not all of his patients would have met the legal requirements for certification as insane: his patients in lodgings included victims of the mesmeric craze, those who sought to contract marriages their relatives considered undesirable, and those who had joined fringe religious groups. On occasion, too, parents employed him to straighten out their wayward children.[82] But many of his patients were clearly deranged, and Morison's diaries provide us with remarkable insights into a subterranean world, largely invisible at the time, and almost wholly ignored by subsequent generations of historians.

For the most part, Morison ignored the new methods of moral treatment and, a few years later, nonrestraint. Some patients, indeed, were kept under an excessive amount of restraint, owing to their potential for violence.[83] Apart from dining with the family with whom they were placed, or occasional rides in a carriage, most patients received little in the way of moral treatment; rather, they were liberally supplied from the traditional pharmacopoeia, had their heads shaved, and were bled.[84]

None of which should be taken as suggesting that—medical treatment apart—they were simply consigned to custody and ignored. On the contrary, Morison's diaries illustrate a personalized level of care not found elsewhere, with a range of services being provided. Unquestionably, Morison often entered into a relationship with patients and their relatives of a much more personal kind than that found in later nineteenth-century doctor/patient contacts in the asylum. This contact, moreover, touched many aspects of his patients' lives.

In 1827, for example, when caring for Mr. Grenfell who was subject to great depression, as a result of a business mistake, he mentions talking to his relatives on several occasions and asking them to soothe him. Grenfell experienced repeated thoughts of suicide but had a horror of the act. He prayed about deliverance from these in Morison's presence and desired Morison to remove his pistols, later making him a present of them. Morison dined with Grenfell and his children regularly during the period of his illness in an attempt to provide as normal an environment as possible for him and even attempted to rectify his business mistake, in conjunction with Grenfell's partner.[85]

It is apparent that in most cases Morison negotiated a great deal with relatives, writing to them regularly to keep them informed of the patient's progress. He also recommended how much contact they should have with the patient, always favouring this unless there were strong contra-indications. Relatives often had their own comments to make about the process. Grenfell's daughter criticized his treatment approach, telling him she was afraid, "I indulged her father too much, especially by saying that at times he might scream involuntarily, which I did and do say, but that it may be excessively indulged and carried beyond bounds by giving way to it."[86] As we have indicated, patients with a huge range of diagnoses were accommodated in this form of care, from frank psychosis to those like the son of his friend and county magistrate, Lawson, who appeared to be wilful teenagers, running up debts and going off the rails.[87] Charles Lawson had been arrested on the point of marrying a Miss Pack, "who had lived with two or three others." After his release from a sponging house for debt he went missing, and Morison was involved with his father in making inquiries at coaching depots and with the local police to establish his whereabouts. He was eventually shipped off to Canton in China to make his way in life without parental support.[88]

With some patients, Morison acted as a broker sorting out access to alternative forms of treatment they wanted for their mental health problems. He engaged lodgings for patients and ensured that the physical environment in them was suitable to their circumstances. This could involve him in haggling over rent and in actually purchasing items for the rooms. He accompanied Miss Simpkinson, a long-standing patient, on numerous visits to Michael La Baume's premises (on occasions with her friend Lady Rose) where a variety of treatments were on offer. She chose a course of galvanism. He advised Mr. Dawson Damer about which continental spas to attend for his nervous debility, and on his behalf he investigated a machine for making artificial Carlsbad Waters. Being a physician, Morison also saw to the other medical needs of his patients, taking a number of them to Mr. Canton, his own dentist.[89] All this confirms Roy Porter's description of the way people shopped around for health care and demonstrates that a parallel market existed for treating the mentally disturbed as well.[90]

The diaries make clear that, as a standard part of his practice, Morison made detailed inquiries about each patient and noted details about their social and family histories. There is also evidence that he employed a primitive mental state examination. In May 1825 for example when asked to assess William Young's mental health, he wrote "examined Latin, counting, drawing, memory of events, dates, days of the week and month. Got a history of care, preceding headaches, convulsive attack after attack of delirium, amendment of position of hands from side like child progressively to placing them on the table—to humming a tune."[91] In deciding how to proceed, he also paid particular attention to patient's likes and dislikes. In September 1835 he met Miss Esdaile's sister, brother-in-law and brother—

Mrs. Thomas, Mr. Winter, and Mr. Esdaile. He was told that Miss Esdaile disliked Dr. Richardson, another brother-in-law, who had been treating her and her sister Mrs. Richardson. Mrs. Thomas was her favourite sister, and Morison thereafter chose to use her as his intermediary. Her relatives were also concerned that the deafness of her companion, Miss Charlton, served to irritate her, a deficiency made worse by the fact that she was insufficiently cheerful. Morison promptly ordered her replacement.[92]

Like many practitioners, Morison did take a few patients into his own home. This proved very stressful for his wife and the family nanny. In May 1828 he agreed to board a relative of his brother's wife, a Miss Jane Fordyce. This lady caused great difficulties by her disordered behaviour, most of it directed against Morison's wife during his frequent absences. She involved Morison's seven-year-old daughter in her religious delusions insisting that she say prayers with her (August 7, 1829) and on occasions came downstairs when they had visitors making an exhibition of herself (August 12, 1829).

Although Miss Fordyce was living as part of the family, there was a clear demarcation between her status and that of the rest of the family. When Morison returned from London in January 1829, he found her spending most of her time in bed in her room. Finally, in July 1829, Dr. Fordyce agreed to remove his daughter; it was not until February 1830 that she actually departed, after much prevarication on his part. Miss Fordyce's brother and parents both came to visit her in this placement, and although she complained a great deal, when Morison drew up a list of five alternative placements, she wrote to her father expressing a wish to remain.[93]

The most famous example of a system of placing patients in single care in nineteenth-century Europe was the Belgian community of Gheel. A religious shrine dating all the way back to the sixth century, the town and surrounding communities had gradually become a centre for the informal treatment of insanity, and during the nineteenth century attracted much attention and commentary as the site of a form of domestic care that differed sharply from the asylum-based care generally characteristic of the age.[94] Morison did visit Gheel but does not seem to have drawn any particular inspiration from it. He remarked on the fact that there was no general medical care there, and his only other comment was that the handsome altarpiece figure of St. Dymphna was too large for a girl of fifteen! His care of the insane in the community had a very different inspiration: a firm belief that individual treatment in a secluded setting would most likely induce recovery in the insane. This may have been the reason why he continued to avoid residential asylum posts, although he was to develop links with many asylums. He was constantly withdrawing attendants from asylum "call" lists to look after patients in the community and acted as a broker for nurses and others securing them patients to look after.[95] Eventually, though, his failure to secure an appointment as one of the Metropolitan Lunacy Commissioners persuaded him to seek some sort of asylum connection.

When the Middlesex magistrates began to build the Hanwell asylum in 1827, Morison was at first tempted to apply for the vacant post of physician, but he withdrew once it became apparent that they intended to appoint a resident medical officer. Within a few months of the asylum's opening, however, he had contacted the new superintendent, William Ellis, and had begun to seek an appointment as visiting physician. More than a year of discreet lobbying brought success, and he finally received the appointment on May 29, 1832.[96] Three years later, following the death of Sir George Tuthill, he secured a similar position as one of the two consulting physicians to Bethlem.[97] These were followed in 1840 by yet a third appointment to the planned Surrey County Asylum. In each case Morison had used his contacts in the Middlesex and Surrey magistracy to help him secure the post. Subsequently, he became as well consulting physician to four private asylums—London House, Southall Park, Earls Court House, and Elm Grove Asylum—each with an annual retainer. Besides the welcome financial boost each appointment brought in its train, these posts had other advantages. Ready access to a variety of establishments was useful for those of his patients who proved unmanageable in private care, and the prestige that accrued from some of these affiliations—advertised on the title pages of each edition of his books—was valuable in the further development of his extrainstitutional practice.

Taken together, Morison's various asylum connections, in addition to payments from his private patients, secured him a relatively handsome living during the 1830s and 1840s. At Hanwell, he had been offered £100 retaining salary, plus fees when his services were called upon. By the end of the 1830s, he had lost this source of income but had more than made up for it on other fronts. His visiting physicianships at Bethlem and the Surrey County Asylum brought him £180 p.a. each, and his relationships with Southall Park and Earls Court private asylums brought in another £125 and £110 p.a., respectively. At Elm Grove Asylum, he was paid between £50 and £110 for each of two or three individual patients, which in an average year brought in the neighborhood of £180. His four pupils at Bethlem paid 20 guineas each, for a total of £84 p.a., and he received £63 p.a. from his longstanding appointment as medical visitor to the Surrey madhouses. Dividends from lunatic stock and payments for attendance on a half dozen or so patients at London House, Hackney, amounted to almost £200, so that before he received any payments for domestic visits to single patients, or income from his lectures, his annual intake verged on £1,000. With these other sources of income added in, his practice by this time was obviously both lucrative and successful.

CONFLICTS WITH CONOLLY

Before 1839 Morison's tenure of his varied posts as Visiting Physician to asylums was largely unproblematical. He covered for Ellis during the latter's absences from Hanwell and kept the required attendances at Bethlem. Similarly, his involvement with private asylums was relatively undemanding and lucrative. But the appointment of Conolly to the superintendency at Hanwell in May 1839 brought a whole series of perturbations in its train.

Unfortunately Morison's diaries for 1837–1840 are missing, but it is evident that from the outset, he felt a great deal of animosity towards Conolly. In 1838 he himself had been knighted and clearly felt he had attained a certain status in the profession. The arrival of an outsider and potential rival on the metropolitan scene was therefore scarcely welcome. Added to the wariness Morison quite possibly felt on these grounds, Conolly's activities at the University of London in the late 1820s may have left some lingering bitterness; and like some of the Middlesex magistrates, Morison may also have disliked Conolly's progressive political views.[98] In any event, the ill-feeling quickly became mutual. Within months of Conolly's appointment, Morison was asked to hand back his key to the Hanwell wards, and his access for the purpose of taking physiognomical drawings and instructing pupils was stopped. Conolly was fifteen years his junior, and whatever verdict history has subsequently placed on their relative importance, these actions were likely to have caused offence.

Worse was to come. The magistrates who served on the governing boards at Bethlem and Surrey immediately began to make invidious comparisons between their own regimes and Conolly's innovations at Hanwell. From the outset Morison, undoubtedly feeling threatened, seems to have decided that rather than investigating Conolly's claims for nonrestraint he would seek to diminish them. In December 1839 when Sir Peter Laurie, chairman of the Bethlem Governors told him about the breaking up of restraint chairs at Hanwell the previous month and how calm the violent patients had been, he merely commented that there were not many violent patients there. Laurie was impressed with an experiment on such a vast scale, and the following August told Morison he would rather have all the windows in Bethlem broken than see a patient in restraint. In a similar vein he commented he would rather have four or five nurses holding a violent patient than have them mechanically held. Morison disagreed, and so did other Bethlem Governors, particularly Mr. Bagallay who felt Hanwell was not being well run.

Whilst the Surrey magistrates were evaluating the new system, Conolly was being assisted by his own justices, particularly Serjeant Adams, who was carrying on a campaign to proselytize those opposing nonrestraint. In

November 1839, Adams began a correspondence with Dr. Poynder, the superintendent at Kent County Asylum.[99] These letters make it abundantly clear that Morison was not alone in perceiving Conolly's system as less revolutionary than was being stated. Adams offered to send Poynder the Lincoln reports and show him round Hanwell, but failed to convert him to the cause. In December the chair of the Kent magistrates, Lord Marsham, told Adams he could not introduce a system that his superintendent opposed. Adams was by now making large claims about the influence of the nonrestraint system, including a statement—which was quite untrue—that restraint had fallen into disuse at Bethlem. A year later Adams was still trying to persuade Poynder to adopt the new system. But Poynder believed many claims made for Hanwell were sheer delusion. He asserted it was not possible to maintain the levels of staffing they had, at the level of expenditure they were stating, and added that he was pleased that Conolly did not go the same lengths as Gardiner Hill in asserting that personal restraint was never justifiable for lunatics. After pointing out that it was absurd to argue against the use of a thing on account of its being abused, he expressed a concern that if restraint were discontinued, something worse would be substituted in its place. His final point was perhaps the most telling of all. After pointing out the problems inherent in getting magistrates to agree to the expense of increased nursing levels, he pointed out that Hanwell's current funding was the result of an "extraordinary state of things—The question is, how will the system work when the excitement and enthusiasm which at present prevail have subsided, and things settle down into an ordinary state."[100]

A full history of the controversy over nonrestraint still remains to be written, but it is clear that Hunter and Macalpine's assertion that Morison orchestrated a campaign against Conolly through the dissatisfied officers at Hanwell is by no means the whole story;[101] this was written with posterity's verdict on nonrestraint in mind. Many contemporaries were unsure that Conolly's reforms were a good idea. The magistrate, Reverend H. S. Trimmer, had asked for Morison's opinion as the Visiting Physician, when Conolly initiated his reforms. Morison felt they were not practicable. His opinion about putting epileptic patients under restraint at night was ignored, almost certainly to the patients' benefit, but following this, two patients suffocated. It seems likely that this was the point at which Morison was asked to leave, as his ideas were clearly in conflict with Conolly's.

The evidence collected by the disaffected Dr. Button, Conolly's assistant, certainly suggests that the nursing of difficult patients was not entirely successful initially. From an average consumption of three crates of glass a year between 1833 and May 1839, Hanwell required twenty-five crates over the following twelve months, and wire mesh was put over the windows.[102] Trimmer reported that in November 1839 a woman who had struck the matron and knocked off her cap was put in a shower bath. Conolly said she could come out if she apologized, and when she did not the shower continued until she fainted.

In such a partisan atmosphere it is difficult to disentangle relative truths, but it is clear that nonrestraint had effected a sea-change in the atmosphere at Hanwell.[103] Moreover, the enormous publicity Conolly's experiment generated in the space of a few months soon gave nonrestraint an almost totemic significance.[104] As "proof" of the practicality and humanity of the reformers' schemes, it soon acquired the status of sacred dogma, a litmus test of progress and modernity.[105]

Morison was soon under still more pressure at Surrey. In April 1841, Mr. Jefferys brought the Hanwell report to a committee meeting. Morison expressed the hope they would not make it their textbook but should receive it with allowance. Meantime, he insisted he had always been in favour of a minimum use of restraint, although he acknowledged that he routinely used straitwaistcoats and muffs where he thought them necessary. In May, Adams wrote suggesting a copy of the Hanwell report go to all Surrey magistrates, in an obvious attempt to get them to adopt Conolly's approach. In the event Morison was supported by his visiting magistrates, but evidently he felt compromised by Conolly's success, which occurred just as he had established himself as an authority on the insane.

As nonrestraint became more solidly entrenched, the battleground switched from disputes over whether the new system was feasible to criticisms of the minimal restraint still used at Hanwell and the associated substitution of seclusion for mechanical restraint. Conolly's reports never disguised the fact that some limited forms of restraint were still in use. Hands were confined when a blister was applied to prevent its removal, and in the cold weather warm boots fastened around the ankle with a small lock were used. Those who were violent wore a dress in which the sleeves terminated in a stuffed glove without divisions for the thumb and fingers. Poynder and Morison challenged this, as did Huxley later at Kent County Asylum, by suggesting that Conolly's reforms were not that revolutionary, but their efforts to minimize his accomplishments appear to have made little headway.[106] In press and in Parliament, the doctrine of nonrestraint was clearly carrying the day.

Conolly also proved a nemesis in other respects. Although Morison had permission to take pupils at Bethlem and Surrey, he later found himself under pressure to lecture as well, in emulation of Conolly's classes at Hanwell.[107] After some initial resistance, Monro and Morison finally gave way in 1849, fearing the loss of their posts. In Morison's case it was with the proviso that they be advertised as general lectures illustrated by cases and not as clinical lectures, which was Conolly's term.

It is easy to see why, having given his own lectures since 1823, Morison did not take kindly to this situation. Conolly's lectures spanned a mere four years, and he did not lecture again after leaving Hanwell, while Morison had been lecturing annually since the early 1820s. Expanding his audience beyond the medical men and magistrates who had formed the primary constituency for his lectures since the early 1820s, in 1844 he proceeded to give the first ever course of lectures to asylum attendants at the Springfield Asylum. Hunter and Macalpine believed this was an "irksome and partisan performance" undertaken in response to the developments at Hanwell. Their account stretches the evidence in Morison's diaries, although the motivation for giving the talks was undoubtedly allied to his wish to counsel caution about nonrestraint.[108]

It is clear from all this that Morison did not care for Conolly and from his perspective had ample reasons for his distaste. His accounts in the Surrey Annual Reports studiously stress that his practice is based on Pinel, and that he has endeavoured to approach, "the beau ideal of Dr Charlesworth." The omission of any mention of his rival at Hanwell is telling. He clearly saw Conolly as a parvenu, and in 1847, when Conolly wanted to place one of his patients at Southall Park, near Hanwell, which was run by Dr. Daniel (and formerly by Dr. Ellis's widow), Morison threatened to discontinue his attendance, giving as his reason that he preferred all the patients to be under his care and Daniel's.[109]

The Defence of Traditional Practice

It must have been galling in the extreme for Morison to observe his rival's extraordinary public success, tied as it was to practices he found dubious and worse. In response, he sought to reassert the value of the kinds of traditional practice he and his allies stood for and to counter the new-fangled notions of the alienists running the reformed asylums. As part of this process, in 1842 Morison founded the Society for Improving the Condition of the Insane.

For more than a decade, until Morison retired from the scene, the Society provided a platform for practitioners who espoused the continued, but limited, use of restraint.[110] Hunter and Macalpine stated that it was set up in imitation of the Association of Medical Officers of Asylums and Hospitals for the Insane (AMOAHI), but there is no evidence for this. Morison was at the time a member of the AMOAHI, and although he did temporarily withdraw his subscription that year, he later rejoined the Association.[111] Of greater significance is that he asked the sixth Earl of Shaftesbury to preside over the new organization. Shaftesbury was a Governor of Bethlem, but

Figure 5.2. New Bethlem—the third hospital, which opened in 1816 in St. George's fields. The dome was added in the 1840s, while Sir Alexander Morison was the Visiting Physician.

more important, he was also well known as an implacable opponent of his son, Lord Ashley's (later seventh Earl) social reforms.[112] One does not have to search very far, therefore, to discern his motivation in seeking to promote an organization that ran counter to his son's obvious support for Conolly at Hanwell. The society operated by offering both prizes for essays related to mental diseases and premiums to attendants for meritorious service.

But the Society's overt function, to reward good practice, and even its role as a centre for opposition to nonrestraint, pale into insignificance along-side the role it played in perpetuating the hegemony of private practice in London enjoyed by Sutherland, Burrows, Monro, Wood, Philp, Millingen, Costello, and others. Its existence, and the forum it provided for informal contact among specialists, helped to cement networks among the elite mad-doctors in the private sector which had been in existence for years.[113] Most valuable of all, meetings at Morison's house provided the opportunity for sharing information about each other's establishments and for keeping track of the Lunacy Commissioners' implementation of policy, a matter of direct and pressing financial concern to those working in this sector.[114]

Morison's alliance with the sixth Lord Shaftesbury almost certainly did not endear him to Lord Ashley, although the latter had a reasonable opinion of Springfield.[115] In his role as Bethlem Governor, the sixth Earl had been instrumental in blocking Ashley's attempts to bring Bethlem under the Lunacy Commission's control,[116] and he had helped to deflect pressure to adopt the nonrestraint system from several of his fellow governors, who were also Hanwell magistrates. Securely entrenched behind the barriers erected by his patronage, Morison and the similarly conservative E. T. Monro, who jointly served as its visiting physicians, had remained tenaciously wedded to a more traditional therapeutics.

But the protection turned out to be less than secure after all. In 1851, barely a month after his father's death, Ashley obtained permission from the Home Secretary to institute an inquiry at Bethlem.[117] The Commission descended on the hospital with the clear intention of bringing it to heel. The letter to the Governors announcing their first inspection arrived the day after they did, and they proceeded to ransack the establishment for evidence of abuse. Even a cursory scan of the evidence they took shows their bias and repeated use of leading questions, a tactic that the Governors fruitlessly pointed out in their own defence:

Q.2718 Where is fault found.
    A. The fault is to be found with Dr Wood.
Q.2719 You think that he is indolent and careless?
    A. Yes.
Q.2720 And he does not take sufficient trouble you think?
    A. No.
Q.2721 He doesn't keep the attendants in sufficient order?
    A. Yes, that is what it is.

The printed reports produced by the hospital also make many other valid comments on the ex parte way the inquiry was conducted. The evidence of former patients was accepted with little question, whilst everything said by the officers of the hospital was presented as being self-exculpatory.

There is little doubt that the hospital, which still attracted many foreign medical visitors, had fallen behind contemporary standards of practice, although the visitor's book comments are almost uniformly fulsome in their praise. In the mid 1830s there are several remarks about the low levels of restraint in use, especially from foreign visitors. This may of course reflect the lower threshold some continental states had for personal coercion, but it also suggests that in some quarters Bethlem continued to be considered a model to be emulated. Not in the eyes of those now scrutinizing its operations, though. Damningly, the Commissioners noted that they had found some dirty patients were still being kept on straw, in a naked condition. All staff members at the hospital were implicated by this, as indeed were the Governors. But other criticisms that were levelled at the hospital were certainly disputable. The Commissioners criticized, for instance, the way in which the casebooks were kept, although comparison with other public asylums at this period would suggest that Bethlem's methods were not in the least unusual. Morison always kept his own record of patients' care, and in a letter he listed the other books he filled in. Quite transparently, however, the Commissioners were not interested in reaching balanced conclusions, but only in finding sufficient evidence to persuade the Lord Chancellor to bring Bethlem in line with other institutions. By now, too, they had adopted the perspective of the Association of Medical Officers of Asylums and Hospitals for the Insane: Visiting Physicians were a thing of the past and did not provide the best method of regulating an asylum. By criticizing Monro and Morison, who were operating in a high-profile institution, they were effectively giving their final seal of approval to the new model of asylum organization, centred on the role of resident medical officers.[118]

Ironically, the presence of Visiting Physicians might have mitigated some negative aspects of degenerationist psychiatry in the later nineteenth century, but by midcentury asylum superintendents had secured a stranglehold on the large-scale management of lunacy. Coincidentally, the Commission's decision to endorse this model of practice occurred just as Ashley was getting his fingers burnt after recommending John Godwin as the nonmedical Governor of Hanwell, the event that had precipitated Conolly's departure. Godwin had been an abject failure, and the Commission now conceded that resident medical officers were the way forward.[119]

From Morison's diaries and the letter he submitted to the inquiry, it is evident that he had been diligent in carrying out his duties but had been overtaken by a wider political struggle within the profession. Conditions at Bethlem were by no means as bad as the Commissioners wished to make out, and Morison had always spent a great deal of time in face-to-face contact with patients and their families.[120] Both he and Monro pointed out, with some justification, that the resident apothecary was largely responsible for the day-to-day management of the hospital, but this merely fed into the Commissioners' line of argument. They chose to highlight the apothecary's role by suggesting that his general supervisory duties had been inadequately carried out because too much medical responsibility had been devolved on to him by the Visiting Physicians. Instead, they recommended the appointment of a Resident Superintendent with overall control of the institution.[121] This post did not interest Morison, who by now was seventy-three, and in 1852 he and Monro were pensioned off.[122]

DOMESTIC TRAVAILS

This crisis in his career came following a period of personal sadness. In 1837 his brother John had died, and in 1846 his wife died after being bitten by an insect. Even after they had obtained a settled residence in London and

Figure 5.3. Portrait of Sir Alexander Morison, 1852, by Richard Dadd, an inmate of Bethlem confined as a "criminal lunatic" after he slew his father in August 1843.

Sutton Vallence, Mary still spent much of her time alone. A letter she wrote to the local vicar at Sutton Vallence suggests strongly that she was careworn after bringing up her huge family and was going through an emotional crisis. Aside from her faithful nanny, she had had little help in coping with the demands of her family.[123] Five years later Alexander remarried. This decision caused enormous anguish to his daughters, and it is likely that they destroyed the diaries that dealt with this period of his life. His second wife was also a distant cousin, Grace Young, and his grandson's biography suggests that she provided a belated comfort to him.

Morison continued as Visiting Physician to the Surrey County Asylum until 1856, and even after that until 1862 he commuted from Scotland to accompany the Surrey magistrates on their madhouse visits.[124] His declining years were marred, however, by various family deaths. In 1859, his son, Alexander Cushnie, returned from twenty-one years service as a surgeon in the East India Company. He had escaped all the conflicts in the subcontinent and during the Mutiny had been based at Peshawar, which did not rise against the British. By the time he got back to England, though, he was already suffering from sprue, a wasting disease, and he died in 1861. Two years later Thomas Coutts, Morison's only other surviving son, died unmarried in Australia, after a failed career as an asylum superintendent at Norfolk, Montrose, and Nottingham and a period of service as a surgeon with the Turkish Contingent in the Crimean War.[125]

Morison's diaries rarely reflect the emotional content of these events, and the picture he presents is of a man immersed in his daily routine. Whatever affection he felt for his family, he was obviously unable to relax his role as paterfamilias. Added to the strain of losing all six sons, he had the extra sadness that his eldest daughter Margaret became mentally ill in the early 1840s and had to be cared for in one of the private asylums he visited. He also clashed with his daughter Somerville, with whom he had always been close, when she insisted on marrying against his wishes.[126]

In October 1861, Morison sold the family home, Larchgrove, to the College of Physicians in Edinburgh, the proceeds being intended to provide for the endowment of a lectureship in his name. This memorial, together with the awards for good nursing practice instituted by his society, have continued to this day.[127] He finally died on March 14, 1866, aged eighty-seven, exactly nine days after Conolly, with whom so much of his career had been intertwined.

ALTERNATIVE MODELS OF PRACTICE

Assessment of Morison's career is difficult so long as it is bracketed with his younger contemporary. Conolly's writings on nonrestraint provided a paradigm for all his contemporaries, but it is unhelpful that Morison's opposition to this doctrine should be taken as the single defining characteristic of a career spanning sixty years. He was a proud, not to mention on occasion prickly, man who faced a radical change late in his career, which on the face of it constituted a critique of much of what he had achieved. The opposition to nonrestraint of much younger doctors, like James Huxley, illustrates why Morison had so much difficulty in accepting what many regarded as a utopian experiment. At the time there was little way of knowing whether the new doctrine would prove as illusory as phrenology or mesmerism. Besides, like many mad-doctors of his generation, Morison believed that a certain amount of restraint was sometimes necessary as part of the modification of asocial behaviour and to teach habits of self-restraint, a view Pinel and Esquirol had also espoused. His pantheon of heroes dated back to a much earlier period, and he was unable to accept Conolly in the same light.

Morison's significance for us lies much more in what his career can tell us about the development of the profession outside the walls of the madhouse and about how that form of practice was and was not linked to asylum care. The whole trend of psychiatry in the wake of the Lunacy Commission's support for first Tuke's, and then Conolly's model, moved towards an almost exclusive dependence on an institutional base. However, the upper and middle classes had always opted for nonasylum care where possible, and from the numbers of pauper single lunatics identified by the Commission in the 1850s and 1860s, it is probable that many working-class people also preferred home care for their mentally disturbed relations. Morison's private practice with the insane grew out of his role as a general physician, caring for people in their own homes. In the absence of raving madness, most affluent people in this period approached a physician or apothecary in the first instance if they had a mad relative, and the surviving evidence suggests they continued to do so throughout the nineteenth and into the twentieth century.

The care Morison offered in the community, with its network of attendants and lodgings, had a number of strengths: families were more or less guaranteed confidentiality; they could have ready access to their sick relative; Morison provided regular reports by letter on their progress; and he often managed the financial aspects of their care.[128] For some critics of the lodgings system, its unregulated nature before the 1860s, was a cause of great concern, as not all those involved were as scrupulous as Morison. Unquestionably, too, some patients resented the dialogue of power that took place between their families and carer over their heads. In the final analysis, though, the most evident feature of Morison's care of private patients is the flexibility and attention to detail that his upper-class clientele was able to demand. His diaries repeatedly document both his willingness to change a treatment regime to suit an individual's needs and his strenuous efforts to negotiate with relatives and patients about the appropriate course of treatment; so much of this was missing in asylum medicine after the initial flush of enthusiasm subsided.

Early alienists like Morison were not products of an asylum system that was tyrannical in its adherence to form. At the Surrey County Asylum at Springfield, his relationship with his Visiting Magistrates was entirely different to that of subsequent superintendents.[129] Initially, Conolly enjoyed a similar relationship with his visiting committee at Hanwell, and it is significant that he did not remain at Hanwell long when exposed to the kind of subordinate position that became commonplace later. Once asylums became noncurative warehouses, however, alienists lost much of the credit they had accumulated, and the vulnerabilities of their position as employees were ruthlessly exposed. By then, memories of alternative models of practice had faded.

The halting and uncertain progress of Morison's early career was obviously in part the product of his own quirks and idiosyncratic choices. On another level, however, the long period of uncertainty he went through before successfully establishing his practice reflects the extraordinary difficulty of creating the conditions for a viable career as an alienist, and the unholy scramble for posts, in which he was so frequent a participant before achieving a measure of professional success is testament to the fierceness of the competition for livelihoods and the limited windows of opportunity that opened up.

Morison's career choices were not those of the mainstream of the mad-doctoring trade in the mid-Victorian era, as it desperately sought respectability and stability. In substantial measure, one could argue that he was simply overtaken by events. The broad cultural appeal of moral treatment was closely linked to an asylum-based model of care, and as his own experience at Bethlem was to show, the Lunacy Commission was ruthless in exacting conformity to this approach once it had found its feet. His preference for visiting rather than residential appointments at an asylum could scarcely survive this change; for while an outsider might visit and dispense prescriptions from the pharmacopoeia, he was scarcely capable of exercising the mundane and all-encompassing supervision over the asylum that moral treatment demanded. As for his extra-institutional practice, it fell afoul of the understandable concern reformers felt about its potential for abuse and hence was driven underground, notwithstanding families' continued strong demand for such services. To be sure, his activities in this area provided a tenuous link to a future generation of private practitioners, who tended to specialize in "nervous" diseases rather than the major forms of insanity, and they usefully remind us that even mid-nineteenth-century alienism was not solely an asylum-based specialty. But the official disapproval with which he wrestled helped to stifle and suppress any significant development of the profession along these lines for an extended period; and, in the process, it likewise decisively reinforced the exodus of alienism from its origins in general medicine.

Chapter Six

THE ADMINISTRATION OF LUNACY IN VICTORIAN

ENGLAND: SAMUEL GASKELL (1807–1886)

> If I have succeeded better than many who surround me,
> it has been chiefly, nay, I say almost solely
> from unwearied assiduity.
> (*John Dalton, 1833*)

SAMUEL GASKELL published virtually nothing of any significance in the course of a professional career that spanned four decades: a handful of annual asylum reports that had an extremely limited circulation;[1] a brief communication for a lay audience on the possibility of educating the "idiotic";[2] and a single article in a professional journal on the need to make better provision for the mentally disordered middle classes.[3] Nor was he responsible for any important innovations in the therapeutics of insanity or the care of the mad. Though a talented asylum administrator, his efforts in this sphere were largely derivative, closely and self-consciously resembling and borrowing from the approaches pioneered by John Conolly at Hanwell.

Yet if neither his practice nor his publications broke significant new ground, Gaskell was nonetheless one of the most influential figures in shaping the transformation of the mad-doctoring trade during the course of the nineteenth century. Through his activities as a Lunacy Commissioner, he played a major role in establishing and defining the context within which his professional brethren operated and in enforcing the legal constraints to which they were subjected. Gaskell was a diligent and indefatigable investigator, and his presence lent teeth to what previously had often proved to be a supine inspectorate. In the process, however, he helped to channel the development of medical psychology in particular directions, to accentuate existing pressures making alienism an essentially administrative specialty, and to foreclose opportunities to develop alternative patterns of professional practice.

PROVINCIAL NONCONFORMITY

The second son of William Gaskell, a well-to-do sailcloth manufacturer, Samuel was born in the prosperous town of Warrington on the coast of Lancashire in 1807. He grew up in a bastion of Nonconformity, a centre of the

early industrial revolution—a manufacturing town whose local elites embraced not merely Dissenting Christianity but the values of science and
"useful knowledge."[4] Institutionally, the dominance of these views among
the Warrington elite was reflected in the Unitarian Chapel, built in 1745,
and the dissenting academy, founded a dozen years later.[5] Baptized in the
former, Samuel grew up in a family with extensive ties, often cemented by
marriages, to a whole network of prominent nonconformists: families like
the Henrys, the Wedgwoods, the Hollands, the Gregs, the Darwins, and the
Rathbones, who together formed "a close-knit, continually intermarrying,
almost dynastic elite."[6]

Two events marred Samuel's childhood: a serious bout of measles left him
with chronic vision problems, which persisted throughout his life; and in
1819, when he was only twelve, his father died, seriously undermining the
family's finances.[7] Three years later, his mother remarried the local Unitarian minister, E. R. Dimmock, restoring a measure of financial stability. But
by then, Samuel, notwithstanding his expressed preference for a medical
career and his eye problems, had already been apprenticed to William
Eyres, a publisher and bookseller in nearby Liverpool.[8]

His older brother William,[9] meantime, precluded by his Nonconformity
from attending Oxford or Cambridge, had instead attended Glasgow University, from which he received an M.A. in classics 1824, and subsequently
had moved to Manchester College, then located in York, to obtain training
in divinity prior to embarking on a career in the Unitarian ministry. By
1828, he had secured an appointment as the junior minister at Cross Street
Unitarian Chapel in Manchester, the institution with which he was to remain affiliated until his death in 1884. Three years later, he met another
Lancashire Unitarian, Elizabeth Cleghorn Stevenson, and within a year, they
were married.[10]

Samuel had, in fact, preceded his brother in moving to Manchester. In
1825, still committed to a career in medicine, he had secured a release from
his indentures to William Eyres,[11] and he had moved to what was by now
the second largest city in Britain,[12] the heart of its new industrial society.
Here, he secured a new apprenticeship as a surgeon in training with Robert
Thorpe, the surgeon at the Manchester Royal Infirmary. Some six years later,
at the age of twenty-four, he supplemented this training with a year in residence at Edinburgh University and obtained an LRCS and MRCS, before
returning to Manchester to establish his practice.

His arrival back in Manchester coincided with an outbreak of cholera on
the east coast of England, an epidemic that allowed him to secure a position
at the very outset of his career as resident medical officer at the Stockport
Cholera Hospital, one of the two institutions specializing in the disease in
the Manchester area. By 1834, his industry and connections had secured
him a much more promising position as resident apothecary back at the

institution where he had begun his training, a post he was to hold till the end of the decade. Here, he had his first sustained contact with insanity, the disorder to which he was to devote the remainder of his career.

The Manchester Royal Infirmary, founded in 1752, had begun admitting lunatics eleven years later, and in 1766, had opened a separate building in the grounds in which to house them. Connection with the general hospital had soon proved a passport to the higher reaches of local medical practice, and when Gaskell had first undertaken his medical apprenticeship there in 1825, it already boasted of treating "2,000 more [patients annually] than the largest hospital in London."[13] Besides the general stream of patients generated from amongst the hordes of inhabitants of Manchester who were mired in poverty, the nearby cotton mills and other factories, with their power-driven machinery, provided no shortage of casualties for its wards. A visitor during Gaskell's tenure at the institution, having praised the mechanical marvels of the new age, described some of their not-so-salubrious consequences: "we saw feet torn off from legs and arms severed from bodies, and hands literally crushed, and heads laid open to the brain. But all was cleanliness, attention, order, neatness."[14]

The infirmary was one of a constellation of three interlocking institutions that linked the Manchester elite. The medical men associated with it, who formed the most prominent segment of the local profession, also occupied leading positions in the Literary and Philosophical Society, where they mingled with the most notable figures in the manufacturing community, many of whom served on the infirmary's board of trustees.[15] For the most part, these men also worshipped together in the third establishment of their particular trinity, the Cross Street Unitarian Chapel, "known locally as the carriage-way to heaven."[16]

Samuel and William Gaskell thus found themselves in close proximity to the dissenting "aristocracy" of the new industrial metropolis and with personal ties to all three of these institutions.[17] During the 1830s, however, their own positions within this world were from some points of view quite marginal and uncomfortable. Despite their impeccable Unitarian credentials and their strong claims to possess the kinds of polite knowledge, of both literature and natural science, that were the warrants of intellectual and social standing in this world of affluent entrepreneurs and professionals, their own positions were ill-paid and scarcely such as to provide a comfortable middle-class existence, let alone to allow them to mingle on terms of equality with the most financially successful medical men or the captains of industry and commerce.

For William, the difficulty was gradually alleviated as he secured additional employment lecturing at Manchester New College, teaching German to young ladies,[18] and eventually succeeding to the post of senior minister at the Chapel, on the death of John Gooch Robberds in 1854. His wife, through the fecklessness of her father, had brought him only the most meagre of dowries—the promise of an annuity of some £80 a year on the death of her aunt Lumb.[19] But Elizabeth ultimately made a major contribution to the household economy, finding fame and fortune as a novelist and securing a national reputation that, while it left him distinctly in her shadow,[20] helped to place the family fortunes on an entirely more satisfactory footing.

Samuel had no wife and family to provide for—he was to remain a lifelong bachelor—but his position at the infirmary, while a promising place from which to launch a career, was ill-paid and scarcely something even a single person could afford to occupy for long. It comes as no surprise, therefore, that when the position of resident superintendent at the County Asylum in Lancaster fell vacant, at a salary of £400 a year, with a house and food provided in addition, Gaskell threw his hat in the ring.[21] Armed with glowing recommendations from his superiors at the infirmary (and possibly another from his fellow Unitarian, John Conolly),[22] to say nothing of his local connections, he was naturally an appealing candidate, and when the magistrates met in Preston in late February, he was elected to the post by a wide margin on the first ballot.[23] Simultaneously, a local Poor Law guardian and physician, Edward De Vitré, was elected to the vacant position of Visiting Physician to the asylum.[24]

SUPERINTENDING A COUNTY ASYLUM

Gaskell's experiences in the lunatic wards at Manchester obviously had much to do with his choice of career and with his successful candidacy for the position at Lancaster. Equally salient, however, were his religious convictions. Unitarians were anxious to work for social and moral improvement in ways that were law abiding and respectable. They prided themselves on their "rational" Christianity, stressing "natural knowledge" and the steady application of self-discipline and self-control as a sure route to personal and social improvement; simultaneously they viewed these endeavours as inevitably leading "the student of Nature back to Nature's God."[25] Self-discipline and self-control were, of course, precisely the values celebrated and striven for within the new system of moral treatment for insanity, and few contemporary social movements more neatly encapsulated the Unitarians' emphasis on rational social progress than the effort to secure lunacy reform.[26] Not so coincidentally, perhaps, the progressive spread of reason and of rationally guided social change were inextricably linked to the progressive rise of the power and status of men like Gaskell himself, whose careers were the joint product of intellect and unremitting effort.

At the asylum whose superintendence Gaskell now inherited, such disciplined and unremitting efforts were to prove indispensable. On taking office, he found himself in charge of what had already become the second largest asylum in England. If Conolly at Hanwell had to find ways to manage almost a thousand inmates, his fellow-Unitarian's task at Lancaster was scarcely less formidable. Among the very first county asylums built under the permissive legislation of 1808,[27] Lancaster had opened in 1816. Originally designed to house no more than 170 patients (and containing only 153 in 1820), it grew remorselessly over the next two decades, so that when Gaskell took over, he found well over 500 inmates confined within its walls.

Physically, like many other county asylums of the period, Lancaster presented a dismal and depressing contrast to the utopian visions of the reformed institution with which the public was now being regaled. Its air of "prison-like gloom" was reinforced by the presence of "strong iron bars . . . fixed to every window, and all the entrances, as well as many of the sleeping rooms, were provided with massive iron gates." Ventilation was grossly inadequate, impeded by "the number and great height of several walls separating and bounding the small yards which, at that time, were the only means for affording exercise to the patients" and made still worse by the fact that, "throughout the greater part of the establishment, the windows were so small and placed so near the ceiling that the patients could not possibly look out." Moreover, a substantial part of the ground floor lay beneath grade level, and the use of flagstone rather than wood floors exacerbated the resulting problems. Huddled together in grossly overcrowded conditions that necessitated that even "the old chapel was used as a sleeping room," the patients suffered from "cold and damp," to say nothing of the stench that permeated the establishment.[28]

In a multitude of other respects, the Lancaster Asylum in early 1840 scarcely served as an advertisement for the reformers' programme. Like his counterparts in the county asylums at Bedfordshire,[29] the West Riding,[30] and at Hanwell[31] in the decade before the advent of Conolly, the Lancaster Asylum's first superintendent, Paul Slade Knight, had made extensive use of a variety of forms of mechanical restraint to maintain order among the patients. Sharing with John Haslam a preference for manacles over the straitjacket, he had won a measure of fame for devising new kinds of wrist- and leg-locks that eliminated "the clinking of the chains"—a noise that "I have known . . . to impress lunatics with the most gloomy apprehension."[32] Knight's dismissal after charges of corruption were raised in 1824 brought little or no change in this regard. To the "nineteen tons of iron bars and gates" that Samuel Gaskell finally managed to remove, two years after he became superintendent, one must add the weight of a remarkable array of locks, chains, and restraining devices with which he had previously managed to dispense.

As a matter of routine, patients who arrived at the asylum in the 1830s were initially chained up at night, a practice that was abandoned only in those cases where it seemed safe to do so.[33] As many as thirty or forty inmates, the "dirty patients" who lacked control over their bowels or bladders, spent their days chained up in so-called "warm rooms," fastened to "seats so constructed as to answer all the purposes of water-closets."[34] Another twenty-nine wandered the galleries wearing handcuffs, leg-irons, or strait-jackets. Throughout the establishment, many inmates went barefoot, and clothing and bedding were generally in short supply, with "loose straw in common use for many of the patients"; and the insufficient quantity and poor quality of the food worsened "the evident feeble condition of the inmates."[35]

With the support of De Vitré and the Visiting Magistrates, Gaskell attacked these practices with a characteristic vigour and determination. A wider variety of clothing, some of it made by the inmates themselves, was made available to the patients. "Warm cloth boots" were provided for those who had previously gone unshod, and "strong shoes were substituted for those of a light description." The use of straw was abandoned, and he secured "a more varied, increased, and improved allowance of food."[36] To deal with the overcrowding, the magistrates had already drawn up plans for "additional buildings," and during Gaskell's first year in office, he also had to cope with the disruptions the construction caused. In fact, he deliberately courted an exacerbation of these problems in the short run, when he persuaded his employers to extend the work to add new exercise grounds and improve the ventilation and cheerfulness of the existing accommodation.[37]

In practice, the need to devote a great deal of attention to the physical fabric of the hospital continued throughout Gaskell's tenure as superintendent. In a pattern that was to repeat itself in other jurisdictions as well, the availability of further space in the asylum was at once more than offset by the arrival of additional patients on its doorstep: "No sooner were the new buildings occupied, than it became necessary to contemplate further enlargement." Old stone walls were demolished, improving "cheerfulness, light, and ventilation," and the building materials thus recovered were recycled and "made subservient to the provision of airy and commodious apartments." Windows were "enlarged and lowered," ironwork removed, wooden floors installed, gas introduced from the town works to light the asylum at night and in the winter, and a new chapel "opened for divine service."[38]

Even after all this work had been accomplished, Gaskell complained that the "greatest inconvenience is daily experienced, from the very inadequate size of . . . the kitchens, laundry, and drying rooms"[39]—a difficulty that became more acute in 1847 "by the failure of the potato crop" and "the alterations in the general diet [the potato famine] rendered necessary."[40] The magistrates now conceded the point, but they found themselves confronted simultaneously with yet more demands for space and accommodation. The asylum census had averaged 523 patients in the first year Gaskell served as its superintendent, and numbers grew steadily and relentlessly during his tenure, reaching an average of 767 in 1848–1849. For all their investment in new dormitories and day-rooms, the Lancashire authorities thus continued to face "the many disadvantages arising from the disparity between the number of patients and the size of the building," and Gaskell constantly grumbled that "obstacles to order and regularity continually arise, which require to be surmounted by temporary expedients."[41]

By any measure, the accomplishment of this continuous programme of expansion and renewal of the fabric of the institution must have cost Gaskell enormous time and labour.[42] In his own view, however, it was subservient to (and cost less effort than) his attempts to bring "into operation throughout the whole establishment, a different system of moral discipline, in relation to the patients generally, as well as to every individual case."[43] Here, he essentially sought to replicate the regime Conolly had established at Hanwell, and, like Conolly, immediately confronted the difficulty that "the efforts of the senior officers [were] not cheerfully seconded by those placed under them"[44]—a euphemism for the considerable resistance he and De Vitré initially encountered from attendants suspicious of their new-fangled notions and reluctant to incur the increased responsibility and workload the new regime now required them to assume.

Gaskell refused to be intimidated. "Increased difficulties were met by increased exertion,"[45] and the attendants were gradually brought into line. They were, he insisted, "so many instruments destined to fulfil, in their various departments, the one great purpose of ameliorating the condition of the inmates," and close attention must thus be paid to their instruction and supervision. Hour by hour, attempts had to be made, "by every means, to render all engaged in the Asylum better capable of exercising over the minds of the patients those regulating and controlling moral influences which it was desired to substitute for the mechanical and degrading contrivances previously employed." Informal education, "the effect of example exercised by the superiors in station and intelligence," "stringent regulations, [and] a rigid and strict discipline" were all employed with the goal of "secur[ing] the most complete order, regularity, and decorum" from work force and patients alike.[46]

Within a year of his arrival at Lancaster, with De Vitré's assistance, he had abolished all forms of restraint.[47] The various elements of moral treatment were likewise introduced. Classification was attempted systematically, for the first time in the asylum's history:[48] clean patients were separated from the dirty; "the convalescent and quiet" from "those who are refractory [and] noisy." A variety of games and amusements was provided for the patients, along with books and newspapers. More important, given the central place work occupied in the moral treatment canon, he began systematic efforts to expand the proportion of inmates employed at various tasks about the asylum. Workshops were constructed, and members of a variety of trades—tailors, joiners, a baker, plumber, painter, and blacksmith—were employed to work around the establishment and to provide instruction to patients. The addition of a weaving room allowed the asylum patients to supply much of their own clothing, providing a useful contribution to the institution's economy. And by purchasing thirty-five acres of moorland adjacent to the previous boundary wall, Gaskell was gradually able to add an array of outdoor activities: work laying out walks for patients; a reservoir constructed by their labour; and a small farm—once again an "obvious benefit in an economical point of view"—but also "the means of recreation and agricultural employment."[49]

One of the more remarkable features of Gaskell's regime at Lancaster was the extent to which he introduced a wide range of improvements without adding to the overall cost of the asylum. Unquestionably, this accomplishment was one important source of the continued support he drew from the local magistrates, for, as was true of almost all county asylums throughout the century,[50] there was continuous pressure from local ratepayers to avoid "unnecessary" expense.[51] To be sure, the additional buildings, necessitated by the remorseless pressure on available space, almost continuously required additional capital investments. But the expenditures per patient per week actually fell during his administration, from 7s. 6d. when he took office in 1840, to only 7s. ½d. six years later.[52]

In matters both large and small, Gaskell laboured incessantly and ingeniously to improve the patients' surroundings and to eliminate the worst features of the establishment he had inherited. The appalling stench, so standard a feature of most such institutions and so vividly represented in the lunacy reformers' complaints about the ancien régime, was due, in substantial measure, to the presence of substantial numbers of inmates who had lost control over their bladders and bowels. At an enormous asylum like Lancaster, "wet and dirty beds were counted by the hundreds," and the "abominable nuisances" that resulted—"the litter, the stench, and the foulness" permeating the atmosphere—"were to be met with in the early morning of every day on many of the wards."[53] Determined to reduce or eliminate the problem, Gaskell instructed his attendants that throughout the night, "each patient, who was liable to be wet or dirty, [must] be aroused, and placed in a situation, to attend to the needs of urination or defaecation at stated intervals, with the result that wet and dirty beds were reduced to units where they had been counted by scores, or even by hundreds."[54]

Many patients understandably saw little difference between confinement in an asylum and imprisonment. Sensitive to this concern and anxious that the alienist not assume the mantle of a gaoler, Gaskell counterattacked on a variety of fronts. Besides tearing out bars, abolishing restraint, enlarging windows, and demolishing high walls enclosing cramped airing courts, he sought other means of disguising "the regulating and controlling power" that inescapably lay just below the surface of even the most benevolent asylum regime. "It appeared," for example, "that the plan of placing an attendant to watch over a body of patients, without himself rendering assistance in the work, was objectionable, as tending to favour an impression, too apt to arise in the minds of the patients in an Asylum, that they are subjected to confinement owing to the commission of crime. An order was issued that every one taking charge of a number of employed patients, should enter actively on the work, so as both to stimulate their exertions, and render the occupation more productive of benefit as a remedial agent."[55] Similarly, he insisted upon "the abolition of the police-like garb given to the attendants, and the substitution of a more economical and suitable dress, as well as the change of the term keeper to that of attendant."[56]

A large proportion of the patient population lacked even the most basic rudiments of an education, arriving in the asylum both illiterate and innumerate. Convinced, characteristically, that here was another means of inculcating a measure of rationality, Gaskell enthusiastically adopted another of Conolly's innovations, establishing "an evening class for reading, writing, and arithmetic . . . in each ward, under the superintendence of the Matron and Chief Attendant."[57] For the large fraction of the inmate population who were idiotic and demented, he established "day-schools . . . conducted on somewhat the same principle as that adopted in infant schools," and he pronounced it "most gratifying to observe the favourable impression produced even on the idiotic mind by well-directed and persevering efforts, where to the casual observer, all prospect of educational benefit would appear to be utterly hopeless."[58] Significantly, while he noted that these efforts "have been serviceable in an educational point of view in individual cases," his prouder boast was that "they have had the effect of promoting discipline and order generally."[59]

Tuke had suggested that the presence of domesticated animals provided salutary benefits to mental patients, giving them objects to care for and drawing them out of their private obsessions. Gaskell early on made use of this tactic,[60] but he soon adopted a far more daring plan: a number of female patients were placed in charge of young orphans, a gesture whose apparently salutary effects on their behaviour produced astonishment among outsiders who had occasion to view the results.[61] And in a variety of other ways, he sought to alleviate the pains and deprivations of the patients' daily existence: water beds were supplied for the bed-ridden; plants and engravings made their appearance to enliven the wards; the floors of "many of the galleries are matted with a material manufactured by the patients from the waste edgings of cloth"; and "the substitution of earthenware plates for wooden trenchers" paradoxically reduced "the amount of breakage" whilst contributing to the general comfort and self-esteem of the inmates.[62]

A MARGINAL PLACE FOR MEDICINE

In attending to this extraordinary whirl of activity and innovation, however, the historian is inclined, like Dr. Watson, to overlook the dog that did not bark. As with Conolly at Hanwell, Gaskell's regime at Lancaster is as notable for what was not present, as for what was. The close attention to every aspect of the asylum's routine; the ingenious adaptation of the principles of moral treatment to the management of a huge and massively overcrowded institution for paupers (the means, as Gaskell put it, "of promoting a more cheerful, contented, and tractable disposition throughout the whole community");[63] the immense labour both men invested in attempting to acquaint themselves with every nook and cranny of the vast operations over which they presided—these are not matched by any remotely comparable commitment to a medical therapeutics for insanity. On the contrary, they both generally exhibited a profound scepticism about the relevance of the conventional medical armamentarium to the treatment and cure of lunacy. To be sure, both emphasized the value of removing concurrent physical disorders and the need to attend to the digestive systems of those afflicted with melancholia. But in a larger view, both saw bleeding, drugs, and the like as at best of marginal significance, of little importance placed alongside the steady application of moral management. "Young and sanguine practitioners," Conolly remarked, "usually feel dissatisfied with candid statements of the possible inefficacy of medicines, resulting from experience; and probably no physician undertakes the charge of an asylum without the pleasing belief that many of the cases considered incurable will recover with the aid of energetic treatment. It is to be regretted that this belief generally yields to repeated disappointments."[64]

When the Lunacy Commissioners conducted a special national survey of alienists' therapeutic practices in 1847—the only such inquiry they were to undertake during the nineteenth century—Gaskell, like Conolly, endorsed the use of the shower-bath as a disciplinary tool, "to check occasional tendencies to violence and destructiveness";[65] but he made no mention of the purges, aperients, emetics, and sedatives many of his colleagues recommended. With respect to phlebotomy, he was more overtly hostile: "general bloodletting is scarcely ever practised in [this] establishment, and . . . even topical bleeding is very rarely resorted to."[66] Internal hospital statistics provide direct confirmation of the small place he accorded such techniques in his daily practice: under his predecessors, the asylum had consistently spent quite considerable sums on medications. In 1840, for instance, the year Gaskell was appointed superintendent, the institution spent £172 14s. 1d. on medicines; six years later, the amount spent had fallen to £38 3s. 0d. Even these numbers understate the magnitude of the change from past practice, for they ignore the substantial rise that was taking place in the patient census. On a per capita basis, the 9s. 1d. that had been spent on medicines in 1833 had fallen to only 1s. 2d. by 1846.[67]

However well-founded the modern reader might feel this therapeutic nihilism to have been, it was greeted in many professional quarters with dissent and alarm. Speaking in a guise that allowed him to cloak alienists' concerns with the authority of the new Lunacy Commission, James Cowles Prichard directly criticized such apostasy: "there is reason to apprehend," he complained, "that the attention of medical men has been of late years too exclusively devoted to what is termed Moral Treatment, to the neglect, in some instances, of the resources of medicine. They appear occasionally to have lost sight of the fact that Insanity never exists without a physical cause, namely, some disturbance of the functions of the brain . . . whence it seems to follow that physical agents ought to be resorted to in the first instance."[68] A few years later, John Charles Bucknill used the pages of the *Journal of Mental Science* to express sorrow that such authoritative figures should lend weight to the idea that "the direct application of therapeutical means [was] most unsatisfactory . . . we"—and he clearly sought to speak for his professional brethren here—"are strongly of the opinion that a small list of active therapeutical remedies frequently afford the happiest results in the treatment of the insane; and that therapeutical means are scarcely more limited in their curative influence upon recent diseases of the brain, affecting the intellectual functions, than upon any other large class of visceral diseases."[69]

Potentially compounding the damage Gaskell's and Conolly's views might do to the fledgling profession's standing were the dismal cure rates both Lancaster and Hanwell produced. For all the remarkable transformations Gaskell had produced at the former asylum, and regardless of the greater tranquillity and comfort that now surrounded the patients, the reported cure rate actually fell, and fell quite substantially, in the years he was in charge. In the decade before his arrival on the scene, cures in most years had amounted to about 20 percent of the average number resident; by 1845, however, the rate had fallen to only just more than 11 percent, and thereafter, it scarcely exceeded 10 percent.[70]

Like Conolly and their counterparts elsewhere, Gaskell blamed this state of affairs on the dismal raw materials with which he had to work. Declining cure rates, on this view, reflected the fact that "a very large majority of the patients now admitted into this asylum are imbeciles, or have laboured under insanity for so long a period [as to be] chronic and hopeless cases."[71]

Apparently, neither patients' families nor Poor Law authorities could be induced to send recent cases to the asylum, and here, it was alleged, lay the major reason for the asylum's failure to fulfil its curative promise.

On some levels, the failure to deliver the expected cures turned out not to matter. The Lancashire magistrates seemed content to oversee a humane if custodial operation, and their complacency can only have been bolstered by the reactions of outside inspectors to conditions in their asylum. In early 1842, the Metropolitan Commissioners in Lunacy—whose powers had previously been limited to the inspection of asylums in the London area—were given a three-year authority to inspect all asylums and madhouses in the country. Their 1844 report finally lent decisive weight to the lunacy reformers' long campaign to secure a national inspectorate, and from 1845 they were replaced by a new, more professionalized body, the Lunacy Commission.[72]

DISCIPLINING THE DISORDERLY

Lancaster was visited on at least three separate occasions by the Metropolitan Commissioners,[73] and subsequently on an annual basis by their successors.[74] Repeatedly, Gaskell's skills were lauded, and the condition of the Lancaster Asylum held out as an exemplary demonstration of what a reformed asylum could accomplish. On the occasion of their first visit, Metropolitan Commissioners Lutwidge and Hume commented that, "having visited and carefully inspected every part of this Establishment, and having personally examined every Patient, [they] feel it a most agreeable part of their duty to express their unqualified approbation of all they have seen."[75] Four years later, when Hume revisited Lancaster as a Lunacy Commissioner, this time accompanied by Mylne, the language was still more complimentary: Gaskell's efforts, his "patience, zeal, and continued perseverance," warranted "our admiration and unqualified approbation."[76] And when Procter and Turner inspected conditions in the final months of his tenure as superintendent, they too concluded that "the state of the Establishment reflects the highest credit on the attention, skill, and judgment of Mr. Gaskell."[77]

In the light of Gaskell's accomplishments, the more remarkable since they required overturning long-established practices and occurred in a severely over-crowded and poorly-endowed pauper establishment, it may seem churlish to question what lay behind these encomiums and what they reveal about the limits of his achievement. For whatever the constraints imposed on us by the surviving sources (and they most certainly do not enable us to penetrate official representations of reality to observe what actually went on in the wards during those long stretches of time when patients and attendants escaped the view of both superintendent and inspectors), it is plain that Gaskell was quite unusually dedicated to and successful at improving the living conditions of his patients. Certainly, during his administration Lancaster Asylum provided a more humane and caring environment than most lunatics would have found in either the workhouse or the "community"; and in affording his patients a refuge from the harsher fate that the most vulnerable elements of Victorian society otherwise confronted, Gaskell had surely earned the gratitude at least some of his charges displayed.[78]

But rather than moral treatment's virtues as a means of restoring the mad to sanity, of which its most enthusiastic proponents continued to boast, the therapy's more enduring if limited value as a set of techniques for disciplining the disorderly, a mechanism for enforcing conformity to a settled institutional routine, came to be emphasized at Lancaster—a subtle shift that prefigured its fate throughout the expanding empire of asylumdom.[79] Gaskell's own reports are quite revealing in this respect, particularly in his unapologetic emphasis on the role of a variety of disciplinary techniques in "promoting a more cheerful, contented, and tractable disposition" among his charges. He consciously sought "to devise and enforce means calculated to prevent . . . interruptions to the order, quietude, and well being of the [patients]"[80] and took great satisfaction in reporting that, "in this large Hospital, receiving patients from a County not noted for either the gentleness or suavity of the populace, and admitting also within its walls a large number of criminal patients, no recourse to mechanical contrivances for restraining the limbs is now found necessary."[81] Still more revealing of the values at the heart of the enterprise, though, were the comments of the various visiting Commissioners, brought face to face with the disciplined regimentation needed to secure such ends.

Where Tuke's version of moral treatment had meant the creation of a stimulating environment in which routine could be sacrificed to the needs of the individual, at Gaskell's establishment the reverse was necessarily the rule. It was, however, precisely the "tranquillity and orderly conduct" of the inmates that the inspectorate found most worthy of note and praise.[82] They emphasized that "the bodily health of the inmates is remarkably good" and the bedding plentiful. The patients were, moreover, "particularly clean and neat in their persons and quiet and cheerful in their demeanour."[83] Most striking of all, and particularly appealing to the Commissioners with Evangelical sympathies, was the disciplined and controlled behaviour of the patients at chapel: "We ourselves attended both morning and evening service yesterday . . . and were much gratified at the serious and orderly way in which the service was performed, and the entire absence of excitement and disturbance among the patients."[84]

Though he faced a never-ending battle against pressures towards disorder and disintegration, Gaskell's unremitting efforts thus produced a well-oiled machine in which both staff and patients had apparently learned their places. Surrounded by hordes of the chronic and the congenitally defective, it would have been easy to despair and to allow his energy and ambition to flag. On the contrary, however hopeless the prospects for cure, however feeble the remnants of their reason might be, Gaskell refused to give in. And he could plausibly claim to have shown that within the highly controlled confines of his asylum, his charges might yet be coaxed and drilled by a firm and watchful authority into a semblance of "self-control."

Perhaps the most striking demonstration of his convictions and commitment were the techniques he developed for coping with the mentally defective. A recurrent theme of Gaskell's reports was "the large proportion of . . . congenital idiots or imbeciles" sent to the asylum, and he was to devote much of what he had to say in 1848 to discussing the results of a survey of poor law medical officers concerning those "mentally deficient from birth."[85] Two years earlier, though, the peculiar problems this group of patients presented had prompted him to visit Paris in order to examine French methods for educating "congenital idiots." On his return, enthusiastic about what he had seen and convinced of its value in "quicken[ing] the feeble and scanty germs of intellectual power bestowed on these forlorn creatures," he disseminated his findings to a general lay audience;[86] and immediately he set about providing schooling for the "idiotic" in his own asylum. The school room, he believed, could serve as a manufactory where certain moral agencies could be brought to bear, their combined effects being to "render serviceable" even these imperfect specimens of humanity. A year later, he claimed considerable success in this venture: "several idiots, formerly considered incapable of amendment, are not only rescued from a miserable state of existence, but are now orderly, cleanly, and daily engaged in some simple occupation."[87] His clearly expressed preference, however, was for "institutions specially adapted . . . to the feeble-minded and idiotic," and together with Conolly and an interested philanthropist, Andrew Reed, he soon sought to create the first English Asylum for Idiots.[88]

PROFESSIONAL PREFERMENT—THE INSPECTOR OF ASYLUMDOM

His commitment and achievements had naturally won Gaskell a considerable local reputation. It therefore comes as no surprise that when the Governors of the Manchester Infirmary decided to build a new subscription asylum outside the city, they turned for advice to their former house officer.[89] More important, however, the repeated approbation of the Lunacy Commissioners, reinforced by their chairman's personal conviction of his merits, now brought him much more significant national recognition and an appointment as one of their number. The death in late 1848 of James Cowles Prichard, the one medical commissioner with direct experience in treat-

Figure 6.1. Samuel Gaskell, brother-in-law of the novelist Elizabeth Gaskell, superintendent of the Lancaster County Asylum, and the most punctilious of Commissioners in Lunacy.

ing the insane, created the necessary vacancy, and Shaftesbury personally approached the Lord Chancellor Lord Cottenham to secure Gaskell's preferment.

The offer of a commissionership brought with it a very substantial improvement in Gaskell's finances. His salary at Lancaster had remained only £400 a year, and he had found this sum barely adequate. Having been one of the prime movers in the founding of a professional association for alienists, the Association of Medical Officers of Asylums and Hospitals for the Insane,[90] he had subsequently hosted its second meeting at Lancaster in 1842, complaining privately that the expenses he incurred were "most hateful."[91] Now, however, he was given a post which carried with it a salary of £1,500, plus expenses, an extremely substantial income to which very few doctors indeed could aspire.[92]

Gaskell's appointment to the Commission in many ways represented a radical departure from past practice. When a national inspectorate had been created in 1845, at Shaftesbury's suggestion, its numbers had been kept quite small: the paid commissioners included three lawyers and three doctors, and five prominent political figures served as unpaid lay commissioners (with Ashley, as one of these, serving as the Commission's chairman). The professional commissioners, chosen from among the larger number who had earlier served on the metropolitan board, all owed their appointments to their social connections and to patronage, with the College of Physicians playing a large role in the choice of the medical men. With the exception of Prichard,[93] none of the medical commissioners had any special claims to expertise in the field; and if anything, their social ties to proprietors of the more exclusive private madhouses and their gentlemanly distaste for the mundane and unpleasant tasks of rummaging about the dormitories and privies in asylums, tasting institutional food, and the like, curtailed the intensity and stringency of their inspections.[94]

By contrast, as a provincial surgeon lacking any substantial metropolitan social contacts, with lengthy experience and strong views about asylum practice, and with no ties or sympathy for the profit-making madhouse sector, Gaskell was an outsider with neither inclination nor incentive to curtail his inquisitiveness. His were inspections with a vengeance. By the time of his death in 1886, he had been retired from his duties for more than two decades. Yet both his obituarists vividly remembered "his very thorough and minute examination of the institutions he inspected from floor to ceiling"[95]—and commented that "proprietors and superintendents who did not look too minutely into details for themselves, were greatly surprised, and not greatly pleased, to find the dignified Commissioner looking into beds and cupboards, and all manner of uninvestigated places."[96]

As one of six professional commissioners, Gaskell's impact on the inspectorate's routines and policies was initially somewhat muted, but with the appointment of a second county asylum superintendent, James Wilkes, to another vacancy in 1856, Gaskell's views and attitudes became increasingly powerful.[97] The job, as the Board itself conceded, was "often an onerous and disagreeable one":[98] the inspection of patients, licenses, casebooks, food, and physical facilities entailing a great deal of drudgery and routine. Not least, it required an immense amount of travel, often under difficult conditions.[99] In the first eighteen months of the Commission's existence, the average medical and legal commissioner travelled 10,776 miles by rail and carriage, and saw 17,749 patients in the course of inspecting 409 asylums and other places taking lunatics.[100] Workhouses, where Poor Law officials persisted in housing a substantial number of harmless lunatics, caused still further difficulties because they were "frequently remote from the great public lines of thoroughfare," difficult of access, and "added most materially to the extent and consequent expense of travelling."[101] Besides the visiting, a great deal of paperwork required regular attention at the London office, where, as early as 1847, "the amount of ordinary business . . . has far exceeded our anticipations,"[102] requiring at least one medical and one legal commissioner to meet there weekly and a monthly meeting of all the professional commissioners.[103] The subsequent growth of the asylum system, without any expansion of the size of the Commission, brought yet further burdens.[104] The number of patients alone virtually doubled between 1845 and 1860, from just over 19,000 when the Commission set about its task to almost 38,000 a decade and a half later, and over the same period, the Commissioners found themselves with almost twenty new county asylums to inspect.

Precisely because its numbers were small, however, the Board proved capable of acting promptly and developed a strong sense of collective identity. Externally, they tended to present a united front, and if Gaskell disagreed with some of his colleagues, those disagreements rarely surfaced in public.[105] Behind the scenes, as one might suspect, all was not completely harmonious. The Evangelical commissioners—Nairne, Campbell, and especially Lutwidge—tended to form one clique, while Gaskell's closest ties were with Procter,[106] and subsequently with Forster[107] and Wilkes.[108] Oddly, Shaftesbury, whose bigotry, Biblical literalism, and rigid fundamentalism[109] ought to have put him sharply at odds with the Unitarians on the Board, maintained friendly relations with Gaskell and was perhaps closest of all to Forster, the "severe and blunt" self-made son of a provincial butcher and cattle dealer.[110]

The routine features of the Commission's activities had become well established in the years before Gaskell joined them. The Commissioners travelled in pairs, a lawyer and a doctor descending together to verify that the increasingly burdensome paperwork was being kept up to date and to rummage around each asylum in search of problems.[111] Initially, they had resisted pressures from the Home Office to implement universal nationwide standards, but Sir James Graham insisted on a measure of uniformity, and within a year, the Board complied.[112] Soon, they themselves began to try to set policy from London and were increasingly inclined to attempt to impose their views about asylum organization and practice on magistrates and asylum superintendents.

Unsurprisingly, in the early years, their efforts often met with considerable resistance. Two years before Gaskell joined the Board, there was a particularly acrimonious exchange of views with the Governors of the Lincoln Asylum over organizational and therapeutic issues. The Commission's complaints that the asylum was too noisy, failed to provide total segregation of male and female patients, neglected classification, and employed a system of "management . . . entirely at variance with the practice of all experienced medical men" were sharply contested by the Governors, who rejected the interference in a manner the former found "exceedingly discourteous."[113]

To Procter's and Turner's complaints about "noise in one of the galleries" the Lincoln authorities responded tartly that the London visitors "seem to be little aware of the chilling, depressing, and fatal influences, which usually promote the stillness they admire; and which they should always look upon with suspicion."[114] So far from conceding the orthodox view on the need for a more systematic arrangement of the patients into classes, they objected that "the ideas of classification, and too many of the practices relative to the insane, have been induced from the economy of prisons. But a Lunatic Asylum is not a penal establishment, and the details should be worked out in a wholly different spirit."[115] They reacted to complaints that male and female patients might catch sight of one another (an obsession with the Evangelically-inclined Commissioners) with something akin to ridicule: the glazed doors to which their official visitors objected were at opposite ends of a fifty-foot corridor and contributed to both cheerfulness and ease of inspection, surely desirable goals.[116] And the Governors insisted that in placing ultimate authority over patient care in the hands of a triumvirate of visiting physicians, who each assumed the management of the asylum for a month at a time (rather than adopting the Commission's preferred model of granting supreme powers to a resident superintendent) they avoided the risks of therapeutic stasis.[117]

If the efforts to impose a central orthodoxy thus met with some temporary opposition and rebuffs, then they were renewed with greater force and determination once Gaskell joined the board. Recruited himself from the ranks of the new breed of asylum superintendents, Samuel had no doubts about the superiority of that mode of asylum administration, and he actively supported moves to impose a uniform management structure. His former colleagues in the expanding county asylum system cheerfully seconded at least this portion of his efforts, closely connected as it was to their own attempts to professionalize the role of the medical superintendent, and by 1854, the Commissioners had issued a circular to county magistrates recommending that there should be no more salaried visiting physicians.[118]

The county asylum superintendents soon came, however, to view Gaskell's activist stance with much more mixed emotions. If the Lunacy Commissioners' near-obsession with securing cleanliness, order, and quiet among asylum inmates was firmly established as the ruling orthodoxy well before he joined their ranks, Samuel brought to the cause the fervour of someone who owed his professional elevation to successful practice along these lines. His accession to the Commission, and his gradually increasing influence with his fellow board members, helped ensure the establishment of the Conollyite model of asylum practice as the ruling ideal in the public sector; and his suspicions about the influences of the profit motive in the private sector likewise challenged the long-standing opinions within the

Commission and prompted a more rigorous inspection and supervision of that sector as well.

Even his fellow Commissioners sometimes protested that Gaskell carried the ideal of diligent, indefatigable, and relentless inspection a little far. Bryan Procter, who often worked with him, periodically voiced muted protests to his colleague, John Forster. On one occasion, clearly somewhat exasperated, he noted that "I went to Brighton under the delusion of holiday making there—but my friend Samuel had me out visiting every day except two."[119] In a more jocular mood, he reported watching Gaskell "writing at another table, intent on some profound work—I see him knit his brows and look as if America were just discovered and I see 'The Baths and Wash-houses' are before him—or rather the Bath Question."[120] And though he praised his friend as "a conscientious and severe Inspector," he also conceded that he possessed the defects of his qualities: "His only fault is that he is too minute—and occasionally too exacting."[121]

If his fellow inspectors sometimes found Gaskell's punctiliousness somewhat wearing, then those he supervised had even more reason to object. With his enthusiastic concurrence, the Commission now increasingly adopted a procrustean approach in which it laid down in an ever more minute fashion the framework within which all alienists had to work. A measure of flexibility and a willingness to engage in tactical retreats when faced with opposition had been fairly common features of the Commission's work before 1850; thereafter, central control became steadily more marked, as the Commission ruthlessly deployed its annual reports as a weapon to shame and pressure the recalcitrant into compliance with their wishes. Where the more "progressive" superintendents had been inclined to complain in the 1840s that several Commissioners were unduly tolerant of the continued use of mechanical restraint,[122] during the 1850s, all alienists came under constant pressure to adopt the dogmas of nonrestraint, on pain of facing sharp disapproval from the central authorities. And once he had the reliable support of James Wilkes,[123] Gaskell aggressively sought to implement his views on night nursing and the proper means of reducing the incidence of "dirty patients," despite their unpopularity with many asylum superintendents.[124]

Towards the close of his years at Lancaster, Gaskell's reports had indicated an increasing conservativism, a growing sense that the basic principles of the new system of asylum management had, for all intents and purposes, been fully realized. As he saw it, there were, in consequence, "few points of novelty" worthy of note.[125] Instead, "the many advantages derivable from a strict adherence to the principles of practice adopted at the outset become more manifest from year to year. The steady occupation of the patients, cultivation of their faculties, avoidance of all coercive or harsh measures, continue to be followed by satisfactory results"—tranquil and tractable patients, if not the hoped-for cures.[126]

The sense that restraint and control were sufficient accomplishments to serve as the primary justification for asylumdom hardened into orthodoxy in the years after Gaskell became a Commissioner. His and Wilkes's fussiness, their officiousness, their minute concern with the mundane, found expression in the Board's emphasis on uniformity in the keeping of casebooks and asylum statistics and registers recording the imposition of mechanical restraint. Bureaucratic means, originally designed to prevent a recurrence of past episodes of maltreatment, became ends in themselves, and as overworked superintendents more and more left their nominal charges to the mercies of their attendants, and as a dull routine settled over the entire system, not even a humane custodialism could be reliably sustained.[127]

Part of the difficulty lay in the fact that the Conollyite model, because it largely eschewed an active role for medical treatment and depended heavily on regimen, left little basis on which the superintendents could resist the Commissioners' incursions into their territory. Gaskell, as we have seen, shared Conolly's sentiments in this regard, and accepted them: "It is not to be supposed that a great number of [asylum inmates] are requiring daily medical treatment; very far from that; they require general superintendence, and the arrangement of everything, so that whatever is done in the asylum, from morning to night, is of a curative tendency. . . . It is not medicine so much as a general regulation of the whole life of the patient."[128] Such views were also readily accepted by Shaftesbury, who displayed a lifelong scepticism about medical claims to special expertise in the treatment of insanity. Once established as orthodoxy, however, beliefs of this sort made it very difficult for county asylum superintendents to resist interference from the centre because the Commission could always claim that its comparative perspective provided a solid basis for the rules it laid down and because individual superintendents, as salaried public employees, could scarcely afford to court official censure. Gaskell and his fellow board members were confident that they were qualified to meddle in the smallest specifics of moral treatment;[129] and the more they did so, the less room for initiative or innovation remained with those they supervised, and the more asylums subsided into cocoons of dullness and despair.

So far as private asylums were concerned, the whole thrust of the lunacy reform movement had been to cast doubt on the profit motive when applied to the provision of care for the insane. The very nature of their business meant that proprietors of private asylums could never escape the stigma of being in "trade"; but deep public suspicion of their motives and integrity—suspicion shared at the very highest levels of the Victorian administration of asylumdom[130]—compounded the damaging effects of this situation on their status. In the first years after the establishment of a national inspectorate, however, its effects on the private sector were relatively limited. To be sure, as the Commission encouraged magistrates to build county asylums under the 1845 Act, the supply of pauper patients diminished, but demand from the upper and middle classes provided a sizeable number of more lucrative private patients and kept most madhouses in business. Meanwhile, as we have previously indicated, the medical commissioners, Prichard, Hume, and Turner, were disinclined to impose strict regulations on professional colleagues with whom they were in many instances closely linked by ties of friendship.

Gaskell and Wilkes, by contrast, were anxious to institute a far tighter measure of central control, and with the support of a number of their legal counterparts, they did not hesitate to use their ultimate weapon to secure compliance with their "suggestions"—the threat to refuse renewal of the proprietor's license.[131] From the mid 1850s onwards, by using this technique, Gaskell and his fellow Commissioners were able to impose steadily more stringent regulation of these establishments.[132] The continued use of mechanical restraint in a number of private asylums brought criticism and pressure for change. Excessive reliance on seclusion also began to attract their attention.[133] Even particular features of the treatment of individual patients on occasion provoked interference (and protests).[134] Less successfully, the Commission sought details about the income and expenditures of each establishment, in part in an effort to ensure a correspondence between the level of care provided in individual cases and the amounts paid by their families. Here, most proprietors dug in their heels and were aided by the persistent reluctance of the families who used their services to permit this degree of governmental intrusion into affairs they were anxious to keep private.[135]

Wrongful Confinement

It is ironic, given Gaskell's prominent role in extending this detailed regulation over the private sector, and his general reputation for diligence as an inspector, that he of all people should have found himself publicly traduced for incompetence in these respects. Allegations of the use of madhouses to confine the sane had surfaced repeatedly in the eighteenth century: in Defoe's pamphlets, in petitions to Parliament, and the polemics of former patients.[136] Recurrently, those who traded in lunacy faced the charge that their cupidity and desire for profit led them to acquiesce in such schemes, and fears of this sort seem, if anything, to have intensified in the nineteenth century, despite ever tighter regulation of the mad business and in the face of persistent legislative efforts to allay them. Paradoxically, indeed, these efforts seem to have fed rather than quieted public anxiety.

On the shoulders of the Lunacy Commission the burden of reassuring the public principally fell, and in many respects the task proved impossible. The boundary between sanity and madness was and remains labile and uncertain; and there were inescapable moral and social components in all such judgements.[137] As periodically became transparent, the very bases of doctors' judgements about questions of lunacy were often heavily value-laden, so that in their eyes insanity, eccentricity, and immorality at times became all but indistinguishable—a situation that naturally provoked considerable public concern. Increasingly, however, alienists insisted that the identification of madness was a judgement experts alone could render, and they sought to define lay intervention in these matters as presumptively illegitimate. And yet it was precisely the motives and competence of the "experts" that large segments of the public seem to have questioned.[138]

The Commissioners, and the asylum superintendents themselves, angrily rejected the charges of improper confinement, and in not a few instances impugned the motives and mental capacities of those who brought them. Periodically given new life by scandalous court cases,[139] by protests from groups like the Alleged Lunatics' Friend Society, and by the complaints of disgruntled former patients,[140] concerns about this issue were nonetheless never far below the surface. In consequence, the Lunacy Commission as a whole found itself on the defensive about this issue throughout the century. It was one of the major concerns animating the parliamentary inquiry into the care and treatment of lunatics which took place in 1859–1860, and it emerged in still more virulent form after Gaskell's retirement, prompting the formation of still another Select Committee in 1877.[141]

Charles Reade exploited and fomented these fears with great success in his best-selling melodrama, *Hard Cash*. We have seen that one of Reade's prime targets was a thinly disguised John Conolly, but his disciple Gaskell and the Lunacy Commissioners as a whole scarcely escaped unscathed. Sarcastically, Reade praised these "gentlemen, who pay an asylum four flying visits a year, know all that passes in it the odd 361 days, and are never outwitted and humbugged on the spot." In reality, he alleged, these "homuncules . . . who had consented to resign feelessness and brieflessness for a snug £1,500 a year at Whitehall"[142] were bumbling, pettifogging incompetents, more concerned with displaying what they saw as their own cleverness, avoiding conflicts, and maintaining cordial relations with asylum superintendents than with performing their nominal duties of protecting patients' rights. When Reade's hero, Alfred Hardie, appeals to the Commission to order his release from Wycherly/Conolly's asylum, it is "Dr. Eskell" (along with a legal Commissioner, Mr. Abbott) who is dispatched to investigate the case. And Eskell constantly makes a fool of himself when interrogating the patient, takes a week to reach the obvious conclusion that Alfred is sane (or, as he prefers to put it, "cured"), and then declines, on behalf of the Commission, to order his immediate discharge: "'The Board has the power,' said Dr. Eskell; 'but for many reasons they exercise it with prudence and reserve. Besides, it is only fair to those who have signed the order, to give them the graceful office of liberating the patient; it paves the way to reconciliation.'"[143]

Perhaps Gaskell's connections to the literary world, or possibly his general reputation as a meticulous if literally short-sighted inspector, induced Reade to make him the prime target of his animus against the Lunacy Commission. More vulnerable targets certainly existed: Thomas Turner, for instance, who served as medical Commissioner between 1846 and 1856, was firmly in the mould of a gentleman physician, strongly opposed any inquiry into medical treatments, and found any prying into the running of asylums personally distasteful; or Robert Nairne, who had been appointed to the Commission in 1857,[144] and was a notoriously lax inspector whose greatest concern was ensuring that a sufficient number of lunatics attended chapel.[145] In any event, regardless of the reasons Gaskell was singled out, in response to the novelist's verbal assaults the Commission publicly opted for a dignified silence, leaving it to various outraged alienists to protest the "unwarranted" slurs on asylumdom's reputation.

LUNACY REFORM IN SCOTLAND

In other quarters, for a time at least, Gaskell's diligence and commitment were obviously more highly regarded. Early in 1855, the American lunacy reformer, Dorothea Dix, following a visit to a series of Scottish asylums and madhouses, had launched a crusade for an official investigation of abuses north of the border. She immediately enlisted the aid of Shaftesbury and the English Commissioners, lobbied the Home Secretary, Sir George Grey, and secured the appointment of the desired Royal Commission of inquiry.[146] Not convinced that this would suffice to secure the results she wanted, Dix made every effort to stack the Commission with men she thought would share her goals; one of her choices was Samuel Gaskell.[147]

Gaskell initially resisted, pleading overwork and lack of time, but his protests were brushed aside. Later the same day, he wrote to accede to her importunings: "Since our interview this afternoon I have given the subject of the Commission to examine the Asylums of Scotland further consideration and it seems to me that [given] the demands on my time here and the opportunity of rendering assistance to those charged with the important task in Scotland [it might be best] if I were associated with them in such a way that I could give help when needed without interfering materially with my duties here." Accordingly, he proposed that he be appointed an unpaid member of the Commission (analogous to the honorary lay members of the English Lunacy Commission), and offered to make "the suggestion . . . to Lord Shaftesbury to-morrow."[148]

In the event, Gaskell was joined on the Commission by another of the English board, W. G. Campbell,[149] and by two Scots, Alexander Montieth and James Coxe.[150] In the ensuing months, the inquiry moved extremely slowly. Both Gaskell and Campbell were, of course, still labouring under the burdens of their English circuits, and Coxe found Monteith "not competent to understand [the Commission's] duties, so that I am forced into inaction [pending their return]. Since Mr. Gaskell and Mr. Campbell left us, we have not crossed the threshold of any *new* asylum or examined any witnesses."[151] Consequently, more than two years passed before the report was finally ready and legislation prepared.

The influence of Gaskell and Campbell on the proposed measures was all-pervasive.[152] In essence, the Royal Commission now proposed to extend the English model north of the border: establish a new Scottish Lunacy Commission; and require local authorities to provide asylum accommodation for pauper lunatics at public expense. Despite the unwieldy nature of their report (it exceeded eight hundred pages, was poorly arranged and filled with "repetition and confusion") it provided a litany of horror stories about the condition of the insane north of the border that echoed the findings of an earlier generation of reformers about the treatment of lunatics in England; reinforced English prejudices about "the inhumanity, the ignorance, the superstition, of poor, 'religious Scotland'"; and did much to secure votes at Westminister for their proposals.[153]

In Scotland itself, however, reaction to what was widely and rightly seen as the handiwork of Gaskell and Campbell was sharply negative. There was resentment that "English influence and ideas unduly predominate over the Scotch," and a widespread view that "there is an evident anxiety to make out a bad case—a strong tendency to paint in the darkest colours the gloomy side of the picture—an ungenerous disposition to depreciate all existing arrangements . . . inaccuracy, unfairness or partiality, and exaggeration."[154] Concerned to resist further control from London and bitterly opposed to proposals that smacked of elements of the despised English poor law, Scottish critics suggested that the interlopers might look a little more closely at the failures of their own system. After ten years, and "after the expenditure by the country of some £160,000 for administering the law," the English Commissioners' own reports provided "abundant evidence . . . of the existence of cases of neglect and abuse, nearly as glaring, if not more so, than those now revealed in the Report of the Scotch Lunacy Commission": the private trade in lunacy continued to treat patients as a commodity from which to extract profits; the English Commission had been unable to make any substantial progress in improving "the disgraceful state of the insane inmates" of workhouses, even in the metropolis, where their authority was strongest; and who could wish to see a proliferation north of the border of vast county asylums on the English model? "We must have no Colney Hatches in Scotland—huge, overgrown, unmanageable establishments, whose interior rivals the gloom and monotony of a prison."[155]

Much of this criticism was surely somewhat disingenuous. The episodes of mistreatment and malfeasance used as evidence of the failings of Gaskell and his colleagues were public knowledge only because of their inspections and were prominently featured in their annual reports as part of the Commission's strenuous (and at least partially successful) efforts to eliminate these kinds of abuse. Regardless of the Commission's views about private asylums, the Victorian governing classes were determined to retain them (both to avoid the stigma and social contamination that would arise from being confined with paupers;[156] and out of concern to maintain the privacy of well-to-do families, who sought to hide a relation who might bring "the taint of insanity upon them").[157] And the English board fought a prolonged campaign against the use of workhouses as substitutes for the asylum[158]— continually hamstrung by its inability to compel parsimonious Poor Law authorities to accede to their wishes; and by the remorseless rise in the numbers of lunatics, always beyond the capacity of even the most ambitious programme of asylum building.[159] (Gaskell, indeed, serving as their spokesman on this issue before the 1859–1860 Select Committee, voiced the Commission's opposition in principle to the idea of keeping lunatics in workhouse wards and unsuccessfully urged legislation to eliminate the financial incentives for parishes to indulge in the practice.)[160]

But the sense that the Lunacy Commission had had some less than salutary effects on the lives of the insane (and those who supervised them) was not entirely misplaced either. A more reflective and self-critical man than Gaskell might have seen in the criticisms roused by his proposals for reform in Scotland some of the very genuine problems inherent in the approach he and his colleagues had adopted. For if moral treatment had initially been Janus-faced, simultaneously embodying elements of both repression and rehabilitation, the imposition of moral discipline and the development of self-government and self-control, English asylumdom under the increasingly inflexible administration of the Commissioners more and more favoured only one side of this equation. In the huge museums of the mad that were the inevitable outcome of the policies the Board pursued, these structural tensions were systematically resolved, as the years went by, in the direction of an oppressive system of moral management, enforced conformity, and disciplined subordination. Initiative and innovation on the part of asylum doctors were stifled, as Gaskell and his colleagues ruthlessly, albeit perhaps unintentionally, fostered a dull, protective environment, where merely keeping the patients alive became an end in itself.

THE VALETUDINARIAN

Some sixteen years after he joined the Lunacy Commission, in 1865, Gas-kell's career came to an abrupt end. Crossing the street, he was run down by a cab.[161] He at first appeared likely to recover completely. On February 2, he called on his retired colleague, Bryan Procter, who reported that "he looks well—but [is] indisposed (by this I mean indisposed for work)."[162] However, it was not until early September that Forster was able to tell Procter that he had returned to the London office,[163] as it turned out for only a few days.

The aftermath of the accident seems to have left him somewhat unbal-anced and unwilling to resume his former life. His letters to his friends grew odd and almost incomprehensible.[164] In the new year, he was no better, (complaining of "so much discomfort in the head that it was not only im-possible for him to pursue his work, but painful to enter into social life"),[165] and it must have come as no surprise to his colleagues that within a few months, he elected to resign his post.

In the years that followed, he began travelling from hotel to hotel, at home and abroad, never seeming to improve and never able to enter upon any substantial activity, trying "to kill time as well as he can."[166] After three decades of almost monastic dedication to his duties, he seems to have slipped slowly into the role of the valetudinarian. At irregular intervals, his former colleagues received reports of his whereabouts. In November 1866, he set off to spend the winter in Cannes and then in Algiers, where, as he reported to the envious Procter (whose inadequate pension allowed no such luxuries),[167] he lolled about under "the palm trees . . . [sitting] without a fire and with the windows open—gorgeous visions. He sees also a vision of a gorgeous female, at some neighbour hotel, where she dispenses smiles and glasses of brandy to the destruction of her thousands of admirers."[168] A long silence, which brought anxious speculation that "he must be ill and alone"[169] only drew to a close when he wrote a brief note to Forster from Rouen in mid-1868.[170] By now he had become a virtual recluse, calling very occasionally on his friends,[171] and otherwise "hoarding his wits" in a series of country hotels, a pattern that persisted unchanged until his death in late March 1886:[172] all in all, a sad and depressing end to a life filled in its earlier years with ambition, hard work, and accomplishment.

Chapter Seven

FROM DISCIPLE TO CRITIC:

SIR JOHN CHARLES BUCKNILL (1817–1897)

> The Physician is now the responsible guardian of the lunatic, and
> must ever remain so, unless by some calamitous reverse the
> progress of the world in civilization should be arrested and
> turned back in the direction of practical barbarism.
> (*John Charles Bucknill, 1853*)

> I affirm that the condition of patients, even in the worst managed
> private asylums, is in every way superior for their present
> comfort and well-being, and for their prospect of recovery,
> to the insane who are scattered over the country
> as single patients.
> (*John Charles Bucknill, "Lunacy Law Reform," 1858*)

> . . . It is in the development of this system of domestic treatment
> that the greatest promise lies of the largest possible amelioration
> of the unhappy lot of those afflicted with mental disease.
> (*John Charles Bucknill*, The Care of the Insane and
> Their Legal Control, *1880*)

FEW BRITISH ALIENISTS of the nineteenth century could match the contributions Sir John Charles Bucknill made to the development and consolidation of the new profession of psychiatry in the course of his lifetime. During the first half of Victoria's reign, he became one of the most energetic and effective spokesmen for alienists' collective interests, did much to codify and present to a wider public the knowledge they claimed to possess, and helped to transform a previously almost moribund professional organization into a vehicle for the creation of a collective identity by unifying what might otherwise have remained an internally divided congeries of practitioners isolated inside the walls of the very institutions over which they presided. He was rewarded for these accomplishments with a lucrative position in the state administration of lunacy, only to turn, unexpectedly, into something of a professional maverick: he criticized many of the orthodoxies to which the majority of his professional brethren continued to cling and publicly attacked the very economic foundations of the system from which a large subset of the most prominent alienists earned their livelihood. Meanwhile, on a broader international stage, his growing taste for controversy manifested itself in a stinging series of criticisms of the practices of American alienists, the outcome of a tour of North American asylums he undertook in the mid 1870s. Simultaneously, now moving for the first time into the private sector, he helped to reestablish on a new and more secure footing a noninstitutionally based practice devoted to the problems of lunacy and nervous disorders.

THE CONVOLUTIONS OF A CAREER

The most salient features of Bucknill's career may be readily summarised. For the first eighteen years of his practice in psychiatry, from 1844 to 1862, he was medical superintendent of one of the newly built county asylums at Exminster in Devon. From 1853 he became the first editor of the new profession's journal, the *Asylum Journal of Mental Science* (subsequently the *Journal of Mental Science*), published by the Association of Medical Officers of Asylums and Hospitals for the Insane (AMOAHI). Together with Daniel Hack Tuke (1827–1895) in 1858 he published *A Manual of Psychological Medicine*, which became established as the first textbook on insanity, having authored key sections on diagnosis, pathology, and treatment. In 1860–1861 Bucknill led the profession nationally, as president of the AMOAHI. Subsequently, from 1862 to 1875, he held public office as one of the Lord Chancellor's Visitors in Lunacy, charged with inspecting the care and treatment of Chancery cases both in and out of asylums. Finally, in the late 1870s, he worked from consulting rooms in Wimpole Street as a lunacy specialist, helping to establish a style of private practice based on office consultancy rather than institutional care. During the same period, from 1878, he was also one of the founding editors of the new journal *Brain*, which fostered a neuropsychiatric approach to understanding the physical pathology of insanity and from 1886 became the journal of the newly formed Neurological Society.

As tempting as it is to see Bucknill's career as representative of, and in some cases as leading, broader professional trends, to concentrate only on this conventional list of accomplishments risks neglecting important paradoxes that mark his progress and complicate any attempt to place his activities in a broader social and professional context. Bucknill may have been one of the pioneering county asylum superintendents and in these years a staunch defender of the crucial role of in-patient treatment: but even at this stage of his career, he was also interested in the boarding-out of patients in less institutional environments. He personally experimented with this sort of arrangement, and in 1861 he went further and publicly recommended that the AMOAHI should investigate the potential benefits of the cottage system, as exemplified by the Belgian lunatic colony at Gheel.[1] Nor was this just a passing fancy. In the later stages of his career, he moved away from the overweening confidence the early Victorian alienists placed in institutional responses to mental disorder, and towards both a more chastened view of their possibilities and limitations and a more sanguine perspective on the state of lunatics left at large. At midcentury, one of the most vocal proponents of institutional care, by the late 1860s Bucknill had begun to entertain serious doubts about its usefulness for at least some of those brought within its ambit.

As we shall see, this apostasy coincided with Bucknill's move outside the walls of an asylum and his efforts to secure recognition from the general medical profession and society at large, instead of his fellow alienists. Equally significant, his experience as a visitor of Chancery lunatics, who were frequently cared for as single patients, meant that he had an unusually broad acquaintance with noninstitutional care, and he himself was to attribute his change of heart to this direct, practical experience. Yet the weight of authority that this might have been expected to add to his otherwise heretical opinions does not appear to have been persuasive. Neither his previous services in behalf of institutional psychiatry nor his claim to rest his new opinions on the solid ground of empirical observation could in any way induce his erstwhile colleagues to embrace such heterodoxy. With both central and local government still committed to mass segregation as the "solution" to the problems posed by the mad, most alienists remained content with their dominion over the expanding empire of asylumdom.

Still, just as the development of institutions for the insane provided an infrastructure within which a specialized profession could develop, we shall suggest that Bucknill's emphasis on the benefits of noninstitutional care from the late 1870s helped to reassert some portion of psychiatry's links with general medicine at a time when in the eyes of both the public and the profession at large its status was distinctly questionable. Likewise, his emphasis on physical pathology and the direct application of scientific medicine in understanding insanity grew out of a wider professional consensus but served a similar purpose. Bucknill's opinions and activities may not always have reflected the mainstream within psychiatry, but an understanding of the way in which paradoxes and tensions were moulded and played themselves out through his individual career unquestionably serves to illuminate certain crucial dimensions of the history of his profession.

BECOMING AN ALIENIST

John Charles Bucknill was born on Christmas Day 1817 at Market Bosworth in Leicestershire, the eldest son of a surgeon who was also called John. His father had been educated at Rugby, and John Charles began his formal education there in 1828, the year that Thomas Arnold became headmaster.

However, he subsequently transferred to complete his schooling as a day pupil at Market Bosworth Grammar School, and it seems likely that he was among those local boys who were excluded from Rugby by the increase in fees that was instituted in the early 1830s.[2] After leaving school, Bucknill worked as an assistant to his father, before beginning his formal medical education in Dublin in 1837.

After only one year in Dublin, Bucknill transferred to University College London. His reasons for doing this are not known, although he joined the College a year after it had been granted powers to award medical degrees, at a time when there was an overall increase in student numbers that some commentators attributed to the popularity of the teaching of the phrenologist and mesmerist John Elliotson, the College's professor of medicine. It is certainly possible that Bucknill could have read correspondence in the *Lancet* in 1838 in which the controversial Elliotson boasted about the liveliness of his teaching and the fact that students in his classes did not fall asleep.[3] However, if the reputation of Elliotson drew him to London, this is not something that Bucknill commented on at a later stage in his career. He would have heard Elliotson lecture on the principles and practice of medicine in the autumn of 1838, when a temporary truce with the College authorities enabled Elliotson to continue lecturing provided that he did not use this as an opportunity to publicise his experiments with mesmerism, but by December Elliotson had been forced to resign.[4] Bucknill stayed at University College to complete his medical education, winning gold medals in anatomy and materia medica, silver medals in surgery and the principles and practice of medicine, and coming top of the list for medical jurisprudence. He then worked as a surgeon's dresser for Robert Liston at University College Hospital. However, in 1841, Bucknill failed to obtain the appointment he applied for as apothecary at the same hospital.[5]

Like Conolly, Bucknill experienced some difficulty in establishing himself on the metropolitan scene early in his career. After failing to obtain the apothecary's appointment at University College Hospital, he next tried to establish a private practice in Chelsea. This attempt seems to have met with at best limited success, however, and following his marriage in 1842, Bucknill felt forced to leave London for the provinces. As with the gregarious Conolly (though for opposite reasons) his problems attracting patients may have been rooted in his personal manner: even a most sympathetic observer had to confess that he was "a man of most reserved habits"; and his own children were to find him "uncommunicative . . . and a difficult man to understand."[6]

His marriage was to the daughter of a local Midlands family, Maryanne Townsend, the only child of Thomas Townsend of Hillmorton Hall near Rugby. Ordinarily, one might expect this sort of alliance with a relatively well-to-do family from the region where he had grown up to be followed by an attempt to establish a practice in the vicinity. Instead (partly, it would

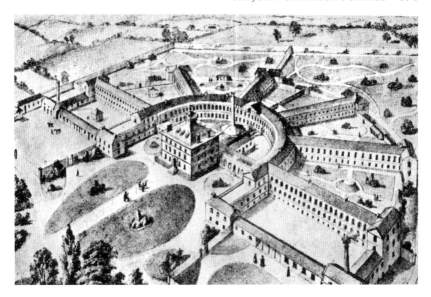

Figure 7.1. Devon County Lunatic Asylum, Exeter: a Victorian museum of madness.

appear, for unspecified health reasons), Bucknill moved to the West Country. Two years later, in 1844, at the age of twenty-six, his fledgling career as a provincial general practitioner took a radically different turn, when he applied for and secured the post as medical superintendent of the newly established Devon County Asylum.

Although not among the first to take advantage of the permissive legislation of 1808 to build a rate-supported asylum, the Devonshire magistrates nonetheless elected to commit to building an institution of this sort more than a year before Shaftesbury's national legislation made such provision compulsory. This initiative suggests that they had been personally converted to the merits of the asylum solution. Possibly reflecting the optimism they would have imbibed from the professional propaganda of the period, they provided their new superintendent with the relatively handsome salary of £500 p.a., as well as laundry and accommodation, which made it better paid than many other county asylum superintendencies. The position provided Bucknill with some measure of professional and financial security, and he remained in post for eighteen years, during which time he and Maryanne had three sons.[7]

For nearly a decade after Bucknill's appointment management of the asylum absorbed his attention fully. Unlike many other medical men who now found work in the new asylum sector, Bucknill was appointed at a sufficiently early stage in the development of the plans to advise on some aspects of internal design. Building work on the Devon County Asylum at Exminster was completed in 1845, and the new asylum opened in July.[8]

The buildings were designed to accommodate 420 patients, and after opening the asylum's population increased steadily, rising from 163 by January
1846, to 351 by January 1849, and overtaking the intended figure in 1852
to reach a total population of 460 by January 1853. Initially a very small
number of private patients were accommodated (always less than 10), but
this policy was soon abandoned as the asylum became more overcrowded,
and, like its counterparts elsewhere, Bucknill's asylum now concentrated
exclusively on the growing ranks of the pauper insane.

Bucknill brought to his asylum duties a conviction of the value of medicine's standard therapeutics in the treatment of insanity, reflective of his
orthodox belief "that the proximate cause of all mental disease is to be referred solely to the abnormal state of the brain."[9] Almost at once, however,
he found his medical skills and training in demand for the treatment of a
more conventional kind of illness. Inadequate sanitation often plagued
nineteenth-century asylums, and less than a year after the Devon County
Asylum opened its doors, its superintendent found himself coping with an
epidemic of cholera. Before it vanished, whether despite or because of Bucknill's efforts, it had affected some of the staff and at least forty patients, a
dozen of whom failed to survive its ravages.[10]

More generally, the frail physical status of many of his charges kept Bucknill occupied with a variety of conventional medical tasks. Like its counterparts elsewhere, the Devon Asylum found itself almost overwhelmed by patients suffering from a whole array of physical disorders. With the character
of his admissions largely a function of those whom the Poor Law authorities
chose to refer to the asylum, Bucknill was soon complaining about the near-
moribund state of many of the chronic cases who arrived on his doorstep:
"Patients have been admitted suffering from heart disease, aneurism, and
cancer, with scarcely a greater amount of melancholy than might be expected to take place in many sane persons at the near and certain prospect
of death. Some have been received in the last stages of consumption, with
that amount only of cerebral excitement so common in this disorder; others
have been received in the delirium or stupor of typhus; while in several
cases the mental condition was totally unknown after admission, and must
have been unknown before, since an advanced condition of bodily disease
prevented speech, and the expression of intelligence or emotion, either normal or morbid."[11]

THE PRACTICE OF NONRESTRAINT

When it came to managing the heterogeneous collection of patients who
found their way to his asylum, Bucknill was an early convert to the virtues
of nonrestraint—a position that was rapidly becoming the orthodoxy and
the distinguishing mark of "progressive" asylum practice, at least in the pub-

lic sector. At first, his allegiance was slightly qualified. In written comments he forwarded to the Commissioners in Lunacy in 1853, Bucknill stressed that in his view, the use of mechanical restraint was only justified in a small minority of cases, suggesting that: "Mechanical restraint in the treatment of the insane is like the actual cautery in the treatment of wounds, a barbarous remedy, which has become obsolete from the introduction of more skilful and humane methods, but which may still be called for in exceptional and desperate cases." To illustrate this point Bucknill cited the case of a violently suicidal male patient at Exminster "who endeavoured to commit suicide by lacerating the veins of the fore-arm with his teeth, and who bit out of his arm large pieces of flesh in the attempt."[12] Such minor exceptions were soon set aside, however, and save for surgical cases, Bucknill was to campaign for the most unqualified Conollyite position on nonrestraint throughout the rest of his career, criticising backsliders among the ranks of English county asylum superintendents, and, late in his career, launching a very public and controversial series of criticisms of American asylum superintendents for "their most unfortunate and unhappy resistance to the abolition of mechanical restraint."[13]

The difficulties associated with managing the violent and the recalcitrant without resort to straitjackets and the like were, of course, a source of considerable concern.[14] At the Devon Asylum, like its counterparts elsewhere, mechanical restraint was in part replaced by the extensive use of seclusion and other means of deterring disruptive behaviour. Bucknill emphasised that solitary confinement should be seen as part of medical treatment and managed directly by the medical superintendent because it might otherwise be resorted to too readily or for punitive reasons by attendants.[15] As was common at other county asylums, including Hanwell itself, showers and other baths were used as another means of managing patients' behaviour, as well as for allegedly therapeutic purposes.[16] Bucknill's annual report in 1848 included a table that showed thirty-five patients had been given baths or showers as "penal remedies" for violent or destructive behaviour, including breaking windows, tearing clothes, fighting, and hitting people, including the medical superintendent.

These substitutes for more overt techniques of coercion were themselves to become a source of official concern. By 1856 the Commissioners in Lunacy were becoming increasingly alarmed about the disciplinary use of baths and showers, following the death of a patient at Surrey County Asylum after a prolonged shower-bath. Bucknill, however, like most of his colleagues who faced the practical difficulties of managing overcrowded public asylums, remained unmoved by their expressions of concern and insisted upon shower-baths' value as part of the asylum doctor's repertoire of treatment, while taking care to stress their therapeutic as well as managerial advantages. In response to the enquiries which the Commission made to all institutions about the use of shower and other baths, he confirmed that these were still used at Exminster and acknowledged one instance in the previous year of a shower-bath being applied for as much as two hours at a time.[17]

None of this seems to have diminished his high standing in the eyes of the inspectorate. For all their expressions of concern about some of the substitutes for restraint asylum superintendents were tempted to adopt, the Commission itself had by now embraced nonrestraint as among the proudest achievements of the reformed asylum system over which they presided; and as they embraced the nonrestraint cause and made it their own, Bucknill's enthusiastic implementation of Conolly's ideas drew approving comments whenever they visited his establishment. His expertise in asylum management likewise attracted increasing praise, notwithstanding the fact that the number of patients confined in the asylum had continued to rise, with only limited additional accommodation provided, till it reached a total of 602 patients by January 1860.[18]

As Nancy Tomes has argued, precisely because nonrestraint could be portrayed as an advance attributable to *medical* intervention, it represented "an opportunity to seize the moral initiative from the lay reformers. By subduing the violent insane without recourse to physical restraint, physicians might give dramatic proof of their superior powers of governing the insane."[19] The labours of Hill and Conolly now allowed the fledgling profession to claim a decisive contribution of its own to the advance of humanity and science; and Bucknill was quick to mark this essential "point of difference between the old and the new systems [of managing the mad] . . . under the old system the insane were controlled by appeals to the lowest and basest motives of human action, and under the new system they are controlled by the highest motive which in each individual case it is possible to evoke."[20]

EXPANDING HORIZONS

As Bucknill acquired confidence in his role as an asylum superintendent, he gradually sought to establish a wider and more substantial professional reputation, as a member of the Association of Medical Officers of Asylums and Hospitals for the Insane, and more important as a spokesperson for the emerging new profession in his role as editor and cofounder of the *Asylum Journal of Mental Science*. The founding of the Association in 1841 had constituted one of the first efforts to create a distinct collective identity for the medical men specialising in the treatment of insanity. Within a few years, however, the enterprise verged upon "complete inanition."[21] The difficulties were multiple. Even securing attendance at the single annual meeting of the Association proved problematic: "The exigant duties of the members, and the system which prevails in this country of vesting in the medical superin-

tendent the entire management of an asylum and the treatment of the patients, have rendered it impossible that any large proportion of these officers
should ever leave home at the same time."[22] Perhaps of still greater significance were the internal rifts and schisms among the membership itself,
most notably the subterranean tensions and antagonisms that created a "distinct line of demarcation between the medical officers of public asylums and
the proprietors of private asylums."[23] The resultant factionalism badly ham-
pered attempts to create a unified profession, and for many years diminished the Association's effectiveness. Indeed, by midcentury, "the meetings
of the Association fell into disuse,"[24] and with no other institutionalized
means of fostering sustained contact and communication among a membership isolated within the walls of the very institutions that constituted its
raison d'être, the organization tottered on the brink of collapse. Unable even
to "claim an existence of decrepitude, it [persisted] in a state of complete
and absolute palsy," holding together only "from very want of the powers of
decomposition."[25]

Earlier in the century, the absence of an organized voice for physicians
treating the mad had perhaps been of less moment than it now threatened
to become. Outside regulation of the treatment of the insane, almost nonex-
istent at the beginning of the century, had remained relatively ineffectual
into the 1840s, particularly outside the metropolitan area. Furthermore,
even without a formal organization to defend their position, those running
private madhouses catering to the upper classes could call upon the social
connections of the families who were their clientele (and who shared their
interest in drawing a discreet veil over their activities) to provide a measure
of protection for their businesses. Nor, in the early part of the nineteenth
century, had the treatment of lunacy been as closely bound up with the
asylum as it was now becoming: during the 1820s and 1830s, leading society physicians had often been involved with the treatment of episodes of
insanity among the aristocrats and plutocrats who routinely purchased their
services, and the prominence of these medical men in the College of Physicians provided yet another avenue for the exercise of influence over the political process.

These older means of collective representation and defence were increasingly becoming obsolete, however. In the moral treatment era, the asylum
was now portrayed as indispensable to effective intervention in the course
of mental disorder, and the new therapeutics was one of a number of factors contributing to the emergence of a more specialised kind of practice,
with a concomitant decline in the involvement of general physicians in the
treatment of the insane. The rapid expansion of the county asylum sector,
particularly in the wake of the 1845 legislation making provision of pauper
asylums compulsory, increased the visibility of full-time specialists in the
treatment of the mad, even as the obvious divergence of interests between

those employed in the emerging public sector and the proprietors of private madhouses further complicated any attempt to represent the specialism's interests in the political arena. Ironically, too, once the Lunacy Commission began to replace the gentlemanly physicians who had first filled the post of Medical Commissioner with former superintendents from the county asylums—a process that began with Gaskell's appointment in 1849—it assumed an increasingly activist and professionalized stance: a development many asylum doctors must have found ominous, as it soon led to efforts to limit their autonomy, to encroach upon their discretion, and even to threaten the very livelihoods of those operating private asylums.[26]

Under the circumstances, that some of the more perspicacious alienists should seek to breathe new life into the Association is anything but a surprise. Taking cognizance of the planned annual meeting of the Provincial Medical and Surgical Association in Oxford—an event likely to bring a fairly substantial number of alienists together—William Ley, the superintendent of the Oxfordshire County Asylum, suggested this could provide the occasion for a possible renewal of collective activity. Crucially, in correspondence during the spring and summer of 1852, several of his fellow superintendents agreed "on the absolute necessity of establishing an Asylum Journal, not only as being in itself a most desirable object, but as affording the only chance of rescuing the association [itself]."[27]

The idea that a professional organ of this sort could play a vital role in advancing professional interests was scarcely confined to the ranks of alienists. Indeed, the explosion of new journals was one of the more remarkable features of the medical scene in the first half of the nineteenth century.[28] Charles Hastings, the founder of the Provincial Medical and Surgical Association (PMSA), the very group whose gathering now formed the occasion for reviving the fortunes of the alienists' own more specialised organization, had from the outset recognized the indispensable role medical journalism could play in his campaign to elevate the status of general practice and had founded what became the *British Medical Journal* as a practical expression of this perception. Coincidentally—or perhaps it was more than a coincidence?—at the PMSA meeting that immediately preceded the alienists' more specialised discussions, a debate had erupted on the future of the *British Medical Journal* itself, and those arguing for its expansion, and the transfer of its editorial offices to London articulated a rationale that was, in precisely parallel fashion, to underpin the new periodical Bucknill and his colleagues were shortly to launch. In the words of Charles Cowan, one of the prime movers in securing the changes in the *British Medical Journal*, "It may with perfect truth be asserted, that on the success of our journal depends the retrogression, stagnancy, or the prosperity of our Association."[29]

The asylum superintendents had, in fact, first contemplated a journal of their own in the early 1840s, but at that time had been unable to find anyone willing to assume the role of editor.[30] That obstacle no longer existed.

In advance of the Oxford meeting, Bucknill printed up and circularized to the other members of the asylum officers' association a prospectus for such a journal, and when the alienists assembled, Ley nominated him as its first editor; the nomination was seconded by John Thurnam, superintendent of the neighbouring county asylum in Wiltshire.[31] With the emphatic endorsement of the sainted Conolly, the fifteen alienists present gave their support, as the *Asylum Journal* was to report rather delicately a year later, *nemine contradicente*.[32]

The matter was indeed delicate—more so than the pages of the new journal let on—for there already existed a specialized periodical devoted to publishing on insanity, albeit one with no connection to AMOAHI and, if not actively hostile to the county asylum doctors, at least very closely identified with the outlook and interests of the proprietors of private asylums. The *Journal of Psychological Medicine and Mental Pathology* was founded as a private speculation by Forbes Winslow, the proprietor of a metropolitan private asylum, as early as 1848. Winslow could scarcely be expected to welcome the advent of a competing publication, particularly a journal officially affiliated with the association, and if his own angry account is to be believed, because Bucknill had anticipated his hostility, he had sent his circular suggesting the *Asylum Journal* and implicitly announced his own candidacy to edit it to every member of the association *except* Winslow. Such rather sharp practice caused deep offence. Winslow protested:

> as an act of courtesy, if for no other consideration, we should have been apprized of the objects [Bucknill and his allies] had in contemplation. . . . We must confess [he continued, that] we do not feel ourselves complimented at the suggestion to establish a periodical of the kind. Our pages have always been open to the communications of members of the Association, and we have done our utmost to promote its well-being, to advance medico psychological literature, and to support the interest of those connected with the public asylums of this country. Having embarked a capital of some thousand pounds in establishing this journal, and having, since 1848, stood nearly alone in fighting the battle for the British psychologist, it cannot be otherwise than mortifying that those who never lifted their little finger to assist us, should, in 1853, attempt to injure the property of this journal by starting a rival publication.[33]

Editor and Spokesman

Heedless of Winslow's protests, the first number of the AMOAHI's new journal appeared on schedule in November 1853, justifying itself as a way "to afford a medium of intercommunication between men engaged in the construction and management of asylums, in the treatment of the insane, and in all subsidiary operations." Sensitive, however, to the need to avoid giving any further offense to Winslow, Bucknill from the outset adopted a conciliatory tone. "Even our choice of the form and mode of publication" was prompted by "the desire to avoid the appearance . . . of establishing a periodical in rivalry or opposition to his own."[34] The *Asylum Journal* appeared every six weeks, on rather flimsy paper in a format somewhere between a journal and a newspaper. Editorially, too, despite an obvious weighting towards the interests and concerns of the county asylum superintendents, Bucknill took pains to acknowledge the interests and concerns of the private sector and to voice sentiments supportive of their interests.

Where the pages of Winslow's journal were open to "the discussion of those higher branches of metaphysical science," Bucknill announced his determination to hew to a much narrower path, only such matters "as have immediate reference to the pathology and therapeutics of insanity, to the construction and management of asylums, and to the diseases, accidents, and difficulties likely to arise therein."[35] Utility and practicality were thus his self-proclaimed watchwords. Within less than eighteen months, his diplomacy had succeeded, and Winslow, abandoning his former hostility to the novel enterprise, had granted it his editorial benediction.

Bucknill's accession to the role of editor of the new journal was to prove of signal importance to his own career and to the fate of the profession at large. His talents and energies were immediately poured into making the new enterprise a success—a rallying point for the newly consolidating profession. To a far greater extent than those who served as the nominal heads of AMOAHI, who were elected to serve a single year as its president, Bucknill was positioned to articulate the profession's interests and to constitute himself as its spokesman. Throughout the 1850s and into the following decade, he was, as Henry Monro put it, "the mainspring of the Association"[36]—a position of dominance that only increased from 1858 onwards, when he and Daniel Hack Tuke together published what rapidly became the standard textbook on insanity.[37]

As its title suggested, the *Asylum Journal* focused on institutional management as well as medical concerns. From the outset Bucknill encouraged asylum superintendents to share the benefits of their everyday practical experience, reminding readers that no less a figure than John Conolly believed "that the case books of asylums contained an unworked mine of golden wealth, which it was their duty to make productive for the public good."[38] Despite the fact that a large fraction of the Association's membership was drawn from the private sector, the interests and concerns of Bucknill's fellow county asylum superintendents were clearly uppermost in his mind. The papers he published, the news of the profession he provided, and the editorials he elected to write were indicative of this preference, as was the roster of writers he attracted to his pages. A dozen public county asylum superintendents contributed to the first volume of the journal,[39] far outnumbering the handful of private asylum proprietors who followed suit.[40] Substantively, Bucknill's staunch and persistent advocacy of nonrestraint and his decision to chastise publicly any backsliders among the county asylum ranks (while remaining largely silent about the profit-making sector, where nonrestraint had been greeted with far less enthusiasm), give a further indication of where his fundamental loyalties lay—the more so when one contrasts his heated advocacy of Conolly's system[41] with the openly sceptical view of the abolitionists offered by Forbes Winslow in the pages of the *Journal of Psychological Medicine*.[42]

Though he boasted in his anniversary issue of having attracted "on an average in each number two original papers, contributed by gentlemen who are or have been the medical superintendents of public asylums,"[43] during the first five or six years of Bucknill's tenure as editor, his colleagues consistently failed to supply him with sufficient matter to fill the journal's pages. Undeterred by this state of affairs, two years after the first issue appeared he opted to move to publishing the journal quarterly, rather than every six weeks. Simultaneously, he expanded the title to the *Asylum Journal of Mental Science* and adopted a more conventional format. Within another two years, the perhaps excessively practical orientation suggested by the word "asylum" was abandoned altogether, and the *Journal of Mental Science* became the preferred title, one that was to be remain in use for more than a century.[44]

Under whatever guise it appeared, however, during these early years Bucknill shouldered the main burden of producing a lively, readable, and useful periodical. Conservatively, he was personally responsible for between 40 and 45 percent of the text that appeared in the first three volumes, covering the years 1853–1857. While his contribution to the whole fell to only 74 out of a total of 532 pages in 1860, it rose again during the last two years of his editorship (he was responsible for 226 pages of volume 7), and throughout his nine years at the helm, the journal bore the unmistakeable stamp of his personality, preferences, and prejudices. It was an accomplishment the more remarkable given that he continued to have charge of a large county asylum and had to stay in touch with events and intellectual developments across Britain, Europe, and North America from an isolated location in the southwest of the country.

Bucknill's contributions in this period covered a broad range of practical issues from asylum architecture, bedsores, and reclining chairs, to use of seclusion as a therapeutical agent and treatment of the insane without mechanical restraint. He wrote extensively on lunacy policy not just in England, but also in Scotland and Ireland, and sought to keep a steady eye on developments in North America. Reflecting his own growing interest in legal issues surrounding insanity (and their importance to the profession at large), he devoted considerable space to medical jurisprudence and included regular summaries of leading legal cases: criminal trials where the insanity defence had been raised, prosecutions of asylum staff for allegedly mistreating patients, as well as some highly publicised "inquisitions" into the mental state of well-to-do individuals subject to the vagaries of the Chancery courts. Alongside all this, and in addition to book reviews and commentary on a host of minor topics, he paid particular attention to the activities and reports of the Lunacy Commissioners—even if the task of writing the major review of their annual reports was on occasion given over to Conolly or J. T. Arlidge. Finally, perhaps in an effort to lighten the tone, and possibly to reach the more leisured and gentlemanly audience who might otherwise have preferred to read Forbes Winslow's literary and philosophical journal, he led the way in writing a series of more speculative pieces about madness in literature, most prominently essays on Shakespeare's treatment of madness in *Hamlet*, *Macbeth*, and *Lear*.[45]

By 1860, in his inaugural address as president of the association, Bucknill could, without undue boasting, proclaim that the journal had "been successful beyond all our expectations as the means of vivifying and extending and uniting this Association of medical men."[46] Unafraid to combat what he termed "mischievous and erroneous opinions,"[47] whether proffered by fellow alienists, the Lunacy Commissioners, or laymen, Bucknill consistently sought to use his editorial voice to advance the interests of the profession as he perceived them. His outspokenness must on occasion have rankled, but whatever resentments he provoked stayed mostly hidden, at least at this stage in his career.

Some of Bucknill's interventions were primarily of interest to his fellow county asylum superintendents. These surely included his reiterated insistence that those with long service in these posts deserved pensions as of right, not as something for which they should have to beg from local magistrates (who were naturally sensitive to ratepayer protests against waste);[48] and his campaigns against the retention of pauper lunatics in workhouses, where they were subject to "the irremediable parsimony of Boards of Guardians."[49] At the same time, he was astute enough to realize that the perpetuation of divisions amongst alienists could only hamper their efforts to defend their interests in the political arena and to seek common ground with the proprietors of private licensed houses.

Perhaps a desire to demonstrate this ecumenical outlook motivated his decision to second Forbes Winslow's nomination as president of the Association for 1857. If so, the political value of the gesture was somewhat wasted when he was absent from the annual meeting at the relevant moment.[50] Less ambiguously, however, when the motives and competence of the alienists in the private sector came under fierce renewed attack in the late 1850s, Bucknill rushed immediately to their defence: "A greater act of injustice has never been perpetrated by the press, than the attack which has been made upon private lunatic asylums." That the distinguished men who practiced in this sector were once more being referred to by the "flattering title" of mad-doctors was yet one more example of "the sewer of calumnious falsehood" emanating from the "panic-mongers" of the press.[51] A few months later, when it came time to address the Association as its president, he sought earnestly to proclaim the theme of unity, by urging his colleagues to recognise that "the welfare of the whole body of medical men practising in lunacy is immediately and indissolubly the same."[52]

Certainly, a number of positions Bucknill took must have been broadly popular among his professional brethren. He consistently objected to the "paltry" salaries some asylum committees offered to medical men,[53] and to arrangements that threatened the medical officers' precarious authority—issues of status and renumeration that were naturally of concern to the profession at large. At Norfolk, for example, the magistrates had hired a former attendant at Hanwell as their lay superintendent, with his wife as matron. When compelled to take on Dr. Foote as their medical officer, the magistrates had made him subordinate to the existing lay officers, and when Foote eventually had the temerity to protest about their interference, he found himself promptly dismissed.

If the Norfolk situation raised *en passant* the issue of feminine authority in the asylum, on other occasions the resentments thus provoked were more directly expressed. Here, too, were matters on which Bucknill found himself at one with virtually all of his colleagues. Winslow and Arlidge had complained that "the ambitious tendency of the matrons of asylums is a very prevalent circumstance at the present day" and that "moderation in the exercise of authority is not a characteristic of the female mind."[54] The arrangements at Hanwell and Colney Hatch—where the matrons were paid as much as the medical men and appeared to be more highly regarded by the magistrates' committee—drew their particular ire. Bucknill objected equally forcibly to seeing licenses of asylums given to "ladies," many of them, as he recognised, widows of the original medical licensees. Not, as he hastened to add, that his campaign would deprive them of the economic benefits of their property: after all, "the license and proprietorship of a good private asylum is a very marketable commodity and will always readily obtain a medical purchaser." But to permit female ownership was to license "the evil of lady speculators in insanity" and implicitly to call into question the notion that "insanity is a disease requiring medical treatment."[55]

Such threats were to be taken the more seriously in Bucknill's mind because "it is but a short day, in the history even of our own country since the diseases of the mind were by no means recognized as the peculiar province of the medical man."[56] Moreover, public scepticism about the extent of medical knowledge of madness still threatened in a rather direct fashion physicians' economic interests. In his more reflective moments, Bucknill acknowledged that "we are not disposed to deny that medical practitioners are in general lamentably ignorant of mental disease, and that their certificates of insanity are of little value except as a legal form."[57] But when pending legislation threatened what he himself termed "the pretensions of medical men to exclusive knowledge of diseases of the mind,"[58] through proposals to diminish the role of doctors in the certification of lunacy, he sprang to the profession's defence: "we maintain that this law is directly advantageous to the medical profession, both from the fees it brings and the power is bestows; it is indeed both profitable and honorable, and the Commissioners in Lunacy, in enforcing this law, although no doubt they are actuated by the desire to watch over the welfare of the insane, do in fact confer a benefit upon the medical profession, for which we ought to be grateful."[59]

This was not the only occasion on which Bucknill sought to remind his colleagues of how much they owed to the presence and support of the Lunacy Commissioners. In his presidential address to the Association, for instance, he urged them to remember that, whatever differences of opinion might exist on other matters, "on the large principle of action, which may be expressed as the supremacy of the medical man in the treatment of the insane," the Commissioners had consistently lined up on the correct side. Indeed, but for their support, "we might still have seen county asylums under the management of lay governors, the former masters of union [work]houses or men promoted from the ranks of attendants."[60] Earlier, he had tried to suppress some of the grumbling from his fellow alienists about the disposition of the Commissioners to interfere in the management of "their" asylums,[61] arguing that "it is the weakness of the medical element, and not its excess, which has been detrimental to that body."[62]

Though he objected to some of his colleagues' complaints about the Commission, it must be said that Bucknill himself was far from uncritical of its actions. He berated it, for instance, for failing to take a tougher approach with the numerous borough authorities who continued to farm out their lunatics to private asylums and resisted moving them to public facilities; and he blamed the Commissioners for insisting, for more than a decade, on "unnecessary" architectural expense in the design and construction of pauper asylums.[63] Most vociferously of all, as someone committed to the critical importance of medical expertise in the management of the mad, he objected that although the Commission counted among its number two of "the most experienced and practically successful of asylum superintendents [in Gaskell and Wilkes] . . . the value of these opinions suffers from being averaged with that of other Commissioners, who know nothing practically respecting the management of asylums, or the treatment of the insane."[64]

Defining a Specialty

In terms of writing and publication, the 1850s were the most productive period of Bucknill's career. Between 1851 and 1860, in addition to editing and contributing regularly to the *Asylum Journal of Mental Science*, Bucknill authored six books and pamphlets on a variety of aspects of insanity.[65] By far the most significant of these was his textbook, *A Manual of Psychological Medicine* written jointly with Daniel Hack Tuke. In the years following the publication of the reports of the 1815–1816 Select Committee on Madhouses, medical men had produced a veritable flood of specialised monographs on the treatment of insanity, at once providing a mark of growing medical interest in the subject and constituting an important cultural resource in support of their efforts to claim exclusive jurisdiction over this territory. The appearance in the late 1850s of a widely adopted and acclaimed textbook can in retrospect be seen to correspond to a further stage in the maturation of alienism as a specialised form of practice, for the book synthesized and at the same time constituted the emerging professional consensus on the theoretical and practical foundations of its activities. *A Manual of Psychological Medicine* thus marks an important moment in the history of British psychiatry, and the manner in which Bucknill and Tuke framed the issues at hand and represented the state of professional knowledge and practice are self-evidently of more than passing significance.

It is not known when or how Bucknill and Tuke first met, although it seems likely that it may have been through the AMOAHI. Daniel Hack Tuke, who was the youngest son of Samuel Tuke, and the great-grandson of William Tuke, the founder of the York Retreat, had qualified in medicine in 1852. He took up an appointment as assistant medical officer at the York Retreat in 1854 and is listed as a member of the AMOAHI in the same year. Bucknill wrote a favourable review of Tuke's essay *On the Progressive Changes Which Have Taken Place Since the Time of Pinel in the Moral Management of the Insane* (1854), which won a prize from Morison's Society for Improving the Condition of the Insane, for the *Asylum Journal of Mental Science*. In this review, Bucknill claimed never to have heard of the Society, but went on to note that he had been told that "it is an old friend with a new name, the quondam Alleged Lunatics' Friends Society."[66] Given the fact that Morison's society was composed of the old London-based elite of private practitioners, who favoured the continued use of mechanical restraint in the treatment of the insane, it is difficult not to see this apparent confusion with a society that was composed primarily of former asylum inmates who claimed to be victimized by the asylum system as a sly attempt at humour, although Bucknill hastily apologized for the mistake in the next edition of the journal.[67]

Whatever the origins of the partnership that led to the production of *A Manual of Psychological Medicine*, the book readily found a niche as a reasonably concise summary of the contemporary consensus on the care of the insane, which continued to be influential for a quarter of a century. In some ways Bucknill and Tuke were uniquely placed to provide this sort of authoritative overview. Tuke's name lent prestige to a project that deliberately aimed at becoming the most definitive statement of what constituted good practice in the care of the insane since Samuel Tuke's *Description of the Retreat* (1813), albeit one—unlike his grandfather's book—which was now written from a medical perspective. As editor of the *Asylum Journal of Mental Science*, however, Bucknill was obviously in a position to have a broad overview of current practice and possessed a clear grasp of what would be of most value to the book's audience.

Within medicine, the intention was to supersede the lingering authority of James Cowles Prichard's *Treatise on Insanity* (1835)[68]—a goal that was swiftly realised—and to provide "a systematic treatise on Insanity, adapted to the use of students and practitioners in Medicine" beyond the ranks of "the specialist physician."[69] The book was sufficiently successful for a second edition to appear within four years of the first, and it eventually ran to four editions, with the last one appearing in 1879. For almost a quarter-century, then, Bucknill's text played a key role in constituting and defining the knowledge base on which the alienists rested their claims to jurisdiction over the treatment of the insane.

The first half of the book represented Hack Tuke's contribution: a lengthy review of the ideas of the "ancients" on the treatment of insanity and of the incidence of the malady from antiquity to the modern world (adopting the conventional position that the advance of civilization itself was perversely productive of a rise in the numbers of lunatics); a survey of the definitions and classification of the various forms of the disease; and a history of the "amelioration of the condition of the insane in modern times," from William Tuke to John Conolly, culminating in the abolition of restraint and the establishment of the hegemony of what the great-grandson of the lay founder of the York Retreat now insisted was properly termed the "medico-moral treatment" of the insane. It was left to Bucknill, however, to explicate the *content* of that medico-moral intervention, in a series of chapters on the diagnosis, pathology, and treatment of insanity.

Two features help to explain the reception of *A Manual of Psychological Medicine*: it was lucidly written; and it was practical, summarising and explaining existing practices rather than proposing innovation. In relation to diagnosis, for example, Bucknill followed the "well-known classification" of insanity under five broad headings (mania, monomania, melancholia, dementia, and idiocy) because it was "convenient," "founded upon the most prominent phenomena of the disease, to be provisionally used, until a more

TYPES OF INSANITY.

FROM PHOTOGRAPHS TAKEN IN THE DEVON COUNTY LUNATIC ASYLUM.

for description see the first seven cases in the appendix.

Figure 7.2. Types of insanity: drawings of patients from Bucknill's asylum, reproduced in *A Manual of Psychological Medicine*. The possible utility of the countenance
and the structure of the cranium in the diagnosis and treatment of mental disorder
fascinated Victorian alienists, many of whom wrote on the physiognomy of insanity.

scientific classification, founded upon the causes and nature of insanity, can be established."[70] This chapter also included guidelines on the factors to be taken into consideration during certification, as well as practical advice on the demeanour which the doctor should adopt towards the insane and the importance of avoiding being drawn into family disagreements.[71]

For those diagnosed as insane, Bucknill advocated a judicious combination of treatments: "the Hygienic, the Moral, and the Medicinal"[72]—an eclectic approach that corresponded closely to the views held by most of his fellow specialists. He left little doubt, however, as to which he considered primary, insisting that in cases of confirmed insanity, "moral agencies, properly so called, possess but a limited efficacy in its treatment."[73] We have seen that he was openly critical of the kind of regime advocated by men like Conolly and Gaskell for concentrating too exclusively on moral means, while failing to give medicine its due, and his publications in the 1850s gave repeated voice to his confidence in the value of a variety of medical interventions in the treatment of at least some cases of insanity, part of his endeavour "to bring the treatment of insanity within the domain of scientific medicine."[74]

Bucknill was convinced that the therapeutic net should be widely cast: "The principle advocated is this, that no manageable remedy ought to be excluded from the treatment of a large and diverse class of diseases [like insanity]. . . . The physician will act wisely in definitely rejecting the use of no manageable force of which he has knowledge."[75] Even bleeding, about the utility of which the profession was increasingly sceptical, drew a cautious endorsement: he himself "in the treatment of some two thousand cases, . . . ha[d] never yet used the lancet"—but the uses of leeches and cupping for "local bleeding" were a different matter.[76] Tartrate of antimony, calomel, and in particular opium drew forth a still more positive endorsement, though with an insistence on tailoring their usage and dosage to the vagaries of the individual case;[77] and stimulants, aperients, and purgatives likewise received his blessing.

The situation was very different when it came to "the moral pharmacopoeia."[78] By the beginning of the Victorian era, the dismissive attitude that medical men had often adopted towards moral treatment in the early nineteenth century had long since been replaced by attempts to assimilate and absorb it into the realm of ordinary medical therapeutics. Moreover, given the central role moral treatment played in the day-to-day management of asylum inmates, and its ideological centrality to the success of lunacy reform itself, even the most aggressive defender of medical prerogatives felt compelled to genuflect in its direction and to employ its techniques. Bucknill was no exception to the rule, but his allegiance on close inspection turns out to be quite remarkably qualified and attenuated.

He poured scorn, for instance, on the empty verbiage that he claimed was characteristic of most discussions of the subject: "If the English physician looks to the writings of his countrymen for some description of that moral treatment with which they boast to have replaced the barbarisms of mechanical restraint, he finds little more than vague generalities." Warming to the task, he then ridiculed the practical import of the prescriptions these men provided: "The most inflexible firmness must be combined with never-failing kindness and gentleness and sympathy; the patient is to be taught habitual self-control, by habitual indulgence; in fact, the alienist physician is to be a veritable lion, but like the notable Bottom in that character, he is to 'roar you as gentle as a sucking dove.'"[79]

Not only were many of the representations offered by the proponents of moral treatment vague and contradictory, but a worse problem loomed: the utility this form of therapy possessed was decidedly limited; indeed, it was simply irrelevant in the treatment of some of the most fundamental manifestations of madness. Even amongst the mad, Bucknill insisted that one must distinguish "between that part of wrong conduct which patients are able, and that which they are not able to control." Moral treatment could certainly be of some considerable value in the former sphere: "On the other hand, that part of their conduct which they are unable to control, and which is neither more nor less than the expression of pathological states of the brain, includes by far the greater part of the most violent and dangerous manifestations of insanity. [Here] this conduct must be resisted solely by physiological and pharmaceutical means; direct moral treatment is as much out of place as in inflammation of the heart, or of any other viscus."[80]

A sustained attempt was thus made to resolve the competing claims of medical and moral treatment as much as possible in favour of the former—and not just by either constraining the sphere of application for moral treatment or making strong claims for the utility of pharmaceutical remedies. Rather the very boundaries of what constituted medical and moral treatment were subtly redrawn, so as to incorporate as many forms of intervention as possible within the domain of the medical. The public at large might be especially prone to identify moral treatment with the introduction of kindness and humanity into the therapeutic regimen, but Bucknill insisted that they were mistaken: "even to be kind and gentle in word and deed to the insane, cannot rightly be called moral, but physiological treatment."[81] And here he sought to invoke the authority of the sainted Conolly. Just as "we seek mild air for the consumptive, and place the asthmatic in an air which does not irritate him, and keep a patient with heart disease on level ground; and on the same prophylactic and curative principles, we must study to remove from an insane person every influence that can further excite his brain, and to surround him with such as, acting soothingly on both body and mind, may favour the brain's rest, and promote the recovery of its normal action."[82]

With kindness now claimed for medicine, what remained as the core of moral treatment? Techniques of management employed by "any officer or attendant, . . . who daily impresses upon [the insane] the influences of his own character to their improvement"; the deliberate creation of "moral emotions opposed to those which cause insanity"; and "the discipline of an asylum," most particularly the "constant surveillance" its organisation and physical arrangements permitted.[83] If not the primary weapons in the cure of insanity, then these forms of moral treatment were nonetheless of great significance in ensuring that "all that part of the wrong conduct of the insane which is under their control becomes controllable by slight means. This is especially the case in asylums of some magnitude, on account of the influence of rule and habit upon the old inmates, and that of example on the newcomers. The influence of example in enforcing obedience to law has a wonderful potency . . . the new inmate of an asylum . . . may resist at first, and his mouth may be as hard as that of an unbroken colt; but after a while, and without any harshness, he will answer to the slightest indications of the rein of discipline."[84]

Deviations from Orthodoxy

If this attempt to mount a vigorous defence of medical prerogatives and to "medicalise" as many of their activities as possible was gratefully received by his colleagues, then some of the other views Bucknill was now beginning to adopt were assuredly more controversial. By the late 1850s, he was displaying an increasing interest in the boarding-out of some patients and in so-called cottage treatment for others. In hindsight, we can see that these views were a harbinger of his later emphasis on the benefits of domestic treatment or care outside an asylum, but already, even in its early, tentative form, his willingness to countenance alternatives to dealing with insanity solely through segregation in specialized institutions put him at odds with the prevailing professional consensus.

Two factors appear to have influenced Bucknill's interest in extra-institutional care. First, as editor of the journal Bucknill was aware of the Commissioners in Lunacy's concern that although more effective regulation and inspection of private and public asylums had been established, lunatics who were cared for at home or as single patients were relatively unprotected, and he also knew that family reluctance to incur the stigma of institutionalization made it unlikely that many of these individuals would readily be placed in an asylum. Second, the mounting pressure of patient numbers meant that Devon County Asylum was becoming overcrowded, and alternative or additional accommodation was required—a situation scarcely unique to Devon, but one which prompted Bucknill to conduct an experiment that decisively reshaped his views on the possibility and desirability of moving some lunatics beyond the walls of the asylum.

In 1855 the increasing number of patients at Exminster led Bucknill to convert two small houses in the grounds of the asylum, which had originally been built as offices, to accommodate patients. These arrangements proved popular with patients and were comparatively cheap.[85] Bucknill accordingly recommended that as asylums became overcrowded, additional accommodation should be provided in houses "built on a simple plan, retaining as much as possible the ordinary arrangements of English homes";[86] and when he needed to add accommodation for about one hundred additional female patients in 1857, Bucknill attempted to follow these principles of design, providing mainly single rooms as sleeping accommodation.

A year earlier, a decision by the Commissioners in Lunacy to close a notorious private asylum at Plympton and transfer the patients to the Devon County Asylum had added a particularly acute source of pressure on the accommodation available at Exminster. In response, Bucknill had begun to experiment with approaches that departed still further from orthodoxy: boarding out quiet, chronic, female patients in neighbouring cottages beyond the asylum grounds, some of which were lived in by asylum attendants;[87] and, more radically still, renting a house in the nearby seaside town of Exmouth, where he boarded forty to forty-five quiet female patients under the care of a resident medical officer, Mr. Symes, and two resident female nurses.

To his evident surprise, Bucknill's attempt to foster some minimal contact between some of his patients and sane members of the community served to demonstrate how thoroughly the public had accepted, and adopted, his fellow alienists' insistence on the imperative need to segregate the insane. As he later recorded in the *Asylum Journal of Mental Science*, when news of this proposed experiment reached them, "Exmouth residents were greatly alarmed." They protested against the seaside annex on the basis that "the hotels and houses let as lodgings would be unoccupied; that the value of house properties would be greatly deteriorated; that the residents would be distressed and terrified by painful scenes, and that in taking their usual walks upon the beach and the sands, they would be in danger from the violence of patients whom they would meet."[88] Local feeling was sufficiently strong to mount a petition to the Secretary of State, but on the advice of the Commissioners in Lunacy, he was not moved by the complaints.

The problem of the rapidly expanding ranks of chronic pauper patients was by this time an ever-increasing source of worry and concern, and it therefore comes as no surprise that after visiting the Devon County Asylum annex in Exmouth in September 1857 the Commissioners added their own support for Bucknill's scheme. In their published report in the following year, they noted that "the prejudice which at first existed against the residence of the patients in this house, has entirely disappeared. . . . It is to be hoped that the Committees of other Asylums may be induced to follow the example thus set by the Devonshire Justices, now that so convincing a proof has been afforded of its practicability and success."[89]

Quite apart from the fact that the fears of local residents had proved unfounded, if Bucknill's description of the patients' experience was accurate, they enjoyed something of a Victorian seaside idyll and "became free of the shore without exciting comment or attracting much notice. They took their daily walks along the sands, picking up shells and weed left by the retiring tide, or they explored the rock pools for anenomes, side by side with other idle folk. Some people took interest in them and talked to them kindly"—a happy outcome, which Bucknill assumed could be explained by the fact that "the insane are vastly like children, and where are children so happy as on the sea shore?"[90]

Despite the apparent success of this initiative, however, the seaside experiment came to an end in 1857 when new female accommodation became available in the asylum itself. With its demise (and even though the boarding out of a handful of quiet, chronic patients on an individual basis quietly continued), one of the few practical attempts to educate public and Parliament out of what Bucknill would later call the "stereotyped prejudice that a lunatic is a lunatic and an asylum is the best place for him"[91] essentially fell by the wayside. Three years later, when the memory of the fierce opposition his efforts had aroused evidently still stung, he commented bitterly that "the feeling and conduct of the British public towards the insane reminds one of nothing so much as that of the enlightened citizens of the free States of America. Noble and just sentiments towards the negro race are in everyone's mouth, but personal antipathy is in every man's heart."[92]

Of course, if the test of antipathy to the insane was an insistence on their sequestration in asylums, hermetically sealed off from the world at large, then the hypocrisy Bucknill complained of was scarcely confined to the general lay population. While his views on domestic care and its possibilities garnered some support from a handful of alienists, most of his colleagues were and remained unalterably opposed to policies that might have lessened the segregation of the insane. Harrington Tuke, Conolly's son-in-law, spoke for the overwhelming majority of the profession in condemning all such schemes as "utopian and absurd"; and when a motion to set up a committee to consider the principle of the cottage system was put before the Association in 1862, it was soundly defeated.[93] Bucknill's apostasy on this question thus marked the beginning of his movement away from the mainstream of his profession.

COMPLAINTS AND DISSATISFACTIONS

Unlike his predecessors as president of the Association, Bucknill elected to give a second major address at the end of his term of office, publishing it in the *Journal of Mental Science* under the revealing title of his "Valedictory Address." Although his departure from the ranks of asylum superintendents, and his resignation as editor of the *Journal of Mental Science* would not occur until almost two more years had passed, his career had in many ways reached a turning point, and there were a number of signs that he himself recognized as much. By 1861, he was the second-longest-serving county asylum superintendent in the country, having spent seventeen and a half years at the helm at Exminster. The job must long since have lost whatever challenges it once held for him, and he had already exhibited a number of signs of restlessness. Before taking on the *Journal*, he had devoted considerable time and energy to the formation, organization, and drilling of a corps of citizen soldiers, the First Exeter and Devon Rifle Volunteers (a project that allowed him to develop extensive social ties to Earl Fortescue and other assorted members of the local aristocracy and gentry).[94] With the appointment of an assistant physician to absorb some of the workload at the asylum, and to cover for him in his absence, he acquired a national reputation for his expert testimony in court cases involving questions of insanity.[95] More significantly still, of course, from late 1853 onwards he had invested enormous amounts of time and energy in the Association and had virtually singlehandedly been responsible for the success of the *Journal of Mental Science*.

From time to time, there had been other signs that he chafed at the limitations imposed by his provincial post and longed for a larger stage on which to perform. His fierce protests about the calibre of some of the medical appointments to the Lunacy Commission were on the surface voiced in behalf of the profession at large, but given his own prominence in the ranks of county asylum superintendents, their self-referential character must have been transparent. When Robert Nairne was appointed to the Commission, Bucknill simply could not contain his anger and disappointment. Beyond some social connections to the proprietors of elite private asylums in London, Nairne's chief—perhaps only—qualification for the post was apparently his Evangelical Christianity, which explains his appeal to Shaftesbury; and to make matters worse, when his appointment was announced, he boasted (as Bucknill reported it) of his "primitive ignorance in all that relates to asylums and the insane." Denouncing the influence of "corrupt dealers in patronage," Bucknill complained bitterly that "the whole class of asylum superintendents justly feels injured and insulted by being placed under the

authority of strange medical men, who have never borne the heat and bur-
then of the day, who have no claims for such preferment and who [are]
practically ignorant of the responsibilities entailed in the management of
asylums and the treatment of the insane."[96] Still worse, the previous appointments of Gaskell and Wilkes from the ranks of county asylum superintendents had raised hopes and expectations that such plum appointments
would go as a matter of course to the most prominent and respected of their
number (and who more deserving than Bucknill himself?). How galling
then, what "a heavy blow and a great discouragement to all medical men
practising in lunacy, and especially to the class of asylum superintendents—
men who upon small stipends devote their lives to onerous and harassing
duties, in the hope that some day they may draw one of the legitimate prizes
of their professional career"[97]—was the decision to ignore their just claims
and instead appoint a complete outsider?

In reality, in serving so effectively as the spokesman for his profession's
interests, Bucknill almost necessarily had occasion to give offence to those
who oversaw the enterprise of asylumdom. Though he sought where possible to offset his criticisms with flattery (proclaiming that "in our opinion,
the public has no servants who discharge their duties with more impartial-
ity, fidelity, and earnestness [than the Lunacy Commissioners]"); and
though he tried to remove the sting from some of his remarks by downplay-
ing their significance and import ("we are sure that if the Commissioners
take the trouble to read these remarks, they will pardon the innocent banter
with which we sometimes refresh ourselves")[98]—the criticisms and complaints he felt compelled to voice cannot have endeared him to the Commission, particularly its notoriously thin-skinned chairman. And complaints
about patronage notwithstanding, absent Shaftesbury's backing, promotion
to the Commissioners' ranks was unlikely in the extreme.

By the time his presidential year came to a close, however, Bucknill's dis-
satisfaction with the limitations of his present position was becoming increasingly clear.[99] Years before, the suicide of the superintendent of the
Worcester Asylum, Dr. Grahamsley, had led Bucknill to warn of "the injurious mental tension of the job" and of the dangers the superintendents' occupation presented to their own mental stability.[100] Such complaints that "we
sacrifice our own welfare to the common-weal . . . , that we consent to
spend our lives in a morbid mental atmosphere" were now voiced in more
melodramatic language: "he who efficiently discharges the arduous functions attendant on the care and treatment of the insane, dwells in a morbid
atmosphere of thought and feeling, a perpetual 'Walpurgis Night' of lurid
delusion, the perils of which he, who walks through even the most difficult
paths of sane human effort, can little appreciate. . . . The number of mental
physicians who have suffered more or less from the seeming contagion of
mental disease, would form, perhaps, if enquired into, a proportion of those

Figure 7.3. Sir John Charles Bucknill, sometime asylum superintendent, journal editor, Lord Chancellor's Visitor in Lunacy, metropolitan consultant on nervous disorders, magistrate, and country gentleman.

who really fight in this warfare which might bear some comparison even with that of men who fall in the strife of the sword."[101] Not unreasonably, Bucknill was not eager to add himself to their number.

Nor were these the only dissatisfactions he now voiced with his career. Despite the "great sacrifice" he and his colleagues made, the public viewed alienists with evident "distaste" and "extends its unreasonable antipathy to the insane to all those who are connected with insanity; even to those who wrestle with the great evil, and to the best of their ability, hold it down!"[102]

"The newspaper press" periodically led "senseless" campaigns "against almost everybody and everything connected with the insane"; Boards of Poor Law Guardians were notorious for their "humiliating . . . treatment of our profession"; and the depressing reality of declining standards of patient care reflected superintendents' "failure to mingle the oil and water of economy and efficiency," as "the management of asylums at a cheap rate, . . . is more and more pressed upon us by local authorities."[103] More alarmingly still, there were proposals abroad, which in the event were to come to nothing, to expand the supervisory powers of the Lunacy Commission on the analogy of the regulatory apparatus already in place for overseeing workhouses, by limiting the role of the Commission itself to oversight of the whole process, and appointing "District Inspectors of Lunatics" to conduct the actual visits to asylums. Such notions horrified Bucknill because they "would tend to degrade the position and estimation of the medical men who are entrusted with the charge of the insane; and it may safely be asserted that no legislative measure would . . . be more calculated to [produce] disgust with their calling, and drive from it the most highly educated and esteemed of the physicians who practice in lunacy, than to subject them to the inspection of an inferior and ill-paid class of government officials."[104]

By this time, it would appear, Bucknill found the pecuniary rewards of his position insufficient to compensate for the travails and abuse it brought in its train. He spoke enviously of how "the income of a general physician increases as his reputation extends, so that golden showers of well-deserved fees fall upon his gray hairs. But the asylum physician, in the full maturity of his experience, can enjoy scarcely more than the modest income which he perhaps has just seen granted to the youngest of his assistants, who may recently have received an appointment similar to his own. These asylum appointments, indeed, are good things enough to young men just entering the profession . . . but they are poor things to end life upon."[105] Soon, he did not have to.

An Extra-Institutional Career

At the peak of his standing among his fellow alienists, Bucknill was naturally one of their major spokesmen before the House of Commons Select Committee that had met between 1858 and 1860, testifying at length in the profession's behalf and successfully helping to stave off legislation inimical to their interests.[106] For all his ability and efforts, however, his salary remained stubbornly static; and his social standing was inextricably linked to a network of pauper institutions founded amid utopian expectations about treatment and cure, but increasingly degenerating into custodial warehouses over-run with the chronic and incurable. Faced with such dismal prospects, and having laboured for almost two decades in the isolation of a provincial asylum, Bucknill now sought to escape his depressing fate.

One legislative proposal widely canvassed in 1859 and 1860 had been the idea of consolidating the operations of the Lunacy Commissioners and the separate body of Chancery Visitors, who possessed legal authority over the care and treatment of those (usually well-to-do) lunatics found insane by inquisition. Whether his opposition had any ulterior motives we cannot know, but Bucknill was a foremost critic of this scheme. In an open letter to Spencer Walpole, chairman of the Select Committee, he attacked the idea as misguided and impractical, and alleged it would leave Chancery lunatics "even more unprovided for than at present."[107] The number of inquisitions in lunacy was large and steadily increasing, so the Court of Chancery was in ever greater need of medical advice. Furthermore, the workload of the Commissioners in Lunacy was "already so onerous that this transference could only be effected by relieving [them] from the duty of visiting the 7000 insane persons confined contrary to law, justice, and humanity in workhouses"[108]—and this hardly constituted sensible social policy.

In the event, whether because of his representations, or more likely from simple inertia, the system of separate visitation for Chancery patients survived the inquiry intact—fortunately so for Bucknill, since two vacancies for Medical Visitors opened up simultaneously only two years later, and one of the prized appointments promptly fell into his lap.[109] The process of preferment that led to what was for him this happy outcome is not clear, though one can readily perceive some attributes that made Bucknill an attractive candidate. Besides his professional prominence and his considerable experience and knowledge about the medical jurisprudence of insanity, Bucknill's moderate views must have commended themselves to the Lord Chancellor, who unquestionably shared his legal brethren's suspicion of alienists' claims to expertise and hostility to their professional jargon. When the Chancellor had finally presented a new Lunacy Bill in 1862, Bucknill had promptly printed a flattering commentary on its provisions. In the process, he conceded that "knowledge of insanity is in its infancy" and lamented "those speculative views, and theoretical opinions which have, in lunacy trials, been the cause of the waste of public time and patience, and of so much discredit to our profession." Alienists, he advised (and the words must have been music in the Lord Chancellor's ears) should strip their testimony of abstract and complicated verbiage, down "to the nakedness of common sense, and of the plainest language" and rely upon "the empirical knowledge which many medical men have acquired by devoting themselves to the daily observation of the characteristics of insanity."[110]

At a public level, Bucknill had established his support for the regulation of single care, both in correspondence and in the evidence he gave in July 1859 to the Select Committee—a form of care objected to by most of his fellow alienists, but the approach to the management of lunacy generally preferred by the affluent classes in whose behalf the Chancery system operated. His letter to Spencer Walpole had also contained a number of sensible and appealing suggestions for reform: for example, that unnecessary duplication of function could be avoided if Chancery lunatics in asylums were visited by the Commissioners in Lunacy, while Chancery lunatics at home or in single care continued to be visited by the Lord Chancellor's Visitors; and that the latter's role should be expanded to include giving advice on the mental state of all individuals whose cases were referred to the Court of Chancery, potentially minimizing some of the expense associated with these often immensely costly proceedings, and avoiding "the dreadful exposure of all that one would wish to keep from the eye of the world."[111]

These recommendations responded astutely both to the tradition of rivalry between the offices of the Lord Chancellor's Visitors and the Commissioners in Lunacy, and to the concern to streamline the cumbersome and costly procedures of the Court of Chancery by moving to a more executive style of decision making. Although neither of Bucknill's recommendations were incorporated in amendments to the law relating to Chancery lunatics in 1862, there can be little doubt that Bucknill's appointment was seen as one that might both ease tension between the offices of the Commissioners in Lunacy and the Lord Chancellor's Visitors and help to facilitate efficiency.

Nevertheless, Bucknill's elevation constituted a break with tradition, insofar as previous medical visitors had been drawn from the elite of London physicians who had well-established and cordial links with private lunacy practitioners.[112] Prior to Bucknill's appointment the two medical visitors were Henry Herbert Southey (1783–1865) and John Bright (d.1870). Southey, who had been a Lord Chancellor's Visitor since the office was created in 1833, was a former physician to George IV and Queen Adelaide, who had been a Metropolitan Lunacy Commissioner from 1828 to 1845, and Commissioner in Lunacy for a brief period in 1845. Bright was a prominent elder of the Royal College of Physicians, who had been secretary to its commission charged with inspecting private madhouses in London prior to the formation of the Metropolitan Lunacy Commission in 1828, as well as a Metropolitan Lunacy Commissioner from 1836. Given the advanced ages of the two men, the 1862 legislation made their resignations almost inevitable, as it became a statutory responsibility that every Chancery lunatic should be visited four times a year. As the *Lancet* explained, the new legislation allowed for pensions "not exceeding one half of their respective salaries, to be paid to the present Medical Visitors, or either of them, in case they or either of them shall be desirous of retiring from the offices held by them, they having already attained the respective ages of seventy-eight and eighty-one years, and having served as Medical Visitors for twenty-eight and twenty years respectively."[113]

The expectation that Bucknill's appointment might help to foster smoother cooperation between the offices of the Commissioners in Lunacy and the Lord Chancellor's Visitors seems to have been borne out. One particular source of tension had been the fact that the Lord Chancellor's Visitors would not disclose the names and addresses of Chancery lunatics to the Commissioners in Lunacy, to assist them in compiling a register of single patients. In 1863, the Lord Chancellor directed that a list of names and addresses of patients found lunatic by inquisition should be sent to the Commissioners in Lunacy and updated regularly. This particular issue does not appear to have caused problems again, although it is questionable whether the Lord Chancellor's Visitors would have benefited significantly from receiving the regularly updated list of private asylums with which the Commissioners in Lunacy supplied them in return.[114]

Whatever its broader impact on the administration of lunacy, though, there can be no question but that in personal terms Bucknill's appointment constituted a considerable financial and social advancement. The salary of £1,500 a year, plus expenses of one pound a day and 9d. a mile, amounted to more than three times as much as the £500 per year which he had earned as a county asylum superintendent and—as with Gaskell's appointment as a Lunacy Commissioner—placed his income on a par with that of leading London consultants.[115] Bucknill promptly took the corner house in Cleveland Square, which had previously been occupied by Lord Playfair (Dr. Lyon Playfair), moving to Wimpole Street, in the heart of medical London, a short time thereafter.[116]

Few offices were more calculated to provide an ambitious medical man with entrée into the private secrets and scandals attending the lives of the rich and the powerful than Bucknill's new position supervising Chancery lunatics. As their families' confidant on a matter of surpassing delicacy, such a man was well placed to win their trust and loyalty, and all but certain to build an extensive network of social connections. Bucknill was socially active on other fronts as well: he joined several clubs, including the Garrick and the Atheneum, and eventually became a Governor of Bethlem, which brought him into contact with leading figures in the City of London. It was perhaps these social connections, and the metropolitan prominence his new position brought with it, that then brought him still another significant mark of distinction, election in 1866 as a Fellow of the Royal Society.[117]

A condition of the appointment to the Chancery post was that the holder should not practice medicine. Nevertheless, both Bucknill and Hood retained strong links with their profession. Although they resigned to become honorary rather than full members of the AMOAHI after their appointments, they continued to socialise with members of the association—attending, for example, the dinner that accompanied the annual meeting of the Association at London in 1863.[118] Nor did the offer of his new post immediately put an end to Bucknill's involvement in professional politics: there can be little doubt, for instance, that the appointment of Charles Lockhart Robertson as Hood's successor in 1870 owed much to his behind the scenes activities.[119]

Notwithstanding his many years spent dealing with paupers, Bucknill's past acquaintance with aristocratic social circles in Devon helped to ensure that he smoothly managed the transition to overseeing the lives of a very different collection of lunatics. Indeed, he proved "eminently suited to his new post, where his commanding presence [he stood over 6' 1" tall] and authoritative manner never failed to impress members of that rather troublesome class of patients."[120] Though obviously conducted over a wider geographical area and on a different financial basis, the pattern of his life as a Lord Chancellor's Visitor bears a striking similarity in some respects to that of Morison's as a Visiting Physician to patients in single care. It was marked by a similar attention to detail and a concern with the minutiae of domestic arrangements, as much as with medical treatment.

As a Lord Chancellor's Visitor, Bucknill's responsibility was partly to ensure that patients were cared for at a standard of living commensurate with that which they might have enjoyed had they been sane. There is evidence that Bucknill took this seriously, suggesting that one wealthy patient should be provided with a carriage and billiard room and complaining that another patient had only one blanket in cold weather.[121] The Visitors also sought to ensure that Chancery lunatics received treatment that might be conducive to recovery. In some cases, this led to a recommendation that a patient should be transferred to an asylum or from an asylum into single care. Much of Bucknill's advice on domestic details fell within the broad spectrum of moral treatment, as when he recommended that one patient should receive a daily copy of the *Times*, and in another case that "the Lunatic should not be allowed to hoard decaying food, but should be so managed that her room may be kept sweet and wholesome."[122] However, he also made more specific recommendations that came within his understanding of what constituted medical treatment. These ranged from advice that a patient should be given a glass of port wine daily, to recommendations that individual patients should be encouraged to engage in agricultural labour or taken on holiday to the seaside.

In principle, the powers of the Lord Chancellor's Visitors were limited because their role was primarily to advise the Masters in Lunacy who separately had access to the financial details of Chancery lunatics' estates and who oversaw the way in which these were managed by the patients' committees. Given Bucknill's strongly held view that the treatment of insanity was strictly a matter for medical men, he could hardly be expected to welcome this arrangement; and indeed, in his evidence to the parliamentary Select

Committee in 1877, he complained that the Masters in Lunacy, who were qualified in law rather than medicine, did not always implement recommendations from the Visitors. In practice, though, the evidence suggests that the Visitors generally prevailed, even when this involved overriding the wishes of patients' relatives. However elevated their social rank, families were liable to find their preferences ignored if they showed themselves reluctant to follow medical advice, particularly in cases where the patient was perceived as at risk or as dangerous. In 1866, for example, after Bucknill had visited a Chancery patient, a letter was sent to the patient's committee warning them of the responsibility they "incurred by giving the Lunatic so much liberty." This patient was subsequently placed in an asylum, and when his committee complained that the proprietor of the asylum was placing too many restrictions on the lunatic's freedom, the Visitors wrote back supporting the actions of the proprietor.[123]

This case is interesting because one way in which the Lord Chancellor's Visitors sought to maintain Chancery lunatics' standard of living and quality of life was by ensuring that they continued to enjoy as much freedom as was compatible with their mental condition. Indeed this provided one influence that encouraged Bucknill to advocate the benefits of domestic care since, as he explained in January 1879, "the tradition of the Lord Chancellor's lunacy offices is opposed to the incarceration of any lunatic in an asylum, for whom due protection and the enjoyment of life can be provided outside."[124] Such views were, of course, anathema to most alienists, but having originally thought it possible to create some advantages of domestic treatment in an asylum setting, Bucknill was increasingly to emphasise the benefits that flowed from restricting the number of lunatics confined together.

Despite his prior dalliance while an asylum superintendent with some limited experiments involving noninstitutional care, it is apparent that, in the first instance, this more thoroughgoing change in his outlook was wrought by his professional experience after leaving Exminster, and more particularly, by the extensive opportunities his new position provided to see examples of single and domestic care. It cannot have been irrelevant, though, that, unlike his former colleagues, his career was no longer tied to the asylum sector. As Chancery Visitor, over a period of fourteen years, Bucknill visited wealthy patients in single care, developing an increasingly high evaluation of such treatment. His protégé and fellow Chancery Visitor, Lockhart Robertson, subsequently came to share his judgement, confessing that, "I could never have believed that patients who were such confirmed lunatics could be treated in private families in the way that Chancery lunatics are, if I had not personally watched their cases."[125]

While in post, perhaps constrained by his official position, Bucknill made few public statements on lunacy policy. Some clues about the evolution of his thinking are provided, though, in the third edition of *A Manual of Psychological Medicine* published in 1874. For the first time, he included an extended discussion of "The Domestic Treatment of the Rich" and "The Cottage Treatment of the Poor," which drew directly on his experience as a Lord Chancellor's Visitor, as well as his earlier experiments in Devon[126]—heretical ideas that would not have gone unnoticed among his former colleagues.[127]

Soon, his apostasy would become more open and obvious. In 1875, Bucknill took an extended leave of absence from his duties as Lord Chancellor's Visitor and spent some months in North America examining asylums in the United States and Canada. On his return, he published reports of this tour, first in the *Lancet*, and subsequently as a collection of *Notes on Asylums for the Insane in America* (1876).[128] This publication provided Bucknill with an opportunity to reaffirm his commitment to the abolition of mechanical restraint, stressing that "his opinions on the subject, published in the eighth Report of the Commissioners in Lunacy in 1854 and republished in the *Manual of Psychological Medicine* . . . remain quite unchanged."[129] He went on to explain that "the coercion of an insane man by means of bands, although mainly a scientific question, is also in great part a moral and social one, mixed up as it is with the rights of society over the individual, and with questions of benevolence and humanity."[130] But these renewed expressions of faith in the very touchstone of alienist orthodoxy were to prove the exception to the rule: over the next decade, Bucknill was to break decisively with the views of asylum doctors on a number of crucial issues and to attack the very basis on which an important and influential segment of that specialty earned its livelihood.

Back in London in 1876, Bucknill resigned his post as Lord Chancellor's Visitor to enter private practice, seeking to carve out a career outside the asylum sector altogether. No doubt he hoped that the network of contacts he had established through his work as a Lord Chancellor's Visitor would assist him in generating private consultations and fees. However, from the mid to late 1870s Bucknill also sought to establish a wider reputation in the medical profession and a higher public profile, which he must also have hoped would help to attract referrals. Together with Ferrier, Hughlings Jackson, and Crichton Browne, he founded *Brain*, a vehicle for developing medically respectable neurophysiological accounts of insanity and the journal around which the emerging specialty of neurology consolidated itself.[131] Where his erstwhile colleagues in asylumdom increasingly looked inward and viewed themselves as an embattled and poorly understood specialty, reviled even by their fellow physicians,[132] it was among the most elite segments of the medical profession at large that Bucknill aimed to move; and the opinions and judgements he now voiced were far more welcome there than among the asylum doctors from whose ranks he had sprung.

In terms of his standing and influence in metropolitan medical circles, his efforts were crowned with a quite extraordinary degree of success. Elected a Fellow of the Royal College of Physicians in 1859 while he was still a county asylum superintendent, he now became more and more active and influential in College affairs. In 1877, he was elected Lumleian Lecturer, and that same year, he gave the presidential address to the Psychological Section of the British Medical Association in Manchester. Two years later, he was chosen as College Censor for a two-year term; and during the 1880s, he was a member of Council and of the College committee dealing with proposed changes in the lunacy law.[133] Very few of his fellow alienists indeed could even dream of achieving this level of acceptance by the medical elite. Together with his fellowship in the Royal Society, his new marks of favour marked the culmination of an astonishing rise by someone who had begun by failing to establish a practice in London and retreated to serve as the head of a provincial pauper lunatic asylum. His accession to his wife's family's country estate, Hillmorton Hall, Rugby; his appointment as a Warwickshire justice of the peace; and his enthusiasm for and spirited participation in fox-hunting, fishing, and shooting completed his transformation into the rank of eminent Victorian physician and country gentleman, to which so many of his fellow medical men aspired and so few acceded.[134]

In Bucknill's publications throughout this period there were several consistent themes: a concern with the protection of the civil liberties and dignity of patients; advocacy of a combination of noninstitutional care and treatment in publicly funded institutions; and an emphasis on scientific medicine and psychiatry's roots in general medicine. Within a year of his resignation from his Chancery post, in evidence to the Select Committee in 1877 Bucknill advocated the use of single care and domestic treatment in appropriate cases, as well as an open-door policy within asylums; and by 1880, he had publicly abandoned much of his earlier optimism about asylum care: "The author's fullest and latest experience has convinced him that the curative influences of asylums have been vastly overrated, and those of isolated treatment in domestic care have been greatly undervalued. . . . It has long been the accepted doctrine [among alienists] that insanity can only be treated in asylums. . . . A wider knowledge of insanity . . . would have taught them that a very considerable number of cases of actual insanity run a short course and recover in domestic life with no great amount of treatment, and that perhaps not of a very scientific kind."[135] If possible, he thought that no more than two or three lunatics should be kept together, an arrangement he saw as "infinitely preferable, both for curative treatment and for happiness." Domestic treatment, besides, afforded privacy, and "Englishmen would rather be pinched in a cottage than pampered in a palace, if the latter implied a crowded life in common."[136]

Even now, there were occasions on which Bucknill believed that the greater level of security provided by an institution was necessary, but this concession in its turn was soon linked to further proposals the asylum doctors considered anathema. For Chancery lunatics, the alternative to domestic care was to be consigned to a private asylum, and the absence of other forms of secure accommodation for patients of this class was sometimes cited as a reason for retaining private asylums. In August 1877, in an attempt to circumvent this objection to the closure of private asylums, Bucknill joined with his former protégé and colleague, Charles Lockhart Robertson, and with James Crichton-Browne, who had succeeded Bucknill as Lord Chancellor's Visitor, to send a joint public memorandum to the Lord Chancellor. In this document, they proposed that three state asylums should be provided for Chancery lunatics for whom single care was inappropriate.[137]

In some ways it is not surprising that Bucknill should have advocated a further extension of the public sector in caring for the insane. Throughout his career Bucknill had prospered as a result of public appointments, first at Devon County Asylum and subsequently as Lord Chancellor's Visitor. Nevertheless it is striking that Bucknill's most forthright attacks on private asylums should come at a time when he was practicing himself as a private lunacy physician. In his evidence to the Select Committee in 1859, and even in 1877, Bucknill had commended the standard of care in private asylums and spoken against their closure; but such views were now cast aside, and from 1879 onward Bucknill called publicly and repeatedly for the total abolition of private asylums.

Bucknill's public statements suggest that he was becoming increasingly mistrustful of the private sector because of what he saw as its vested interest in prolonging treatment. His oppositional stance is evident in the very critical comments he offered about proposals that would have enabled drunkards to be compulsorily detained for treatment in private inebriate asylums, proposals he attributed to the fact that "members of his profession were taking hold of the stick by the wrong end, and were considering drunkenness not as a cause of disease, but as a disease in itself . . . he looked upon inebriate asylums as an unfortunate attempt to coddle drunkenness, and patch up a wide and fruitful social mischief."[138] Bucknill objected to these schemes for two reasons. First, he was now prepared to suggest that "if there were no vested interests to consider, private lunatic asylums could not be permitted; and yet this fragment of legislation would establish a new class of asylums, in which the liberty of the subject would be submitted to determinations, biased by self-interest, of private adventurers."[139] Second, he feared that "unless stringent measures are taken to prevent it, these new asylums will be resorted to as places of detention for real lunatics." Indeed, he went so far as to allege that this was already happening: for example, when he visited patients in one inebriate asylum on behalf of the Lord Chancellor he found a lady whose state of lunacy was obvious and unquestionable and for whose detention without certificates the keeper of the asylum was prosecuted and punished.[140]

A PROFESSIONAL HERETIC

Three years after he entered private practice, in 1879, Bucknill began to mount increasingly outspoken attacks on private asylums in the general medical press. In a series of articles in the *British Medical Journal*, which were initially published anonymously, Bucknill described licensed houses as "private places of imprisonment" and quoted Conolly's early dictum that "every lunatic asylum should be the property of the State, and be controlled by public officers."[141] Bucknill finally identified himself as the *British Medical Journal*'s anonymous correspondent at a meeting of a branch of the British Medical Association in January 1880, at which he reiterated that "no change of the law can be satisfactory which does not contemplate the eventual abolition of all private lunatic asylums."[142] The articles were collected and published under Bucknill's name in the same year as *The Care of the Insane and Their Legal Control*.

Although there were consistent preoccupations in Bucknill's publications between 1874 and 1880, at first sight it seems paradoxical that Bucknill began to criticize private asylums at the time at which he entered private practice himself. The shifts in Bucknill's attitudes to asylums and noninstitutional care seem less puzzling, however, when placed in the context of the needs of his particular career path. Bucknill entered private practice at a time when private asylums were the subject of widespread public criticism. The recurrent public panics about the improper confinement of the sane surfaced with renewed force in the 1870s, prompting the formation of still another Select Committee.[143] In such an emotionally charged climate, Bucknill may have hoped that a purposeful distancing of himself from private asylum practice, together with his years of experience of public office, would help to establish his integrity as a private physician capable of giving disinterested advice. The same intention may also have lain behind Bucknill's claim in *The Care of the Insane and Their Legal Control* that domestic treatment was not "for the advantage of the rich alone, but for that of all lunatics who are easily manageable and are not dangerous, and it is in the development of this system of domestic treatment that the greatest promise lies of the largest possible amelioration of the unhappy lot of those afflicted with mental disease."[144]

By 1880, when Bucknill summarized his views for a broad audience, he was reflecting to a considerable extent a consensus that had emerged among similarly placed consultant physicians attempting to specialize in the treatment of lunacy and nervous disorders—men such as Henry Maudsley and George Fielding Blandford. He also continued to be supported by his erstwhile colleague Charles Lockhart Robertson and by James Crichton-Browne. Whilst Bucknill's attacks on private asylums cost him the support of some members of the Medico-Psychological Association, he and Maudsley were able to use the Royal College of Physicians as an alternative power base from which to lobby government on proposed new lunacy legislation. As early as 1880 Bucknill had praised the work of general practitioners with mental and nervous cases, stressing that this form of intervention often went unrecognized and unacknowledged by advocates of asylum treatment. One notable editorial in the *Lancet* in May 1881 went so far as to compare the average asylum to the zoo in Regents Park; it stressed that the asylum function was custodial and ridiculed moral treatment as a system of management and containment rather than therapy and cure.[145] Such views were not uncommon among the medical elite to whose ranks Bucknill now belonged; but to the asylum superintendents from whose midst he had risen, and whose collective consciousness he had once done so much to create and shape, his endorsement of these profoundly heretical opinions must have seemed a peculiarly painful kind of treachery.[146]

From retirement in 1885 Bucknill published a final attack on private asylums in the popular periodical *Nineteenth Century*, in which he called for their immediate closure.[147] This article caused a sufficient stir for the Lord Chancellor, Lord Selborne, to write anxiously to Lord Shaftesbury that "this seems to me to be the view of a man who is carried away by his enthusiasm to the total disregard of practical considerations. . . . I should not infer, from anything which you have said on the subject—either in 1877, or last year—that you would be prepared to go Dr Bucknill's length." Shaftesbury was able to reassure the Lord Chancellor that "In the principle of extinction of proprietary madhouses, I agree with my friend Dr Bucknill; but his mode of operation would amount to violent, and needless, confiscation."[148]

As new proposed legislation was debated, the issue of patients in single care prompted Bucknill to write to the Lord Chancellor and advocate that the principle of voluntary treatment should apply to cases in single care as well as in private asylums because "there are many insane persons whose mental condition makes it inadvisable that they should reside in their own families, who are yet quite capable of exercising a rational choice as to their residence in other families, and of enjoying all the amenities of domestic life, and I know that such patients do sometimes feel pained and humiliated by being confined as lunatics even as single patients."[149] In the event, the legislation that finally emerged as the 1890 Lunacy Act did not incorporate Bucknill's amendment. Nor did it close private asylums, although it forbade the issue of new licences with a view to eventual closure. Representatives of the Royal College of Physicians, including Henry Maudsley, were instrumental in ensuring that this act also permitted doctors who were not licensed as private asylum proprietors to in some circumstances receive more than one certified lunatic into their homes for domestic care and treatment.

After the death of his wife in 1889 Bucknill moved from Rugby to Bournemouth. He lived not only to be belatedly knighted in 1894 but also to hear of the premature death of his youngest son in Australia in 1895. Two years later, on July 20, 1897, his own life came to a close.

In summarizing Bucknill's career James Crichton-Browne perhaps too generously suggested that "for twenty years he was the acknowledged and dignified head of his department in this country, and mingled on an equal footing with all the finest intellects of his times."[150] In a more extended historical perspective the scale of his achievements seems rather more modest. Whereas Bucknill's decision to edit the *Asylum Journal of Mental Science* was prescient, his public statements from 1876 onwards frequently appear ill-timed and at odds with the consensus of his profession. Their direct impact on social policy was unquestionably slight, and for that reason their significance may be either overlooked or dismissed as eccentric. They constituted, however, some of the intellectual foundations on which Bucknill and others uncertainly sought to build an alternative basis for psychiatric careers, one outside and even pursued to some degree in conscious opposition to the still expanding realms of asylumdom. It is nonetheless ironic that someone who played such a central role in building a new profession based on asylum treatment should now be of renewed interest partly because of his historically less popular advocacy of noninstitutional care.

Chapter Eight

DEGENERATION AND DESPAIR:

HENRY MAUDSLEY (1835–1918)

> To me, the Universe was void all void of Life, of Purpose, of
> Volition, even of Hostility: it was one, huge, dead, immeasurable
> Steam-engine, rolling on, in its dead indifference, to grind me
> limb from limb . . . the foredone soul drowning
> slowly in quagmires of Despair.
> (*Thomas Carlyle*, Sartor Resartus, *1834*)

> It is plain that biography which estimates both the individual
> and his circumstances, and displays their reactions, can alone
> give an adequate account of the man.
> (*Henry Maudsley*, Physiology and Pathology of Mind, *1867*)

> Our concern as medical men is with the body. If there be such
> a thing as disease of the mind, we can do nothing for it.
> (*John Hughlings Jackson, "Remarks on the Evolution and
> Dissolution of the Nervous System," 1887–1888*)

> I have said that the practical religion of the day, the real guiding
> gospel of life, is money-getting; the professed religion is
> Christianity. . . . With a profession of faith that angels
> might adopt, there is too often a rule of practice
> which devils need not disdain."
> (*Henry Maudsley*, The Physiology and Pathology of Mind, *1867*)

IF JOHN HASLAM was perhaps the most famous (or infamous) mad-doctor of the early nineteenth century, and John Conolly the best-known
alienist of the optimistic mid-Victorian era, Conolly's son-in-law, Henry
Maudsley, must surely be reckoned the dominant medico-psychological
specialist of the last third of the century. Maudsley's materialism and his
positivism, his determinism and his Lamarckian evolutionism, not to mention his profound pessimism, were more thoroughgoing and unabashed
than can be found among most of his fellow alienists; but in all these respects late Victorian medico-psychological theorizing is nonetheless indelibly marked by his influence. Not that exerting a profound influence in these
quarters mattered much to Maudsley; for he was a man who had a profound

contempt for the intellectual qualities and practical accomplishments of most of his erstwhile colleagues, and by the mid 1890s, he was openly questioning whether alienists' interventions were producing more harm than good. By this time, too, his cynical and hypercritical manner and his calculated distancing of himself from the dominant forms of practice in the specialty had ensured his withdrawal into an ever deeper personal and professional isolation.

Maudsley's alienation from his psychiatric colleagues enabled him to be an exceptionally astute, if bitter, critic of the wishful thinking and self-interest that underpinned some of the Medico-Psychological Association's policies. However, his personal isolation and the wide spectrum of people he had succeeded in offending help to explain why he never achieved the public honours awarded other medical psychologists less intellectually distinguished and socially well-connected than he. Finally, though his prolific pen and the power that he drew from his position as editor of the *Journal of Mental Science* enabled him to become the dominant figure in the profession for almost a quarter century, in the longer view his role in founding the Maudsley Hospital and his comparatively isolated pioneering of lunacy consultancy based outside the walls of the asylum constituted his most significant contributions to the making of the mad-doctoring trade.

A DESOLATE UPBRINGING

Henry Maudsley was born at Rome Farm in Giggleswick in the Yorkshire Dales on February 5, 1835.[1] He was the fourth of eight children of a moderately well-to-do yeoman farmer, Thomas Maudsley, and of his wife Mary, née Bateson.[2] Though his childhood was not marked by the material deprivation endured by his future father-in-law, John Conolly, Maudsley shared with him (and with W.A.F. Browne and Samuel Gaskell) the emotionally wrenching experience of losing a parent at a very young age. But whereas Conolly, Browne, and Gaskell lost their fathers, in Maudsley's case it was his mother who died, just after he had turned ten years of age. A little more than a year after this catastrophe, three siblings—his sister Jennet and his twin brothers Richard and James—also succumbed to the tuberculosis that had killed her.

The emotional toll this must have taken on the young boy was all the greater since he now found himself in the hands of a father who, even before his wife's demise, was known to be of "a retiring character and remarkably reticent and reserved of speech, not inclined to be what is called sociable." Henry now endured "a succession of sombre and dreary years, for my father was so profoundly affected by my mother's death, to whom he was ardently attached, that his natural silence was increased and hardly a word passed between us boys and him except when absolutely necessary." The local school provided little respite, his days there being filled with rote learning of Greek and Latin, interspersed with an equally mechanical encounter with Euclidian geometry, undertaken "without any comprehension of the problems, learning the letters of the lines and angles by heart and repeating them offhand and instantly forgetting them."[3]

Only his mother's unmarried sister, Elizabeth, provided some relief from the emotional dreariness and emptiness of these years. His aunt, Maudsley recalled, "spent her whole life in beneficent work . . . teach[ing] reading writing and sewing to the village girls, and . . . training a body of them who were much sought after as servants." She now took her young nephew under her wing, providing some nourishment for "the emotional part of my nature." Generally not one to acknowledge his intellectual debts to others, Maudsley made an exception in this instance: "I owed more to her than I can reckon for the poetry which she used to repeat to me, and I, having got it by heart, used to rush into the kitchen and declaim to the servant. To that early and useful instruction I owe, I believe, my quality of style in my writings which has been ascribed to them; and my regret now is the frequent regret of maturity—that I can never express my gratitude to her. It would certainly appear that I owed much to the emotional quality of my maternal stock, which I inherited in a degree not displayed by my brothers."[4]

It was at Elizabeth's urging (and perhaps with some assistance from her purse) that four years later, the precocious young man escaped the confining and intellectually stultifying atmosphere of the village schoolhouse, being

> sent as a private pupil to the Rev. Alfred Newth [a friend of the Bateson family] who kept a small school for dissenting dayboys [at Oundle] and received four or five pupils into his house. He was a good classical and mathematical scholar, and well read in general literature, being made afterwards a Professor in the Manchester Independent College. I remained there with him for over two years, and benefitted immensely by the classical studies and the general opening and development of my mind. During that period, I learnt something of Homer, Herodotus, Thucydides, Aeschylus, Sophocles, and Euripides, and among Latin authors Sallust, Cicero, Tacitus, Horace, Livy, Thucydides [sic], Aeschylus [sic], Prometheus Vinctus and Tacitus [sic] were the authors whom I remember to have made some impression on my mind.[5]

It was a literary education that was to leave its mark on his own voluminous writings, while providing him with the ornamental classical learning that was de rigueur in the gentlemanly and upper-class circles from which his future patients would be drawn.

The Making of a Medico-Psychological Career

His dissenting background next drew Maudsley to matriculate at the University of London. Apparently on his own, he had now "decided that I should become medical" (rather than entering upon the clerical career his mother had intended for him). Once again, his aunt took an active role: "After due consideration of plans, it was decided to apprentice me to University College Hospital for five years. The apprenticeship was nominally to Mr. J. T. Clover, who was Resident Medical Officer at the time."[6]

Headstrong and difficult, and sardonic and sarcastic besides, Henry was a pupil few would have warmed to. He boasted that he arrived in London "self-assertive and stubbornly rebellious against all control, as I have always been"; and it was perhaps fortunate, in consequence, that his nominal mentor was "very much [pre]occupied with building up a private practice for himself outside the Hospital" so that he "did not take much pains to guide and teach me at the time, . . . and what little he took he soon abandoned." Clover saw enough of young Maudsley, however, that in later years he swore that "he never had but one pupil and would never have another."[7] When he left his post for full-time private practice, it was perhaps understandable, therefore, that no one stepped forward to take his place; the young Yorkshireman was left essentially to his own devices.

Possessed of an extraordinarily retentive memory, Maudsley had little difficulty impressing his examiners: he was able to regurgitate the contents of their texts on command and was rewarded for such performances with an impressive tally of ten gold medals for achieving "first place in all the classes in which I competed," afterwards exchanged at "Deutsch the clockmakers for a gold watch which I leave behind me to tick when my heart shall cease to tick."[8] Characteristically, though, he did only the work that suited him, ignoring or circumventing requirements he judged onerous and unpleasant. His attachment to the University College Hospital meant that "I had, of course, good opportunities of seeing patients who had suffered from accidents, of attending post-mortem examinations, and of pursuing clinical study; and it was entirely my own fault if I did not adequately avail myself of them, as assuredly I did not." So far as other aspects of his training were concerned, "I neglected practical work, did little dissection, and learnt my anatomy and botany from books. Worse still, I never attended a midwifery case, although attendance on six cases was obligatory by the regulations for the Licence of the College of Surgeons. The obstetric Physician-Assistant at the Hospital was my friend, and he managed to secure for me the requisite number of cases."[9] Small wonder that the only one of his teachers not bowled over by his feats of memory commented acerbically that "Maudsley has great abilities but he has chosen to throw them into the gutter"[10]—to which the target of his criticism responded in later years: "Happily I managed to pick some of them up again before they entirely rotted."[11]

Picking them up was not easy, however. As his expensive apprenticeship came to an end, Maudsley found he lacked "the resources necessary to stay in London to wait until I might get attached to a Hospital. But as my bent was to surgery, and I intended to become a surgeon, I applied for an advertised House Surgeonship at the Liverpool Southern Hospital, which I should have obtained but for the fact that a letter therefrom was sent to my London address and not forwarded to me in Yorkshire where I had gone temporarily after my application to await the reply. Thus, in the result the purposed tenour of my life was completely changed."[12]

By a quirk of fate, the aspiring surgeon now found himself diverted in a wholly unlooked-for direction. "Disheartened and disgusted" by his stroke of bad luck, Maudsley decided to abandon England altogether and to embark upon a career as a medical officer with the East India Company—a post which "required at that time experience of six months in an asylum." Coincidentally, at that very moment the local county asylum in the West Riding needed a temporary assistant medical officer, the incumbent superintendent having taken a six-month leave of absence for health reasons. Maudsley's apparently stellar academic record easily sufficed to secure him the appointment, and his experiences in asylums over the next four years— his only sustained contact with the institutionalized insane—formed the foundation for his career as a practitioner of psychological medicine.[13]

In the event, Maudsley's stay at Wakefield lasted nine months, until the resignation of the ailing superintendent (and the election of his deputy, John Cleaton, to head the asylum), brought about his departure. His newfound interest in insanity survived the rejection of his application for the post of medical officer at the York Asylum and even an unhappy few months as an assistant physician at the Essex County Asylum in Brentwood. (He subsequently complained that "the character of the Essex people, sly, secret and insincere, [was] distasteful to me.") Soon enough, however, his exile to the Home Counties came to a welcome close, when he received (with the aid of a strong recommendation from Cleaton) an appointment as superintendent of the Manchester Royal Lunatic Asylum in Cheadle.[14] At only twenty-four years of age, he found himself in charge of a small charity asylum, recently removed from Manchester to new buildings—an establishment which, quite unusually among asylums at this time, was somewhat underprovided with patients.

Maudsley's two predecessors at the Manchester Asylum had each lasted only a few months; neither satisfied the management committee.[15] His own tenure, by contrast, was unquestionably a success. Within a year, the committee had raised Maudsley's salary from £200 to £300 per annum. Patient

Figure 8.1. Henry Maudsley in his twenties, in his own words, "self-assertive and stubbornly rebellious against all control, as I have always been."

numbers rose steadily, as the asylum's reputation improved, and demand soon outran the supply of beds.[16] Despite his limited prior acquaintance with the plethora of pathology now facing him, and his even more striking lack of previous administrative experience, Maudsley succeeded in imposing a modicum of order on the establishment over which he presided, while finding time for extensive reading in the existing medical literature—British and Continental—on insanity and the treatment of the insane. What the patients made of him we do not know, but the testimonials his employers provided on his departure show that they, at least, were well satisfied. As one of the board of managers wrote, "If I knew what words of mine would be of most use to you, those are the words I should employ in expressing the entire satisfaction which I am sure every member of the committee has felt in the manner with which you have discharged the duties, medical and administrative, of the Resident Superintendent of the Manchester Lunatic Hospital."[17]

By 1860, Maudsley felt sufficiently confident of his grasp of his new specialty to venture into print by contributing two substantial articles to the *Journal of Mental Science*.[18] Three more papers followed over the next two years,[19] by which time he had resigned his post and was preparing to move back to London. Even more quickly than a number of other ambitious alienists, he seems to have tired of the isolated life of an asylum superintendent and to have become determined to seek some other means of pursuing his chosen vocation.[20] Quite what the alternative path to success might be was unclear, however, even to him.[21] With extremely limited financial resources, he was dependent upon his wits and his talent to make his way in the crowded and competitive metropolitan medical marketplace.

Main-chancing It in the Metropolis

Maudsley's essays had already received critical acclaim from his fellow specialists before his arrival in London. His retentive memory and his extensive knowledge of French and German as well as British writings on insanity lent great authority to his interventions, even though he was still less than thirty years of age. Within a matter of months he had established himself as someone who knew "more about the 'literature' of insanity than anyone else in England."[22] Immediately plunging into active participation in the affairs of the Association of Medical Officers of Asylums and Hospitals for the Insane (soon to be renamed, probably at his instigation, the Medico-Psychological Association),[23] he deftly cultivated close relationships with the small group of insiders who dominated its affairs. Due to deliver a paper, for instance, at the first annual meeting he had attended, in the summer of 1862, he noticed that time was short and ceded his place to the well-connected Lockhart Robertson, superintendent of the Sussex County Asylum (slightly spoiling the gesture by commenting mockingly that he was sure that "the members would be more generally interested" in what the latter had to say about the utilization of asylum sewage than in his own more abstruse remarks).[24] In October, he contributed an essay on "Middle Class Hospitals for the Insane" to the *Journal of Mental Science*, supporting what had long been one of John Conolly's pet projects.[25] Soon thereafter, drawn into the great man's intimate circle, he dined frequently with the group of ambitious younger alienists who met to pay court to Conolly at his small private madhouse, "The Lawn," in Hanwell.[26] A respectful notice of his future father-in-law's book on *Hamlet* in the *Westminster Review*,[27] endorsing in a qualified fashion Conolly's idée fixe that Hamlet was mad, must have further endeared him to the doyen of the profession. No doubt, too, Maudsley's spirited attack on routine confinement of the insane in his paper on "Delusions" would have reminded Conolly of his own youthful ideal of noninstitutional care for the insane, so that he may have seen Maudsley as a sympathetic intellectual successor.[28] Not long afterwards, the ambitious young man secured the ultimate mark of Conolly's favour, marriage to his remaining unmarried daughter.[29]

Maudsley's talent and political maneuvering brought him swift rewards. Within months of his arrival in the metropolis, Bucknill was compelled to resign as editor of the *Journal of Mental Science* on being appointed Chancery Visitor in Lunacy. Too junior and too recently arrived on the scene to aspire to succeed Bucknill directly, Maudsley promptly offered his services as an assistant to the new editor, Lockhart Robertson,[30] and was formally installed as coeditor a year later, in October 1863. The post was the more desirable since, in addition to providing its incumbent with a potentially powerful platform at the very centre of the Association's affairs, it brought with it a small stipend, thanks to the journal's growing success over its first decade of existence.[31] His energy and prolific pen made Maudsley ideally suited to exploit the opportunity this position represented, so that by the end of the 1860s, he had established himself by most measures as the dominant voice in the profession—rather anomalously in some respects because he lacked a position at the head of a public asylum or of a sizeable private institution at a time when the profession was virtually coextensive with men occupying such positions.

Maudsley had sought in these years a variety of institutional affiliations of the sort that could contribute to the development of a successful metropolitan practice. Initially, however, he met with only mixed results. Two years after arriving in London, he obtained a post as Junior Physician to the West London Hospital in Hammersmith, the kind of unpaid position that was vital to any medical man trying to build his credibility and visibility among the moneyed classes. He made an unsuccessful application for the chair of materia medica at his alma mater, and after that failure, agitated for University College to become the first English medical school to provide a regular "Course of Clinical Instruction in Mental Diseases . . . [for] all Candidates for the second M.B. Pass Examination." "Success" on this second occasion did not have the expected result: instead of being invited to deliver the lectures himself, Maudsley found that the opportunity instead passed to W.H.O. Sankey, a rival of whose abilities he was characteristically scornful. He then found himself faced with still another rejection early in 1866, when his application for the vacant position of physician to Bethlem was spurned, despite eloquent testimonials from such luminaries as Bucknill, Conolly, Thurnham, Lawrence, and Jenner (the Queen's surgeon and physician respectively), not to mention the eminent German alienist, Griesinger.[32]

On other fronts, though, the gamble he had taken in moving back to London now began to pay dividends. For a few years following his marriage, he found himself in competition for preferment and visibility with his newly acquired brother-in-law, Thomas Harrington Tuke,[33] nine years his senior and the proprietor of a more substantial and successful private asylum than Lawn House, Manor House in Chiswick.[34] Both men were elected honorary members of the Medico-Psychological Society of Paris in 1866 and of the Imperial College of Physicians in Vienna in 1868. Harrington Tuke became a Fellow of the Royal College of Physicians in 1868, Maudsley one year later in 1869.[35] But the contest between the two of them, if such it was, rapidly proved unequal. By the end of the 1860s, at the latest, Maudsley's intellectual reputation dwarfed his brother-in-law's, and he had established himself as *the* preeminent figure among British alienists.

Supported in the first instance by the stipend he received as editor of the *Journal of Mental Science* supplemented by the income from Conolly's former private practice, Maudsley made use of his prolific pen and the strategic advantages conferred by his position as coeditor of the *Journal of Mental Science* to heighten his professional visibility and influence. In the first year after he married, he published five clinical papers, three in his own journal and two in the *Lancet*. Remarkably, he also succeeded in completing and publishing his first book, *The Physiology and Pathology of Mind*, in January 1867—a treatise he repeatedly revised and republished in expanded and modified form over the three succeeding decades.[36] If the reviewer of the book in the *Lancet* sounded a warning note about Maudsley's "pugnacious intolerance," the *British Medical Journal* felt "confident that by its means Dr Maudsley will establish for himself the reputation of being a thoughtful and accomplished physician."[37]

The very title of his first book announced with characteristic aggressiveness Maudsley's uncompromising materialism, and in its preface he expressed his determination "to treat of mental phenomena from a physiological rather than from a metaphysical point of view."[38] Throughout his long career, he was to devote much of his considerable intellectual energy to a sustained and consistently hostile polemic against the "absurdity" of metaphysical musings about insanity, denouncing again and again as "fruitless" and "unscientific" all attempts to study mind "from the psychological point of view" and insisting that it could only be understood "inductively . . . from a physiological and pathological basis."[39] That his own views, consistently presented as the rigorous findings of the unsentimental man of science, themselves rested upon the flimsiest and most speculative of empirical foundations was seldom acknowledged,[40] "the apostle of heredity and of temperament"[41] dogmatically insisted instead that "no one whose opinion is of any value pretends now that [the phenomena of insanity] are anything more than the deranged functions of the supreme nervous centres of the body" and celebrated this advance in understanding as the product of medicine freeing itself from "the bondage of false theology and mischievous metaphysics" and of its "emancipat[ion] from the fables and superstitions of the vulgar."[42]

Maudsley's unflinching materialism and hostility to religion unquestionably discomforted many of his colleagues, who had nonetheless long since joined him in insisting on the centrality of the somatic. In his hands, their shared conviction that madness was rooted in disordered bodily functions now acquired a harder edge and was elaborated in a variety of novel directions.[43] Even in the early nineteenth century, alienists had pointed to defective heredity as an important etiological factor, predisposing the vulnerable to madness;[44] but in Maudsley's reworking of traditional views, hereditarian explanations of the origins of defective inhibitory control acquired a new force and significance. Drawing on his knowledge of the contemporary French literature on insanity, and particularly of the work of B. A. Morel,[45] he constructed a "physiological psychology" that used the language of degeneration to provide a rhetorical link between madness and the new theories of evolution. Likewise, there was no more formidable spokesman for the late Victorian consensus that the psychological symptoms of insanity, though they constituted the visible manifestations of the disorder and the features that provoked social intervention, were, from the "scientific" point of view, purely epiphenomenal, mere surface reflections of the underlying morbid state of the brain and nervous system.[46] "It is not our business," he asserted truculently, "it is not in our power, to explain *psychologically* the origins and nature of any of [the] depraved instincts [manifested in typical cases of insanity] . . . it is sufficient to establish their existence as facts of observation, and to set forth the pathological conditions under which they are produced: they are the facts of pathology, which should be observed and classified like other phenomena of disease. The explanation [of madness], when it comes, will come not from the mental, but from the physical side—from the study of the *neurosis* [the brain and nervous system], not from the analysis of the *psychosis*."[47] With equal bluntness, he drew a professionally comforting conclusion about the respective roles of the physician and psychologist in the therapeutics of insanity: "That which . . . has its foundation in a definite physical cause must have its cure in the production of a definite physical change . . . no culture of the mind, however careful, no effort of will, however strong, will avail to prevent irregular and convulsive action when a certain degree of instability of nervous element has, from one cause or another, been produced in the spinal cells. It would be equally absurd to preach control to the spasms of chorea, or restraint to the convulsions of epilepsy, as to preach moderation to the east wind, or gentleness to the hurricane."[48]

Metaphysical or theological views of the origins of insanity, as he saw it, were not merely therapeutically useless and scientifically wrong, but bore a heavy burden of responsibility for the mistreatment of the mad in earlier days. In Maudsley's eyes, "the iniquities practised upon the insane in olden times, the countless unnecessary and cruel sufferings which they underwent," could be attributed directly to the fears and hostility of the vulgar. Popular attitudes in their turn derived from "false views" of the nature of insanity that were quite possibly "legacies from that ancient superstition which regarded an insane person as tormented with an evil spirit in consequence of some great sin committed by him or his parents."[49] It was to the labours of a "few earnest members of the medical profession" and to the advance of medical science, he contended, that one could attribute the slow and painful improvement of the condition of the insane, for among society at large prejudice persisted, and "to be a lunatic, as public sentiment goes, is to be cut off socially from humanity."[50]

Paradoxically enough—though this was something of which Maudsley himself seemed utterly oblivious—his own materialistic and "scientific" view of madness simply recast this popular "shame, horror, and dread of insanity" and the attribution of madness to sin in a different and in many respects still more damning idiom. A convinced neo-Lamarckian, Maudsley repeatedly stressed the intergenerational transfer of acquired morbid characteristics as the explanation of both insanity and other forms of social pathology. Madness, his "science" demonstrated, was the penalty to be paid for vice and immorality, because "the so-called moral laws are laws of nature which [men] cannot break, any more than they can break physical laws, without avenging consequences. . . . As surely as the raindrop is formed and falls in obedience to physical law, so surely do causality and law reign in the production and distribution of morality and immorality on earth."[51] Excess of any sort threatened the mental integrity, if not of the sinner, then of future generations, and "the wicked man" must be brought "to realise distinctly the fact that his children and his children's children will be the heirs of his iniquities."[52] Predictably and inescapably, Maudsley argued, moral causes wrought physical changes on people's bodies, and these degenerative modifications of the organism were successively "transmitted as evil heritages to future generations: the acquired ill of the parent becomes the inborn infirmity of the offspring. It is not that the child necessarily inherits the particular disease of the parent, . . . but it does . . . inherit a constitution in which there is a certain inherent aptitude to some kind of morbid degeneration . . . an organic infirmity which shall be determined in its special morbid manifestations according to the external conditions of life."[53]

Within this harsh discourse, Maudsley's insistence on "kindness and consideration" towards the lunatic, and on the importance of "the humane system of treatment"[54] consorted uneasily, at best, with his view of the mad as inferior beings, the product of "literally an *unkinding* . . . a change from a higher to a lower kind . . . from a more to a less complex organization, a process of dissolution . . . [which produced] the transformation . . . into a new or abnormal kind which, incapable of rising in the scale of being, tends naturally to sink lower and lower."[55] As "a degeneration of the human kind," lunatics were the waste products of the evolutionary process, "morbid varieties fit only for excretion." Moreover, just as "in the body morbid elements cannot minister to healthy action, but, if not got rid of, give rise to disorder, or even death; so in the social fabric morbid varieties are themselves on the way of death, and if not sequestrated in the social system, or extruded from it, inevitably engender disorder incompatible with its stability."[56]

PROFESSIONAL DOMINANCE

Success followed rapidly after the appearance of *The Physiology and Pathology of Mind*. Most crucially of all, in May 1867 Maudsley was invited, together with the leading French and German alienists Morel and Griesinger, to give an opinion on the highly publicised question of the mental state of the Hapsburg Archduchess Charlotta, Empress of Mexico—an invitation that played a central role in establishing his credentials in aristocratic circles as the man to consult where questions of mental instability were at issue.[57] Other marks of his growing stature in the profession followed in dizzying succession: he secured a lectureship in insanity at St. Mary's Hospital in London in 1868; became professor of Medical Jurisprudence at University College London in 1869; and was invited to give the Gulstonian lectures to the Royal College of Physicians in 1870 (lectures that were subsequently published as *Body and Mind*).[58] The same year, Lockhart Robertson's resignation to assume the post of Lord Chancellor's Visitor in Lunacy allowed Maudsley to become senior editor of the *Journal of Mental Science* (jointly with John Sibbald until 1872, and thereafter with the assistance of Thomas Clouston).

The appearance of German and Italian translations of *The Physiology and Pathology of Mind* in 1870 meant that, in seconding Maudsley's nomination as president of the Medico-Psychological Association, Clouston could assert with confidence that Maudsley's "reputation [was] European" and that in elevating him to the presidency "we do ourselves honour . . . to a much greater extent than we honour him. . . . He is our President in fact and we ought to make him so in form." Barely thirty-five years of age, Maudsley found himself feted before his colleagues as "a man who has done more than any living Psychologist in this country for our science."[59]

Maudsley's first proposer had, conventionally enough, been G. W. Mould, the man whom Maudsley had recommended as his successor to the medical superintendency of Cheadle Royal in Manchester in 1862.[60] However, in basing Maudsley's claim to the presidency on his intellectual and scientific stature, Clouston broke with a tradition in which patient years of service to the Association had been rewarded with nomination for the presidency. Maudsley may have been editor of the *Journal of Mental Science* for seven years (as Bucknill had been before he was elected president at the age of forty-two), but he was still exceedingly young, and his election displaced and probably displeased those who were considerably senior to him and had many more years of service behind them. In particular, Harrington Tuke had been biding his time as general secretary of the Association since being narrowly defeated for the presidential nomination by David Skae, when he himself had been only thirty-six.[61] Their contrasting fates at the hands of their fellow alienists may have given Harrington Tuke yet one more reason to resent his brother-in-law, a resentment that was to surface very publicly before the end of the decade.

Having elected Maudsley to head their Association, and after lavishing praise on his standing as the real as well as nominal leader of their profession, his colleagues must have been mortified by the contents of his presidential address. "Insanity and Its Treatment," delivered on August 3, 1871, at the Royal College of Physicians, was nothing less than a sustained assault on the raison d'être of the specialty as it then perceived itself, a slaughter of sacred cows that undoubtedly left his audience squirming in their seats. In swift succession, Maudsley held up to scrutiny and mercilessly mocked doctrines and practices "physicians engaged in the care and treatment of insane persons" had spent half a century establishing and legitimizing, all the while protesting that he was only "asking, in the Socratic spirit, what we really know, and what we only think we know."[62]

He began with an examination of the "startling fact" of the "regular increase . . . in the insane population for the last twenty years" and asked whether the profession might contribute significantly to "the prevention of insanity."[63] The answer, he suggested, was essentially negative. One could take for granted, of course, "the important part which hereditary disposition plays in the causation of insanity," but this knowledge scarcely solved "our practical difficulties":

> It is certain that if we were interested in the breeding of a variety of animals, we should not think of continuing to breed from a stock which was wanting in those qualities that were the highest characteristics of the species. . . . But to my mind very great difficulties lie in the way of declaring what are rational grounds unfitting a person for marriage . . . it is impossible to determine what ancestral influences are of so baneful a character as rightly to preclude an individual from continuing his species. . . . [Besides] if all persons in whose families there was the history of some nervous disease were placed under the ban of a compulsory continence, or at any rate were debarred from marriage, it is clear that there would be some danger of unpeopling the world.[64]

The impossibility of the mental hygienist's task was made even more manifest by the sheer variety of

> predisposing causes of mental degeneracy in the offspring. Take, for example, that deterioration of character which is produced in the individual by a life of mean and petty deceit and grasping selfishness in business, where there is no conscience in work, where there is not a single great or generous aim, where the highest aim is the acquisition of riches, the highest ideal the appearance of worldly respectability, and the result of its pursuit a life-long hypocrisy, conscious or unconscious;—and can we have at work more powerful causes of degeneracy in the next generation? It is the man who spends six days of the week in that sort of occupation, and on the seventh day appears as deacon in a chapel or as teacher in a Sunday school whom, had we knowledge enough to warrant interference, we should do well to prevent propagating his kind. Of course no one would think of doing so, but this *reductio ad absurdum* of the matter may serve to show how little justified science is, in its present state, in interfering in the dearest interests and nearest relations of human life.[65]

Taken together, Maudsley concluded, these considerations made it plain that although "rather loose assertions are sometimes made confidently, as if they were well-established facts of observation," in reality "[they] have no better foundation than conjecture." And so far from being in a position to offer practical advice, the profession must concede that its role "for some time to come must be to learn rather than to teach, to practice observation until it has acquired much more exact data than it is yet in possession of."[66]

If on this front the profession's intellectual and practical resources were depressingly thin and insubstantial, perhaps it redeemed itself through its successful treatment of those who had actually gone mad in the asylums of which alienists were so proud? Not in the view of its iconoclastic president.

Well aware of the fact that, although his own connections to the world of the asylum were by now tenuous in the extreme, his audience depended for their very livelihood and social standing on the existence and legitimacy of these establishments, Maudsley was nonetheless utterly unsparing in analyzing the deficiencies of such places. He referred scornfully to "the old notions regarding insanity" (that is, the conventional wisdom his colleagues had spent a half century and more establishing): "first, that the best means to promote the recovery of an insane person was to send him to an asylum; and secondly, that so long as he remained insane there was no better place for him than the asylum."[67] In their place, he ventured two of his own: "The first is, that not many persons recover in asylums who might not recover equally well out of them; and the second is, that the removal of an insane person from the asylum sometimes conduces to his recovery."[68]

Certain cases, he conceded, "cannot be treated satisfactorily out of asylums. But," he immediately added, "this is not because there is any special virtue in asylum treatment." Rather, it was simply that pauper lunatics could not be dealt with as cheaply elsewhere and that even for the rich an asylum provided an "efficient means of exercising proper care and control, where great care and watchfulness are necessary to prevent the patient doing harm to himself or others."[69] Therapeutically, he found little that was positive to say about specialized institutions. The acknowledgement that "the discipline of the establishment counts for a great deal in some cases" was immediately undercut by the observation that this came at the price of the neglect of "the patient's individuality . . . he becomes one of a crowd, the majority of whom are not expected ever to get well, and his moral treatment is little more than the routine of the establishment and the dictatorship of an attendant."[70] In all too many cases, the asylum actually made the patient permanently worse: "The confinement, the monotony, the lack of interest and occupation, the absence of family relations, which are inevitable in an asylum, . . . do, after a certain time . . . more than counterbalance the benefit of seclusion. The patient has no proper outlet for his energies, and an outlet is made for them in maniacal excitement and perverse conduct; he goes through recurrent attacks of that kind, and finally sinks into a state of chronic insanity—becomes an asylum-made lunatic."[71]

For all Maudsley's occasional diplomatic gestures—his claim, for instance, that "in making these remarks, I do not overlook the value of the skilled attendance and of the supervision which asylums furnish"[72]—his speech constituted a devastating assault from within on the very foundations of the profession at whose head he now stood.[73] Not yet finished with his wholesale criticisms, he turned at the last to the question of "the use and abuse of sedatives in the treatment of insanity." Here, as elsewhere, he contended, "we are grievously in want of exact information."[74]

Judging by their practices, he recognized that his colleagues had an extraordinary faith in these chemicals, though "no one, so far as I know, has ever yet tried the experiment of treating one case of acute insanity without giving any sedative whatever, and of treating another case, as nearly like it as possible, with sedatives, and of observing the results."[75] For his own part, he granted that "drugs will, no doubt, generally quiet a patient, but the question is whether they promote recovery. In fact, the question is a larger one—whether the forcible quieting of a patient by narcotic medicines does not diminish his excitement at the expense of his mental power,—whether it is not, in fact, 'to make a solitude and call it peace' . . . whether putting the patient's brain into chemical restraint, so to speak, does really benefit them?"[76]

With the arrogant sense of intellectual superiority and blithe disregard of ordinary social conventions that would end up distancing him from virtually all his fellow professionals, Maudsley finally turned his fire on the very man who had nominated him in such fulsome terms for the presidency. Clouston's attempts to measure the value of various drug treatments experimentally were initially praised as "admirable" and worthy of imitation, but stinging criticism rapidly followed. His colleague's claims of success were dismissed as misleading and overblown ("although 80 per cent. are reputed to have been more or less benefitted, I do not find that many got well; in fact, only one recovered"); and Maudsley then concluded on an even more insulting note: "I should like to ask Dr. Clouston whether he feels quite sure that his experiments for nine consecutive months with bromide of potassium and cannabis Indica have not helped his patients down hill, and burdened the rates of Cumberland and Westmoreland with some incurable lunatics."[77]

Small wonder that at the conclusion of this swingeing and stinging verbal assault, Clouston himself rose to complain of his distinguished colleague's "utter and entire scepticism."[78] Other comments from the floor were equally hostile. William Wood, for example, himself a former president of the Association, chided Maudsley for inflicting grave damage on the specialty's already fragile public reputation: "The fact is, any physician connected with an asylum is to a certain extent tabooed [sic]. A mad physician is a dangerous character, and if we find in our own class men who are occupying high positions, saying anything to encourage the popular notion that we are unworthy of the trust that is reposed in us, I think we ought to try and set ourselves right."[79] And as Maudsley was soon to find, the hornets' nest he had stirred up would not go away.

One of the numerous hostages to fortune he had offered up in his speech was an attack on religion as the source of morality, coupled with the suggestion that its place ought to be taken by "the method of positive science"—a stance he conceded others might find "sacrilegious."[80] As he ought to have expected, here, too, his views came under severe criticism. In the following year the incoming president, Sir James Coxe, devoted his address to the Association to a direct riposte, emphasizing the effectiveness of Christian moral training in preventing insanity. This speech was in fact an elegant restatement of Christian phrenology, with its emphasis on "living" rather than "old" religion;[81] but the response of his colleagues made plain their eagerness to embrace a renewed assertion of the fundamental compatibility of mental science and religious teaching. It seems more than a coincidence, for instance, that at the same meeting Thomas Clouston, who among his other objections had criticized Maudsley's presidential address for ignoring the therapeutic value of spirituality, was elected to work alongside Maudsley as coeditor of the *Journal of Mental Science*.

A year later, perhaps in an attempt to stem the reaction against him in the MPA, Maudsley proposed Harrington Tuke's nomination as president.[82] Despite this mollifying gesture, when his brother-in-law took the presidential chair in 1873, a first attempt was made to remove Maudsley as editor, when another former president of the Association, Robert Boyd, proposed that the editorship of the journal should become a function of the presidency. This amendment to the by-laws would of course have ousted Maudsley in favour of Harrington Tuke, and, though the motion did not pass, it suggests that the disquiet aroused by his heterodoxy was not dying down.[83]

MOUNTING CRITICISM AND THE ABANDONMENT OF ASYLUMDOM

It seems clear, at least in retrospect, that by the early 1870s, Maudsley had entirely abandoned any lingering idea he may once have had of resuming a career at the head of an asylum. He complained bitterly about "the old and bad theory that insanity is a disease quite out of the category of other diseases, demanding a sort of incarceration," about attempts to create an asylum-based "monopoly" over the treatment of lunatics, and about efforts "to render it impossible for any physician to practice with much success in the treatment of mental disorders who has not set up for himself an asylum."[84] Refusing to accept these limitations and making use of his university and hospital connections and the prominence he obtained from his writings, he began to cultivate his connections with the general medical elite and to try to construct an alternative career path for himself, one built almost exclusively around the consulting room. Possibly as early as 1870 (and certainly by 1872) Maudsley and his wife moved from Hanwell to a more suitable address for a metropolitan consultant, 9 Hanover Square, immediately adjacent to the Royal Medical and Chirurgical Society, and in close proximity to the residence of Sir James Paget (perhaps the most prominent surgeon of the age, and a man who numbered both the Queen and the Prince of Wales among his patients). By 1874, he had taken steps to divest himself of "The

Lawn," ultimately arranging for the transfer of its lease and licence to Emma Dixon,[85] who, together with her niece and companion, set herself up as the "proprietor" of a "private asylum for ladies" and soon expanded its lunatic population to a total of eight. Once he was physically present on a regular basis at the centre of the London medical scene, he immediately sought on various fronts to heighten his visibility in both lay and medical circles, an essential step if his gamble on establishing this novel form of specialized practice was to succeed. As well as his Gulstonian Lectures to the Royal College of Physicians, he managed to be chosen as the first president of the new "psychological section" of the British Medical Association.[86] His articles appeared frequently in general medical journals,[87] as well as more occasionally in periodicals with a predominantly lay audience.[88] A number of his books, too, acquired a distinctly more polemical tone and were obviously aimed at a far wider audience than the few hundred specialists in psychological medicine.[89]

Increasingly distant from the world of the asylum within which most alienists plied their trade, and never much interested in the mundane administrative chores and details that absorbed so much of their lives, Maudsley's position as editor of the *Journal of Mental Science* became ever more anomalous. Nonetheless, until the late 1870s, few of his erstwhile colleagues seemed to have the stomach to take on such a formidable opponent, someone whose considerable intellect was more than matched by the savagery of his pen and a harshly dismissive way with those who disagreed with him.[90] At the Association's annual meeting in August 1877, however, the long-simmering discontent with him finally moved explosively into the open.

The assault on Maudsley's position had obviously been planned in advance and involved several members of the Association's inner circle. Bucknill, who had resigned his position as Chancery Visitor two years earlier, had been persuaded to write to the Secretary, Rhys Williams, before the meeting to offer to resume his previous position as editor of the *Journal of Mental Science*. When the proceedings themselves began, Harrington Tuke rose on cue to propose that Dr. Bucknill should "offer himself as Editor of the Journal in the event of the resignation of Dr. Maudsley. . . . I am not myself personally entirely satisfied," he continued, "with the way the Journal is at present conducted. The great literary abilities of the editors are unquestionable; I think no one could say the Journal could be better edited, or done with greater pains, and perhaps better success, but there are certain doctrines taught there, certain tenets, which are contrary and repugnant to me, and I may say, to some others here . . . the present editor or editors of the Journal in their doctrines do not represent the majority of the Association . . . [and] I understand that Dr. Maudsley proposes to resign next January." Murray Lindsay immediately seconded the motion, by complaining that in Maudsley's hands, "the Journal has not done for the Association what it might have done, what it ought to have done, and what it was expected to have done. It has not advanced our interests, not been of that practical use we have looked for. . . . I regret to say its weight has not been very much felt in high quarters, if we may judge from the results." In response, Maudsley pronounced himself "not in the least anxious to continue the job" and "entirely in the hands of the Association," but after a prolonged and confused debate, he and Clouston, somewhat surprisingly, were reelected by a margin of twenty-eight votes to nine, with the formal vote having been forced by Harrington Tuke "as a lesson to the present editor."[91]

This unseemly episode must have made clear to Maudsley, if he was somehow unaware of the fact, how deeply his dominance was resented by some of the more powerful alienists in the Association. He was, besides, but little inclined to risk further humiliation at the hands of people for whom he had, for the most part, a thinly veiled contempt. By the time the Association reassembled in July 1878, faced with the prospect that Harrington Tuke would again force the issue of his editorship to a vote, he had accordingly decided to submit his resignation, a course he persisted in even when Bucknill, of all people, urged him to reconsider his position.[92]

After two such painful experiences and his forced departure, Maudsley rarely published in the journal that he had edited for fifteen years. Even his attendance at Association meetings became somewhat erratic, before he abandoned his membership entirely in 1890. Apparently he was not, like Savage, invited to become a founder member of the Neurological Society in 1886, nor, as Charles Mercier was, asked to contribute to the journal *Brain* from 1878. Effectively, he was therefore compelled to publish articles on "The Physical Conditions of Consciousness" (1887), "The Double Brain" (1888), and "The Cerebral Cortex and Its Work" (1889) in the philosophical and psychological *Mind* (founded 1876), where he must have been mortified to find himself described by one reviewer as a "*Metaphysicien malgré lui.*"[93]

What led to Henry Maudsley's estrangement from his fellow professionals, and what accounts for the extraordinary role his brother-in-law played in bringing about his departure? The bitterness and extreme lengths to which the latter went in trying to undermine his position suggests that some deep and long-standing animosities were at work. Harrington Tuke possessed, in fact, no shortage of possible motives. Trained at Hanwell Asylum, married to one of Conolly's elder daughters, Sophia Jane, since 1852, and proprietor of Manor House private asylum in Chiswick, he must for a long time have seen himself as the natural heir to Conolly's private medical practice in London. Conolly's eldest daughter was married to a Chinese missionary, his nonmedically qualified son had emigrated to New Zealand in 1865, and his remaining daughter was seemingly destined for the life of a spinster. Since 1863, Conolly had shared Harrington Tuke's consulting rooms at 37

Figure 8.2. Lawn House, Hanwell, used by both John Conolly and his son-in-law, Henry Maudsley, as a private asylum for the reception of insane ladies.

Albemarle Street, and given his father-in-law's failing health, the younger man had every reason to expect that the entire practice and the valuable connection to the Conolly name would soon be his.[94] At the very last, however, barely a month before Conolly's death, Maudsley married his hitherto unmarriageable youngest daughter; and, when the will was read, it emerged that the newcomer, not Harrington Tuke, was to take over as proprietor of Conolly's private asylum, Lawn House in Hanwell—the lease having been transferred to Anne Caroline prior to her marriage. Simultaneously, Maudsley also took over Conolly's positions as visiting physician to Moorcroft House and Wood End private asylums.

Having arrived on the scene so late and snatched away the prizes his brother-in-law may justly have thought were his, Maudsley then rubbed salt in the wounds by taking advantage of his position as coeditor of the Journal to write the official obituary of his father-in-law. It was not just a matter of presumption: the recently acquainted man-on-the-make elbowing aside someone who had a far longer and more intimate knowledge of his subject. Rather, it was that the "memoir" Maudsley produced was such an extraordinary and offensive document, breaking with the conventions of the obituarist to dwell minutely on Conolly's failings and deficiencies, personal and professional, while according his accomplishments only the most grudging of praise. Conolly was described as a weak man, one who "never seemed heartily to recognise or accept the stern and painful necessities of life." A poor physician undistinguished "in either the investigation of disease or in its treatment," a man for whom "the actual practice of his profession was not agreeable" and whose writings were "vague and diffuse, wanting in exact facts and practical information," Conolly (in Maudsley's portrait, at least) was a feckless creature who had "a liking for enjoyment without a liking for paying the painful cost of it." Easily flattered, impulsive, prone to shrink "from the task that was painful to him" and disinclined "to renounce a gratification which appealed to [him]" even when he lacked the resources to afford it, much of his life was marked by "energy misspent in cultivating talents that never could be brought to perfection, and in vague activities which, though benevolently aimed, were practically aimless." At the last, even the great success he ultimately enjoyed was "without conscious design of his own, driven by the necessities of failure arising partly out of defects of character."

By any normal standards of etiquette and propriety, this obituary was an odd, in some respects an odious, performance, scarcely calculated to endear its author to anyone linked by ties of blood or marriage to its subject. Moreover, still other factors made a clash between Harrington Tuke and Maudsley likely. In his own obituaries, Harrington Tuke is described as "a genial host, a cheery physician and an amiable companion," whose "gentleness and generosity secured for him the affection of a wide circle of friends."[95] No one would have thought to apply such adjectives to Maudsley. Indeed, it is difficult to imagine a personality more at odds with Maudsley's "hypercritical," "sententious," "cynical and rather unfriendly" temperament.[96] Whilst Maudsley's marriage was childless, the size of Harrington Tuke's family is variously estimated by his obituarists as somewhere between six and eight. These personal differences are nicely paralleled by the contrast in their styles of clinical practice. Whilst Harrington Tuke enjoyed playing paterfamilias to his patients at Manor House, Maudsley's distaste for close association with his patients may have provided one personal motivation to gradually develop his private practice into consultancy.[97] There were, moreover, some fundamental disagreements in the way in which they conceptualized mental disorders and their own therapeutic role as asylum physicians. Where Harrington Tuke was Christian and optimistic, Maudsley was materialist and pessimistic. Despite their relative closeness in terms of age, this difference between them is almost generational. Harrington Tuke worked from a mid-Victorian psychophysiological perspective where attention to medical and moral treatment were considered equally important and faith and prayer might be beneficial in restoring mental equilibrium. In contrast, Maudsley helped to fashion late-Victorian perceptions of mental illness as the result of hereditary degeneration, a disease that might be inhibited through moral vigilance, but that given the contemporary state of medical knowledge, was tragically incurable.

These differences, however, were all of long standing and cannot explain either the timing of the attack on Maudsley's position or Harrington Tuke's ability to muster substantial support from other active members of the MPA. Maudsley's materialism, and to a lesser extent his therapeutic nihilism, have sometimes been blamed for his sudden loss of favour with his colleagues,[98] but again, these beliefs of his were scarcely revealed for the first time at the end of the 1870s. Both, as we have seen, were prominently featured in Maudsley's presidential address in 1871, where he suggested that ethical principles were best derived from science rather than Christianity and questioned the therapeutic benefits of chemical sedation.[99] Such arguments, however, were generally controversial and undoubtedly served to thin the ranks of Maudsley's defenders when his position came under attack. Likewise, the sting of his sarcasm, which may have deterred many from overtly criticizing him while his position seemed impregnable, made him numerous enemies and few friends, and hence heightened his vulnerability in the long run.

So what *had* changed by 1877? The answer may lie in the third main point of Maudsley's presidential address, his criticism of institutional care and his suggestion that the insane had as much chance of recovery outside as inside an asylum. Although this led to fewer immediate reactions in 1871, by 1877 it had become a central issue, with the appointment of a Select Committee by the House of Commons to consider the lunacy laws from the point of view of civil liberties. For those alienists making their livings in the long-stigmatized private asylum sector, the threat of restrictive legislation, and perhaps even the abolition of the profit-making sector, was an extremely worrisome development; and Maudsley's status as the editor of the profession's journal gave his heterodox views on this subject a professional legitimacy his colleagues could well have done without.

Harrington Tuke had particularly pointed reasons for leading the attack on Maudsley's editorship at this time. By 1876 Maudsley had transferred the licence of Conolly's private asylum, Lawn House, to an outsider. If Harrington Tuke had felt that he had been cheated of his own inheritance of Conolly's medical practice, then he may have hoped that his own sons might one day fare differently with the childless Maudsley,[100] and those hopes were now permanently dashed. Worse still, the licence had been handed over to a woman—an asylum matron no less—though Maudsley was scarcely an advocate of women's entry into medicine or other professional careers. Contemptuous of his colleagues, Maudsley was implicitly suggesting that if the chronic insane were incurable, and only required feeding, bathing, and nursing in an ordinary homelike environment, the careful domestic management of mid-Victorian asylums could properly be left to women; it was unimportant for private asylum proprietors to be medically qualified.

This was an unpopular point of view when, as a *British Medical Journal* editorial complained in March 1877, the Lunacy Commissioners' refusal to issue new licences in the metropolis gave existing proprietors a virtual monopoly on private practice.[101] In his evidence to the Select Committee in April 1877 Harrington Tuke repeatedly argued that medical men were in every respect more desirable as the heads of private madhouses.[102] Maudsley, by contrast, stressed only that it was important for new cases to receive early treatment from someone who was medically qualified, and in fact he recommended that this should be in single medical care rather than in an asylum.[103]

Even without the personal offence caused by the transfer of the licence of Lawn House out of the family, Harrington Tuke may well have felt that it was inappropriate for someone with Maudsley's publicly expressed doubts about asylum treatment to be editing the *Journal of Mental Science* at this crucial time in the profession's history. Furthermore, one case of alleged wrongful confinement investigated by the Select Committee, Louisa Lowe, had been a patient of Maudsley's at Lawn House, so that Maudsley might be implicated personally by the report and would be unable to appear as a neutral professional commentator.[104] Both were concerns the profession at large would have broadly shared.

By the time of the annual general meeting of the Association in August, however, Harrington Tuke had still more pressing personal reasons to fear the outcome of the Select Committee's hearings. In July 1877, he had been hauled up before the Lunacy Commissioners to explain the death of a suicidal patient at Manor House, who had managed to strangle himself from his bedposts despite being mechanically restrained. This patient's attendant was prosecuted for wilful neglect, after admitting that he had restrained the patient without Harrington Tuke's knowledge and then left him unattended. However, during the trial the attendant alleged that, in order to prevent a scandal, Harrington Tuke had offered to pay his fine if he pleaded guilty and had promised he would also pay the attendant and his family to emigrate to America once the case was over. Although the Lunacy Commissioners decided that this had been no more than a malicious allegation, Harrington Tuke's denunciation of Maudsley's editorship came one week before this case became public knowledge in the Lunacy Commissioners' Annual Report.[105] In the light of that report, Manor House would be particularly vulnerable to any Select Committee recommendation for the closure of private asylums where patients' civil liberties had been shown to be at risk.

In August 1877, other members of the Association naturally shared Harrington Tuke's concern about the outcome of the Select Committee's hearings. The very vagueness of Harrington Tuke's unspecific allusion to "certain doctrines" and "certain tenets" advanced in the *Journal of Mental Science* which were "contrary and repugnant to him" invited members to vote about whatever most concerned them: materialism, therapeutic nihilism, or Maudsley's attacks on asylum treatment. In seconding Harrington Tuke's proposal, however, Murray Lindsay specifically homed in on the fact that under Maudsley's editorship the journal had failed to represent the interests of the Association.

In view of the level of concern about the government enquiry, it was in fact a tribute to Maudsley's standing in the MPA that Harrington Tuke was unable to muster a majority.[106] However, events during the following year may have increased Maudsley's unpopularity. Whilst Maudsley was still acting as coeditor with Clouston, and technically was the senior editor, Clouston published a summary of evidence to the Select Committee that included a scathing and satirical account of Harrington Tuke's testimony.[107]

In answer to the Select Committee's questions, Harrington Tuke had claimed that private asylums had a higher cure rate than registered hospitals, which of course included Maudsley's former asylum, Cheadle Royal, and Clouston's present one, Morningside Asylum in Edinburgh.[108] However, Clouston went beyond the evidence collected by the enquiry in publishing details of low cure rates at the two private asylums with which Harrington Tuke was connected and in drawing attention to the recent suicide at Manor House as evidence of alleged mismanagement and excessive reliance on mechanical restraint.[109] Harrington Tuke responded by sending a solicitor's letter, accusing Clouston of a malicious attempt to damage his professional reputation. After a further exchange of letters, in which Harrington Tuke showed himself to have been particularly upset, as Conolly's son-in-law, by the allegations about mechanical restraint, Clouston published the entire correspondence in the final issue of the *Journal of Mental Science* for which Maudsley served as coeditor.

These letters suggest that Maudsley and Harrington Tuke had had very little contact in the early summer of 1877, so that Harrington Tuke was hardly in a position to know, as he had informed the MPA, that Maudsley was thinking of resigning as editor. Though at the next annual meeting of the Association in July 1878, Harrington Tuke emphasized that he had intended to criticize Maudsley's editorship rather than Clouston's, and Maudsley made a point of saying that his contribution as editor during the previous year had been only nominal,[110] some members of the Association may nonetheless have suspected that Maudsley's hand had been pushing Clouston's pen. Certainly, the personal vindictiveness of the attack, which constituted a serious breach of professional ethics, was far more characteristic of Maudsley's style than of Clouston's.[111]

MUTUAL ALIENATION

Maudsley's resignation failed to dissipate the substantial hostility amongst those who had joined Tuke in criticising his editorship. George Fielding Blandford (1829–1911), who had published a critical reply to Maudsley's presidential address in 1871, and as president had chaired the meeting where Maudsley's resignation was debated, remained a particularly fierce opponent. Educated at Rugby and Oxford, he had many reasons to disapprove of Maudsley. A former private asylum proprietor, who lectured at Harrington Tuke's former medical school, St. George's (which had strong Evangelical affiliations), Blandford was a sincere Christian who operated a private consultancy practice with a similar clientele to Maudsley's. In 1877, Blandford must have been disturbed to learn that, in his evidence to the Select Committee, the Evangelical Earl of Shaftesbury had singled out not only Blandford and Bucknill, but the materialist Maudsley, for especially appreciative praise of their talents as private physicians.[112] It may well have been Blandford who, as one of a tiny minority of Oxford-educated members of the MPA, authored the frankly hostile reviews of Maudsley's publications that appeared in the *Journal of Mental Science* over the name of "Oxon" from 1879 onwards.[113]

After 1878, as we have noted, Maudsley continued to attend meetings of the MPA very occasionally, mostly when friends or former colleagues were presiding, or when his critics were likely to be absent. In 1880, the annual general meeting was held at University College London, where Maudsley had been professor of medical jurisprudence until 1879. Maudsley's successor at Cheadle, and proposer as president of the MPA, George Mould, was in the presidential chair. In 1884, Henry Rayner, a convinced devolutionist who had become medical superintendent of the male wards at Hanwell in the early 1870s, and had therefore been a neighbour of Maudsley's until 1876, chaired the annual general meeting. Maudsley revealed himself as unrepentantly belligerent at this meeting. In reply to Rayner's address, Maudsley commented first that the therapeutic benefits of chemical sedation had been grossly exaggerated and second that the insane might recover more quickly in cottages than asylums.[114] His next attendance was in 1887, when Harrington Tuke was absent on account of illness. Maudsley's subsequent appearance at quarterly meetings in January and April suggests that he may have regarded Harrington Tuke's continuing, and in the event terminal, illness as an opportunity to reestablish friendly relations with the Association, but if so he had underestimated the strength of feeling against him.

In April, Hack Tuke deployed gentle sarcasm in thanking Maudsley for reading a paper to the quarterly meeting, commenting that: "Although Dr Maudsley will probably not care to be associated with angels, there was one particular in which they bore a certain resemblance, Dr Maudsley's visits to the meetings of the Association were like theirs, few and far between."[115] It is surely significant, too, that with the exception of this paper on "Crime and Criminals," Hack Tuke and Savage never published any papers by Maudsley during their seventeen-year editorship of the *Journal of Mental Science*. Maudsley's next contribution to the journal appeared in 1895 in the first issue to be coedited by Henry Rayner.[116]

Hack Tuke's Quaker background may explain his opposition to the materialist Maudsley, but Savage's is less easy to understand. Nevertheless, a clash with Savage may have led to Maudsley's final rift with the MPA. Despite the facts that Harrington Tuke died in June 1888 and Maudsley's former ally Thomas Clouston was in the presidential chair at the annual meeting in August 1888, Maudsley did not attend. His name disappeared from the list of members of the Association in 1890, and he was not to attend another meeting of the Association until he was invited to read a paper on "The New Psychology" in 1900.[117] No direct evidence exists of what happened to provoke Maudsley's resignation or removal from the Association, but circumstantial evidence suggests a possible link between these events and Maudsley's strained relations with Savage.

In the late 1880s while new lunacy legislation was being drafted in slow response to the 1877 Select Committee's report, the question of the use of mechanical restraint became publicly controversial, and Savage was closely identified with the group that favoured greater freedom to use restraint. Maudsley, however, consistently opposing the use of mechanical restraint throughout his career,[118] had insisted that in advocating less chemical sedation he had not been proposing a return to mechanical restraint. In the 1870s, despite the murder of one Commissioner in Lunacy by a violent patient in 1873, the prorestraint movement had made little headway. By the late 1880s however several factors made change possible. Lord Shaftesbury, always a keen and powerful proponent of nonrestraint, died in 1886; within the psychiatric profession increased fears about the damaging effects of prolonged chemical sedation encouraged some asylum physicians to reconsider their attitude to mechanical restraint; and, under Savage's and Hack Tuke's editorship, the *Journal of Mental Science* helped to shape a change in attitudes such that mechanical restraint once more appeared respectable.

Harrington Tuke's obituary, for example, used the ambiguities surrounding his use of restraint in 1877 to praise him as someone who had not been a rigid follower of his father-in-law's advocacy of nonrestraint, which was now disparagingly dubbed "Conollyism."[119] Later in the same year Savage was placed at the centre of the debate on the subject when Bucknill wrote to the *Times* criticizing Savage's reliance on mechanical restraint at Bethlem.[120] Bucknill may have hoped to provoke an investigation into the abuse of restraint. Instead a clause was drafted into the lunacy bill at the committee stage which aimed to set limits to the use of mechanical restraint by only permitting its use for medical or surgical purposes—a clause that Savage and Hack Tuke welcomed on the grounds that "medical superintendents of asylums will now have legal authority for applying 'instruments and appliances' in the treatment of patients without the doubts and misgivings they have long suffered from as to whether mechanical restraint is or is not a legitimate form of treatment."[121]

Maudsley's name did not appear in these debates, but at the annual general meeting of the MPA in 1887, he had voiced concern that "during the last 2 years [he had] seen restraint practiced which [he had] never seen in his life."[122] Although he was referring in this instance to the use of restraint in single cases Maudsley also had a particular interest in criminal insanity which led him to visit Bethlem—whereas Bucknill, in retirement at Bournemouth, apologised in his letter to the *Times* for the fact that he had not been able to verify Savage's use of restraint personally. Ill-health had prevented him from being as active as he would have liked as a governor of Bethlem.[123] Perhaps Maudsley had alerted Bucknill to Savage's use of restraint. This could explain why, in his obituary of Maudsley, Savage recalled that he had once accused Maudsley of having more affection for humanity than the individual man, going on in the same passage to acknowledge that Maudsley was "jealous of any return to undue control being used over [the insane]."[124] Since Bucknill's correspondence with Bethlem about the extent of use of restraint began in July 1888, Maudsley's engagement in this controversy could also explain the otherwise unexpected timing of his withdrawal from the Association.[125]

Maudsley's criticism of the use of mechanical restraint was consistent and from every indication sincere, but he could also have been suspected of having personal motives for attempting to damage Savage's reputation at this time. Like Maudsley in the 1870s, in the late 1880s Savage had been gradually building up a consultancy practice. One of Bucknill's criticisms of Savage, which he could not have gleaned from Bethlem's annual reports, was of Savage's repeated absences from Bethlem on private business. As with the appearance of Clouston's article and correspondence with Harrington Tuke in 1878, a decade later Maudsley's hand seemed to be pushing someone else's pen in an attempt to damage the professional reputation of a colleague whom he perceived as a rival.

Undeterred, Savage emulated Maudsley's use of popular journalism in the 1870s to establish a reputation for himself. In the late summer of 1888 Savage took the Jack the Ripper murders as a platform for an article on "Homicidal mania" in the *Fortnightly Review*, which only fleetingly acknowledged Maudsley's work on criminal insanity.[126] By November, Savage was able to resign as physician at Bethlem and concentrate exclusively on private practice.

As with the events of 1877 and 1878, it is unclear how far Maudsley's resignation or withdrawal from the Association was voluntary. It was certainly not out of keeping with his character to invite martyrdom in the name of principle, as is clear from his 1863 essay on "Delusions." In this article, where the twenty-eight-year-old Maudsley first expounded his opposition to asylum treatment, he self-righteously compared his position to that of Christ before his trial and crucifixion. He knew that what he had to say would give offence, but he must bear witness to the truth.[127] If this paper encouraged Conolly to see Maudsley as a potential successor, the choice seems in retrospect distinctly peculiar.

Unlike the genial Conolly, Maudsley almost perpetually found himself at odds with the mainstream of his own profession. Largely isolated from his fellow specialists from about 1880 onwards, the cynicism and pessimism that were always so prominent a feature of his outlook on the world became even more apparent, and his published work stressed ever more insistently the hopelessness of insanity, the degeneracy of the mad and the criminal classes, and the grimness of man's fate:

> There is a destiny made for each one by his inheritance; he is the necessary organic consequent of certain organic antecedents; and it is impossible he should escape the tyranny of his organization. All nations in all ages have virtually confessed this truth, which has affected in an important manner systems of religion, social and political institutions. . . . The dread, inexorable destiny which played so grand and terrible a part in Grecian tragedy, and which Grecian heroes are represented as struggling manfully against, knowing all the while that their struggles were foredoomed to be futile, embodied an instinctive perception of the law by which the sins of the father are visited upon the children unto the third and fourth generations.[128]

In later years, he issued a series of stern warnings that "new products of an asocial or antisocial kind are formed in the retrograde metamorphosis of the human kind."[129] A decade earlier he had assumed that degeneracy would naturally diminish over time, given that it inexorably led over three or four generations to sterility and death. Now, having lost even this degree of faith in the future, he suggested that the pressures towards degeneration might well triumph over healthier impulses.[130] "Crime and madness," he proclaimed, "are both antisocial products of degeneracy . . . [and] it is not possible to draw a distinct line between [them]."[131] Insanity constituted nothing less than a form of phylogenetic regression—which accounted, of course, for its social location ("There is most madness where there are the fewest ideas, the simplest feelings, and the coarsest ideas and ways");[132] and for the lunatic's loss of civilised standards of behaviour and regression to the status of a brute: "Whence came the savage snarl, the destructive disposition, the obscene language, the wild howl, the offensive habits displayed by some of the insane? Why should a human being deprived of his reason ever become so brutal in character as some do, unless he has the brute nature within him?"[133]

Such lugubrious sententiousness was less than universally admired. While few had ventured to criticise him in print so long as he occupied the editor's chair, Maudsley now found himself the target of much hostile commentary. Within a year of his resignation, he was mocked in the pages of the *Journal of Mental Science* as someone who "fearlessly, in a paragraph, disposes of questions that have puzzled wise men since the world began" and for having "no theory of life that does not end by speciously denying the patent facts it started to describe."[134] Four years later, his *Body and Will* was denounced in the same pages as a "hymn of pessimism"[135] and even more savagely taken apart by Charles Mercier in the pages of *Brain*. (Mercier was particularly biting about Maudsley's efforts to "physiologize" the mind by turning it into "an all-pervading mentiferous ether" and about his pretensions to "intelligibility" and "practicality.")[136]

And yet if Maudsley's place in the profession was increasingly isolated, and his own books apparently more appreciated by the public at large than by his fellow alienists, one should not conclude that his ideas themselves were bereft of influence among his erstwhile colleagues. On the contrary, as asylums silted up with chronic lunatics and earlier expectations of cures proved almost wholly evanescent, Maudsley's claim that the insane constituted "morbid" or "degenerate" varieties of human beings whose problems were rooted in "an inward and invisible [and incurable] peculiarity of cerebral organization"[137] proved ever more appealing to those who had charge of asylumdom. The embrace of his rigid and pessimistic somaticism, while it appeared to leave but little scope for positive forms of intervention, had the invaluable compensating virtue of explaining away psychiatry's dismal therapeutic performance.[138] In the words of one asylum superintendent, "the unhopeful prospect has been due, not to want of recourse to early treatment [or to the deficiencies of psychiatric therapeutics], but, so to speak, to the inherent unfavourableness determined from the very outset of the mental symptoms."[139] In fact, in a wider view, so it was now alleged, it was a blessing that few were discharged cured, for those confined and then released still carried the taint of insanity in their blood and would pass it down to succeeding generations, adding to the pool of degenerates and increasing "the tale of lunacy in the next [generation]."[140] Paradoxically, then, as a bitter and thoroughly jaundiced Maudsley distanced himself from the world of the asylum and, like Bucknill, depended instead on his ties to mainstream medicine, many of the ideas he had championed were embraced by those who continued to care for the institutionalized insane,[141] which suggests, perhaps, that much of the criticism he received in these years was aimed more at the man than at his ideas.

ENGENDERING CONTROVERSY

Maudsley's attitudes towards gender differences and gender roles permeate his writing throughout his career, and the peculiarly personal salience of these issues to the man himself were equally evident when he spoke in a more directly autobiographical vein. Showalter has perceptively drawn attention to the way in which Maudsley's repudiation of asylum practice may have been based partly on a rejection of the feminine associations of the domestic routine of asylum management, and in this connection, one may recall Maudsley's decision to hand over the management of his own establishment for lunatic ladies to a female proprietor. The infamous obituary of Conolly, replete with barely disguised autobiographical elements, further illustrates how closely Maudsley associated femininity and weakness.[142] Describing Conolly's mind as being "of a feminine type; capable of a momentary lively sympathy, which might even express itself in tears, such as enemies, forgetful of his character, might be apt to deem hypocritical," Maudsley added his own harsh assessment of his father-in-law's vulnerabilities: "a character most graceful and beautiful in a woman is no gift of fortune to a man having to meet the adverse circumstances and pressing occasions of a tumultuous life."[143]

Maudsley wrote this obituary at the age of thirty-one, a few years after his return to London, where his purposeful and surefooted entry into the psychiatric profession contrasted readily enough with the struggles that characterized his father-in-law's early career. Notwithstanding the obvious differences, however, Maudsley's own life had not been without "adverse circumstances" and tumultuous moments, which likely contributed to his perceptions of the consequences of biological sex and gendered identity. As Maudsley recorded in the autobiographical fragment he set down at the age of seventy-two, as an eleven-year-old boy on the Yorkshire moors, he had seen his mother die of consumption after giving birth to tubercular twins, "which, all things considered, was not to be wondered at, seeing that she had eight children . . . at intervals of two years."[144] The brief sketch that follows is highly informative, redolent with Maudsley's personal anxieties and revelatory of the way in which the particular circumstances of his life may have sharpened his sensitivity to gender differences and perception of the dangers of reproduction for the female of the species. His parents "were . . . half cousins or something like," and Maudsley broods upon the personal consequences of this too unboundaried, genetically and emotionally similar, fragilely gendered mix. He insists that he "inherited chiefly the emotional part of my nature" from his mother and that "my intellectual faculties savour most of my father's family," despite the fact that he describes his mother as being "of good intellect, firm character," and his father as not showing any intellectual "distinction . . . though he had sound understanding and quiet solid sense in the management of his affairs."[145] He then reassures himself: "I presumably hark back to my [paternal] grandfather, who was . . . sardonic and sarcastic; so much so as to have earned him the sobriquet of 'the old philosopher.' In which connection I may relate that when I began my literary career by contributing to the *Journal of Mental Science* under J. Bucknill's editorship I was nicknamed 'the young philosopher.'"[146] Subsequently, he complained that "I am a tormenting critic of myself. This is ascribable perhaps to the paternal judgement censoring the maternal impulsion. I have always thought and said that the paternal and maternal were never vitally *welded* in me but only *rivetted*. My hat shows that the placing of my cerebral halves is not uniform."[147] For Maudsley, then, masculinity depended on the prerogative of critical intellect, which might be experienced as destructive by others, as well as steadiness of purpose, whilst femininity was characterized by emotionality and acute vulnerability to the crises of life, particularly childbirth.

In the light of these views and experiences, it is perhaps not wholly surprising that on one of the first occasions on which Maudsley sought a broader audience beyond the ranks of his professional colleagues, he should have chosen to write on the topical subject of "Sex in Mind and Education."[148] The article was ostensibly prompted by publication of a book on *Sex in Education* by Edward Clarke, an American doctor who was critical of coeducational initiatives in the United States, and as Maudsley doubtless intended, Maudsley's own intervention led to widespread comment and debate, for the whole question of women's place in society and, more particularly, the agitation of some upper-class women for access to higher education were becoming matters of increasing controversy. It provided, moreover, a splendid opportunity for him to illustrate the contributions an alienist might make in bringing his science to bear on questions of public health and welfare, precisely the sort of widening of his sphere of activity and influence that was vital if he himself were to develop a practice that extended beyond the walls of the asylum.

Few issues, one might reasonably conclude, presented a more suitable opportunity for him to demonstrate the "soundness" of his views, both to his colleagues in the medical mainstream and to the conservative upper-class men, who—it goes without saying—constituted the two most vital audiences for someone determined to establish his bona fides as an adviser on matters of mental hygiene. Joan Burstyn has reminded us that "medicine was the first occupation to be assailed by women in their attempts to enter the professions, and it was medical practitioners who made the strongest attack against higher education for women."[149] In assuming a prominent place in this argument, and in suggesting the relevance of psychological medicine to its resolution, Maudsley was thus quite certain to find a receptive audience among his fellow medical men.[150]

Like others who were critical of ambitious women, Maudsley insisted that he viewed their arguments "without prejudice, or with some sympathy."[151] The constrictions of women's lives were real and must be frankly acknowledged: "A system of education which is framed to fit them to be nothing more than the superintendents of a household and the ornaments of a drawing-room, is one which does not do justice to their nature, and cannot be seriously defended. Assuredly, those of them who have not the opportunity of getting married suffer not a little, in mind and body, from a method of education which tends to develope [sic] the emotional at the expense of the intellectual nature, and by their exclusion from appropriate fields of practical activity."[152] Yet "those who pant for other careers" were but "a small minority of women" and "cannot be accepted as the spokeswomen of their sex."[153] The destiny of the overwhelming majority of women remained marriage and childbearing, and their education and upbringing must be designed accordingly. Besides, notwithstanding the selfish and misguided protests of a few, there remained the inescapable "fact that the male organization is one, and the female organization another, and that, let come what may in the way of assimilation of female and male education and labour, it will not be possible to transform a woman into a man."[154] When all was said and done, "they . . . cannot rebel successfully against the tyranny of their organization"; they cannot escape the fact that a woman "labours under an inferiority of constitution by a dispensation which there is no gainsaying. . . . This is not the expression of prejudice nor of false sentiment; it is a plain statement of a physiological fact."[155]

In invoking the facts of physiology to prove that the existing social and moral order was rooted in the stern realities of the natural world, Maudsley was employing a rhetorical tactic that he would repeatedly use in other contexts, as he sought to establish his authority as an alienist to diagnose and prescribe for a whole host of social ills. Nor did he shrink from open discussion of "matters it is not easy to discuss out of a medical journal" because "the gravity of the subject can hardly be exaggerated," making it "a duty to use plainer language than would otherwise be fitting in a literary journal."[156] A woman must attend to "the periodical tides of her organization."[157] Otherwise, "the important physiological change which takes place at puberty . . . may easily . . . pass into pathological change . . . nervous disorders of a minor kind, and even such serious disorders as chorea, epilepsy, insanity, are often connected with irregularities or suspension of these important functions."[158] In "an enthusiasm which borders on or reaches fanaticism," the advocates of higher education for women all too easily overlooked the fact that "the energy of the human body [was] a definite and not inexhaustible quantity" which could "not bear, without injury, an excessive mental drain as well as the natural physical drain which is so great at that time."[159] The evolutionary, as well as individual medical consequences, of their schemes might be deadly, leading to the creation of "a race of sexless beings" who would "carry on the intellectual work of the world, not otherwise than as sexless ants do the work and fighting of the community."[160]

Maudsley's intervention in this controversial arena led to widespread comment and debate, particularly after the *Fortnightly Review* printed a reply by Elizabeth Garrett Anderson, the first woman to qualify as a doctor in Britain. As a professional, wife, and mother, Garrett Anderson might well have cited herself as a living refutation of many of Maudsley's contentions (though by helping to maintain existing barriers to women's entry into the universities, and by revising the constitution of the Society of Apothecaries to prohibit women taking its examinations, medical men had done their best to ensure she remained an isolated counterexample).[161] Instead, she chose to fight on Maudsley's own terrain, attacking his views as scientifically indefensible. Though sharing the conventional Victorian view that "there is grave reason for doubting whether such a subject can be fully and with propriety discussed except in a professional journal," she argued that Maudsley had left her no choice: "As, however, the usual reserve has been broken through, it would be out of place for those who approve the changes against which Dr. Maudsley's argument is directed to be silent in obedience to those considerations he has disregarded. We will therefore venture to speak as plainly and directly as he has spoken."[162]

"When we are told," she remarked (with pardonable asperity), "that in the labour of life women cannot disregard their special physiological functions without danger to health, it is difficult to understand what is meant, considering that in adult life healthy women do as a rule disregard them almost completely."[163] Working-class women, she pointed out, had no alternative but to work without interruption throughout the menstrual cycle and did so without apparent difficulty. Nor were the developmental strains and difficulties associated with puberty necessarily any greater for girls than for boys. Most tellingly of all, she pointed to those "thousands of young women, strong and blooming at eighteen, [who] become gradually languid and feeble under the depressing influence of dulness [*sic*] . . . till in a few years they are morbid and self-absorbed, or even hysterical."[164] "From the purely physiological point of view," she shrewdly suggested, turning the logic of Maudsley's own arguments against him,

> the stimulus found in novel-reading, in the theatre and ball-room, the excitement which attends a premature entry into society, the competition of vanity and frivolity, these involve far more dangers to the health of young women than the competition for knowledge, or for scientific or literary honours, ever has done, or

is ever likely to do. . . . It is not easy for those whose lives are full to overflowing of interests which accumulate as life matures, to realise how insupportably dull the life of a young woman just out of the schoolroom is apt to be, nor the powerful influence for evil this dulness has upon her health . . . where the days drag along filled with make-believe occupations and dreary sham amusements.[165]

Intellectually, modern observers have had few doubts about who had the best of this particular exchange.[166] Without the benefit of hindsight, however, and viewing the debate as something more than an abstract intellectual exercise, for the next quarter century, Maudsley might plausibly be said to have "won" the argument. For his views remained entrenched as the medical orthodoxy till the close of the nineteenth century and beyond; and while leading male physicians[167] (and not a few women doctors)[168] continued to insist that the facts of physiology made imposing limits on female ambition all but essential for the well-being of society at large, Maudsley's pioneering statement of this position won him applause rather than criticism among those whose opinion mattered.[169] As late as 1897, discussing the vexed issue of the admission of women to Oxford and Cambridge universities, the Tory *Quarterly Review*'s correspondent could essentially echo Maudsley's views of the limitations of female physiology: "To anyone who has seriously considered the facts of sex in the light of physiology and psychology, it must appear extremely improbable that an education which duly fits girls for women's duties can be identical with an education which fits boys for the duties of men. Either sex is an appalling blunder, or else it must have been intended that each sex should have its own work to do, not merely in the physical economy of the race, but also in the social and intellectual world."[170]

Physician to Society

"Sex in Mind and Education" was only one of a whole series of essays Maudsley wrote for a popular educated as well as medical audience during his decade as professor of medical jurisprudence at University College London. From the early 1870s onwards, he published a range of articles on such topics as "Is Insanity on the Increase?"[171] "Judges, Juries and Insanity,"[172] "Stealing as a Symptom of General Paralysis,"[173] and "Hallucinations of the Senses."[174] During the same period, he published a book on *Responsibility in Mental Disease* (1874), as well as a new and enlarged edition of *The Physiology and Pathology of Mind* (1867), which now appeared in separate volumes as *The Physiology of Mind* (1876) and *The Pathology of Mind* (1879).

In precisely the years when he was progressively losing the support of the psychiatric profession for his editorship of the *Journal of Mental Science*,

Maudsley was thus, paradoxically enough, establishing himself as an authoritative psychiatric voice on a range of topical issues with the general medical profession and a wider public. Among his medical colleagues (though scarcely among members of the legal profession) his strenuous defence of the essentially *medical* character of insanity and of its diagnosis was obviously popular.[175] As professor of medical jurisprudence, Maudsley had both a licence and a responsibility to pronounce on questions of insanity in relation to criminality, and he did not hesitate to make his feelings known. Insisting that "it is useless to say smooth things when things are not smooth," he denounced "the inquity of the law [on the insanity defence] as laid down by judges." "One cannot justly complain," he added, "that judges should be ignorant of insanity, seeing that only by long experience and study is a true knowledge to be acquired; but it is a fair ground of complaint that, being ignorant, they should speak as confidently and foolishly as they sometimes do."[176] As for asking lay juries to judge the question of insanity, "Had the wit of man been employed to devise a tribunal more unfitted for such a purpose, it might have exhausted itself in the vain attempt. . . . The ground which medical men should firmly and consistently take in regard to insanity is, that it is a physical disease; that they alone are competent to decide upon its presence or absence; and that it is quite as absurd for lawyers or the general public to give their opinion on the subject in a doubtful case, as it would be for them to do so in a case of fever."[177]

Maudsley's polemics about the insanity defence were only part of a much wider ranging set of commentaries on the physiological origins of the ills afflicting Victorian society. Judging by the work of a whole spectrum of writers in the closing decades of the nineteenth century—novelists and social commentators alike—respectable Victorians were haunted by the spectre of the "dangerous classes."[178] Maudsley's theorizing about degeneration provided a naturalistic account of the constitutional infirmities that underlay all such varied species of social pathology and that gave rise to "entire semi-barbarian sub-cultures, maintaining themselves apart from and beyond the reach of the moral empire of civilised society in particular vice-and crime-ridden slum districts of great cities, or in vagrant criminal bands."[179] In principle, when joined to his claims about the inheritance of acquired characteristics, such theories supplied scientific warrant for a greatly expanded role for the alienist as social diagnostician; and when allied to Hughlings Jackson's theory of nervous dissolution, also developed during the 1870s and 1880s, they obtained still greater scientific credibility and cultural authority.[180] In other (less misanthropic and pessimistic) hands, at least, they laid the groundwork for the mental hygiene movement, permitting the hope that conscious intervention by expert practitioners of psychological medicine might reverse the threatening tide of degeneration and bring about the improvement of the race.

With their privileged access to what Clouston termed "the laws of mind

and brain," alienists could claim to rest their prescriptions on the incontrovertible foundation of modern cerebral anatomy and physiology, and such
leading figures as Crichton-Browne, Mercier, Hack Tuke, and Clouston
himself actively sought to provide guidance on the upbringing and education of children, the choice of marriage partners, and the organization of
family life, as well as the problems associated with overwork and overpres-
sure, and, at the opposite extreme, with intemperance and other forms of
self-indulgence and vice. Maudsley approved of such endeavours in principle, but remained far more sceptical than most of his colleagues about
whether they yet possessed the necessary knowledge to implement wide-
ranging plans for "social prophylaxis" and racial improvement.[181] Whatever
his personal doubts on this score, though, his essays and monographs unquestionably contributed powerfully towards efforts at redefining "the theoretical object of [psychiatric] practice [at least among the professional elite]
away from the clinical study of the major psychoses and the custodial care
of the chronically insane towards the comparative study, preventive and 'hygienic' treatment of other, related but less severe 'nervous' disorders."[182]

Practically speaking, too, from the early 1870s onwards, Maudsley had
already begun to demonstrate the possibility of creating a career in psychological medicine based solely upon the consulting room. Some time in 1874
or 1875, as we have already noted, he had begun to disentangle himself
from his residual ties to the world of the asylum, the small collection of
female lunatics at Lawn House. His evidence to the Select Committee in
1877 would make clear his distaste for living in close proximity with lunatic
cases like Louisa Lowe, but he may have had an additional motive for finally
taking the radical step of severing his connection to a secure source of income.[183] On the death of William Hood in 1870, Charles Lockhart Robertson, the joint editor of the *Journal of Mental Science* with Maudsley and former medical superintendent of Haywards Heath asylum, had followed
Bucknill from the editorship of the journal to assume the lucrative post of
Lord Chancellor's Visitor in Lunacy. When Maudsley decided to transfer the
licence of Lawn House to Emma Dixon, changing his own role initially to
one of Visiting Physician, it is possible that he was purposefully shedding
the private interests that would otherwise have impeded him from following
in Bucknill's and Robertson's footsteps, as Bucknill prepared to retire in
1875. In the event, however, another former county asylum superintendent,
James Crichton-Browne, one of the editors of the new journal *Brain*, rather
than Maudsley, was appointed to succeed Bucknill.

Without the range of private lunacy contacts Bucknill had established
through his role as Lord Chancellor's Visitor, Maudsley nevertheless succeeded in building up a substantial private consultancy—just how substantial would be revealed by the size of his estate at his death in 1918. The
autobiographical fragment he wrote at the age of seventy-two records simply
that "the rest of my life in London was spent in getting such practice in

lunacy as I could, which increased gradually, and in writing the books which I published in succession."[184] The two activities were, of course, not unconnected, for Maudsley's publications, among other things, constituted a subtle and regular advertisement for his professional standing and expertise. In general, however, the details of his practice remain sketchy and for the most part beyond recovery, for his private papers seem not to have survived him.

Trevor Turner has plausibly suggested that the absence of clinical records and private papers is no accident. Maudsley's clientele was predominantly upper class and aristocratic, and "the essence of keeping such a clientele would have been absolute discretion and the guaranteed disposal of any damning documents or notes. The secrets of the mad rich proved safe with Henry Maudsley, in his time and our own." Ironically, as Turner further argues, in attracting his clients in the first place, Maudsley's estrangement from colleagues in the MPA may have been a positive blessing, for it limited the contamination of his medical identity which association with asylums and a stigmatized medical group would inevitably have brought in its train.[185] Perhaps even more important, though, from the time he abandoned the superintendency at Manchester, Maudsley had consistently argued in favour of nonasylum treatment of insanity under medical supervision, long the upper classes' preferred way of handling their mad relations; this was a position he, like Bucknill who was now also bent on developing a practice of this sort, publicly endorsed yet again in his testimony before the 1877 Select Committee.

We simply cannot reconstruct, though, the extent of Maudsley's involvement in this type of practice after the transfer of the licence for Lawn House. We can say, from his role as a consultant physician to wealthy and aristocratic patients at Ticehurst House in Sussex, that on occasion he also referred some of his patients to conventional asylums. Maudsley is known to have been associated with eight cases there in a variety of capacities, which ranged from signing certificates to being called in as a consultant on the treatment of inmates.[186] It seems highly probable that this practice would have been mirrored by contacts with patients in other private asylums and lunatics in single care, and Shaftesbury's specific commendation of Maudsley in his evidence to the Select Committee of 1877 suggests that Maudsley was well regarded in upper-class social circles.

Certainly Maudsley was well placed to use a range of contacts to establish a wealthy and aristocratic clientele. Apart from his friendships with Bucknill and Robertson, who had extensive knowledge of Chancery cases, Maudsley was friends with his immediate contemporary and highly successful fellow Yorkshireman, William Broadbent (1835–1907). In the late 1860s, Broadbent was a physician and lecturer in physiology at St. Mary's, where Maudsley lectured on insanity. Despite their different specialisms, Broadbent and

Maudsley shared medical interests, both publishing for example on aphasia. Broadbent's correspondence in the late 1860s expressed some envy at Maudsley's earlier election to the Royal College of Physicians and subsequent invitation to give the Gulstonian lectures.[187] Nevertheless, it is noticeable that Maudsley's move from consulting rooms in Hanover Square, which he had occupied since the early 1870s, to the still more fashionable Mayfair in 1892, coincided with Broadbent's appointment as Physician to the Prince of Wales.

Like Bucknill, in the 1880s Maudsley stressed his links with the general medical rather than psychiatric profession, through not only personal associations like that with Broadbent but also active membership of the Royal College of Physicians. Maudsley, for instance, was one of a group of delegates from the Royal College of Physicians who lobbied Parliament during the passage of the 1890 Lunacy Act and helped to introduce amendments to liberalize the proposed legislation in relation to single care, so that it allowed "double" as well as single care—that is, for more than one patient to be received for treatment by medical practitioners in houses that were not licensed as private asylums.[188] Personal ties to the medical elite were obviously useful in securing the referral of suitable patients, but like every other physician who sought to "practise . . . medicine in the highest social circles," Maudsley was moving in a world where "the public chose their doctors by evaluating their class attributes rather than their medical skills."[189] Though, in Sir George Savage's words, "he was not a clubbable man,"[190] he became a member of both the Reform and the Savile clubs, and his acceptance in these circles provided one important marker of gentlemanly status, as well as regular contact with the social circles from which his clientele were drawn. Fortunately, his classical education and the ornamental literary allusions that were so prominent a feature of his writings, his aloof and self-assured manner, and his handsome appearance, which he complemented by being "carefully dressed and scrupulously careful of his hands,"[191] all in their various ways provided the necessary further warrants of his status. Of the financial rewards which these in their turn brought him there can be no doubt, for in addition to the £30,000 he had previously donated to the London County Council, to launch the hospital that still bears his name, he left in the region of £100,000 in his will (the equivalent of well over £1 million in contemporary terms).

A HOSPITAL, NOT AN ASYLUM

His hospital, of course, has ensured that (almost uniquely among the ranks of the nineteenth-century alienists whose careers we have surveyed) Maudsley's name continues to be known today outside the narrow circle of psychiatric historians. Once it finally opened in 1923, it rapidly emerged as the political centre of British psychiatry, its associated Institute of Psychiatry, with its links to the University of London, at last providing the profession with a measure of the academic respectability within medicine that it had long craved.[192] With the hospital's focus on acute forms of mental disorder, whether mild or malignant, its outpatient department, its stress on avoiding asylum treatment, and its emphasis on combining clinical instruction with research into the causes and pathology of insanity, Maudsley anticipated and helped to generate the gradual shift in the profession's centre of gravity—away from the barracks asylum and towards noninstitutional forms of practice—that has been one of the dominant features of its evolution over the course of the twentieth century.

Soon after the turn of the century, Maudsley began to relinquish much of his practice. By now, he had bought a large house in Bushey Heath and was dividing his time between his townhouse and his "country residence." Watching cricket absorbed much of his leisure time, and in 1903, he supplemented his frequent visits to Lords with a long sea voyage to Australia "to see the best of cricket in its best home."[193] The occasional patient still consulted him in Mayfair,[194] but for the most part Maudsley, who had "allowed his hair and beard to grow long, and . . . had rather the aspect of an aged prophet,"[195] had become a recluse, pessimistic as always, and by now somewhat embittered besides.

According to Frederick Mott, it was at his suggestion, fresh from a visit to Kraepelin's clinic in Munich, that Maudsley first conceived of the idea of endowing a similar facility in London.[196] Perhaps so, but Maudsley, who had been, as we have seen, a consistent and fierce critic of the defects of traditional asylums, may well have viewed the scheme as a final gesture of his contempt for his erstwhile colleagues. As he must have known, given the publicity it had generated at the time, an earlier plan of a very similar sort had been floated before the newly established London County Council (LCC) in 1889 by Robert Brudenell Carter,[197] only to be denounced by furious asylum doctors from all over the country. Carter's justification for his proposed hospital had explicitly detailed his disdain for the scientific and therapeutic failings of asylumdom and his conviction that alienists were an intellectually bankrupt fraternity; Carter had proposed a hospital for the treatment of acute insanity wholly independent of the existing asylum system, staffed solely by specialists in other branches of medicine. Perhaps influenced by the enormously hostile response from asylum doctors, the LCC Asylums Committee had promptly shelved the plan, which was nonetheless denounced by David Yellowlees, in his 1890 presidential address to the Medico-Psychological Association, as "a wholesale slander" on his profession.[198]

The new plan, whose guiding spirit was very similar to Carter's,[199] had the decisive advantage, however, of being backed by a substantial portion of Maudsley's fortune. The £30,000 he offered on July 16, 1907, at first anonymously, constituted a powerful inducement to the LCC to implement his scheme. Yet it took four more years, considerable political maneuvering by the astute Mott, and ultimately a threat by Maudsley to withdraw his offer, before the council "procured a site at Denmark Hill . . . within the stipulated distance of four miles from Charing Cross" and announced publicly the plan to build what was now officially called "the Maudsley Hospital."[200] In the interim, Maudsley had published a lengthy prospectus on "A Mental Hospital—Its Aims and Uses" in the *Archives of Neurology*, a piece whose peroration cannot have failed to serve as a reminder of, and a further occasion for, his alienation from his fellow specialists. While asylum doctors preferred to portray their institutions as humane and therapeutic, Maudsley once again insisted on the evil and pernicious effects of compulsory incarceration in a large asylum:

> A complaint often bitterly made by persons who have been discharged recovered from asylums is of the coarseness, roughness and indifference of attendants, and of the degrading humiliation of being ordered about by them in daily routine like so many sheep, without the least regard to personal feeling. Such system of routine is no doubt more or less unavoidable in a large asylum crowded with patients in all stages of disease, but it is nonetheless apt to be accompanied by an utter want of the sympathetic imagination which might realise what the particular patient, not deadened into stolid indifference by his surroundings, may feel. . . . It may reasonably be expected [he concluded] that besides the prevention of incipient insanity by wise counsel and treatment in its out-patients' department, the early treatment of acute insanity in a special hospital will prevent the necessity and perhaps lasting expense of placing some patients in a lunatic asylum—the very name of which is perhaps a terror, the remembrance a sort of nightmare, the social consequences a life-long prejudice.[201]

Maudsley's donation and the plans to build the hospital were reported in the *Journal of Mental Science* in 1911. Shortly afterwards, the same journal contained news that Thomas Clouston and George Henry Savage had been awarded knighthoods for their contributions to British psychiatry and recorded Maudsley's election to honorary membership of the MPA, thirty-five years after he was forced to resign as editor of the Association's journal and twenty-two years after his name unaccountably disappeared from the list of ordinary members.[202] If Maudsley had not been so profoundly humourless about himself, he might have been tempted to remark to Clouston or Savage, as one asylum inmate did to her visiting physician, c.1840, "Well, Sir! Since we last met I have been benighted and you have been knighted."

Figure 8.3. Henry Maudsley in old age. A misanthropic recluse who had essentially despaired of the future of civilization and—almost incidentally—of his own chosen profession, Maudsley in retirement had "allowed his hair to grow long and . . . had [acquired] rather the aspect of an aged prophet."

DESPAIR

It is surely a testimony to the deep antipathies Maudsley had accumulated over the years that, notwithstanding his reputation as a private physician, his aristocratic and general medical contacts, his stream of influential publications, and his bequest to the LCC, he was not, like Broadbent, Clouston, or Savage, honoured for his services to medicine. Nor did he mellow with age. Among his final publications were two 1917 articles on "Optimism and Pessimism" and "Materialism and Spiritualism," which Alexander Walk described as "gestures of reconciliation" to his psychiatric colleagues but which were in fact trenchant restatements of the philosophy that had helped to divide him from the Medico-Psychological Association many years before.[203]

Maudsley's wife, Anne Caroline, had died on February 9, 1911, of "senile decay," at the age of eighty-one. Alone and essentially friendless, Maudsley would survive until the closing months of the First World War, an isolated, cynical, and bitter man, and by now something of an intellectual fossil. The closing lines from the final edition of his *Pathology of Mind*, though written more than two decades earlier, surely still captured the essence of his outlook on a world and a form of professional work of which he had come to despair:

> A physician who had spent his life in ministering to diseased minds might be excused if, asking at the end of it whether he had spent his life well, he accused the fortune of an evil hour which threw him on that track of work. He could not well help feeling something of bitterness in the certitude that one-half the disease [*sic*] he had dealt with never could get well, and something of misgiving in the reflection whether he had done real service to his kind by restoring the other half to do reproductive work. Nor would the scientific interest of his studies compensate entirely for the practical uncertainties, since their revelation of the structure of human nature might inspire a doubt whether, notwithstanding impassioned aims, paeons of progress, endless pageants of self-illusions, its capacity of degeneration did not equal, and might some day exceed, its capacity of development. Fain, though in vain, would he question the Genius of the human race, mute and inscrutable, musing of the seeds of time and dreaming prophetically of things to come.[204]

Chapter Nine

CONCLUSION

> A young medical man, who has received a complete medical and
> surgical education, must either be very sadly situated, or very
> advantageously, who can make up his mind to devote himself to
> the study and treatment of Insanity.
> *(John Conolly, "On the Prospects of Physicians Engaged in Practice*
> *in Cases of Insanity," 1861)*

> Not the least of the evils of our present monstrous asylums is
> the entire impossibility of anything like individual
> treatment in them.
> *(Henry Maudsley,* The Physiology and Pathology of Mind, *1867)*

> It must be frankly granted that Psychological Medicine can
> boast, as yet, of no specifics, nor is it likely, perhaps, that such
> a boast will ever be made. It may be difficult to suppress the
> hope, but we cannot entertain the expectation, that some future
> Sydenham will discover an anti-psychosis which will as safely
> and speedily cut short an attack of mania or
> melancholia as bark an attack of ague.
> *(Daniel Hack Tuke, "Presidential Address," 1881)*

ADDRESSING HIS colleagues in 1857 as the newly elected president of
the Association of Medical Officers of Asylums and Hospitals for the
Insane, Forbes Winslow was in a characteristically ebullient mood.
To hear him tell it, alienists were a revered and near saintly fraternity:

> How noble is the study in which we are engaged! how important the duties which
> devolve upon us! how solemnly responsible is our position! Is it possible to exag-
> gerate or over-estimate our character, influence, importance and dignity?[1]

Alienists were, on his account, "a body of men engaged in a holy and sacred
office"—so much so that "the angels in heaven might well envy us the enno-
bling and exalted pleasures incidental to our mission of love and charity."[2]
  A half century later, his own son, Lionel Forbes Winslow, hinted at a very
different and much more dismal reality:

> The monotony of asylum life is of such a nature that there is every danger of those
> who constantly associate with the inmates themselves becoming mad. . . . The
> constant association with the insane I have found terrible to contend with.[3]

His jaundiced view soon found confirmation from a more authoritative source. The reports of an official task force of the Medico-Psychological Association complained bitterly of the profession's low status and standing and spoke in equally scathing terms of "the grave defects in the present position of psychiatry . . . [and] the reproach at present attached to our specialty."[4] "The lunacy service," the committee acknowledged, existed in a twilight world "divorced from ordinary medical education and practice. . . . Psychiatry as a branch of medicine is in a decidedly inferior position to practically every other branch [of the profession]."[5]

Most psychiatrists, as some medical psychologists had begun to call themselves by the closing years of Victoria's reign, continued to work in the county asylum system that had once been lunacy reformers' proudest accomplishment, in the establishments in which men like Conolly, Gaskell, and Bucknill had launched their careers. The empire of asylumdom had grown larger and larger as the century wore on and contained more than one hundred thousand inmates by the dawn of the Edwardian age. Yet the remorseless rise in the numbers of the mad had not produced a comparable expansion in the numbers of asylum superintendents, for the average asylum, which had contained fewer than three hundred patients at midcentury, had grown to house a thousand and more some fifty years later, forming part of a national network of vast receptacles largely devoted to the confinement of those without hope. For those attempting to build a career in this sector of the mad-doctoring trade, the climb up the ladder to the prize of an asylum superintendency had accordingly become far longer and much more uncertain and arduous, even as the optimism with which the whole enterprise had been launched steadily receded from memory.

Where men like Gaskell, Bucknill, Browne, and Maudsley had obtained posts as asylum superintendents in their twenties and early thirties, their successors faced a much bleaker set of life chances; such diminished prospects were ironic in a way because the pathway into the profession, haphazard and unstructured for the first generation, had become steadily more organized and predictable. The remorseless rise in the size of pauper asylums brought with it a steady expansion in the ranks of assistant doctors who were employed to ease the administrative and clinical burdens falling on the superintendents, occupying posts that functioned in effect as apprenticeships in asylum medicine. In turn, this development created a reservoir of experienced men from which the more senior positions could be filled. But with their superiors entrenched for decades at a time, and the number of superintendencies sharply limited by the authorities' preference for the massive barracks asylum, the assistant "sees the best years of his life slipping away from him, without any advancement of his interests and prospects."[6] Poorly remunerated and with only slender hopes for advancement, these doctors also found themselves almost as much at the mercy of autocratic superintendents as were the castes beneath them, the attendants and the untouchables of the asylum world, the patients. Hours were long, isolation from the outside world almost complete, and celibacy was enforced, either directly, by edict of the superintendent, or indirectly, by pitifully inadequate salaries that precluded the acquisition of dependents.[7] Nor did the daily routine itself offer many intrinsic rewards by way of compensation. As the official task force led by Bedford Pierce acknowledged, "the work assigned to Junior Medical Officers is in the majority of cases monotonous, uninteresting, and without adequate responsibility [which] leads to a gradual loss of interest in scientific medicine." Besides, in the average asylum, "no organised research work is carried on, and clinical and pathological investigations are often ill-directed, haphazard, [and] consequently fruitless"—producing an environment that tended "to kill enthusiasm and destroy medical interests [as well as] to produce a deteriorating effect upon those who remain long in the service."[8]

A few brave or foolhardy assistants openly complained of their fate, comparing their circumstances with those of "dutiful relatives, most patiently await[ing] the falling in of their estate" on the death of a rich relation. They protested that the contrast of "the fat salaries of the Superintendents with the lean ones of the assistants" had perhaps been bearable "when the Assistant Medical Officers were few and superintendencies ripened in four or five years, but [their superiors' counsel to be patient and wait their turn] loses all its sweet reasonableness when we have to wait ten, twelve, or more years for the golden fruit, and even run the risk of its being plucked by some outsider from over the [asylum] wall just when we thought it about to drop."[9] Vocal dissent of this sort was, however, the exception rather than the rule. The more ambitious and energetic who had ventured into asylumdom could scarcely be blamed for perceiving the situation to be all-but-hopeless and contemplating only a dispiriting future of being worn down by the demands of a job that required them to wrestle daily with the depressing problems of legions of the lost—the pauperized flotsam and jetsam of society, an anonymous mass of people who suffered from what their superiors insistently proclaimed was a congenital and essentially incurable condition. Not surprisingly, such men usually opted simply to abandon the field altogether and to seek a more rewarding career in the greener pastures offered by other branches of the medical profession. For those who remained behind, long years spent in humdrum routine tasks wore away whatever initiative and independence they may once have possessed, thereby ensuring the complacent and unimaginative conservatism of those who finally succeeded to a superintendency.

Another segment of the profession, the proprietors and medical staff of private asylums, escaped the stigma that attached itself to salaried employees of poor law institutions, but only at the cost of incurring their own unwelcome set of disabilities. To be sure, this portion of the marketplace for the services of alienists tended to be far more lucrative—at least for those who possessed the large capital sums a suitable physical plant and staff required—but it was indelibly contaminated by its overtones of trade and the endemic suspicions among the well-to-do about the motives of those who ran such establishments. Conolly's complaints that "in the very beginning and to the very end, the law merely treats the [alienist] as one of the dangerous classes, exercising a suspected trade, and solely intent on gain," that "the practitioners in this department of medicine are depreciated, or exposed to derogatory observations," and that their lives are "full of affronts and discouragements,"[10] could as well have been uttered in 1900 as in 1860.[11] Indeed, the hostility and suspicion that swirled about this segment of the mad-doctoring trade were so powerful—notwithstanding the services elite asylums rendered to the British upper classes[12]—that the 1880s had seen serious attempts (to which Bucknill among others had lent his support) to abolish private asylums altogether. And although this extreme measure was not part of the legislation eventually passed in 1890, the Lunacy Act of that year did make statutory the Lunacy Commissioners' longstanding refusal to countenance any further expansion of the private asylum sector. In effect, while granting a monopoly of this market segment to the existing institutions and their proprietors, the legal system had set itself up as a powerful barrier to the expansion of the specialty in this direction.

As we have seen, Bucknill and Maudsley, together with men like Savage, Blandford, and Crichton-Browne, had begun to pioneer still another form of psychiatric practice in the closing decades of the nineteenth century, one based primarily on the consulting room. In interesting ways, as ironic as it may appear, their approach might be said to hark back to a style of practice characteristic of some of the more prominent general medical practitioners and physicians who had begun to focus on the insane in the eighteenth and early nineteenth centuries. Like Sir Alexander Morison, whose career in some ways epitomized this pattern of practice, these late Victorian and Edwardian alienists exhibited considerable scepticism about the merits of asylum treatment and often placed their patients in alternative settings. Similarly, their primary reference group within the medical profession was the Royal College of Physicians, rather than the Medico-Psychological Association, and one major concern of this elite group of psychiatrists was the search for ways to develop stronger and more coherent links with general medicine.

However, on this front, too, the profession—or rather this fraction of the profession—found itself beset with difficulties. The stigma that attached so firmly to asylums[13] and to mental illness[14] in the public mind cast a deep shadow over the efforts these men made. An editorial in the *Journal of Mental Science* spoke eloquently of the obstacles they faced:

> a large proportion of the public, owing to its prejudice against insanity, avoids, until compelled by the direst necessity, any approach to a physician who has experience in treating it. To avoid doing so, they will often resort to the treatment of persons whose knowledge of insanity is practically *nil*, and who practise as specialists on the strength of a certificate from some medical man or hospital that they have learned massage, Swedish drill, medical electricity, Weir Mitchelling, etc., in endless variety. . . . If a medical man is consulted, care is taken, in the large majority of cases, that he is not one whose name is associated with mental diseases; it is only in the last resort, when means are exhausted and the mental breakdown is complete that an alienist is resorted to.[15]

In competing with "these quasi-quacks" (as they angrily called their competitors),[16] alienists who sought to build extra-institutional practices were simultaneously forced to confront the dismaying fact that "British medical circles continued to harbor deep pockets of prejudice against psychiatry"[17]—disdain that persisted well into the 1920s and beyond.[18] They were handicapped, too, ironically enough, by some of the efforts they themselves made to legitimize their place in the profession, as well as by the ever more evident limitations of their own knowledge and therapeutics. Paradoxically, for example, in the very process of voicing their own criticisms of asylumdom, men like Maudsley, Bucknill, and Crichton Browne—while symbolically distancing themselves from the system's suffocating and stigmatizing embrace—were simultaneously diminishing the public standing of the specialty as a whole,[19] even if such views brought them into closer accord with the prejudices and preferences of both their upper-class clientele and the medical elite.

Similarly, as the intellectual leaders and most prominent spokesmen for the psychiatric profession, their insistence on somatic explanations of madness and their emphasis that insanity was the product of degeneration, although these did not always lead to the extremes of Maudsley's nihilism and despair, nonetheless shed little light on the troubles of the still functioning, albeit symptom-bearing patients who could form the foundation of an office-based practice. Unfortunately, too, such accounts of the origins of mental disturbances also provided only the slimmest of guides for practical intervention. It may seem remarkable, therefore, that "disillusioned though they were by the failure of somatic hypotheses to elucidate the ailments they examined, Edwardian psychiatrists were not prepared to accept . . . psychological solutions" to the puzzling disorders with which they grappled.[20] Ultimately, it would take the seismic upheavals associated with the "war to end all wars," and the resulting epidemic of shell shock, before a significant fraction of the specialism began to countenance purely psychological theories and therapeutics of nervous collapse.[21]

One suspects that such conservatism did not come at the expense of therapeutic efficacy, because psychoanalysis and other forms of psychotherapy provided (and in many ways continue to provide) few evident advantages in this regard. In other respects, however, it would seem that Freudian ideas, in particular, might have offered some distinct benefits to the profession, especially to those bent on developing the new realm of office practice. Most notably, Freud's system "made sense" of a whole range of phenomena that the somatic theorists previously left outside the realm of systematic observation, and in the process (from some perspectives, at least), created "understandable order out of chaos."[22] It is hard to overestimate the potential significance and power of this ideological accomplishment. For madness is fundamentally behaviour too unintelligible to be accorded the status of human action, and psychoanalysis now offered to provide accounts, constructable only by experts, which replaced commonsense judgements that something was "irrational"—literally did not make sense—with interpretations that were at once remarkably systematic, symbolically highly elaborated, and—once its premises were granted—both plausible and internally coherent. Freud offered, as well, an elaborate technology of treatment, "certain definite methods of procedure of a rational sort,"[23] which could underpin and give substance to an outpatient practice—a form of psychotherapeutics that its practitioners solemnly compared to "a surgical operation of the most dangerous sort."[24] It is thus a measure of just how deep-seated British psychiatrists' resistance to overt psychologising remained (even if their own chosen alternative offered few advantages beyond an increasingly threadbare link to orthodox somatic medicine), that they so resolutely refused to engage in any serious exploration of these approaches to the explanation and treatment of mental disorder,[25] and that they reacted with so much ridicule and venom towards the handful of renegades who broke ranks over this issue.[26]

The mad-doctoring trade had in many ways transformed itself by the close of Victoria's long reign, not least through the struggles and efforts of the men whose lives and careers we have explored here. When John Haslam entered upon his practice, certification procedures were wholly informal, the law afforded medical men little or no special role in deciding who was and was not insane, and the medical profession was far from possessing a monopoly over the treatment of the insane. In all these respects, the legal and cultural authority of doctors was transformed over the course of the nineteenth century. Simultaneously, the creation of an association of alienists, the rapid growth of a monographic literature on insanity, and the emergence and consolidation of professional periodicals devoted solely to the pathology and treatment of mental disturbance marked the emergence of a self-conscious and organized specialty, one whose discourse about madness and its relations to the social order was, without question, quite strikingly influential among the educated classes in late Victorian Britain.

For all its evident advances of this sort, however, alienism remained from several points of view a quite marginal specialty, uncertain of its own profile and prospects, and riven by sharp internal divisions and disputes. The bulk of the profession, trapped almost as surely as its patients within the walls of the isolated institutions over which it presided, was almost wholly cut off from the medical profession at large; and those who ministered in private asylums to lunatics drawn from the privileged classes occupied a relatively lucrative, but inevitably a small and declining niche in the medical marketplace. Significantly, the men who aspired to form the profession's elite sought, as and when they achieved such standing, to leave the institutional sector behind them; they opted for either a lucrative position in the state inspectorate that supervised some portion of the empire of asylumdom or a place among those who aspired to create an extra-institutional market for psychiatry's wares. Whichever path they took, though, these men, who formed the profession's natural leadership, all too frequently were then led to adopt intellectual positions that put them at odds with the interests and outlook of the rank and file. In word and deed, many of them proceeded to undermine the legitimacy of the very institutions that had given birth to medical psychology as a distinctive enterprise; and in the process, ironically enough, they did their part to inhibit the development of a strong and unified psychiatric profession. Mad-doctoring transformed thus remained a hobbled and stigmatized enterprise—handicapped not just by the limitations of its own knowledge and capacities, but also by its own internal divisions, and by the disdain and distrust that (regrettably as many may see it) have long marked society's attitudes to the mad and their keepers.

NOTES

CHAPTER ONE
THE TRANSFORMATION OF THE MAD-DOCTORING TRADE

1. See Andrew Scull, *The Most Solitary of Afflictions: Madness and Society in Britain, 1700–1900* London and New Haven: Yale University Press, 1993; Roy Porter, *Mind Forg'd Manacles: A History of Madness in England from the Restoration to the Regency* London: Athlone, 1987.

2. For defences of the biographical approach, see Thomas L. Hankins, "In Defense of Biography: The Use of Biography in the History of Science," *History of Science* 17, 1979, pp. 1–16; and the commentary in Charles Rosenberg, "Science in American Society," *Isis* 74, 1983, pp. 365–366.

3. For a similar insistence that "individual biography is a sociological and social-historical topic," see Steven Shapin, *A Social History of Truth* Chicago: University of Chicago Press, 1994, chap. 4, esp. pp. 127–130; and idem, "Personal Development and Intellectual Biography: The Case of Robert Boyle," *British Journal for the History of Science* 26, 1993, pp. 335–345.

4. C. Rosenberg, "Science in American Society," p. 365.

5. Cf. Harold Perkin, *The Rise of Professional Society: England since 1880* London: Routledge, 1989. See also Magali S. Larson, *The Rise of Professionalism: A Sociological Analysis* Berkeley: University of California Press, 1977; W. J. Reader, *Professional Men: The Rise of the Professional Classes in Nineteenth-Century England* New York: Basic Books, 1967.

6. The term "mad-doctor" now carries overwhelmingly pejorative connotations, but it was once the standard English expression for those medical men who sought to make a living from the treatment of the mentally disordered. Its modern replacement, "psychiatrist," which originated in Germany, did not come into widespread use until the last third of the nineteenth century and was not generally preferred by the profession itself until the twentieth century.

7. H. Perkin, *The Rise of Professional Society*, p. 16.

8. Anthony Trollope's (or rather, Sir Lionel Bertram's) definition of a profession. See *The Bertrams* London: Chapman and Hall, 1859, vol. 1, p. 154.

9. See M. Larson, *The Rise of Professionalism*.

10. For a superb recent analysis of "the role of trust and authority in the constitution and maintenance of systems of valued knowledge," see Steven Shapin's *A Social History of Truth*. Our emphasis here is on a different but related sense in which trust is constitutive of the place of the professional in the social order.

11. The problems were deeply embedded in the structure of the mad-doctors' enterprise: madhouses were "trading speculations [operated] with a view to pecuniary profit . . . the extent of the profit must depend on the amount that can be saved out of the sum paid for the board of each individual." Commissioners in Lunacy, *Further Report Relative to the Haydock Lodge Lunatic Asylum* London: Spottiswoode and Shaw, 1847, p. 14. For this reason alone, proprietors must "have a strong tendency to consider the interests of the patients and their own at direct variance."

S. W. Nicoll, *An Enquiry into the Present State of Visitation in Asylums for the Reception of the Insane* London: Harvey and Darnton, 1828, pp. 2–3. Worse still, it was alleged that the prospect of a lucrative stream of income in return for confining the inconvenient might induce medical men either to connive in the corrupt confinement of the sane or to delay releasing patients who recovered for fear of losing their fees. (See the discussion in Peter McCandless, "Liberty and Lunacy: The Victorians and Wrongful Confinement," in A. Scull (ed.), *Madhouses, Mad-Doctors, and Madmen: The Social History of Psychiatry in the Victorian Era* Philadelphia: University of Pennsylvania Press, 1981, pp. 339–362.) Worst of all, perhaps, the overwhelming taint of trade attendant on the way most mad-doctors made their living severely damaged their claims to professional status, clashing as it did with any attempt to acquire the veneer of gentlemanly standing the members of the major professions so eagerly sought. Nor did the other branch of the proto-profession find itself much better off: directly dependent upon often ill-paid salaried careers in the public sector, where they dealt all-but-exclusively with a poor and stigmatized clientele and were subordinated to the whims and authority of the laymen who made up the magistracy, their subservient position sharply constrained any and all attempts to secure their standing as professionals.

12. The seventh Earl of Shaftesbury, who played a major role in the reform movement from the late 1820s onwards, and who served as the chairman of the national Lunacy Commission from its establishment in 1845 to his death in 1885, was only the most prominent of these sceptics.

13. Harrington Tuke commented that "the study of mental disorders is studiously excluded from the medical curriculum" (quoted in Richard Hunter and Ida MacAlpine, *Three Hundred Years of Psychiatry* London: Oxford University Press, 1963, p. 1053); and subsequent presidents of the Medico-Psychological Association acknowledged despairingly the reality that "we seem to be very Levites among our medical brethren." W.H.O. Sankey, "Presidential Address," *Journal of Mental Science* 14, 1868, pp. 297–304; T. L. Rogers, "Presidential Address," *Journal of Mental Science* 20, 1874, pp. 327–351; W. T. Gairdner, "Presidential Address," *Journal of Mental Science* 28, 1882, pp. 321–332; Herbert Hayes Newington, "Presidential Address," *Journal of Mental Science* 35, 1889, pp. 293–315.

14. W.A.F. Browne, quoted in the *Journal of Mental Science* 4, 1857, p. 201.

15. Andrew Wynter, *The Borderlands of Insanity* 2d edition, London: Renshaw, 1877. It was, of course, their very status as members of the profession's elite that at once made Bucknill and Maudsley so conscious of the drawbacks of asylum practice and allowed them the luxury of becoming the most outspoken and articulate detractors of asylumdom. At best but a handful of their professional colleagues were as yet in a position to follow their examples and build extra-institutional careers. Here again, then, attention to the activities of the professional elite proves advantageous, throwing into relief strains and tensions lurking beneath the surface of professional life that ordinary practitioners perforce had to suppress.

16. Adrian Desmond, *The Politics of Evolution: Morphology, Medicine, and Reform in Radical London* Chicago: University of Chicago Press, 1989, p. 3.

17. On the external-internal distinction, see Steven Shapin, "Discipline and Bounding: The History and Sociology of Science As Seen Through the Externalism-Internalism Debate," *History of Science* 30, 1992, pp. 333–369.

CHAPTER TWO
A BETHLEMETICAL MAD-DOCTOR: JOHN HASLAM (1764–1844)

1. Haslam's will is reproduced and discussed in Richard Hunter and Ida Macalpine, "John Haslam: His Will and His Daughter," *Medical History* 6, 1962, pp. 22–26.

2. *The Lancet* i, 1844, p. 571. The longest and most detailed obituary was published in the *Literary Gazette* for July 27, 1844, pp. 484–485; a briefer summary in the *Gentleman's Magazine* n.s. 22, part 2, September 1844, pp. 322–323, simply borrowed portions of this text. Yet Haslam self-identified first and foremost with the medical profession, and here his death largely went unnoticed and unmourned.

3. Francis Scott, "English County Asylums," *Fortnightly Review* 32, 1879, p. 138.

4. Haslam's father lived to the age of ninety-two, dying on March 19, 1828, at his son's house.

5. Irvine Loudon, "The Nature of Provincial Medical Practice in Eighteenth-Century England," *Medical History* 29, 1985, pp. 1–32; idem, *Medical Care and the General Practitioner 1750–1850* Oxford: Clarendon Press, 1986.

6. Neil McKendrick, John Brewer, and J. H. Plumb, *The Birth of a Consumer Society* Bloomington: Indiana University Press, 1982; see also Roy Porter, *English Society in the Eighteenth Century* Harmondsworth, Middlesex: Penguin, 1982.

7. See *Observations of the Physician and Apothecary of Bethlem Hospital Upon the Evidence Taken Before the Committee of the Hon. House of Commons for Regulating Madhouses* London: Bryer, 1816, p. 54.

8. Loudon provides data that suggest the average apprenticeship premium for London apothecaries in the period immediately preceding Haslam's entry into the profession was of the order of £100, the annual income of a moderately successful lawyer or minor clergyman. *Medical Care*, pp. 42–44, 113–114. See also Joan Lane, "The Role of Apprenticeship in Eighteenth-Century Medical Education in England," in W. F. Bynum and R. Porter (eds.), *William Hunter and the Eighteenth-Century Medical World* Cambridge: Cambridge University Press, 1985, pp. 57–103.

9. Loudon, *Medical Care*, p. 48.

10. On Fordyce and Pitcairn, see Denis Leigh, *The Historical Development of British Psychiatry* Oxford: Pergamon Press, 1961, vol. 1, pp. 97–99.

11. Haslam, *Observations of the Physician and Apothecary*, p. 54.

12. See Anonymous, *A Narrative of Some Late Injurious Proceedings of the Managers of the Royal Infirmary* Edinburgh, 1785.

13. Dennis Leigh (*Historical Development*) wrongly asserts that Haslam attended Cambridge *after* his disgrace in 1816. Both *Observations of the Physician and Apothecary* and the title page of Haslam's first book, published in 1798, demonstrate the contrary.

14. Cf. D. Leigh, "John Haslam," *Journal of the History of Medicine* 10, 1955, p. 19.

15. Quoted in Leigh, *Historical Development*, p. 101.

16. For some contemporary commentary, cf. William Rowley, *Truth Vindicated, Or, The Specific Differences of Mental Diseases Ascertained, and Reasons for Declaring the Case of a Great Person to Have Been Only a Fever or a Symptomatic Delirium* London: Wingrave, 1790; and for a modern concurrence in this judgement, cf. Ida Macalpine and Richard Hunter, *George III and the Mad Business* London: Allen Lane, 1969.

17. See Porter, *Mind Forg'd Manacles*; and Scull, *The Most Solitary of Afflictions*.

18. Thomas Arnold (1742–1816), author of *Observations on the Nature, Kinds, Causes, and Prevention of Insanity, Lunacy, or Madness* 2 vols. Leicester: Robinson and Cadell, 1782–1786, owner of Belle Grove Asylum and physician to the Leicester Lunatic Asylum.

19. John Ferriar (1761–1815), author of *Medical Histories and Reflections* 3 vols. London: Cadell and Davies, 1792–1798, and physician to the Manchester Infirmary and Lunatic Hospital.

20. Joseph Mason Cox (1763–1818) author of *Practical Observations on Insanity* London: Baldwin and Murray, 1806; owner of the Fishponds Lunatic Asylum near Bristol.

21. Sir Alexander Crichton (1763–1856), author of *An Inquiry into the Nature and Origin of Mental Derangement* 2 vols. London: Cadell and Davies, 1798.

22. Edward Long Fox (1761–1835), owner of Cleve Hill and subsequently of Brislington House private madhouses.

23. William Saunders Hallaran (?1765–1825), author of *Practical Observations on the Causes and Cure of Insanity* Cork, Ireland: Hodges and M'Arthur, 1818, physician to the Cork Lunatic Asylum and owner of a private asylum at Cittadella, near Cork.

24. See chapter 4 below.

25. Sir Andrew Halliday (1781–1839), author of *A General View of the Present State of Lunatics, and Lunatic Asylums* London: Underwood, 1828, and consulting physician to the Crichton Royal Asylum, Dumfries.

26. See William Pargeter, *Observations on Maniacal Disorders* Reading: for the author, 1792.

27. The most famous of these was the Lincolnshire clergyman, Francis Willis, brought to London to treat George III. Willis had obtained an M.D. degree from Oxford in 1759, when his treatment of bodily disease among his parishioners brought threats of prosecution from local doctors (hence his derisive nickname, Dr. Duplicate). Lewis Southcombe, rector of Rose Ashe, Devonshire, and author of *Peace of Mind and Health of Body United* London: Cooper, 1750, enjoyed a local reputation for skill in treating the mad; and the Reverend John Lord owned a small madhouse in Drayton Parslow, Buckinghamshire. Among nonconformists, the Baptist Joseph Mason founded the Fishponds madhouse (later taken over by his grandson, Joseph Mason Cox) in 1760.

28. Two of the best known were Benjamin Faulkner, owner of a private madhouse in Chelsea and author of *Observations on the General and Improper Treatment of Insanity* London: for the author, 1790; and Thomas Bakewell, proprietor of Spring Vale Asylum in Staffordshire and author of *The Domestic Guide, in Cases of Insanity* London: Allbut, 1805. Among female proprietors, a Mrs. Sarah Minchin (d. 1778) ran a madhouse at Hook Norton in Oxfordshire for nearly half a century.

29. See William Parry-Jones, *The Trade in Lunacy* London: Routledge and Kegan Paul, 1972; and for additional discussion, Charlotte MacKenzie, *Psychiatry for the Rich: A History of Ticehurst Private Asylum* London: Routledge, 1993, chap. 1.

30. Porter, *Mind Forg'd Manacles*, p. 164.

31. John Haslam, *A Letter to the Metropolitan Commissioners in Lunacy* London: Whittaker, Treacher, 1830, p. 6. To cite just three undoubtedly exceptional examples: William Battie, physician to St. Luke's Asylum and owner of private madhouses

in Islington and Clerkenwell, was a self-made man who left an estate of between £100,000 and £200,000 pounds at his death, largely derived from his practice as a mad-doctor; by 1815, Thomas Warburton received as much as £1,500 a year to confine the Duke of Atholl's son at Hoxton House; and Anthony Addington's private madhouse at Reading, opened in 1749, provided an important source of funds for his upwardly mobile family (his son subsequently became Prime Minister as well as a governor of Bethlem).

32. Cf. J. Haslam, *Observations on Madness and Melancholy* London: Callow, 1809, p. 282.

33. Haslam, *A Letter to the Metropolitan Commissioners*, pp. 1, 6.

34. Ibid., pp. 6–7.

35. Jonathan Andrews, "Bedlam Revisited: A History of Bethlem Hospital c.1634–c.1770," Ph.D. diss., London University, 1991, p. 353.

36. William F. Bynum, "Physicians, Hospitals, and Career Structures in Eighteenth Century London," in Bynum and Porter (eds.), *William Hunter*, pp. 118, 121. Bynum rightly emphasizes the *general* significance of this phenomenon in the development of medical careers in this era: hospital appointments were a *means* to, rather than a recognition of, professional success.

37. James Monro began the dynasty in 1728, and his great grandson, Edward Thomas, took it into the 1850s.

38. For discussion of this pattern of nepotism among Bethlem appointments, see J. Andrews, "Bethlem Revisited," pp. 251–258. On the establishment of a general pattern of endogamy in the recruitment of eighteenth-century professions, see Geoffrey Homes, *Augustan England: Professions, State and Society* London: Allen and Unwin, 1982, p. 217.

39. Bethlem General Court of Governors Minutes (hereafter Bethlem GCGM), in manuscript, Bethlem Hospital archives. Haslam was perhaps fortunate to have such a small field of competitors: between 1656 and 1772, the average number of applicants on each occasion the position fell vacant had been nearly eight.

40. *Select Committee on Madhouses*, 1815, evidence of John Haslam, p. 102.

41. Bethlem GCGM, April 30, 1795. In November, this was supplemented by a £50 allowance to buy furniture and linens, and a further £15 for the purchase of a bed and furniture. See also November 26, 1795.

42. Bethlem GCGM, July 16, 1795. The Governors reaffirmed the respective duties of their medical officers in the minutes of March 4, 1802. Like his father and grandfather before him, Monro seems to have devoted much of what limited effort he expended on the mad-business to the family's lucrative private madhouse, Brooke House in Clapton.

43. See the details provided in Andrews, "Bedlam Revisited," pp. 278–282.

44. *Select Committee on Madhouses*, 1816, p. 41, evidence of James Simmonds, the head keeper at Bethlem.

45. House of Commons, *Select Committee on Madhouses*, 1816, evidence of John Watts, the superintendent of Miles's house.

46. The Governors of the hospital were induced to accept this arrangement by the promise of a state subsidy for rebuilding the hospital, a development to which we shall return.

47. The numbers involved were quite substantial. For instance, James Veitch, the

surgeon to Miles's madhouse, testified that, of 180 seaman, soldiers, and marines kept in the establishment at government expense since his appointment on June 27, 1815, 104 were transfers from Bethlem. *Select Committee on Madhouses, 1816,* pp. 65–67. This amounted to more than a fifth of the total number of patients in the establishment.

48. *Select Committee on Madhouses, 1815,* p. 106; 1816, p. 48, evidence of John Haslam.

49. Ibid., 1816, p. 48.

50. John Dunston subsequently formalized the family connection by marrying Warburton's daughter.

51. The diaries of Thomas Monro's son, Edward Thomas, provide a remarkable window into this hitherto obscure set of relationships. Monro, George Man Burrows, Thomas Mayo, Alexander Sutherland, and John Warburton—the top echelon of madhouse keepers—met regularly at the Royal College with their nominal supervisors, such as Sir Lucas Pepys, Sir Henry Halford, and Drs. Powell, Tierney, Baillie, Heberden, Maton, Bree, and Hue. All these Commissioners also sent patients to Monro's asylum, Brooke House. For examples of Monro dining with Commissioners, see Diaries, August 16, 1811 (Dr. Pemberton); September 29, 1815 (Drs. Latham and Turner); December 23, 1820 (Drs. Warren and Nevinson); September 30, 1825 (Drs. Turner and Halford); and July 25, 1826 (Heberden). For a joint consultation with Halford, then a Commissioner, Diaries, July 25, 1826. (We would like to thank Dr. F.J.G. Jeffries, a descendant of Monro's, for providing us with photocopies of these diaries.)

52. Compare the casual allusion in Alexander Pope's *Dunciad:*

Close to those walls where Folly holds her throne,
And laughs to think Monro would take her down,
Where, o'er the gates, by his famed father's hand,
Great Cibber's brazen brainless brothers stand.

53. See Joseph Girdler to Lord Fermanagh, in Margaret Verney (ed.), *Verney Letters of the Eighteenth Century from the Manuscripts at Claydon House* London: Benn, vol. 2, p. 202.

54. A surviving casebook for 1766 records a hundred cases at this madhouse alone.

55. Some idea of John Monro's business acumen and success can be deduced from his will, which details pecuniary legacies and gifts totalling £12,500, quite apart from his property and madhouses in Clapham and Clerkenwell, which generated sufficient income to allow him to require his sons to pay his widow an annuity of £500.

56. A talented amateur painter himself, he also served as a patron to others, including J.W.M. Turner. For details, see G. W. Thornbury, *Life of J.W.M. Turner* London: Chatto and Windus, 1904; and the Victoria and Albert catalogue, *Dr. Thomas Monro (1759–1833) and the Monro Academy, Prints and Drawing Gallery, February–May 1976.*

57. In his testimony before the 1815 *Select Committee on Madhouses* (p. 95), he was to contrast his infrequent and glancing attention to the patients at Bethlem with

his far more assiduous attention to his paying patients at Brooke House, where "I have forty odd patients, and as many servants." This evidence needs to be treated with some scepticism because Monro was clearly attempting to distance himself from the scandal which by then was engulfing Bethlem. But his infrequent attendance at the hospital was confirmed by a number of other witnesses, and he had no obvious reason to dissimulate about the nature of his other professional activities. Independently, his son's diaries reveal a network of private practice that extended to a substantial number of other madhouses, including Peckham House, Fox's house at Edmonton, and the Red and White Houses at Hoxton, as well as consultations in Guilford, Cheltenham, Tewkesbury, Bristol, and Witney. He also serviced patients in Hertfordshire and Essex.

58. *Select Committee on Madhouses*, 1815, p. 104.

59. Ironically, immediately after Haslam's dismissal, the apothecary *was* given the power to hire or suspend the male keepers, subject to the approval of the house committee. Bethlem GCGM, June 28, 1816.

60. House of Commons, *Select Committee on Madhouses*, p. 106.

61. Even when the matron and steward approached senescence, the Governors proved extremely reluctant to replace them, and Haslam was left to cope as best he could.

62. Andrews, "Bedlam Revisited," pp. 174–175.

63. Classification was to be a central component in the new system of managing the mad emerging at this time, usually referred to as "moral treatment," and constituted a vital part of the advance in management techniques that permitted a diminution and ultimately the complete abandonment of "mechanical restraint"—gyves, handcuffs, chains, straitjackets, and the like. Haslam's inability to experiment along these lines—and classification is accorded no place in his extensive writings on the treatment of insanity—may have helped to sustain his traditional belief in the vital and salutary effects of physical restraint, a belief that cut him off from what was to become the new orthodoxy in the field.

64. *Report Respecting the Present State and Condition of Bethlem Hospital* London: Richardson, 1800.

65. Bethlem Court of Governors' Minutes (hereafter Bethlem CGM), July 6, 1809.

66. *Select Committee on Madhouses*, 1815, pp. 117–118, evidence of Richard Clark, treasurer of Bethlem.

67. Ibid., pp. 99–100 (Monro), p. 104 (Haslam). Neither man evidenced the least concern about this lack of consultation. The proponents of moral treatment were to place much emphasis on architecture itself as a means of remoralizing and resocializing the insane, but Haslam had obviously neither absorbed nor accepted these novel notions. (Nor, equally obviously, did the Bethlem Governors.) The insouciance displayed on this subject by both Haslam and Monro is one further mark of the gulf that separated them from the next generation of alienists.

68. In practice, the emphasis on candour and openness was not always easily sustained. Thomas Bakewell, for instance, in the midst of an otherwise straightforward account of his practice, apologized "for the extreme shortness of the list of medicines used," pleading that he was "under strong family obligations not to dis-

close" certain secrets. *The Domestic Guide*, quoted in Richard Hunter and Ida Macalpine (eds.), *Three Hundred Years of Psychiatry* Oxford: Oxford University Press, 1963, p. 705.

69. John Haslam, *Observations on Insanity* London: Rivington, 1798, pp. vii, viii. Battie had been instrumental in setting up St. Luke's as a rival to Bethlem in 1751.

70. See W. Perfect, *Methods of Cure, in Some Particular Cases of Insanity* Rochester: for the author, 1778; idem, *Cases of Insanity and Nervous Disorders, Successfully Treated* Rochester: for the author, [1780]; and *Select Cases in the Different Species of Insanity, Lunacy, or Madness* Rochester: Gillman, 1787.

71. Haslam, *Observations on Insanity*, p. 14.

72. Shrewdly, Haslam insisted that "as my plan extends only to a description of that which I have observed, I shall neither amplify, nor embellish my volume by quotations" (ibid., p. 14)—a strategy that maximized the strength he could draw from his Bethlem appointment.

73. Philippe Pinel, *Traité médico-philosophique sur l'aliénation mentale* Paris: Richard, Caille and Ravier, [1801].

74. *A Treatise on Insanity* trans. D. D. Davis, London: Cadell and Davies, 1806.

75. Ibid., pp. 49–51, 184, 189. This final passage was immediately followed by a lengthy quotation from Haslam himself. Ibid., pp. 190–191. For other approving commentary on Haslam's work, see pp. 179–80; 214–216, 251, 252, 255, 263–264. Only Ferriar was accorded a similar measure of respect, though in his case it was mixed with a substantial amount of criticism and dissent.

76. Haslam, *Observations on Madness*, pp. v, vi.

77. Ibid., pp. 282, 273.

78. Pargeter, *Observations on Maniacal Disorders* pp. 50–51; also pp. 52, 58–59.

79. See the account provided in *The Life and Times of F. Reynolds, Written by Himself* London: Colburn, 1826, vol. 2, pp. 23–24.

80. Haslam, *Observations on Madness*, p. 276.

81. Joseph Mason Cox, *Practical Observations on Insanity* London: Baldwin and Murray, 1804, 1806. Subsequently, the book was to appear in a further enlarged third edition (London: Baldwin and Underwood, 1813), as well as in American (1811) and German (1811) editions.

82. See Haslam, *Observations on Madness*, pp. 303, 307, 330–331, 340–341.

83. John Haslam, *Illustrations of Madness* London: Rivington, 1810, p. 3. Five years later, the patient in question, one James Tilly Matthews, was to play an important role in Haslam's disgrace.

84. Ibid., pp. 15–16.

85. *Select Committee on Madhouses*, 1815, p. 106—a situation he must have found galling in the extreme.

86. Haslam, *Observations on Insanity*, pp. ix, 12–13, 102–103, 104–106.

87. See ibid., pp. 136–147.

88. For Battie's emphasis on the utility of "bodily pain" and "fear," cf. *Treatise on Madness*, pp. 84–85.

89. Haslam, *Observations on Insanity*, pp. 122–123, 125, 126–127, 128, 133. See also the similar passages in *Observations on Madness*, pp. 283–297, with their stress on "the mild and rational practice of Bethlem Hospital."

90. See Samuel Tuke, *Description of the Retreat* York: Alexander, 1813, and the

review by Sydney Smith in the *Edinburgh Review* 23, 1814, pp. 189–198. The definitive history of the Retreat is Anne Digby, *Madness, Morality, and Medicine: A Study of the York Retreat, 1796–1914* Cambridge: Cambridge University Press, 1985.

91. See Tuke, *Description of the Retreat*, pp. ix, 113, 122–123, 133, 134–135, 163, 164, 170, 204–205, 210, 213–215. Only the indiscriminate medical treatment at Bethlem (which, as we have seen, Haslam had publicly attributed to Monro) was the occasion for criticism. Cf. ibid., pp. 119–120. None of which should be taken as suggesting that Haslam had discovered moral treatment *avant la lettre*: many of the key features of Tuke's regime were entirely absent from Haslam's therapeutic practice. Tuke placed great stress on the importance of labour in the treatment of insanity; the Retreat's architecture (extending to such minute details as the construction of its windows) and the layout of its grounds were portrayed as a vital part of its regime; and classification of patients according to the degree to which their behaviour approached "rationality" was likewise an absolutely central element in his approach. Haslam displayed no interest whatsoever in the relevance of work, of architecture, or of classification as therapeutic tools—which perhaps should come as no surprise, since none of them were techniques he could conceivably have employed at Bethlem, given the physical arrangements and condition of the hospital and its level of staffing.

92. Edward Wakefield, "Plan for an Asylum for Lunatics," *The Philanthropist* 3, 1812, pp. 226–229.

93. Oddly enough, this was the very day the General Court of Governors met to go through the formality of reelecting the hospital's officers, including Haslam and Monro, for the next twelve months.

94. This regulation had been introduced in 1770, when Bethlem abandoned its long-standing practice of allowing the general public to enter its galleries and view the patients on payment of a nominal fee.

95. *Select Committee on Madhouses*, 1815, p. 11.

96. [Edward Wakefield], "Extracts from the Report of the Committee Employed to Visit Houses and Hospitals for the Confinement of Insane Persons. With Remarks. By Philanthropus," *The Medical and Surgical Journal* 32, August 1814, pp. 122–128.

97. *Select Committee on Madhouses*, 1815, pp. 12, 36.

98. Ibid., pp. 11, 12, 36.

99. Ibid., p. 12. Wakefield mistakenly referred to him as *William* Norris. On this second visit, he had brought an artist with him, and a sketch of Norris in his cage was to become an extraordinarily effective piece of propaganda. The Bethlem Court of Governors Minutes reveal that Norris's confinement in this apparatus actually dated from June 16, 1804.

100. Ibid.

101. Bethlem CGM, June 23, 1814.

102. Bethlem GCGM, June 28, 1814. (Both Haslam and Monro were later to attempt to use this Governors' report as a key element in their defence against charges of mistreatment of patients).

103. Ibid. Norris, they contended, was "by no means seriously out of health at this time"—an unfortunate judgement, for he was to expire in a matter of months, dying of the consumption he had contracted while confined.

104. Between April and July, 1814, Rose busily tried to secure the passage of

legislation creating a tighter system of regulation for madness. The Bethlem governors, sensing a serious infringement on their authority, fought this proposal fiercely, lobbying Rose, and the Home Secretary, Lord Sidmouth, for an exemption from the bill's provisions. See Bethlem CGM, April 21, May 6, July 8, 1814.

105. The hospital surgeon, Bryan Crowther, had just died, and that office was accordingly declared vacant, pending the nomination of candidates and the election of a replacement. (On July 7, 1815, William Lawrence was selected to replace him.)

106. At least four members of the Select Committee, Lord Robert Seymour, the Honourable Henry Grey Bennet, Charles Callis Western, and William Smith, had formed part of Wakefield's inspection party and were later to testify directly about what they had seen.

107. *Select Committee on Madhouses*, 1815, pp. 93, 95.

108. Ibid., p. 99.

109. Ibid., pp. 95, 97, 99.

110. May 10, 12, 19, 1815; March 8, 15, 1816.

111. See, for example, Bethlem Governors' Sub-Committee Minutes, March 18, 25, May 6, 1797 (banning Mrs. Matthews from the hospital); Lord Chancellor's Office to Bethlem Governors, December 23, 1808; Bethlem Governors' Sub-Committee Minutes, August 12, 1809; CGM, August 11, 1814. The family's affidavits and certificates attesting to Matthews's sanity from Drs. Clutterbuck and Birkbeck, together with the mass of evidence the hospital assembled to secure dismissal of a habeus corpus case before Mr. Justice Leblanc in December 1809 are also preserved in the Bethlem archives.

112. On admission, and for some time thereafter, Matthews had exhibited a remarkable array of delusions and hallucinations. By his own account, he was persecuted by a team of ferocious ruffians who tormented him from a distance by means of a device called an "Air Loom," an apparatus fuelled by "effluvia of dogs—stinking human breath—putrid effluvia . . . stench of the sesspool [sic]—gaz from the anus of the horse—human gaz" and so forth, by means of which they endeavoured to control his thoughts and to inflict on him all manner of tortures. All of this dastardly activity was allegedly designed to foil Matthews's attempts to reveal a plot by the French revolutionaries "for . . . republicanizing Great Britain and Ireland, and particularly for disorganizing the British navy"—a plot in which he sought to implicate a member of the Cabinet, Lord Liverpool. Interventions by Lord Liverpool in 1809, and by Lord Sidmouth (then Home Secretary) in 1813 and again in 1814, were explicitly aimed at securing his continued confinement. See Lord Liverpool to the Bethlem Governors, September 7, 1809, Bethlem archives; letter from J. Poynder (clerk of Bethlem) to Haslam, June 10, 1813; and Bethlem CGM, August 11, 1814.

113. Haslam, *Illustrations of Madness*. Haslam's animus cannot be concealed: "if . . . the Reader, throughout this narrative, should suspect a sneer, the benevolence of the Writer allows him to soften and correct it by a smile." p. vi.

114. Cf. Charles Dickens, *Little Dorrit* London: Bradbury and Evans, 1857.

115. *Select Committee on Madhouses*, 1815, p. 14, evidence of Richard Staveley. John Blackburne, one of the Bethlem keepers, subsequently confirmed that Matthews was "much respected by the patients and servants of the Hospital. No man more so." Ibid., 1816, p. 91.

116. Haslam, *A Letter to the Governors*, p. 30.

117. Ibid., p. 31. The jab at "those who passed for persons of sound mind" is vintage Haslam and was scarcely likely to endear him to his critics.

118. Similarly, his *Illustrations of Madness*, presented Matthews's own views verbatim to the reader, on the assumption that the lunatic protesting his sanity would condemn himself out of his own mouth, mad speech being a nonsense to be discarded rather than scrutinized. As Allan Ingram has recently noted, throughout the seventeenth and eighteenth centuries, "the testimony of the mad was regarded as being without meaning." *The Madhouse of Language* London: Routledge, 1991, p. 22.

119. As Haslam now realized, "This manuscript . . . had fascinated certain of the honourable members of the mad-house committee; it had been carefully perused, and doubtless fully digested; for I found the questions proceed in the same order they were detailed in the lunatic's journal; in some of their enquiries they condescended to employ his peculiar expressions: and in one instance, an honourable member left his seat to refresh his recollection at this authentic source." *A Letter to the Governors*, p. 31.

120. *Select Committee on Madhouses*, 1815, pp. 62–63. They were, he repeatedly insisted, the best means of rendering even the most violent madman "an innoxious animal."

121. Ibid., pp. 63–67, 82–90, 104, 106.

122. Ibid., p. 104; ibid, 1816, pp. 49–50.

123. Haslam, *A Letter to the Governors*, pp. 27, 28; emphasis in the original.

124. *Observations of the Physician and Apothecary*, p. 43.

125. Bethlem CGM, April 5, 1816.

126. *Observations of the Physician and Apothecary*, pp. 2 (Monro), 37 (Haslam).

127. Ibid., p. 50.

128. Bethlem CGM, May 15, 1816.

129. The governors had decided in the interim to elect *two* visiting physicians. E. T. Monro was nonetheless the top vote-getter, receiving 160 votes, compared to 151 and 106 for the two runners-up—one of several indications that the governors rejected the reformers' criticisms and had simply offered up Thomas Monro and Haslam as sacrificial victims to quiet their critics' complaints.

130. Bethlem CGM, July 19, 1816. Wallett received 76 votes, Haslam 1. Three years later, Wallett was himself dismissed when he was found guilty of financial corruption.

131. Ibid., June 28, 1816.

132. *A Catalogue of the Entire Library of John Haslam, Esq.* London: Leigh and Southeby, 1816.

133. Leigh, *Historical Development*, p. 114.

134. John Haslam, *Considerations on the Moral Management of Insane Persons* London: Hunter, 1817.

135. Tuke, *Description of the Retreat*, pp. 110–111, 115. For similarly pessimistic conclusions, see Pinel, *A Treatise on Insanity*.

136. *Select Committee on Madhouses*, 1815, p. 24.

137. See, for instance, the sarcastic comments of Godfrey Higgins, the Yorkshire magistrate who had helped to expose abuses at the York Asylum. *The Evidence Taken Before a Committee of the House of Commons Respecting the Asylum at York* Doncaster: Sheardown, 1816.

138. Haslam, *On the Moral Management of Insane Persons*, pp. 2–3, 5–7.

139. Ibid., pp. 23–24, 25, 26, 28, 30–31. For similar views, see, for example, Paul Slade Knight, *Observations on the Causes, Symptoms, and Treatment of Derangement of the Mind* London: Longman, 1827, p. 16.

140. For details of these bills, and an even more far-reaching measure introduced in 1819, see Hervey, "The Lunacy Commission, 1845–60," pp. 64–67. All three bills were defeated.

141. John Haslam, *Medical Jurisprudence as it Relates to Insanity* London: Hunter, 1817, preface, pp. iv–vi. A year later, he was to return to the attack, condemning the reformers' schemes as "involving prodigious, but useless expense—of oppressive operation—tending to retard the progress of medical science, and fabricated to confirm and extend the horrors of insanity." *A Letter to the Governors of Bethlem Hospital, Containing an Account of their Management of that Institution for the Last Twenty Years* London: Taylor and Hessey, 1818, p. 41.

142. For examples of others engaged in the same endeavour, see George Man Burrows, *Cursory Remarks on a Bill Now in the House of Peers for Regulating of Madhouses* London: Harding, 1817; and Anon., *Insanity* London: Underwood, 1817.

143. Haslam, *Medical Jurisprudence*.

144. Haslam, *A Letter to the Governors*; idem, *Sound Mind; or Contributions to the Natural History and Physiology of the Human Intellect* London: Longman, Hurst, Rees, Orme, and Brown, 1819.

145. Hence he always made sure, in whatever he wrote, to emphasize the central requirement for *experience* in those who sought to treat the insane and his own credentials in this respect. On his awareness of the latent functions of medical publications, compare the comments of Dr. Diddleum, one of the characters Haslam invented for his satirical series of articles, "The Barley-Corn Club": "medical books are mere lures, hooks nicely bated for the sport and emolument of the author." *London Literary Gazette*, August 16, 1823, p. 525.

146. This claim was, in fact, an overstatement. There was at least one earlier book on this topic: John Johnstone's *Medical Jurisprudence: On Madness* Birmingham: Johnson, 1800, published in the immediate aftermath of James Hadfield's trial for his assassination attempt on George III.

147. These oddly named and very expensive proceedings, held before a Master in Lunacy, were designed for propertied persons who were suspected of being insane. Such lunatics were known as Chancery lunatics, and, as we shall see, a separate system of regulation and inspection surrounded their persons and their property.

148. In Haslam's words, a means "to shelter crime under the pretence of insanity." *Medical Jurisprudence*, p. 47.

149. Ibid., p. 4.

150. Ibid., pp. 61, 63, 64.

151. Ibid., pp. 4–5, 7, 62.

152. Quoted in W.A.F. Browne, *What Asylums Were, Are, and Ought to Be* Edinburgh, Black, 1837, p. 7.

153. On the other hand, his skills as a forensic witness received fulsome praise in the *Lancet*, which cannot have hurt his earning power. Referring to the muddled and contradictory medical testimony in a series of "Commissions of Lunacy" on

mad scions of the aristocracy, Wakley commented that "*such* evidence is one of the opprobia of our profession, and with the single exception of the testimony of Dr. Haslam, we have seen none that ought to have weighed more than a feather in the scales of justice." *The Lancet* 12, 1827, p. 18.

154. Hunter and Macalpine's contrary conclusion that his income was always "meagre" in the years after his dismissal from Bethlem (*Three Hundred Years of Psychiatry*, p. 632) seems to depend largely on the small sum he left at his death, ignoring the inferences that can be drawn from the other evidence that survives. We know from their own researches that Haslam was earning sufficient income in the late 1820s to support not just himself and his aged father, but his widowed daughter, Henrietta Hunter, and her two children, Henrietta and Harriet Eliza, at his house on Lambs Conduit Street. Cf. Hunter and MacAlpine, "John Haslam: His Will." Haslam survived late into old age (he was eighty when he died), and it is likely that his long life, and not any lack of success in his practice, ultimately left him in reduced circumstances.

155. See, for example, *London Literary Gazette*, July 26; August 16, 23, 30; September 13, 1823, pp. 475, 525–526, 542–543, 557–558, 588–589.

156. Cf. Francis Schiller, "Haslam of 'Bedlam,' Kitchiner of the 'Oracles': Two Doctors Under Mad King George III, and their Friendship," *Medical History* 28, 1984, pp. 189–201.

157. Unlike Haslam, however, Morison was awarded a pension of £150 a year by the Governors.

158. As one measure of the circles within which Haslam was moving, when his new friend Alexander Morison wanted to draw the attention of the Duke of York to his course of lectures on insanity, it was Haslam to whom he turned for assistance, asking him to use his good offices to lay the syllabus before the Duke. See Morison Diaries, Royal College of Physicians, Edinburgh (hereafter RCPE/MD), January 24, 1824. Another of Haslam's close friends was Sir Anthony Carlisle (1768–1840), a courtier knighted by the Prince Regent in 1820, who was to serve as president of the Royal College of Surgeons in 1818 and again in 1837.

159. St. Bartholomew's Hospital, Governors Minute Books, May 5, 7, 19, 1824.

160. See *The Lancet* 9, 1825–1826, pp. 823–829—a lecture received, Wakley informed his readers, "with reiterated shouts of applause."

161. *The Lancet* i, 1827–1828, pp. 38–44, 71–76, 119–125, 207–212, 288–294, 335–341.

162. Wakley publicly termed him "an enlightened and honourable man"—perhaps a quid pro quo for Haslam making a speech as president of the London Medical Society in which he called the *Lancet* "not only the most extensively circulated, but also the best conducted of all the medical journals, not only of this country but probably of Europe." *The Lancet* 11, 1826–1827, pp. 837, 850. Never one to overlook a slight, real or imagined, Wakley was equally susceptible to flattery.

163. The London Medical Society had been founded in 1773 by John Coakley Lettsom with the deliberate intention of breaking down some of the barriers in a tripartite profession. Its initial constitution laid down that the society was to have thirty physicians, thirty surgeons, and thirty apothecaries as members. Election to its presidency demonstrates that Haslam had obtained considerable standing among his peers, particularly the reform-oriented segments of the profession opposed to the

narrow exclusivity of the medical corporations. On the society, see Thomas Hunt (ed.), *The Medical Society of London 1773–1973* London: Heinemann, 1972; and Sir St. Clair Thomson, *John Coakley Lettsom and the Foundation of the Medical Society [of London]* London: Harrison, 1918.

164. Hunter and Macalpine, "John Haslam: His Will," p. 22.

165. *Minutes of Evidence, Taken Before the Select Committee of the House of Lords on the Bills Relating to Lunatics and Lunatic Asylums*, 1828.

166. See the Diaries of E. T. Monro, March 17, 25; April 3, 12, 29; May 14, 16, 17, 1828.

167. "Lunatic Asylums," *London Medical Gazette* 1, May 17, 1828, p. 732.

168. Ibid., February 9, 1828, p. 278.

169. See the lengthy objections put forward by Sir Henry Halford, longtime president of the Royal College of Physicians: Halford Manuscripts, DG24/835/1, "Report on and suggested regulations for the keeping of lunatics," n.d.; and Halford's subsequent correspondence with the Marquess of Landsdowne, August 24, 1830, Halford Manuscripts, DG24/895/2, Leicestershire County Record Office.

170. Haslam, *A Letter to the Metropolitan Commissioners*, pp. 1–2; emphasis in the original.

171. Ibid., p. 3.

172. Ibid., p. 23; the autobiographical overtones are evident.

173. Ibid.

174. Ibid., pp. 7, 8–9.

175. Ibid., pp. 9, 13–14.

176. Metropolitan Commissioners in Lunacy, *Report*, 1830, pp. 4–5.

177. This prompted another withering remark by Haslam: surely, "it would be a whimsical inference, that the Bill was passed, and the Metropolitan Commissioners appointed, for the probable advantage of the keepers." *A Letter to the Metropolitan Commissioners*, p. 18.

178. Ibid., p. 17.

179. Alienists' attitudes towards those who supervised them, and who held individual careers and livelihoods in their hands, were naturally ambivalent at best. For the most part, however, they adopted the prudent course of grumbling only covertly and in private. Public criticism of the Lunacy Commission would thus come from general medical periodicals—the *Medical Circular*, *Medical Times*, and *British and Foreign Quarterly*—whose editors could voice objections to the interference of outsiders in medical judgements and in the financial affairs of proprietors of private asylums, without fear of subsequent retribution.

180. RCPE/MD, May 28, 1830.

181. *Tenth Report of the Directors of the Dundee Lunatic Asylum for the Year Ending 31st May 1830*, p. 5, quoted in Hunter and Macalpine, "John Haslam: His Will," p. 25.

182. Both Hunter and Monro were targeted for criticism by the Lunacy Commissioners, when the latter finally won access to Bethlem in 1851 (see *Report of the Commissioners in Lunacy to the Secretary of State on Bethlem Hospital*, 1853), and by 1853 both of them, recapitulating the careers of their fathers, were forced out of the hospital. (E. T. Monro was subsequently admitted as a patient to his family's private madhouse, Brooke House, where he remained until his death in 1856.)

183. See chapter 3 below.

184. The paper is reprinted in John C. Somers, *A Selection of Papers and Prize Essays on Subjects Connected With Insanity, Read Before the Society for Improving the Conditions of the Insane* London: for the Society, 1850, pp. 1–5. Haslam also delivered two other papers to the Society, "An Attempt to Institute the Correct Discrimination Between Crime and Insanity" and "On the Increase in Insanity, with an Endeavour to Detect the Causes of Its Multiplication," both also reprinted in the Somers volume, pp. 6–9 and 10–17.

185. Ibid., p. 11.

186. Ibid., pp. 1–2.

187. Ibid., pp. 3, 8.

188. RCPE/MD.

CHAPTER THREE
A BRILLIANT CAREER? JOHN CONOLLY (1794–1866)

1. *The Lancet* i, 1843–1844, pp. 71–72, quoting the *Morning Chronicle.*

2. *Select Committee on Lunatics,* 1859, pp. 45–49.

3. Sir James Crichton-Browne, *Victorian Jottings* London: Etchells and Macdonald, 1926.

4. Sir Benjamin Ward Richardson, "Medicine under Queen Victoria," *The Asclepiad,* 1877, vol. 4, pp. 203–214.

5. Richard Hunter and Ida Macalpine, "Introduction," to John Conolly, *An Inquiry Concerning the Indications of Insanity* facsimile ed. London: Dawsons, 1964, p. 1.

6. John Conolly, "Autobiographical sketch," reprinted in Leigh, *British Psychiatry,* pp. 211–215.

7. Conolly's first career choice was the subject of invidious comment among his relatives, the Tennysons. Writing to her brother, Ann Raines informed him that "John Conolly has got an Ensign's commission in the Cambridgeshire Militia and has joined the regiment at Leith, it is but a poor prospect for a young man but better than being idle." Ann Raines to George Tennyson, Lincolnshire Archives, Tennyson d'Eyncourt Papers, 4/71/61, quoted in Elizabeth Burrows, "Dr. Conolly and the Tennyson Family," unpublished paper, 1993, p. 7.

8. Henry Maudsley, "Memoir of the Late John Conolly," *Journal of Mental Science* 12, 1866, p. 161.

9. M. Jeanne Peterson, *The Medical Profession in Mid-Victorian London* Berkeley: University of California Press, 1978.

10. Anthony Trollope, *The Vicar of Bullhampton,* quoted in ibid., p. 194.

11. On the importance of possessing either a family tradition of medical practice and/or the means to short-circuit the otherwise laborious and uncertain business of building a general practice by purchasing an existing one, see Peterson, *Medical Profession,* passim., esp. pp. 91 ff.

12. Ibid., pp. 24 ff.

13. *Edinburgh Medical and Surgical Journal* 75, 1851, p. 255.

14. In later years Forbes was appointed physician to the Queen's household. For his career, see *Lives of the Fellows of the Royal College of Physicians of London 1826–1925* London: for the College, 1955, pp. 34–35 (hereafter cited as *Munk's Roll*).

15. Maudsley, "Memoir," p. 164.

16. Ibid., p. 172.

17. On medical incomes in this period, compare Peterson, *Medical Profession*, pp. 207 ff; and Loudon, *Medical Care*, chap. 11, 12.

18. H. H. Bellot, *University College London 1826–1926* London: University of London Press, 1929, p. 37.

19. There were some famous names, however, including Charles Bell, A. T. Thomson, and D. D. Davis. For biographical details, see *Munk's Roll*.

20. Peterson, *Medical Profession*, p. 161.

21. Conolly to Horner, July 21, 1827, College Collection, University College London Library (hereafter cited UCL).

22. Conolly [to Messrs Longman] July 21, 1827; May 28, 1828 (Wellcome Institute for the History of Medicine Collection, London). See also Conolly to Thomas Coates, April 3, 1828, Society for the Diffusion of Useful Knowledge Collection (hereafter cited SDUK Coll.), University College, London.

23. Conolly to Horner, September 26, 1827, November 7, 1827, UCL.

24. He had been preceded by Charles Bell.

25. *Morning Chronicle*, October 3,4, 1828. See also *The Life and Times of Henry Brougham by Himself* London: Blackwood, 1871, vol. 2, pp. 498–499. Towards the end of his lecture, however, Conolly took to task certain "injudicious, or selfish, or reckless men" whose divisive assaults on their professional brethren he deplored. The target of these remarks was Thomas Wakley, the crusading editor of the *Lancet*. *Pace* Wakley, he proceeded to inform his students that in building their careers, "probity and honour" were quite as vital as science: "not *knowledge* alone, but *character* is power; . . . knowledge without character can procure no more than temporary and very transient preeminence." As Conolly must have hoped, his criticisms won him support from the mouthpiece of the traditional medical elites, the *London Medical Gazette* (2, 1828, p. 568), which praised his "most eloquent" remarks. But he may not have counted on the cost—the bitter enmity of Wakley, which was to last until Conolly's triumphs with nonrestraint in the 1840s. "The Professor," the *Lancet* (i, 1828, pp. 50–51) promptly observed, "is . . . a master of that branch of rhetoric, which has been aptly denominated *twaddle* . . . he has commenced most inauspiciously."

26. Conolly, *Introductory Lecture*, p. 16.

27. Maudsley, "Memoir," pp. 165–166.

28. Conolly, *Introductory Lecture*, pp. 16–17.

29. "Review of *An Inquiry into the Indications of Insanity*," *Medicochirurgical Review* 13, 1830, pp. 289–308.

30. Robert Gardiner Hill, *A Lecture on the Management of Lunatic Asylums* London: Simpkin Marshall, 1839, pp. 4–5.

31. Conolly, *Inquiry*, pp. 8–9, 31.

32. Ibid., pp. 1, 4–5, 17, 28.

33. Ibid., pp. 7, 17–18, 25.

34. Ibid., pp. 30–31.

35. Michael Clark, "Victorian Psychiatry and the Concept of Morbid Introspection," in W. F. Bynum, Roy Porter, and Michael Shepherd (eds.), *The Anatomy of Madness* London: Routledge, 1988, vol. 3, pp. 71–101.

36. J. Conolly, *Inquiry*, pp. 18, 22–23.

37. Ibid., p. 22.

38. Ibid., pp. 7, 13–14, 37–38, 483.

39. "Review of *An Inquiry into the Indications of Insanity*," *The Lancet* ii, 1829–1830, pp. 646–652, 695–696.

40. *Medicochirurgical Review* 13, 1830, pp. 289–308.

41. For a solitary exception, see Maximillian Jacobi, *On the Construction and Management of Hospitals for the Insane* London: Churchill, 1841, pp. 77–80.

42. Bellot, *University College London*, p. 191.

43. University College London, Minute-book of the Faculty of Medicine, Inaugural Meeting, October 26, 1827.

44. Conolly to Horner, July 10, 1830, UCL.

45. Hunter and Macalpine, "Introduction" to J. Conolly, *Inquiry*, pp. 25–26.

46. Conolly to Horner, August 18, 1828, UCL.

47. Conolly to the University Council, May 5, 1830; see also John Hogg to Horner, May 8, 1830, UCL.

48. Horner to Conolly, July 8, 1830, UCL.

49. Conolly to Horner, July 10, 1830, UCL.

50. Conolly to Horner, July 19, 1830, UCL.

51. Bellot, *University College London,* p. 177; see also Desmond, *The Politics of Evolution*, p. 84. To make matters worse, the shareholders who had subscribed the University's capital expected the professors to generate sufficient surplus from student fees to provide a return on the money they had subscribed.

52. *A Letter to the Shareholders and Council of the University of London on the Present State of that Institution* London: Taylor, 1830, pp. 12–15, 23, 28.

53. *The Sun*, April 21, 1830.

54. Conolly to Horner, April 21, 1830, UCL.

55. Conolly to Horner, November 16, 1830, UCL.

56. Conolly to Horner, March 1, April 28, 1831, UCL.

57. Maudsley, "Memoir," p. 172.

58. Charles Knight, *Passages from a Working Life*, quoted in D. Leigh, *British Psychiatry*, p. 219.

59. Maudsley, "Memoir," pp. 173–174.

60. "Obituary of John Conolly," *Journal of Mental Science* 12, 1866, p. 148.

61. Maudsley, "Memoir," pp. 172–173.

62. *Correspondence between Mr Granville Sharp-Pattison and Dr N. Chapman* 3rd ed., Philadelphia: Webster, 1820.

63. Bellot, *University College London*, pp. 198–199.

64. *London Medical and Surgical Journal* 5, November 1, l830, pp. 443–448.

65. See *The Lancet* ii, 1830–1831, pp. 693–695, 721–727, 747, 753–757. Conolly's public support of a colleague closely identified with the conservatism of the College of Surgeons can only have compounded the dislike and contempt Wakley felt towards him.

66. Quoted in Hunter and Macalpine, "Introduction," to J. Conolly, *Inquiry*, p. 29.

67. Bellot, *University College London*, pp. 207–208.

68. Conolly to Horner, March 30, April 8, 1831, UCL.

69. For a recent analysis of the broader sociopolitical and intellectual issues at stake in these disputes, cf. Desmond, *The Politics of Evolution*, esp. chap. 2.

70. *Morning Chronicle*, October 23, 1828.

71. Conolly to the University Council, December 4, 1830, UCL.

72. Ibid.

73. He had previously been an unsuccessful candidate for the appointment as first superintendent at the new Hanwell Lunatic Asylum—ironically, a job John Conolly was to seek and obtain some years later.

74. Maudsley, "Memoir," p. 161.

75. Bellot, *University College London*, pp. 250–251.

76. Conolly to Horner, December 4, 1830, UCL.

77. Ibid. Thomson, indeed, was to succeed to Smith's chair in Medical Jurisprudence in 1832, holding this position in addition to his prior appointment as professor of Materia Medica and Therapeutics.

78. John Conolly to University Council, December 4, 1830—his official resignation. UCL.

79. John Conolly, "Valedictory Lecture on Retiring from London University," *London Medical Gazette*, 1831, vol. 8, pp. 161–162 ff.

80. Pouring salt on his wounds, Thomas Wakley jeeringly drew the attention of the profession at large to his resignation: "The chair of Medicine has been lately vacated by Dr. Conolly, whose absence we believe will prove no loss to the University." *The Lancet* ii, 1830–1831, p. 210.

81. Peterson, *Medical Profession*, p. 25.

82. Maudsley, "Memoir," p. 173. As Maudsley waspishly commented, this was "an amiable sentiment, which however, when closely analyzed, might be made to resolve itself into a liking for enjoyment without a liking for paying the painful cost of it."

83. Conolly to Coates, October 13, 1831, SDUK Coll., UCL.

84. Conolly to Coates, October 27, 1831, SDUK Coll., UCL.

85. Conolly to Coates, December 27, 1831, SDUK Coll., UCL.

86. Conolly to Coates, December 18, l831, SDUK Coll., UCL.

87. Conolly to Coates, October 13, 1831, SDUK Coll., UCL.

88. See, for example, Conolly to Coates, February 14, 1832; February 2, 1833 ("I venture to promise to finish forthwith my part of the Book of Gin"); May 13, 1834 (it would be done in three weeks if he could but get rid of his patients); January 14, 1836; till he finally abandoned the project later that year. SDUK Coll., UCL.

89. Conolly to Coates, January 17, 1832, SDUK Coll., UCL.

90. Conolly to Coates, May 7, 1832, SDUK Coll., UCL.

91. Conolly to Coates, May 7, 1832, SDUK Coll., UCL.

92. Conolly to Coates, May 13, 1834, SDUK Coll., UCL.

93. Conolly to Coates, January 14, 1836, SDUK Coll., UCL. His ambition still flickering, Conolly had been actively engaged on other fronts trying to secure a measure of professional visibility, at least in provincial circles. Charles Hastings, whom Conolly had known since 1822, was busily trying to organize an association of provincial doctors. Conolly had contributed to his journal, the *Midland Medical and Surgical Reporter*, in November 1831 and subsequently attended (together with his brother William) the inaugural meeting of the new Provincial Medical and Surgical Association—the ancestor of the British Medical Association—at Worcester on July 19, 1832. Together with his old friend from Chichester days, John Forbes, he had planned while in London to edit a *Cyclopedia of Practical Medicine*, and this appeared

in four volumes between 1833 and 1835 (with Hastings contributing a chapter on diseases of the chest). And early in 1836, Forbes again involved him in a new project, as joint founder and editor of the *British and Foreign Medical Review*.

94. Maudsley, "Memoir," p. 167.

95. A year later, Conolly discovered that his progressive politics and association with efforts to educate the working classes had cost him the job. Suitably chastened, he declined Coates' invitation to lecture for the SDUK at Lewes. Conolly to Coates, August 26, 1839, SDUK Coll., UCL.

96. Maudsley, "Memoir," p. 167.

97. Conolly, *Valedictory Lecture*, p. 161.

98. Maudsley, "Memoir," p. 173.

99. *Hanwell County Lunatic Asylum Visitors' Report* No. 45, 1838, pp. 187–188. The existing superintendent, Sir William Ellis, resigned rather than submit to the change.

100. *Hanwell Visitors' Report* No. 49, 1839, pp. 12–13.

101. *The Times*, May 15, 1839, p. 3.

102. *Hanwell Visitors' Report* No. 50, 1839, p. 26.

103. Maudsley, "Memoir," p. 172.

104. Looking back on this period at the very end of his life, he contrasted the expectations of some of the magistrates with his own view of the job: "I recollect being told when I took charge of the Hanwell Asylum that I could not find more than two hours' duty in the course of the day; I can only say that the duties began as soon as I was dressed, and never ended until I was nearly asleep." *Select Committee on Lunatics* 1859, p. 167.

105. Bakewell, *Domestic Guide*, p. ix.

106. Edward Jarvis to Almira Jarvis, May 31, June 5, 1860, Jarvis Papers, Concord Free Public Library, Concord, Massachusetts. We are grateful to Gerald Grob for this reference.

107. Maudsley, "Memoir," p. 169.

108. Tuke, *Description of the Retreat*, p. 163.

109. John Conolly quoted in Maudsley, "Memoir," p. 169.

110. Conolly, quoted in Granville, *The Care and Cure of the Insane*, vol. 1, p. 111.

111. Conolly, *Treatment of the Insane*, p. 323.

112. Conolly, quoted in Sir James Clark's *A Memoir of John Conolly, M.D., D.C.L.* London: Murray, 1869, pp. 22, 28.

113. *The Times*, December 10, 1840, p. 6.

114. J. G. Millingen, *Aphorisms on the Treatment and Management of the Insane* London: Churchill, 1840, p. 106.

115. *The Times*, January 25, 1841. This was perhaps an unfortunate comparison, given the subsequent fate of the bulk of the nineteenth-century pharmacopoeia.

116. "Editorial," *The Lancet* i, April 4, 1840, p. 58. There were some fifty contributions of one sort or another to this debate during the first six months of 1840.

117. Ibid.

118. Samuel Tuke, Introduction to M. Jacobi, *On the Construction of Hospitals for the Insane*, p. xxxv.

119. *Hansard's Parliamentary Debates*, 3rd series, 16 July, 1842, vol. 65, column 223.

120. *Illustrated London News*, May 21, 1843; see also January 15, 1848.

121. See, for example, *The Times*, November 18, December 10, 30, 1840; December 8, 14, 1841; January 5, 1842.

122. *The Times*, December 8, 14, 1841.

123. *The Times*, January 5, 1842. The praise may strike modern readers as misplaced, even itself bizarre, but the Victorians exhibited an unalloyed delight in the reduction of the vicious, the depraved, and the unruly to at least a simulacrum of order and decorum. Such practical demonstrations of the power of "reason and morality" evidently possessed great symbolic power, and those who successfully staged them could count on widespread approval and acclaim.

124. *The Times*, March 8, 1842.

125. *Morning Chronicle*, October 5, 1843.

126. Leigh, *British Psychiatry*, p. 227.

127. See *The Lancet* ii, August 10, 1850, pp. 181–182; August 17, 1850, p. 224.

128. *The Lancet* i, April 3, 1852, p. 339; Clark, *Memoir*, pp. 44–51.

129. Sir G. E. Paget, *The Harveian Oration* Cambridge: Deighton, Bell, 1866, pp. 34–35.

130. John Conolly, *On the Construction and Government of Lunatic Asylums* London: Churchill, 1847, p. 143.

131. Clark, *Memoir*, pp. vii–viii.

132. For example, *Hanwell Lunatic Asylum Annual Report*, 1840, p. 52; Conolly, *Treatment of the Insane*, pp. 177–178; idem, "President's Address," *Journal of Mental Science* 5, 1859, p. 74; Clark, *Memoir*, p. 49.

133. Hill, *Management of Lunatic Asylums*, p. 147.

134. He arrived in May 1839, with his brother William, proprietor of a licensed asylum at Cheltenham, and noted in the Visitors' Book, "Having read Mr. Hill's lecture . . . we visited this asylum with feelings of unusual curiosity and interest; we have been deeply impressed." Quoted in Hunter and Macalpine, "Introduction," to Conolly, *Treatment of the Insane*, p. x.

135. See, for example *The Lancet* ii, November 28, 1840, pp. 337–341; *The Lancet* i, January 9, 1841, pp. 532–540; *The Lancet* i, January 30, 1841, p. 659; *The Lancet* i, January 15, 1842, pp. 544–546.

136. Robert Gardiner Hill, *A Concise History of the Entire Abolition of Mechanical Restraint in the Treatment of the Insane* London: Longman, 1857, pp. 13–14.

137. Alexander Walk, "Lincoln and Non-restraint," *British Journal of Psychiatry* 117, 1970, p. 481.

138. *The Lancet* ii, August 24, 1850, pp. 247–248.

139. Charlesworth had died before this occurred, on February 20, 1853.

140. Compare C. W. Brook, *Battling Surgeon*, p. 149. Hill's claims were dismissed as "the audacious assaults of envy," and his sanity was subsequently called into question. (*The Lancet* i, March 4, 1854; *The Lancet* ii, October 10, 1857, p. 365.) Wakley's venom may in part have reflected his by now friendly relations with Conolly. It certainly also derived from the fact that Hill had the misfortune to have his cause adopted by the rival *Medical Circular*, a journal that attacked Wakley as a liar given to "senile ranting," "as insensible to evidence as he is to shame," a "licensed reviler" who was "an offense to professional nostrils." (*Medical Circular*, August 11, 1852, p. 304.) Wakley was only too ready to respond in kind.

141. Robert Gardiner Hill, *Lunacy: Its Past and Present* London: Longman, Green, 1870, p. 53.

142. Walk, "Lincoln and Non-Restraint," p. 494.

143. Maudsley, "Memoir," p. 174.

144. John Hitchman, quoted in Clark, *Memoir*, pp. 40–43. Hitchman, later superintendent of the Derby County Asylum, had begun his career under Conolly at Hanwell.

145. Edward Jarvis to Almira Jarvis, June 22, 1860, Jarvis Papers.

146. In 1842, he even managed to gain permission to introduce the clinical teaching of medical students in the asylum.

147. Conolly, *Construction and Government*, p. 10.

148. J. M. Granville, *The Care and Cure of the Insane*, vol. 1, p. 154. Only in his declining years did Conolly vigorously protest the tendency of county asylums to be little more than "museums for the collection of insanity." See J. Conolly, "President's Address," esp. p. 75; idem, *A Letter to Benjamin Rotch, Esquire, on the Plan and Government of the Additional Lunatic Asylum . . . About to be Erected at Colney Hatch* London: Churchill, 1847, p. 18.

149. Ironically, given his public praise of Conolly's role in introducing nonrestraint, this scheme was secretly supported by Shaftesbury, who remained sceptical of medical claims to expertise in the diagnosis of insanity throughout his life. See National Register of Archives, Diaries of the seventh Earl of Shaftesbury, SHA/PD/3, November 15, 1844.

150. Conolly, *Letter to Benjamin Rotch*, p. 18.

151. *Hanwell Visitors' Report* No. 69, 1844, p. 4.

152. *Hanwell Visitors' Report* No. 70, 1844, pp. 3–7.

153. Metropolitan Commissioners in Lunacy Report, 1844, p. 28; our italics.

154. *Hanwell Visitors' Report* No. 69, 1844, p. 5.

155. *Hanwell Visitors' Report* No. 72, 1844, p. 13.

156. *Hanwell Visitors' Report* No. 73, 1845, p. 1.

157. *Hanwell Visitors' Report* No. 75, 1845, p. 3.

158. Hunter and Macalpine, "Introduction," to J. Conolly, *The Treatment of the Insane*, p. xxxii.

159. In 1859, the two physicians at Hanwell were still being paid only £200 each per annum, the same salary as the matron. House of Commons, *Select Committee on Lunatics* 1859, pp. 169, 242. Sir Alexander Spearman, chairman of the magistrates overseeing Hanwell, testified that the board saw no need for the services of more than two doctors for one thousand patients, given the overwhelming preponderance of chronic, incurable patients.

160. See chapter 8 below.

161. Sir George Savage (1842–1921), formerly physician superintendent of the Royal Bethlem Hospital, editor of the *Journal of Mental Science*, and president of the Medico-Psychological Association and the Neurological Association, was one of the most fashionable consultants on mental diseases in late nineteenth-century London. For Savage's role in treating Virginia Woolf, see Stephen Trombley, *"All that Summer She Was Mad": Virginia Woolf and Her Doctors* London: Junction Books, 1981.

162. For example, when the confinement of Lady Rosina Bulwer Lytton in a private asylum threatened to become a scandal of major proportions, her husband

sought advice from "the most experienced and able physicians" specializing in psychological medicine, choosing Conolly and Forbes Winslow. By a curious coincidence, Lady Lytton, whose sanity they confirmed, was an inmate in Robert Gardiner Hill's asylum, Wyke House. *The Times*, July 19, 1858, p. 12. Conolly also testified at such well-publicized commissions in lunacy as W. F. Windham, Sir Henry Meux, and Mrs. Catherine Cummings.

163. For example, Robert Tate, Edward Oxford, Luigi Buranelli. On this aspect of Victorian psychiatric practice, see Roger Smith, *Trial by Medicine: Insanity and Responsibility in Victorian Trials* Edinburgh: Edinburgh University Press, 1981.

164. The Morning Post, quoted in Hunter and Macalpine, "Introduction," to Conolly, *The Treatment of the Insane*, p. xxxvii.

165. Conolly, *Inquiry*, pp. 8–9, 35, 386; emphasis in the original.

166. John Conolly, *A Remonstrance with the Lord Chief Baron Touching the Case Nottidge versus Ripley* 3rd ed., London: Churchill, 1849, p. 3.

167. T. T. Wingett, *The Law of Lunacy* Dundee: Chalmers, 1849.

168. Conolly, *Remonstrance*, pp. 3, 4–5, 6–7.

169. *Daily Telegraph*, January 7, 1862; *The Times*, January 7, 21, 31, 1862; *British Medical Journal*, January 11, February 8, 1862.

170. "Report on the Ruck Case," *Journal of Mental Science* 4, 1858, p. 131.

171. Charles Reade, *Hard Cash: A Matter-of-Fact Romance* London: Ward, Lock, 1864.

172. Ibid., p. 335. The reference to nonrestraint makes transparent who the target is, but Conolly's identity becomes still more blatantly obvious in later passages.

173. Ibid., pp. 203, 208, 211, 212, 335, 339. Here, the reference to Conolly was unmistakable, for the latter's *A Study of Hamlet*, addressed to precisely this issue, had appeared but a few months earlier. Reade maliciously takes his vendetta a step further: Wycherly readily debates the sanity of Alfred Hardie, the young man he has wrongly incarcerated, "with a philosophical coolness, the young man admired, and found it hard to emulate; but this philosophical calmness deserted him the moment Hamlet's insanity was disputed, and the harder he was pressed, the angrier, the louder, the more confused the Psychological physician became; and presently he got furious, burst out of the anti-spasmodic or round-about style and called Alfred a d——d ungrateful, insolent puppy, and went stamping about the room; and, finally, to the young man's horror, fell down in a fit of an epileptic character, grinding his teeth and foaming at the mouth." Alfred, by now well acquainted with the face of lunacy, has discovered Wycherly's secret: he was himself a monomaniac! (Reade, *Hard Cash*, p. 340.)

174. Reade, *Hard Cash*, p. 453. For someone with a powerful animus against the pretensions of Victorian alienists, Conolly was a tempting target, because of both his eminence and his general reputation as a great humanitarian; and in attacking him, Reade was at once ruthless, unscrupulous, and resourceful, not shrinking from quoting Conolly out of context and putting his behaviour in the worst possible light.

175. For instance, papers at the Warwickshire County Record Office reveal that Conolly, together with his disciple Samuel Gaskell, the superintendent of the Lancaster County Asylum, was paid £50 to give advice on the setting up of the new County Lunatic Asylum.

176. The annual reports of the Commissioners in Lunacy reveal an average of five

or six "ladies" present at any one time. Given that Conolly was prohibited from engaging in any form of private practice during his years as superintendent at Hanwell, it is not clear where he obtained the capital to launch this operation.

177. In 1859, he had to rescue this enterprise from bankruptcy.

178. Hunter and Macalpine, "Introduction" to J. Conolly, *Treatment of the Insane*, pp. xxxv–xxxvi.

179. House of Commons, *Select Committee on Lunatics*, 1859, p. 185.

180. Conolly, *Inquiry*, p. 481.

181. Maudsley, "Memoir," p. 172.

182. To Thomas Harrington Tuke, one of Conolly's former pupils and the proprietor of Chiswick House private asylum.

183. To Henry Maudsley. See chapter 8 below.

184. John Conolly to Lord Brougham, June 19, 1846, Brougham Collection, UCL.

185. Edward Conolly to Lord Brougham, November 10, 1846, (a request he reiterated on November 27, 1846), Brougham Collection, UCL.

186. Edward Conolly to Lord Brougham, February 3, 1851, Brougham Collection, UCL. In the interim, John Conolly had again tried unavailingly to intercede on his behalf. In 1849, when a post as Inspector of Factories fell vacant, he approached not only Brougham (whom he claimed "has written to Lord John Russell soliciting the appointment for him in the strongest terms"), but also his wealthy relative, Charles Tennyson d'Eyncourt: "I trust you give me credit for being extremely averse to encroaching in any way on your kindness, but it has occurred to me that you may well be acquainted with Sir George Gray, to whom, no doubt, a word or two might be very useful, and to whom I have no direct access." John Conolly to Charles Tennyson d'Eyncourt, November 16, 1849, Lincolnshire Archives, Tennyson d'Eyncourt Papers 2, H/51/36, quoted in E. Burrows, "Dr. Conolly and the Tennyson Family," p. 19. Even with such powerful support behind him, Edward failed to secure the preferment.

187. Edward Conolly to Lord Brougham, December 27, 1853, Brougham Collection, UCL.

188. Edward Conolly to Lord Brougham, December 6, 1855, Brougham Collection, UCL. The vacancy occurred when one of the legal commissioners, James Mylne, died on November 24, 1855. After exerting considerable effort to influence the Lord Chancellor (who was inclined to appoint his secretary, William Spring-Rice), Shaftesbury obtained the position for R.W.S. Lutwidge, an Evangelical and long-time secretary to the Commission. John Forster (who was backed by Brougham, Granville, Bulwer Lytton, and Lord John Russell for a commissionership) was then made secretary, leaving Edward Conolly still without official preferment. By now, his father was clearly wearing down under the burden of feeding so many mouths. Not yet sixty, he described himself to Dorothea Dix as become old, feeble, and wracked with pain. John Conolly to Dorothea Dix, November 16, 1855, Dix papers, Houghton Library, Harvard University.

189. Edward Conolly to Lord Brougham, August 8, 1857. Brougham Collection, UCL. "I do not know if I am asking too much." He was.

190. John Conolly to Thomas Harrington Tuke, quoted in Hunter and Macalpine, "Introduction," to J. Conolly, *Treatment of the Insane*, p. xxxvi.

191. Leigh, *British Psychiatry*, p. 227; Burrows, "Dr. Conolly and the Tennyson Family," p. 29.

192. John Conolly, "On Residences for the Insane," *Journal of Mental Science* 5, 1859, pp. 412–413.

193. Ibid., p. 413.

194. Ibid., p. 412.

195. Ibid., pp. 415–417.

196. Ibid., pp. 417–418.

197. Bucknill, *The Care of the Insane*, p. 128.

198. Edward Jarvis to Almira Jarvis, May 31, 1860, Jarvis Papers. "Dr. Conolly is apparently seventy or more [sic], yet hale and vigorous; very kind, bland, affectionate in his manners. Having ever cultivated the higher moral and intellectual [sic], he manifests a beautiful spirit. He is retired from active practice and devotes himself to study, writing, social enjoyment, and some consultation practice."

199. London: Moxon, 1863. For alienists' recurrent fascination with Shakespeare, see W. F. Bynum and M. Neve, "Hamlet on the Couch," chap. 12 in Bynum, Porter, and Shepherd (eds.), *The Anatomy of Madness*, vol. 1.

200. "Obituary of John Conolly," *Journal of Mental Science* 12, 1866, p. 146.

201. Scull, *The Most Solitary of Afflictions*, esp. chaps. 3 and 6.

202. Granville, *The Care and Cure of the Insane*, vol. 1, p. 15.

203. Conolly, *Inquiry*, p. 3.

204. Bucknill, *The Care of the Insane*, p. 60.

205. Peter Sedgwick, *Psychopolitics* London: Pluto Press, New York: Harper and Row, 1982, p. 141. For a critique of modern "community care," see Andrew Scull, *Decarceration* 2d ed., Oxford: Polity Press/New Brunswick, N.J.: Rutgers University Press, 1984.

CHAPTER FOUR

THE ALIENIST AS PROPAGANDIST: W.A.F. BROWNE (1805–1885)

1. Larson, *The Rise of Professionalism*.

2. Loudon, *Medical Care*.

3. Ibid., pp. 183–185, 270–271, et passim. Between 1801 and 1850, Oxford and Cambridge produced only 273 doctors. During the same period, 8,000 doctors were produced in Scotland.

4. W.A.F. Browne, "Application and Testimonials for the Superintendency of the Montrose Royal Lunatic Asylum," quoted in C. C. Easterbrook, *The Chronicle of Crichton Royal (1833–1936)* Courier Press: Dumfries, 1940, p. iv.

5. Cf. G. Cantor, "The Edinburgh Phrenology Debate: 1803–1828," *Annals of Science* 32, 1975, pp. 195–218; S. Shapin, "Phrenological Knowledge and the Social Structure of Nineteenth Century Edinburgh," *Annals of Science* 32, 1975, pp. 219–243; idem, "The Politics of Observation: Cerebral Anatomy and Social Interests in the Edinburgh Phrenology Disputes," pp. 139–178 in R. Wallis (ed.), *On the Margins of Science* Keele, Staffordshire: Sociological Review Monograph No. 27, 1978.

6. Cf. Roger Cooter, "Phrenology and British Alienists, ca. 1825–1845," in A. Scull (ed.), *Madhouses, Mad-Doctors, and Madmen*, pp. 58–104.

7. Shapin, "The Politics of Observation," p. 147.

8. E. H. Ackerknecht, *Medicine at the Paris Hospital 1794–1848* Baltimore: Johns Hopkins University Press, 1967, p. 172.

9. Shapin, "Phrenological Knowledge," p. 232.

10. Shapin, "The Politics of Observation," p. 145.

11. Ibid., p. 143.

12. Cooter, "Phrenology and British Alienists," p. 67.

13. Browne, "Application and Testimonials," p. iv.

14. Andrew Combe to George Combe, March 22, 1834, reprinted in George Combe, *Life of Andrew Combe*, pp. 228–229.

15. Eliot Freidson, *The Profession of Medicine* New York: Dodd, Mead, 1970, p. 10.

16. C. Easterbrook, *Chronicle*, p. 616.

17. W.A.F. Browne, "The Moral Treatment of the Insane: A Lecture," *Journal of Mental Science* 10, 1864, pp. 312, 313.

18. Browne, *Asylums*, p. 1.

19. See "Facts Regarding the Statistics of Insanity," *The Lancet* ii, July 8, 1837, pp. 543–544, pp. 555–556; [John Conolly], "Review"; Anon., "Review of *What Asylums Were, Are, and Ought to Be*," *Edinburgh Medical and Surgical Journal* 48, 1837, pp. 513–518; *Phrenological Journal* 10, 1836–1837, pp. 687–695.

20. Andrew Abbott, *The System of Professions* Chicago: University of Chicago Press, 1988, p. 40.

21. [W. H. Fitton], "Lunatic Asylums," *Edinburgh Review* 28, 1817, pp. 431–471.

22. See Scull, *Social Order, Mental Disorder*, pp. 80–94; and Porter, *Mind Forg'd Manacles*, esp. p. 277.

23. S. Tuke, *Description of the Retreat*, pp. vi, 158. In W.A.F. Browne's words, the task of those employing moral treatment was "to offer temptations to the lunatic to cooperate in his own restoration." Quoted in the *Phrenological Journal* 10, 1836–1837, p. 248.

24. Tuke, *Description of the Retreat*, pp. 110, 111, 115.

25. Among other misfortunes, the hearings revealed the profession's utter inability to agree on even the most basic issues. The spectacle of internecine bickering and the wildly discrepant and contradictory assertions made by medical witnesses could only have served to undermine public confidence in their claims to possess expertise in the treatment of the mad.

26. Bynum, "Rationales for Therapy," p. 43.

27. See Godfrey Higgins, *A Letter to the Right Honourable Earl Fitzwilliam Respecting the Investigation Which Has Lately Taken Place, into the Abuses at the York Lunatic Asylum* Doncaster: Sheardown, 1814; idem, *The Evidence Taken Before a Committee of the House of Commons Respecting the Asylum at York*.

28. Jonathan Gray, *A History of the York Asylum* York: Hargrove, 1815.

29. Samuel Nicoll, *An Inquiry Into the Present State of Visitation in Asylums* London: Harvey and Darton, 1828.

30. Wakefield, "Plan of an Asylum"; idem, "Sir George O. Paul on Lunatic Asylums," *The Philanthropist* 3, 1813, pp. 214–227.

31. T[homas] H[ancock], "Tuke's *Description of the Retreat*," *The Philanthropist* 3, 1813, pp. 326–338.

32. *Select Committee on Madhouses*, 1815, p. 24. Wakefield was to modify this

judgement the following year, after a visit to William Finch's establishment at Laverstock House, near Salisbury (see *Select Committee on Madhouses* first report, 1816, p. 36), but his earlier judgement was reflected in the bills introduced into Parliament over the next three years.

33. Godfrey Higgins, *The Evidence Respecting the Asylum at York*, p. 48.

34. R. A. Cage, *The Scottish Poor Law, 1745–1845* Edinburgh: Scottish University Press, 1981, pp. 84–89.

35. The impetus for change was the splitting apart of the Church of Scotland in 1843, when the so-called Disruption led two-fifths of the clergy to leave to form the Free Church of Scotland, fatally undermining the ability of the established church to administer poor relief and putting "to the hazard the pitifully small sums available for poor relief." Even then, despite an official inquiry that revealed widespread and abject poverty, legislative changes were minimal, and the fundamental opposition to the provision of relief for the able-bodied remained as firm as ever. Cf. Cage, *Scottish Poor Law*, pp. 133–142.

36. E. P. Thompson, *The Making of the English Working Class* New York: Vintage Books, 1963, p. 82, et passim.

37. Besides the Montrose Asylum, founded in 1781, these were located at Aberdeen (1800); Edinburgh (1813); Glasgow (1814); Dundee (1820); Perth (1826); and finally, at Dumfries (1839).

38. The term is Ellen Dwyer's: see her *Homes for the Mad* New Brunswick, N.J.: Rutgers University Press, 1987.

39. Thomas Mayo, *Remarks on Insanity* London: Underwood, 1817, p. v.

40. Francis Willis, *A Treatise on Mental Derangement* London: Longman, 1823, p. 2.

41. William Lawrence, *Lectures on the Physiology, Zoology, and Natural History of Man* London: Callow, 1819, p. 114.

42. "Insanity and Madhouses," *Quarterly Review* 15, 1816, p. 402.

43. Haslam, *Considerations on the Moral Management of Insane Persons*, pp. 2–3.

44. See Burrows, *Cursory Remarks*.

45. See the *Minutes of Evidence Taken Before the Select Committee of the House of Lords on the Bills Relating to Lunatics and Lunatic Asylums* London: 1828, esp. the testimony of William Finch, E. T. Monro, and Edward Long Fox. See also E. T. Monro's diaries.

46. Mayo, *Remarks on Insanity*, p. v.

47. Browne, *Asylums*, p. viii.

48. Ibid., p. 99.

49. Ibid., pp. 1–2.

50. [George Combe], *Essays on Phrenology* Edinburgh: Bell and Bradfute, 1819, pp. 304–306.

51. Shapin, "Phrenological Knowledge," p. 228; David de Giustino, *The Conquest of Mind: Phrenology and Victorian Social Thought* London: Croom Helm, 1975; Cooter, *The Cultural Meaning of Popular Science*.

52. Andrew Combe to an unknown correspondent, 1830, quoted in G. Combe, *Life and Correspondence of Andrew Combe*, p. 189.

53. Combe, *Observations on Mental Derangement*, p. 353.

54. Conolly was, of course, the most prominent English alienist of his generation; Ellis was superintendent successively of the West Riding Asylum at Wakefield, and of the Hanwell Asylum in Middlesex and was the first alienist to be knighted; Alexander succeeded him at Wakefield; Poole was Browne's successor at Montrose (as well as being the first editor of the *Phrenological Journal*); Uwins was the physician to the Peckham Asylum in London and wrote regularly for the *Quarterly Review* on matters psychiatric; and Forbes Winslow, who owned two private madhouses in Hammersmith, later published the first English psychiatric periodical, the *Journal of Psychological Medicine and Mental Pathology*.

55. Cf. Cooter, "Phrenology and British Alienists."

56. Ibid., p. 62.

57. See W.A.F. Browne, "On the Morbid Manifestations of the Organ of Language, as Connected with Insanity," *Phrenological Journal* 8, 1832–1834, pp. 250–260, 308–316, 414–423; idem, "Observations on Religious Fanaticism," *Phrenological Journal* 9, 1834–1836, pp. 289–302, 532–545, 577–603; idem, "Pathological Contribution to Phrenology: Case of a Patient in the Montrose Lunatic Asylum," *Phrenological Journal* 10, 1836–1838, pp. 45–52.

58. Andrew Combe to Browne, January 28, 1837, reprinted in G. Combe, *Life and Correspondence of Andrew Combe*, pp. 280–281.

59. Browne, *Asylums*, [p. v].

60. Ibid., p. viii.

61. Andrew Combe to Browne, January 28, 1837, in George Combe, *Life and Correspondence of Andrew Combe*, p. 281.

62. Browne to Andrew Combe, January 3, 1845, reprinted as an appendix to Andrew Combe, *Phrenology—Its Nature and Uses* Edinburgh: Maclachan, Stewart, 1846, p. 30.

63. Shapin, "The Politics of Observation," p. 142.

64. de Giustino, *Conquest of Mind*, p. 100.

65. L. S. Jacyna, "Somatic Theories of Mind and the Interests of Medicine in Britain, 1850–1879," *Medical History* 26, 1982, p. 248.

66. Browne, *Asylums*, p. viii.

67. [John Conolly], "Review," p. 70.

68. Browne, *Asylums*, p. 3.

69. Ibid., p. 4.

70. Ibid., p. 7.

71. Compare David Skae's revealing commentary on the significance of a somatic etiology: "Unless insanity is *a disease*, a disease of the brain affecting the mind, I do not see what we have to do with it more than other people: but if it is a disease, I maintain that we are bound to know more about it than other people." "On the Legal Relations of Insanity: The Civil Incapacity and Criminal Responsibility of the Insane," *Edinburgh Medical Journal* 12, 1867, p. 813.

72. Browne, *Asylums*, p. 91.

73. Ibid., p. 69. As Roger Smith notes, routinely in the discourse of nineteenth-century alienists, "Spiritualist theories of insanity were denigrated by association with therapeutic pessimism." *Trial By Medicine*, p. 41.

74. Browne, *Asylums*, p. 178.

75. Ibid., p. 5.

76. William Nisbet, *Two Letters to the Right Honourable George Rose, M.P., on the State of the Madhouses* London: Cox, 1815, pp. 21–22.

77. William Neville, *On Insanity* London: Longman, Rees, Orme, Brown, Green, and Longmans, 1836, p. 18.

78. See the account of these events in Howard E. Gruber and Paul H. Barrett, *Darwin on Man* New York, Dutton, 1974, pp. 39–41, 479. Sitting in the audience was the young Charles Darwin, whom Browne had just proposed for membership in the Society.

79. See the discussion in Desmond, *The Politics of Evolution*, pp. 114–121.

80. George Man Burrows, *An Inquiry Into Certain Errors Relative to Insanity* London: Underwood, 1821, p. 7.

81. Browne, *Asylums*, p. 4.

82. Smith, *Trial by Medicine*, p. 43.

83. A few broke ranks and adopted a more thoroughgoing materialism. William Lawrence, for instance, spoke dismissively of the "hypothesis or fiction of a subtle invisible matter, animating the visible textures of animal bodies." (See William Lawrence, *An Introduction to Comparative Anatomy and Physiology* London: Callow, 1816; idem, *Lectures on Physiology, Zoology, and the Natural History of Man*). Such heterodox and atheistic opinions almost cost Lawrence his appointments at Bethlem and Bridewell and at St. Bartholomew's Hospital (and did force him to submit his resignation as a lecturer to the College of Surgeons). Either because their own theological convictions barred such materialism, or from motives of prudence, few of Lawrence's medical colleagues (with the notable exception of Wakley and his fellow radicals) publicly adopted his stance.

84. Browne, *Asylums*, p. 4.

85. Ibid.; Morison, *Lectures on Insanity*, pp. 35–37.

86. Browne, *Asylums*, p. 4. For variations on this line of reasoning, which more starkly reveal the ultimately theological basis on which most alienists sought to validate their claim that insanity was a somatic disorder, see Morison, *Lectures on Insanity*, pp. 34–44; and Halliday, *General View*, pp. 5–8.

87. Ibid., pp. 54–55, 63.

88. George Man Burrows, *Commentaries on Insanity* London: Underwood, 1828, pp. 21–23, was one of the few dissenters from the ruling orthodoxy. Of course, the connections between artificiality, overstimulation, luxury, and madness had been a staple of speculation on the causes of nervous distempers at least since the publication of George Cheyne's *The English Malady* London: Wisk, Ewing, and Smith, 1733.

89. Browne, *Asylums*, pp. 52–53.

90. Ibid., p. 55.

91. Ibid., pp. 56–57, 59, 61.

92. Henry Maudsley, *The Pathology of Mind* London: Macmillan, 1879, pp. 105, 115.

93. Daniel Hack Tuke, *Insanity in Ancient and Modern Life* London: Macmillan, 1878, p. 152. In Tuke's words, "On admission, 'No good' is plainly inscribed on their foreheads." By the mid 1860s, Browne, too, had revised his earlier judgement: "although the blight of alienation falls upon the purest and highest spirit, the blight

falls heaviest and most poisonously upon those of imperfect character, or ungoverned passions, and degraded propensities." Consequently, "in many senses an asylum should be a grand moral school and reformatory, as well as an hospital." "Moral Treatment," pp. 314–315.

94. Browne, *Asylums*, pp. 172, 177.

95. Ibid., pp. 99, 101. More complex portraits of the ancien régime madhouse may be found in Parry-Jones, *The Trade in Lunacy*; and in Porter, *Mind Forg'd Manacles*.

96. Browne, *Asylums*, pp. 101, 107, 128, 133.

97. Ibid., p. 138. The description Browne gives here of Pinel liberating the insane at the Bicêtre had rapidly become one of the most hackneyed images in the alienists' own version of their history. That modern scholarship has demonstrated its almost wholly mythical character (see J. Goldstein, *Console and Classify*, pp. 72–119) does not detract in the least from its rhetorical and practical importance in the constitution of Victorian asylumdom. One should note here the political significance of Browne's choice of Pinel as the founding father of moral treatment and thus of alienism. William Tuke has at least equal claim to the title, and his work at the Retreat was far better known to a British audience. Perhaps the choice in part reflects Browne's Parisian experiences and his extended contact with Pinel's most famous pupil, Esquirol. But Browne, as his later career and writings were to reemphasize, was centrally concerned to make the treatment of madness an exclusively medical prerogative. (He was subsequently to accuse medical men who were insufficiently active in this cause of "treason" to the profession.) The shadowy presence, throughout the book, of the Retreat, and of the tea and coffee merchant who founded it, is thus wholly unsurprising; as is the choice to emphasize a rival who, however sceptical he may have been of the value of a medical therapeutics for madness, at least had the merit of being one of the two or three best known physicians in Revolutionary France.

98. Browne, *Asylums*, p. 139.

99. Ibid., p. 176.

100. Ibid., pp. 203, 213.

101. Ibid., pp. 183, 191.

102. Ibid, p. 203.

103. See Conolly, *Indications*, p. 31; and George Nesse Hill, *An Essay on the Prevention and Cure of Insanity* London: Longman, Hurst, Rees, Orme, and Brown, 1814, pp. 222, 220.

104. Browne, *Asylums*, p. 207.

105. Ibid., pp. 169, 199, 201.

106. Ibid., p. 181.

107. W.A.F. Browne, quoted in "Miscellaneous Notices—Dundee and Montrose Lunatic Asylums," *Phrenological Journal* 10, 1836–1837, p. 248.

108. Browne, *Asylums*, p. 156.

109. Ibid., pp. 50, 155, 178, 180.

110. "Review of *What Asylums Were, Are, and Ought to Be*," *Phrenological Journal* 10, 1836–1837, p. 697.

111. The centrality and the necessarily untrammelled power of the asylum superintendent are consistently insisted upon by Browne throughout his career as a vital

"element in curative discipline. He is not merely a dispenser of advice and medicine, he is a moral governor, who identifies himself with the happiness as well as the health of those around; a referee in all disputes and difficulties; a depository of all secrets and sorrows; a source of pleasure, as well as of power and direction, and who gives a tone to every proceedings." (*Crichton Royal Asylum, 11th Annual Report* 1850, p. 39.) In his 1864 lecture on "The Moral Treatment of the Insane" (p. 334), the royal analogy is made overt: "The power or government by which such communities are ruled should be monarchical. The details, as well as the principles, should emanate from one central will; while much must be left to the spontaneous good sense and good feeling of subordinates, these subordinates should be chosen, their views and acts should be influenced, their whole bearing determined by the supreme official."

112. Browne, *Asylums*, pp. 229–231.

113. Karl Polanyi, *The Great Transformation* Boston: Beacon Press, 1957.

114. [Conolly], "Review," p. 74.

115. The Crichton Royal owed its existence to a very substantial bequest from Elizabeth Crichton's husband, Dr. James Crichton, the bulk of whose fortune derived from his service in the East India Company. On his death in 1823, he left the residue of his estate, amounting to well over £100,000, for charitable purposes, its precise use or uses to be determined by his widow. Her initial plans to found a university at Dumfries were blocked by the existing Scottish universities, and it was not until 1833 that she decided to build a lunatic asylum instead. Her plan was not popular locally: "The Building was commenced amidst much ridicule, and in so far as public opinion went, even some opposition." *Dumfries and Galloway Courier*, August 29, 1838.

116. His many years at the head of a sizeable asylum form a marked contrast with John Conolly's career.

117. There is, nonetheless, something distinctly odd about his incessantly reiterated insistence on his own selflessness and un(self)conscious references to his "Godlike" qualities. The self-congratulatory tone is evident, for instance, in the following passage from his *12th Annual Report* of 1851, p. 36: "if it be recollected that there is no suspension of these offices and ministrations; that there is no holiday from the vagaries and caprices, and sufferings of the insane, nor from the supervision and anxiety which these exact; that every new case creates new cares; that the seclusion of the guardians is nearly as complete as that of their charges; it must be a matter of satisfaction that individuals have been found capable of such self-denial, and of discharging such complicated and arduous duties, who interpret aright the Godlike act of giving a hand to the lunatic and raising him up, and whose chief reward consists in seeing him seated, clothed, and in his right mind." Browne was not alone, as it turns out, in viewing alienists as "a body of men engaged in a holy and sacred office." Cf. Forbes Winslow, "Presidential Address," *Journal of Mental Science* 4, 1857–1858, p. 8.

118. *Crichton Royal Asylum, 13th Annual Report*, 1852, p. 36.

119. *Crichton Royal Asylum, 3rd Annual Report*, 1842, pp. 15–16.

120. Sir James Crichton-Browne, "Some Early Crichton Memories," foreword to C. Easterbrook, *The Chronicle of Crichton Royal*, p. 4.

121. *Crichton Royal Asylum, 5th Annual Report*, 1844, p. 23.

122. Ibid., p. 24.

123. Easterbrook, *Chronicle of Crichton Royal*, p. 24; *Crichton Royal Asylum, 12th Annual Report*, 1851, pp. 22–28.

124. In 1842, for example, he reported that "sixteen men have been almost constantly employed in the gardens and grounds; and this is a very large proportion of the male pauper inmates of the Establishment." If inclement weather kept them indoors, mat-making, basket-weaving, mattress making, shoe mending, and watch and clock repairing all provided occupation. "The female patients of all classes are more easily provided with employment, and are, perhaps, from previous custom and the nature of their avocations, more capable of continuous exertion." *Crichton Royal Asylum, 3rd Annual Report*, 1842, p. 24. Between 1842 and 1844, patient labour was used to construct large sand filter beds to purify the water drawn from the River Nith, a precaution that preserved the asylum from cholera, when an epidemic broke out in Dumfries in 1848.

125. *Crichton Royal Asylum, 3rd Annual Report*, 1842, p. 22.

126. *Crichton Royal Asylum, 11th Annual Report*, 1850, p. 7; see also *14th Annual Report*, 1853, p. 11; *16th Annual Report*, 1855, p. 9.

127. *Crichton Royal Asylum, 3rd Annual Report*, 1842, pp. 25–26.

128. *Crichton Royal Asylum, 8th Annual Report*, 1847, p. 20; *9th Annual Report*, 1848, p. 23. The disease remained defiant.

129. W.A.F. Browne, "Moral Treatment," p. 335.

130. *Crichton Royal Asylum, 8th Annual Report*, 1847, pp. 19–20.

131. *Crichton Royal Asylum, 18th Annual Report*, 1857, p. 18.

132. *Crichton Royal Asylum, 11th Annual Report*, 1850, p. 39.

133. *Crichton Royal Asylum, 3rd Annual Report*, 1842, p. 17.

134. *Crichton Royal Asylum, 7th Annual Report*, 1846, p. 35; *11th Annual Report*, 1850, p. 31.

135. Cf. W.A.F. Browne, "Moral Treatment," pp. 311–312, et passim. At an early stage, he insisted on "the necessity for rigid, stringent, even stern discipline among the insane." *Crichton Royal Asylum, 3rd Annual Report*, 1842, p. 21. Elsewhere, Browne boasted that the use of dormitory accommodation for pauper patients "continues the discipline and inspection exercised during active pursuits into the night, and during silence and sleep. Control may thus penetrate into the very dreams of the insane." *10th Annual Report*, 1849, p. 38.

136. *Crichton Royal Asylum, 5th Annual Report*, 1844, p. 5.

137. A.B.C. [W.A.F. Browne], "Letter to the Members of the Royal Commission of Inquiry into the Operation of the Poor Laws in Scotland, on the Condition of the Insane Poor," *Dumfries and Galloway Herald*, December 21, 1843, reprinted in *The Phrenological Journal* 17, 1844, p. 258.

138. Ibid., pp. 255, 256.

139. *Crichton Royal Asylum, 14th Annual Report*, 1853, p. 7.

140. Revealing in this regard are two incidents cited in his 1849 report: "so fully impressed do relatives sometimes appear to be as to the inevitable result of seclusion, that upon one occasion the grave clothes were found to have been added to the ordinary wardrobe; and upon another the construction of a coffin negotiated for when its intended occupant was alive, and she still fortunately is." *Crichton Royal Asylum, 10th Annual Report*, 1849, p. 6.

141. *Crichton Royal Asylum, 9th Annual Report*, 1848, p. 5.

142. *Crichton Royal Asylum, 8th Annual Report*, 1847, p. 23.

143. *Crichton Royal Asylum, 10th Annual Report*, 1849, p. 5.

144. *Crichton Royal Asylum, 12th Annual Report*, 1851, p. 5. Earlier he had commented that "much is to be gained if captivity be rendered bearable: it is a great achievement, if it can be divested of its bitterness." Ibid., *3rd Annual Report*, p. 25.

145. *Crichton Royal Asylum, 12th Annual Report*, 1851, p. 28.

146. W.A.F. Browne, "Moral Treatment," p. 322.

147. *Crichton Royal Asylum, 9th Annual Report*, 1848, p. 35.

148. *Crichton Royal Asylum, 13th Annual Report*, 1852, p. 40.

149. *Crichton Royal Asylum, 15th Annual Report*, 1854, p. 5.

150. *Crichton Royal Asylum, 13th Annual Report*, 1852, p. 40.

151. *Crichton Royal Asylum, 17th Annual Report*, 1856, p. 37. Elsewhere in the same report, he urged legal changes to allow "retreats," separate from existing asylums, to be set up for those in "the premonitory stages, or under the milder forms of the malady." Otherwise, as he revealingly put it, such a patient would find himself or herself reduced to the same status as the unambiguously mad already under confinement, "treated as a culprit and a captive." Ibid., p. 6.

152. *Crichton Royal Asylum, 18th Annual Report*, 1857, p. 5.

153. Ibid., pp. 5, 7, 8.

154. Ibid., pp. 12-13.

155. Ibid., pp. 24-26.

156. Ibid., p. 40.

157. See W.A.F. Browne, "Cottage Asylums," *Medical Critic and Psychological Journal* 1, 1861, pp. 213-237.

158. For the Commission's proceedings and report, see *Report of Her Majesty's Commissioners Appointed to Inquire into the State of Lunatic Asylums in Scotland* Edinburgh: Thomas Constable for Her Majesty's Stationery Office, 1857.

159. See James Coxe to Dorothea Dix, April 11, 16, 24, May 14, 21, June 12, August 2, 12, 1855, September 10, 1856, June 4, June 20, 1857; Samuel Gaskell to Dix, April 7, May 10, 1855, August 10, 1856; Sir George Grey to Dix, April 9, 1855; Sir Walter Trevelyan to Dix, June 29, 1857; William George Campbell to Dix, June 16, 1855; George Douglas Campbell, eighth Duke of Argyll, to Dix, April 12, 1857. (Coxe, Campbell, and Gaskell were all members of the Commission itself.) In manuscript, Dix Papers, Houghton Library, Harvard University (hereafter cited DPHL).

160. Coxe to Dix, May 21, June 12, 1855. DPHL.

161. Coxe to Dix, September 10, 1856; see also Gaskell to Dix, August 10, 1856; Trevelyan to Dix, June 29, 1857. DPHL.

162. Coxe to Dix, June 4, 1857. DPHL.

163. Coxe to Dix, June 20, 1857. DPHL.

164. In the United States, Dix was quite ruthless in advancing the careers of alienists who curried favour with her and blocking the advancement of those with whom she had disagreements.

165. Browne to Dix, April 10, 1855. DPHL.

166. For their opposition to proposed legislation of this sort in 1848 and 1849, see Easterbrook, *Chronicle of Crichton Royal*, pp. 48, 51-52.

167. Ibid., p. 64. Browne's adherence to this position was the subject of acerbic criticism in the *Journal of Mental Science* 2, 1856, pp. 413-416. Bucknill, its editor,

particularly objected to Browne's claim that room could be found for pauper lunatics in charity asylums, which ought to maintain their monopoly by arranging "to
undersell private speculators" (i.e., proprietors of private madhouses). He pointed
out that "when it comes to a matter of underselling, the screw of parsimony can be
pressed tighter in the obscurity of a private asylum, than it will be possible to do in
a public one." And he found equal fault with Browne's references to "the hard and
severe simplicity which necessarily and properly, and the ignorance and vulgarity,
if not the wild turmoil and debasement which naturally characterize a pauper asylum," seeing such passages as confirmation of a long held opinion among English
alienists "that too large a share of the attention of the officers and governors [of
Scottish asylums] has been devoted to patients [of the wealthier classes], and that
the state of the pauper patients has been such as to form a striking and painful
contrast, not only to the wealthier patients in the same institutions, but to that of
insane paupers in this country."

168. Browne to Dix, September 3, 1857. DPHL.

169. See, for example, W.A.F. Browne, "Epileptics: Their Mental Condition,"
Journal of Mental Science 11, 1865, pp. 336–363 (delivered at the Inverness District
Asylum); and his lecture on "Moral Treatment," delivered the previous year at the
Crichton Royal. Laycock, professor of the practice of physic at Edinburgh University
since 1855, was to serve as president of the Medico-Psychological Association in
1869. Earlier in his career, while a lecturer at the York Medical School, he had exercised a formative influence over Hughlings Jackson, and his advocacy of psycho-
physical parallelism and of the notion of cerebral reflex action appealed to Browne
as a scientific replacement for a now-discredited phrenology. See, for example, Browne to George Combe, April 30, 1857, Combe Papers, National Library of
Scotland.

170. Browne's address, "On Medico-Psychology," *Journal of Mental Science* 12,
1866, pp. 309–327, marked the change in the official title of the alienists' organization from the Association of Medical Officers of Asylums and Hospitals for the Insane to the Medico-Psychological Association, a transformation of obvious symbolic
importance for the emerging profession.

171. Browne, "Moral Treatment," p. 311.

172. Browne, "On Medico-Psychology," p. 311.

173. Browne, "Moral Treatment," p. 311. The reiterated emphasis is precisely
proportional to the flimsiness of the evidentiary basis on which these assertions
rested.

174. Browne, "On Medico-Psychology," p. 312.

175. Browne, "Moral Treatment," p. 311.

CHAPTER FIVE
TREATING THE MAD OUTSIDE ASYLUM WALLS:
SIR ALEXANDER MORISON (1779–1866)

1. Morison also gave the first lectures to nursing staff. See Morison Diaries (hereafter RCPE/MD), September 4, 1844.

2. *Medical Times and Gazette*, January 16, February 6, March 6, 27, April 17, May
15, June 19, July 24, August 28, October 9, December 25, 1858, and February 19,
1859. Conolly directly criticized Morison's (and Esquirol's) earlier books as "more

calculated to produce a temporary interest than to impart important instruction."
Ibid., February 2, 1858, p. 3. Conolly's discussions were indeed more extensive,
though it is not clear that they were more useful.

3. Morison, "Obituary," *Journal of Mental Science* 12, 1866, pp. 296–297.

4. A reading list extracted from Morison's diaries and published works shows
that he had read many of the major psychiatric texts of the nineteenth century, in-
cluding works by Bardenat, Bayle, Bell, Broussais, Burrows, Calmeil, Charlesworth,
Combe, Crichton, Cullen, Dugald Stewart, Esquirol, Ferrier, Ferrus, Fodere, Gall,
Georget, Haslam, Locke, Monro, Pinel, Reid, Rush, Spurzheim, Thurnham, and
Winslow.

5. Information about Morison's early life can be found in an unpublished biography by his grandson, Alexander Blackhall Morison. Copies exist at the Royal College
of Physicians, Edinburgh, and in the Morison papers at Bethlem Hospital (hereafter
BRH/MP).

6. Russia 1805; France 1818; France 1819; France, Nice, Piedmont, Lombardy,
Switzerland 1820–1821; France, Switzerland, Lombardy, Parma, Modena, Tuscany,
Papal States, and Rome 1822; France, Belgium, Netherlands 1825; France 1827.

7. Morison to Andrew McCrae, October 1865, BRH/MP.

8. Lisa Rosner, *Medical Education in the Age of Improvement: Edinburgh Students
and Apprentices 1760–1826* Edinburgh: Edinburgh University Press, 1991.

9. Alexander and his elder brother dedicated their theses to Alexander Wood.
Alexander's dissertation topic, "hydrocephalo phrenetico," led to an enduring interest in the physiology of brain disease. As late as 1846, he compiled a long review of
eighteenth- and nineteenth-century work done on morbid appearances in the brain
that were apparent from postmortems performed on the insane. RCP London, SR/
471.

10. Morison to his wife at Duke Street, Edinburgh, November 7, 1800, telling her
he is to dine with Dr. Crichton, BRH/MP/6/v.

11. See Blackhall Morison, "Alexander Morison," p. 7. Also Papa's letter to
A. McCrae, October 1865, BRH/MP.

12. March 9, 1817, RCPE/MD.

13. May 1, 1817, RCPE/MD.

14. This was £60,000, which would equate to a sum of over £2 million today.

15. Barbara Forbes to Alexander Morison, March 7, 1799, BRH/MP/5/vi.

16. Anne Burnes (aunt) to Mary Morison, August 30, 1798, BRH/MP/6/ix.

17. With the constant movement between Scotland and England it is hard to
escape the feeling that his children's emotional life must have suffered. Between
1815 and 1825 the Morison's children were deposited all over the country with
friends and relatives. Often they were left with relative strangers. Andrew certainly
rebelled against this treatment, and Morison's daughter Somerville, who was sent on
long holidays to the household where her future husband lived, appears to have
developed a relationship in the absence of any guidance from her family. Margaret,
Anne, and Charlotte all remained single, but his other daughters married and stayed
in contact with their father.

18. These included the Farquhars (his brother John's wife's family) among them
Sir Walter Rockliffe Farquhar; the Youngs (distant cousins of his mother's); Dr. Alexander Crichton; the Fordyces; and the Longlands.

19. They also educated his children in their school.

20. They finally bought 26 Cavendish Square in 1832 and for a while in the 1830s also rented a large cottage at Sutton Vallence in Kent.

21. The lease of Bankhead had long been in the possession of Adam Fergusson, the professor of Moral Philosophy, but Morison purchased it from a parvenu coach builder named Wilson. Other parcels of land he later resold to his brother John and brother-in-law William.

22. John Southey Somerville (1765–1819) inherited estates from both the Scottish and English branches of his family. A close friend of the fifth Duke of Bedford, he was an original member of the Board of Agriculture and became a noted agriculturalist. He and Morison shared an interest in angling. See *Dictionary of National Biography* (hereafter DNB).

23. Similarly in Scotland he was introduced to Sir Humphrey Davy, Sir Walter Scott, the Earl of Erroll, and the Scotts of Malleny, who were his local neighbours.

24. This was the first of many posts that Morison sought assiduously through his connections, and his courting of patronage has often been cited as indicating a lack of ability on his part. However such canvassing for positions was standard for the early nineteenth century, and he was certainly as well qualified as most other doctors of the period. Morison later sought positions for his children in the same way, and in the overcrowded medical market of the first half of the nineteenth century, it was often the only way to secure work.

25. In his diary, Morison notes that he told Lord Somerville he was "sometimes a month without being sent for, and that I was afraid I should never have sufficient business." January 20, 1810, RCPE/MD.

26. For Maton reference, January 17, 1817, RCPE/MD. For Halford's and Somerville's efforts on his behalf, February 21, March 13, 1818, RCPE/MD. Morison had been restrained from going abroad before this because he was physician to HRH Princess Charlotte, although he was never called to attend her. She died in childbirth in November 1817. University College London, Brougham Correspondence, September 10, 1831; July 21, 1832; March 9, 1833. Morison also applied to Lord Brougham in 1831, 1832, and 1833 for posts as a Lunacy Commissioner.

27. Falret went round Hanwell with Morison, March 15, 1818, September 2, 1835, RCPE/MD.

28. March 28, April 8, 1818, RCPE/MD.

29. April 16, 1818, RCPE/MD.

30. April 4, 11, 17, 1818, RCPE/MD.

31. March 26, 27, 31, April 2, 3, 4, 7, 8, 10, 14, 17, 1818, RCPE/MD.

32. March 22, 28, April 4, 17, 18, 1818, RCPE/MD.

33. May 13, June 9, 13, July 24, 1818, RCPE/MD.

34. December 8, 1818; March 13, 1819, RCPE/MD. There are few references to Mary in Morison's diaries, but it is clear that she was never fully reconciled to living in England. She wrote on this occasion, that it would need many £100s to keep his numerous family (nine children at this point), "even with the strictest frugality—you must judge entirely for yourself in those matters—I have had so much trouble and anxiety in moving from place to place with the care of young children, the certain and great expense attending it, the hitherto little success—I cannot describe the agitation and uneasiness these changes give me."

35. Somerville died of dysentery at Vevey in August, and Morison was appointed trustee of part of his estate. September 8, 1819, RCPE/MD. Once again, while in Paris Morison dined with Esquirol and his circle and accompanied them around the Salpêtrière.

36. September 14, 25, 28, 30, 1819, RCPE/MD.

37. August 20, 1820, RCPE/MD. Morison's contract was for his board and lodging, and £400 p.a. He was given permission to acquire other medical practice provided it did not interfere with his attendance on Lady Bute.

38. March 18, 20, December 12, 1821, RCPE/MD.

39. December 19, 1820; February 13, 1821; March 1, 1821; May 30, 1821, RCPE/MD. for examples of each of these.

40. Harriet Mellon's mother was from Cork and worked as a dresser in Kena's theatrical company. Harriet herself appeared on stage as a juvenile. At the height of her career she vied with Mrs. Jordan for public popularity. Her affair with Thomas Coutts caused a lot of unfriendly comment. On the death of his first wife in 1815, they married. In 1822 he died and left her his whole fortune. In 1827 she married William Aubrey de Vere, ninth Duke of St. Albans (DNB).

41. March 19, 27, 1823; October 9, 1824, RCPE/MD.

42. Rosner, *Medical Education*, passim.

43. With remarkable persistence, as late as 1845 he was still giving these annual lectures on both sides of the border.

44. A fifth edition, edited by his son, T. C. Morison, appeared in 1856.

45. Morison often changed the venue, and the times of his lectures, and they were advertised publicly in the newspapers. It was hardly surprising then that they were often badly attended. For example, November 1, 7, 22, 27, 1826, RCPE/MD. Compounding the problems this situation created, it seems likely, from the comments of one or two of his auditors, that his presentation was not very exciting.

46. Royal College of Physicians Edinburgh, Papers of the Society for Improving the Condition of the Insane, uncatalogued, contains a complete list of those who attended the lectures. February 1, 1827, RCPE/MD. MacGregor secured twenty-one pupils for Morison, and after Thornhill's intervention, eight attended from the East India Company. Towards the end of his career, Morison gave a paper to the Society for Improving the Condition of the Insane (hereafter SICI) in which he suggested that attendance on a course of lectures on mental diseases should be compulsory for medical students. See "A Paper suggesting the propriety of the Study of the Nature, Causes and Treatment of Mental Diseases as forming part of the Curriculum of Medical Education," London 1844 (RCPE/Uncat. papers of the SICI).

47. Eliot Freidson, *Professional Dominance* New York: Atherton, 1970, pp. 134–135.

48. Another important cohort who came to the lectures, though, were those who either were, or became, asylum visitors or governors. Many of these were Morison's personal friends among the gentry and magistracy and saw this course as a means of improving their understanding of the issues they were expected to address in their inspection visits. An important secondary audience thus were indoctrinated in the elements of medicine's claims to expertise in the treatment of insanity.

49. See, for example, Halford Papers, Leicestershire County Record Office DG24/793/3 (consultation re. Lady Westmorland); and DG24/905/1–4 (consultation re. Lord Derby).

50. Among those who attended were Southey, Maton, Macmichael, Haslam, Sutherland, Burrows, Dunston, Spurzheim, Thomas, Willis, and Wastell.

51. November 4, 1823, RCPE/MD.

52. February 9, 10, 13, March 9, 1827; November 15, 1835, RCPE/MD. This was, of course, Conolly's unfortunate colleague at the University of London.

53. October 26, 27, 29, 1835; November 14, 1835, RCPE/MD.

54. June 9, 1828, RCPE/MD.

55. Interestingly, Sutherland also offered Morison the facility of clinical instruction at St. Lukes, should he be offered something by Horner. Subsequently Conolly spent two fruitless years attempting to obtain facilities for students to observe clinical practice in a London asylum, at a time when Morison had negotiated such openings elsewhere. It is quite possible that his progress was deliberately blocked by Morison's friends. See September 8, 1828, RCPE/MD. (In 1828 Morison was simultaneously asking his connections to put him forward for Kings College, the King's Physicianship in Scotland, and as a Lunacy Commissioner. His patrons could obtain none of these positions for him.)

56. Parliamentary Papers, *Report of the Commissioners on the Universities of Scotland*, vol. 1, pp. 216, 348.

57. February 8, March 27, 1827, RCPE/MD.

58. Here was yet another instance of his inability to decide whether to make Edinburgh or London the focus of his efforts to build his career. Two years earlier, he had spurned another opportunity to build an Edinburgh practice. April 9, 1825, RCPE/MD: a proposition was put to Morison to help set up a new Infirmary in Edinburgh. Lizars and Liston were to be the surgeons, he and Poole the physicians, and Abercromby and Thompson consulting physicians.

59. Similarly, his later opposition to Conolly was never expressed in an open forum.

60. May 18, 20, 1830, RCPE/MD.

61. Reports on Madhouses and Notes of cases 1824-1829, RCP London, SR/471. The visitation of madhouses near Edinburgh was on the same basis as those in London, before the new English legislation of 1828. Morison was active on a variety of fronts during his presidency, chairing, for example, the committee that formulated and forwarded to Sir Robert Peel the College's response to the exposure of the Burke and Hare murders in Edinburgh.

62. For a detailed discussion of this subject see, Cooter, *Cultural Meaning*; see also January 27, February 6, 14, May 26, June 15, 1823, RCPE/MD. Interestingly a large proportion of Gall's lectures were read straight from his book.

63. James Deville (1777-1846) was the leading phrenological manipulator and cast maker in London in the 1820s and 1830s, among whose customers were Charles Bray, Richard Carlisle, George Eliot, Harriet Martineau, Prince Albert, and the Duke of Wellington.

64. May 19, 20, 1825, RCPE/MD.

65. June 2, 4, 1825, RCPE/MD.

66. June 2, 4, 8, 1825, RCPE/MD; Morison, *Outlines* 2d ed., London: Longman, 1826, pp.125-126. Even at this stage he talks of "those who adopt the phrenological ideas of Dr Gall" as if distancing himself. The use of lithography, developed in the late eighteenth century, permitted a more impressionistic sense of the mobility of the features than was possible in earlier engravings. For a fuller discussion see,

Sander Gilman, *Seeing the Insane* New York: Brunner/Mazel, 1985, pp. 72–98; also A. Boime, "Portraying Monomaniacs to service the Alienist's Monomania: Gericault and Georget," *The Oxford Art Journal*, January 14, 1991.

67. His book, *The Physiognomy of the Insane*, was an extension of the plates illustrating his *Outlines*. It failed to explore the historiography of physiognomy, especially the ideas of Lavater, Holcroft, and Bell, and his references to Pinel and Esquirol are in relation to their classification of *folie raisonnante* and monomania, rather than their exploration of physiognomy.

68. Morison often noted the physiognomical appearance of his patients in his diaries, and French influences inform the discussion throughout his book on physiognomy. This is particularly evident in his strong adherence to Esquirol's category of monomania.

69. These etchings and paintings (and the photographs later produced by one of Morison's students, Hugh W. Diamond) form part of a continuing iconography of madness that can be traced backwards to Hogarth and the mediaeval grotesques of central Europe and forwards to the work of Duchenne, Darwin, and Lombroso. The portrayal of the insane in this tradition reveals more about contemporary attitudes to the insane than about the individuals with which it is nominally concerned.

70. Morison, *Outlines of Lectures* 2d ed., 1826, p. 125.

71. In a sense, this turned out to be true because the need for close observation for purposes of phrenological diagnosis did foster close contact with patients and legitimized programmes of individualized treatment—features that were to disappear under the regimented routines of the emergent county asylum system.

72. February 14, 16, 28, March 7, 1826, RCPE/MD.

73. Charles Bell and John Haslam were both opposed to Spurzheim's doctrines, and their views evidently carried considerable weight with Morison. His friend Wardrop also mentioned a variety of contradictory evidence, as did the French alienist, Foville, when Morison revisted Paris in 1827. See March 16, 18, 23, 25, 30, June 30, 1826; January 10, April 11, June 3, 7, September 12, 1827, RCPE/MD. Haslam's opposition may have been particularly significant, since he was planning to give six lectures in October on perception, memory, imagination, thought, reason, and volition from a nonphrenological perspective. See May 31, 1827, RCPE/MD.

74. See Cooter, *Cultural Meaning*.

75. Morison, *Outlines*, pp. 77–84. Morison always believed in ready access for relatives, in both lodgings and asylums.

76. See Scull, *The Most Solitary of Afflictions*, pp. 138–146.

77. Initially, notification of single patients went only to a small subcommittee of the Commission, who alone were empowered to inspect single patients, but by 1853 this had proved unworkable, and the authority was transferred to the whole Commission.

78. See the discussion in MacKenzie, *Psychiatry for the Rich*, pp. 98–99, and, for example, Susanna Winkworth, *Letters and Memorials of Catherine Winkworth*, Clifton: for the author, 1883, vol. 1, p. 67; also G. N. Ray (ed.), *The Letters and Private Papers of William Makepeace Thackeray* London: Oxford University Press, 1945, vol. 2, p. 81.

79. As an anonymous writer (possibly John Conolly) explained in 1850, this ac-

counted in part for the fact that the animus of families against asylum confinement was greater amongst the wealthy classes than among the poor, "who have already been more accustomed to have their movements controlled; they are moreover, very often better off with regard to bodily comforts than they were when at large." *Familiar Views of Lunacy and Lunatic Life* London: Parker, 1850, p. 80.

80. In fact, the hypocrisy of the inspectorate's public pronouncements had a far more intimate foundation. Publicly, Lord Shaftesbury insisted that private lodgings constituted the worst possible system of care for lunatics, asserting "from the bottom of [his] heart" that he would advise anybody, "if it should please Providence to afflict any member of his family [with insanity], to send him or her to a private asylum." Were one of his own near relatives to go mad, he insisted he "would consign him to an asylum in which there were other patients and which was subjected to official visitation." See E. Hodder, *Life of Shaftesbury*, p. 308, quoting Shaftesbury speaking before Parliament in 1844; and Shaftesbury's later testimony before the 1859 Select Committee (*Report*, pp. 30–32). In fact, when his son Maurice became mentally disabled with epilepsy, asylum care was not considered for a moment. Rather, after the expenditure of hundreds of pounds in an attempt to cure him at home, he was placed in private lodgings, first in the Hague and then in Lausanne, Switzerland. In his diary Shaftesbury noted: "Fits, Lunatic Asylums, 'private charge' pass before me; 20 years of labour have made me well to fear them. Fits are treated as madness and madness constitutes a right as it were to treat people as vermin." September 5, 1851, SHA/PD/6.

81. He supervised lodgings in many locations: Maidstone, Sevenoaks, Tonbridge, Gravesend, Canterbury, Plaistow, and Farley, as well as many in London itself. In addition, he would obtain patients for doctors, clergymen, and others to care for at home, most of whom were not registered. Nor was he averse to keeping more than one patient at a single location, though this was most definitely illegal.

82. September 4, 1844; April 10, 1850, RCPE/MD. In 1844, a Captain Greathorpe approached Morison about his daughter, who wanted to marry a common soldier. Morison recommended Dr. Belhomme in Paris as someone who had an "Institution for the children of parents who had difficulty in managing them."

83. The Reverend W. G. Howard, whom Morison placed with a former Hanwell magistrate, Mr. Trimmer, was under restraint almost continuously for eight years, before he was finally transferred to Ticehurst. (Howard was a Chancery case, who paid £650 p.a. when he was admitted to Ticehurst in 1846. He became the eighth Earl of Carlisle in 1864, when he was still in Ticehurst.) In 1842, Morison recorded that another patient was "still requiring restraint, although nearly reduced to a skeleton and his back excoriated with sores." November 11, 1842, RCPE/MD.

84. Morison was willing, too, to try other standard medical treatments: leeches, the insertion of an issue, emetics, bathing with warm or cold vinegar, the use of shower baths, and so forth, subject to certain limits: "generally speaking, . . . all remedies which act powerfully on the system are to be resorted to with extreme caution especially in the early stage of this complaint. The Brain is an organ of too delicate a texture to suffer with impunity violent treatment." Ms. 471, notes on the case of Miss F., Royal College of Physicians, London.

85. February 3, 12, 17, 20, March 3, 29, April 3, 7, June 2, 1827, RCPE/MD.

86. June 14, 1827, RCPE/MD.

87. John Perceval, famous author of *A Narrative of the Treatment Experienced by a Gentleman During a State of Derangement* (London: Effingham Wilson: 1838, 1840) was cared for in lodgings after his release from Ticehurst asylum. See letter from Robert Stedman to the Home Secretary, PRO/HO40/40.

88. March 11, 18, 23, June 4, 1828, RCPE/MD.

89. February 10, March 13, 17, 1835, RCPE/MD.

90. Cf. Roy Porter, *Health for Sale: Quackery in England 1660–1850* Manchester: Manchester University Press, 1989.

91. May 13, 1825, RCPE/MD.

92. September 13, 1835, RCPE/MD.

93. October 20, 1828; January 14, July 12, August 7, 9, 12, 1829; February 18, 1830, RCPE/MD.

94. On the reaction of British alienists more generally, see William Ll. Parry-Jones, "The Model of the Geel Lunatic Colony and Its Influence on the Nineteenth-Century Asylum System in Britain," in Scull (ed.), *Madhouses, Mad-Doctors, and Madmen*, pp. 201–217. See also Chapter 7 below.

95. June 23, 1825, RCPE/MD; for "call" lists, see Hervey, "A Slavish Bowing Down."

96. For the progress of his candidacy, see March 19, 23, April 11, November 1, 1831; January 18, May 29, 1832, RCPE/MD. At the beginning of 1832, he had also sent complimentary tickets to his forthcoming annual lectures to Ellis and magistrates on the visiting committee.

97. Halford supported one of Morison's opponents in this election, which tends to confirm the impression one receives elsewhere that his support for Morison was always lukewarm.

98. These views had, of course, cost Conolly the superintendency on the first occasion he applied for the post, and they were resurrected by his enemies among the magistrates and staff when the controversy over nonrestraint erupted. On that occasion, the chaplain, the Reverend Francis Tebbutt, who was closely associated with Morison, publicly attacked "the conduct of Dr. Conolly . . . who had been in the habit of speaking . . . very disparagingly of the tenets and discipline of the Established Church, and upholding the Unitarians as the most moral and religious people. . . . Dr. Conolly has expressed . . . his approbation of the people called Chartists. . . . Dr. Conolly did . . . receive at his residence in the asylum, and there entertains as his guests, Owen the notorious founder of Socialism, and one Pare, of Birmingham." See his *Letter to the Magistrates of the County of Middlesex* London: for the author, [1841]. These were views and associates of which the conservative and deeply religious Morison could hardly be expected to approve.

99. Correspondence between John Adams and George Poynder, Kent Marsham Papers, Romney of the Mote, MSS (1461–1957), CRO/U1515/OQ/LI.

100. Adams to Poynder, November 28, 1839; Adams to Marsham, December 7, 1839; Poynder to Adams, November 6, 1840; Poynder to Adams, January 5, 1841, Kent CRO/U1515/OQ/LI. This last was an important point. Conolly's subsequent departure to private practice resulted from the magistrates' appointment of a Governor to manage the administrative side of Hanwell, to leave the doctor free to carry out the medical treatment. Hunter and Macalpine were undoubtedly correct in stating that this move was to stop escalating costs, a large portion of which were due to the system of nonrestraint.

101. Although Begley handed Morison the evidence he gathered at Hanwell relating to nonrestraint, there is no evidence that Morison solicited this behaviour. Begley, Button, Tebutt, and Trimmer probably thought Morison had been shabbily treated, and all had their own doubts about the new system. For file of cuttings and information about Hanwell collected by Begley, see RCP Edinburgh, Morison MSS. For Hunter and Macalpine's discussion of these events, see their introduction to the reprint edition of Conolly's *Construction and Government*, pp. 25–29.

102. J. Conolly, *The Reports of J Conolly M.D. The Resident Physician of the County Lunatic Asylum* London: M'Gowan & Co, 1842, Second Report, p. 59. Conolly's report confirms this but contends it reflects patients coming to terms with their new-found freedom. Button's apostasy brought a quick response from the majority of the magistrates who backed Conolly: in July 1840, he was informed "that his services would be dispensed with" from the beginning of 1841, allegedly because the asylum board had decided that it could do without a house surgeon for the five hundred or so patients on the female side of the asylum.

103. *The Times*, February 16, 1841, report on nonrestraint controversy. February 4, 1842, RCPE/MD: "met Dr Begley, he fears Serjeant Adams means to discharge him, that Conolly is at the bottom of it—says he goes a great way in the no restraint but not the whole length, blames Button and Tebbutt for bringing his affidavit forward. Was on his way to speak to Pownall about remaining."

104. It even received the royal imprimatur: following a visit by George III's son Adolphus, the Duke of Cambridge, he wrote to the chair of the Visiting Magistrates to express his gratification at what he had seen, and to add that "Dr. Conolly appears to me to be the most proper person to conduct such an important concern."

105. See the discussion in Nancy Tomes, "The Great Restraint Controversy: A Comparative Perspective on Anglo-American Psychiatry in the Nineteenth Century," in Bynum, Porter, and Shepherd (eds.), *The Anatomy of Madness* vol. 3, pp. 190–225.

106. April 30, 1841, May 28, 1841, RCPE/MD.; J. Conolly, *The Reports of J. Conolly M.D.*, pp. 67–74. Conolly was very alert to the possible abuses of seclusion and addressed these from the outset in his reports.

107. On Conolly's classes, see Hunter and Macalpine, "Introduction" to Conolly, *Construction and Government*, pp. 29–31.

108. See Hunter and Macalpine's "Introduction" to Conolly's *Treatment of the Insane*, p. xvi. There is no evidence that Morison gave these lectures reluctantly, as they state. In fact they may well have been linked to his Society for Improving the Condition of the Insane, which attempted to promote better practice amongst nurses by rewarding meritorious service.

109. Surrey County Asylum, *1st Annual Report*, 1843, p. 25; *3rd Annual Report*, 1845, p. 26; June 29, 1847, RCPE/MD. Earlier in the year when Daniel had proposed bringing Conolly into partnership with him at Southall Park, Morison had been against the idea; March 18, 1847, RCPE/MD.

110. The records of this society are deposited at the Royal College of Physicians, Edinburgh, in a box which came to light during a recent visit there. Included with the papers, are the original plates done by Richard Dadd for the society's award certificates.

111. As late as 1857, he is listed as a member of the AMOAHI and in fact hosted a large conversazione attended by four hundred doctors. Remaining a member of the Association must have created problems for Morison as a number of their policies—

in particular their opposition to the role of Visiting Physicians—ran counter to his interests.

112. On the mutual hatred that existed between the seventh Earl and both his parents, see Finlayson, *The Seventh Earl of Shaftesbury*, passim. The younger Shaftesbury experienced an abusive and neglectful childhood, even by the standards of the British aristocracy. He once referred to his mother as a "fiend." "What a dreadful woman our mother is," he wrote on another occasion. "Her whole pleasure is in finding fault." National Register of Archives (NRA), Shaftesbury Diaries, April 28, 1826; September 18–23, 1825, SHA/PD/1. His father he thought guilty of "malignity and horror" towards his children, creating "constant fear" with his "very great severity, moral and physical." For most of his adult life, the two were scarcely on speaking terms and when the son attempted a reconciliation, he soon found himself turned out of the house: "cannot, by word or deed, do good," he noted, "My presence even is hateful." Shaftesbury Diaries, November 16, 1828; December 3, 13, 16, 1844, SHA/PD/1; Hodder, *The Seventh Earl of Shaftesbury*, p. 51.

113. For membership of the Society, see Hervey, "A Slavish Bowing Down." Its existence allowed those who endorsed often illegal single lodgings to exchange patients, to set up joint consultations, and to trade favours, undermining the independence of those certifying the insane in ways that were difficult for the Lunacy Commissioners to detect.

114. RCPE/Society MSS.

115. NRA, Shaftesbury Diaries, March 23, 1845, SHA/PD/4: "to Surrey Lunatic Asylum. A noble establishment and admirably conducted. A sight to make a man who cares a fig for his fellows jump for joy . . . surely we are on the advance to better things."

116. Bethlem and Guy's paid out considerable sums of money to get an exemption from inspection by the Lunacy Commission in 1828 and 1845. See Guy's Papers, November 12, 1828, H9/Gy/A72/1; As "Father of the House of Lords" the sixth Earl was in a prime position to block his son's legislative efforts. See seventh Earl's diaries on the passage of his lunacy bills, July 23, 1845, SHA/PD/4: "now we have the Lords; we must pass from Scylla to Charybdis—my father, as usual and of course taking the lead in hatred and resistance to anything of mine. God turn his heart."

117. Cf. Procter to Forster, Forster Papers, F.48.E.32/29, November 14, 1852, Victoria and Albert Museum: "it has been at our solicitation that we obtained a special order from the Secretary of State to visit it." The seventh Earl personally took charge of the investigation.

118. See *Asylum Journal* 1, no. 3, February 15, 1854, pp. 33–36. This issue arose again in the 1850s in Ireland where there were still Visiting Physicians and the resident medical officers enlisted the support of the Lunacy Commission and AMAOHI to strengthen their position. See Finnane, *Insanity and the Insane*, pp. 39–47.

119. See November 15, 1844, SHA/PD/3: "sad news of Godwin's complete unfitness for the post to which I had so greatly contributed to raise him—the Governorship of Hanwell—unfit in every way and yet what testimonials from the Horse Guards!! on those and on William's [his brother] credentials I relied—this is painfully humiliating and shatters the little confidence I had in my own judgment."

120. Morison was able to list hundreds of visits he had made to Bethlem. His

diligence is confirmed by Offley Martin's Charity Commissioners Report on Bethlem, *An Account of Bethlem Hospital* London: Pickering, 1853, pp. 24–25; see also Blackhall Morison, "Alexander Morison," pp. 146–154.

121. *Bethlem Hospital: The Report of the Lunacy Commissioners to the Secretary of State* London: Spottiswood and Shaw, 1852, pp. 5–16. The Commissioners commented that the system of two Visiting Physicians "encourages carelessness and destroys responsibility."

122. Monro became mentally ill himself in 1855 and was eventually made a Chancery patient. See record of Chancery Inquisitions, PRO Chancery Lane/ C211/ 30. Monro was looked after in one of the cottages attached to his asylum, Clapton House. Also Docket Book March 1840–February 1855, J/103/2.

123. Reverend James Hamer to Mrs. Morison, Sutton, October 11, 1837, BRH/ MP/6xiii. The family nanny, Nanny Ross, who had been with them throughout their married life, was buried three years later, in the family kirkyard at Currie, aged seventy-four.

124. He was a madhouse visitor for fifty-three years.

125. For this see *Medical Directory*, 1854.

126. See January 10, 1846, RCPE/MD: brought Margaret up from Elm Grove to see her mother (who had just died); also March 8, 1844. Haslam certifies Margaret to go to Elm Grove, March 8, 1844, also September 12, 1844, RCPE/MD.

127. Among those who lectured were David Skae, Thomas Clouston, John Batty Tuke, and Sir Frederick Mott. For full list see Blackhall Morison, "Alexander Morison," pp. 165–167.

128. For an example of other doctors providing the same service, see letters of Winslow to Robert Peel concerning his brother, 40609, f.149, 151, 208, 215, 221, 258, 259, 268, 277, 279, and 314, Peel MSS, British Museum.

129. Morison's children were friends and stayed with the families of several of the county magistrates. Morison himself was invited onto the Board of the Equitable Life Assurance Company through one of the Surrey magistrates. This board included the Bethlem Governors Ralph Price and E. R. Adams; the Surrey Asylum Visitors, Henry Kemble, E. R. Adams, and William Shadbolt; and the Kent Asylum Visitors, Edmund Henry Lushington, and Charles Pott.

CHAPTER SIX
THE ADMINISTRATION OF LUNACY IN VICTORIAN ENGLAND:
SAMUEL GASKELL (1807–1886)

1. Copies of these are preserved in the Lancashire Record Office, Preston.

2. [Samuel Gaskell], "Visit to the Bicêtre," *Chambers's Edinburgh Journal* n.s. no. 158, January 9, 1847, pp. 20–22; "Second Article: Education of Idiots at the Bicêtre," *Chambers's Edinburgh Journal* n.s. no. 161, 1847, pp. 71–73.

3. Samuel Gaskell, "On the Want of Better Provision for the Labouring and Middle Classes When Attacked or Threatened by Insanity," *Journal of Mental Science* 6, 1860, pp. 321–327.

4. On the embrace of science and useful knowledge by provincial elites, particularly those in Lancashire, see Arnold Thackray, "Natural Knowledge in Cultural Context: The Manchester Model," *American Historical Review* 79, 1974, pp. 672–709.

5. The Gaskell family played a major role in both institutions. Among the masters at the Academy were Dr. John Aikin, Joseph Priestly, and Gilbert Wakefield, and the pupils included Thomas Malthus. The Academy closed in 1786, temporarily transferred to Manchester, and then was moved to York in 1803, where it was renamed Manchester New College. It was here that Gaskell's older brother William subsequently trained for the Unitarian ministry.

6. A. Thackray, "Natural Knowledge," p. 698. On the clannish tendencies of the Unitarians, cf. A. B. Hopkins, *Elizabeth Gaskell, Her Life and Work* London: Lehmann, 1952, p. 43. Jennifer Uglow refers to "the bewilderingly entwined Unitarian community." *Elizabeth Gaskell: A Habit of Stories* New York: Farrar, Straus, and Giroux, 1993, p. 56.

7. "Obituary: The Late Samuel Gaskell, Esq.," *Journal of Mental Science* 32, 1886, p. 235. There was sufficient money to provide a £100 annuity for his mother, and he left some additional funds to help with the education of the surviving children. See Barbara Brill, *William Gaskell 1805–1884* Manchester: Manchester Literary and Philosophical Publications, 1984, p. 12. (Brill describes these, oddly, as "considerable assets.")

8. The apprenticeship was for seven years. It seems a perverse choice of career given Samuel's vision problems. His obituarist in the *Journal of Mental Science* (p. 235) attributes the family's decision to the influence of the family doctor, who emphasized "the weakness of his eyes" and sought "to discourage the adoption of medicine as his profession."

9. On William, see Brill's brief biography, *William Gaskell 1805–1884*.

10. Winifred Guerin, *Elizabeth Gaskell, A Biography* Oxford: Clarendon Press, 1976, pp. 45–58; Hopkins, *Elizabeth Gaskell*, pp. 43–53. This marriage provides an example of the clannishness of the Unitarians, alluded to above. Elizabeth's maternal grandfather was Samuel Holland, and her cousin, (Sir) Henry Holland, became one of the most prominent London physicians of his generation. One of Samuel and William's two sisters also married a Holland, and several Hollands, in turn, married into the Wedgwood family.

11. "Obituary," *Journal of Mental Science*, p. 235.

12. By 1831, Manchester's population had grown to some 250,000 and was increasing at a rate twice as fast as London's.

13. Thomas Turner, *An Address to the Inhabitants of Lancashire on the Present State of the Medical Profession* London: Longmans, 1825, pp. 19–20.

14. "A Week in Manchester," *Blackwood's Magazine* 45, 1839, pp. 481–496. Cleanliness, attention, order, and neatness were to be a hallmark of Gaskell's establishments and the features he most insisted upon when he was later charged with supervising asylumdom.

15. On the place of the Manchester Literary and Philosophical Society in the local social structure, cf. A. Thackray, "Natural Knowledge." In its earliest years, the society met in a room at the back of the Cross Street Chapel.

16. Hopkins, *Elizabeth Gaskell*, p. 45.

17. A variety of evidence points to a close and continuing connection between Samuel and his brother. Mrs. Gaskell provides an amusing anecdote of her brother-in-law being pulled hither and thither at the altar during her wedding service (where

he was best man), as her two cousins, Kate and Susan Holland, fought for his affections by tugging on his arms. During the 1830s and 1840s, Samuel and William spent holidays together in the Lake District and were together on many social occasions. Samuel served as medical adviser to the family, caring for the Gaskell babies and providing advice on such matters as which seaside resort to visit for the summer. Elizabeth Gaskell grew especially close to him, dropping in to dine with him at the Infirmary during her husband's absence, sharing her correspondence with him, and seeking his opinion on a variety of subjects. "I believe I am," she once confessed to her sister-in-law Elizabeth, "more open with Sam than I dare to be with William, and I love Sam as a dear brother." Even after his appointment to the Lunacy Commission removed him from the local scene, Samuel stayed with his brother and sister-in-law whenever his duties as an inspector made this possible, and his friendship with his fellow Commissioners, John Forster and Bryan Procter (the minor poet, Barry Cornwall) brought him into the same literary circles as Mrs. Gaskell. See J.A.V. Chapple and Arthur Pollard (eds.), *The Letters of Mrs. Gaskell* Manchester: Manchester University Press, 1966, letters 2, 10, 11, 13, 14, 16, 92, 93, 96, 117, 134, 135, 145, 202, 203, 211, 214, 217, 218, 252, 259, 422; and Guerin, *Elizabeth Gaskell*, pp. 56, 305 (for his attendance at Mrs. Gaskell's funeral).

18. Angus Easson, *Elizabeth Gaskell* London: Routledge, 1979, p. 29.

19. Guerin, *Elizabeth Gaskell*, p. 48. Elizabeth's father had thrown up a secure position as resident preacher to the Dobb Lane Unitarian Chapel at Failsworth, when he developed scruples about being paid to preach the gospel. He subsequently developed a similar distaste for his other occupation, teaching classics, tried experimental farming, failed miserably, and practically bankrupted the household, before ending his days as a petty civil servant.

20. William Gaskell, while steadily more prominent in Manchester affairs, had by contrast a purely provincial reputation.

21. He had earlier demonstrated his interest in lunacy by visiting Hanwell during Sir William Ellis's tenure as superintendent (1831–1838). As recorded in the visitor's book, though "forty-one of his patients were in almost constant restraint of some kind or other, . . . Mr. Gaskell thought the amount of this restraint moderate and satisfactory." [John Charles Bucknill], "Dr. Conolly and Mr. Pownall," *Asylum Journal of Mental Science* 2, 1856, p. 383. (Unfortunately, Bucknill does not give the date of this visit.)

22. G. P. Button, Conolly's assistant at Hanwell, was one of his rivals for the post. Button produced a testimonial from his superior in support of his candidacy and, by his own account, was mortified to discover that Conolly had written a far stronger endorsement of Gaskell's application, in the course of which he pointedly noted that "I know of no candidate whose qualifications are altogether to be compared with those of Mr. Gaskell." Quoted in Hunter and Macalpine, "Introduction," to Conolly, *Construction and Government*, p. 26.

23. Samuel's successor at the Manchester Infirmary was another Unitarian, Joseph Holland, related to him both through his sister's marriage into the Holland clan and through his brother's wife, Elizabeth. Joseph Holland would subsequently become the superintendent of the second Lancashire County Asylum at Prestwich.

24. John Walton, "The Treatment of Pauper Lunatics in Victorian England: The

Case of Lancaster Asylum, 1816–1870," in Scull (ed.), *Madhouses, Mad-Doctors, and Madmen*, p. 173. Walton provides a detailed account of Gaskell's years at Lancaster, on which we have drawn extensively in the following paragraphs.

25. Thackray, "Natural Knowledge," p. 692. For a discussion of the ways in which Unitarians linked science, the alleviation of suffering, and moral progress, see J. Raymond and John V. Pickstone, "The Natural Sciences and the Learning of the English Unitarians," in B. Smith (ed.), *Liberty, Truth, Religion: Essays Celebrating Two Hundred Years of Manchester College* Oxford: Manchester College, 1986, pp. 129–164. Also useful for the broader context is Desmond, *The Politics of Evolution*.

26. Quakers formed another sizeable portion of Manchester's Nonconformist elite, and there was close contact between the two sects. During William Gaskell's time at Manchester College in York, it is difficult to imagine that he failed to have some direct contact with the by now famous York Retreat, and this, too, may have played some role in stimulating his younger brother's interest in insanity.

27. It had been preceded only by the asylums built in Nottinghamshire (1811), Bedfordshire (1812), and Norfolk (1814).

28. Lancashire Record Office, QAM 5/1845, p. 4.

29. See Scull, *The Most Solitary of Afflictions*, p. 89.

30. J. S. Bolton, "The Evolution of a Mental Hospital, Wakefield 1818–1928," *Journal of Mental Science* 74, 1928, pp. 588–596.

31. Hanwell's first superintendent, W. C. Ellis, who was recruited from his previous position as head of the West Riding Asylum, employed restraint liberally, utilizing its most modern forms, including Paul Slade Knight's restraining chair and the so-called "Charenton Basket." See March 29, 1832, RCPE/MD. His successor, J. G. Millingen (who informed Conolly that "it would be impossible for the Physician to find occupation for more than two hours in the day") placed even greater reliance on such devices.

32. P. S. Knight, *Observations on [the] Derangement of the Mind*, p. 116.

33. J. Walton, "The Treatment of Pauper Lunatics," p. 171. Gaskell subsequently boasted that "The locks formerly used to restrain the patients in bed at night were converted to a useful purpose, in fastening back the bed room doors during the day time, so as to prevent any accidental or unnecessary seclusion of a patient." Lancashire Record Office, QAM 5/1845/9.

34. Lancashire County Asylum, Medical Officers' Report for 1841, p. 4, Lancaster Public Library.

35. Lancashire Record Office, QAM 5/1845/6.

36. Ibid.

37. Lancashire Record Office, QAM 5/1845/4–5.

38. Ibid.

39. Lancashire Record Office, QAM 5/1846/5.

40. Lancashire Record Office, QAM 5/1847/7.

41. Ibid. By 1847, as a temporary expedient, some of the pressure on available space was being relieved by farming out "a large number of patients into the Haydock Lodge [private] asylum"; and work was under way on two additional public asylums for the county.

42. Wearily, he at one point informed his readers that "no adequate idea can be conveyed of the anxieties felt, or the amount of mental and bodily exertion required, in carrying out a milder system of treatment, amidst the noise, confusion and exposure to danger, consequent on extensive alterations in a building in which the insane are confined." Lancashire Record Office, QAM 5/1845/8.

43. Lancashire Record Office, QAM 5/1845/7.

44. Lancashire Record Office, QAM 5/1845/8.

45. Ibid.

46. Lancashire Record Office, QAM 5/1845/10–11. For the revised regulations themselves, which provide a good deal of insight into the attendants' work routine, cf. QAM 5/1848/17–22. For an assessment of the attendants' performance, see Walton, "The Treatment of Pauper Lunatics," pp. 178–182.

47. In John Conolly's attempt to create an authorised version of the history of the nonrestraint movement, he deliberately accords Gaskell pride of place, listing him as the first to adopt the Hanwell system in the years when "the progress of this method in England generally remained very slow." Conolly further indicates that, prior to doing so, Gaskell had visited Hanwell and spent an extended period "watching the results of non-restraint." Cf. *Treatment of the Insane*, p. 295. The similarities between the social organization of Lancaster and Hanwell and Gaskell's subsequent role as a proselyte for Conollyite ideas, are thus rooted quite as much in early and direct contact and imitation as in their shared religious background and intellectual outlook.

48. The Lunacy Commissioners subsequently indicated their approbation: "The Asylum of Lancaster has been generally looked upon by us as affording one of the best specimens of proper classification." *Further Report*, 1847, p. 228.

49. Lancashire Record Office, QAM 5/1847/5–6. In 1847, he reported that 479 out of 663 patients were employed, full or part-time, over the course of the year.

50. See Scull, *The Most Solitary of Afflictions*, pp. 165–168, 267–269, 311–315.

51. See, for example, R. Hindle, *An Account of the Expenditure of the County Palatine of Lancaster for a Period of 23 Years* London: Whittaker, 1843.

52. Lancashire Record Office, QAM 5/1846/9.

53. "Obituary. Samuel Gaskell, F.R.C.S. Eng.," *British Medical Journal* 1, 1886, p. 720.

54. Ibid. See also Gaskell's own testimony about this system before the House of Commons, *Select Committee on Lunatics*, 1859, p. 144.

55. Lancashire Record Office, QAM 5/1845/9.

56. Lancashire Record Office, QAM 5/1845/14.

57. Lancashire Record Office, QAM 5/1846/3–4; QAM 5/1848/6. For the favourable impression formed by the official inspectorate, cf. Commissioners in Lunacy, *Further Report*, pp. 226–227.

58. Lancashire Record Office, QAM 5/1847/4–5.

59. Lancashire Record Office, QAM 5/1846/3. The following year, he reported that 220 males and 268 females (out of a total asylum population of 663) were involved in classes where they were taught the alphabet, reading, writing, and arithmetic. QAM 5/1847/11.

60. Lancashire Record Office, QAM 5/1845/24.

61. Shaftesbury vividly recalled the sight almost four decades later. It was

what first attracted my attention to . . . my friend, Mr. Gaskell. . . . It happened to be the
meat day when I visited the Lancaster Asylum. To my astonishment I saw about forty women
sitting at dinner, each with a child in her arms. I said, "What is this?" "Well," he said, " it is
an experiment I am making. Here are several women wanting occupation, and there are
several children wanting care. So these women have the exclusive care of the children day
and night." It was positively a stroke of inspiration in the man. It was his aim to develop in
the women the great principle of maternal love—that those women should receive the blessings of children and the children receive the blessings of motherly care. I never was so
pleased, and this is a proof of it. When I went away, I said, "By God's blessing, if I ever have
the opportunity, that man shall be a Commissioner."

Lord Shaftesbury, "Vote of Thanks to the President of the Medico-Psychological Association," *Journal of Mental Science* 27, 1881, pp. 444–445.

62. Lancashire Record Office, QAM 5/1845/24; QAM 5/1846/4.

63. Lancashire Record Office QAM 5/1847/3–4.

64. Conolly, *Treatment of the Insane*, p. 73.

65. Commissioners in Lunacy, *Further Report*, p. 430. Conolly's recommendation
of "a cold shower bath, efficiently applied . . . in violent cases" appears in ibid.,
p. 444.

66. Ibid., p. 183. Compare Conolly's response: "I consider the direct treatment
of any form of insanity, by mere medicinal applications, to be very limited." General
bloodletting, he continued, was both dangerous and useless, and purges often
"needlessly employed." Ibid., p. 444.

67. Lancashire Record Office, QAM 5/1846/9.

68. Commissioners in Lunacy, *Further Report*, p. 229. Prichard, the one medical
commissioner who had written extensively on insanity, was the prime mover behind
this survey of contemporary therapeutics.

69. J. C. B[ucknill], "Review of *The Treatment of the Insane Without Mechanical
Restraints*," *Journal of Mental Science* 3, 1856–1857, p. 257.

70. Lancashire Record Office, QAM 5/1848/14–15. Gaskell himself quite openly
acknowledged the inescapable, that "a striking diminution in the number of recover-
ies has taken place" (QAM 5/1845/19). By 1860, the cure rate was to fall as low as
4.6 percent, and from 1850 onwards, the death rate at Lancaster almost always exceeded the cure rate.

71. Lancashire Record Office, QAM 5/1846/7; and, for reiteration of this point,
see QAM 5/1847/6; QAM 5/1848/3.

72. For details, see Scull, *The Most Solitary of Afflictions*, chap. 3.

73. On October 25, 1842, by R.W.S. Lutwidge and J. R. Hume; on September 13,
1843, by J. W. Mylne and Hume; on August 23, 1844, by Bryan Procter and Thomas
Turner. The manuscript reports of these visits, and the subsequent visits of the national commissioners, are preserved in the Lancashire Record Office, QAM 1/33/11.

74. By Turner and John Hancock Hall, on September 15, 1845; by Hume and
Mylne, on September 22, 1846; by W. G. Campbell and Hume, on September 13,
1847; and by Procter and Turner on August 29, 1848. Shaftesbury, who chaired the
commission from its founding to his death in 1885, subsequently indicated that he
had also visited the asylum to view Gaskell's administration. See *Journal of Mental
Science* 27, 1881, pp. 444–445.

75. Lancashire Record Office, QAM 1/33/11, October 25, 1842.

76. Ibid., September 22, 1846.

77. Ibid., August 29, 1848. For other testimony from outsiders about Gaskell's skills as a superintendent, see Thomas Greene, M.P., to Dr. William Baly, July 20, 1842, Library of the Royal College of Physicians ms. 716/44 (which describes the asylum as "in a dreadfully crowded state" but praises Gaskell as "a most intelligent and skillful man"); and the "Report by Professor Crommelinck to the Belgian Minister," partially reprinted in Lancashire Record Office, QAM 5/1845/25–26.

78. We echo here the sensible conclusions reached in Walton, "The Treatment of Pauper Lunatics," pp. 191–192.

79. See the discussion in Scull, *The Most Solitary of Afflictions*, pp. 169–174, 277–293.

80. Lancashire Record Office, QAM 5/1847/3–4. For Conolly's comparable emphasis on "tranquillity . . . cleanliness, order," see his comments in Commissioners in Lunacy, *Further Report*, pp. 444–445.

81. Lancashire Record Office, QAM 5/1848/4.

82. Commissioners in Lunacy, *Further Report*, p. 224, summarising "several years" of inspection of the Lancaster Asylum. Report of the Metropolitan Commissioners Procter and Turner, Lancashire Record Office, QAM 1/33/11.

83. Visit of the Metropolitan Commissioners Mylne and Hume, September 13, 1843; and for almost identical comments, visit of the Lunacy Commissioners Turner and Hall, September 15, 1845, and Mylne and Hume again, September 22, 1846, Lancashire Record Office, QAM 1/33/11.

84. Visit of the Lunacy Commissioners Campbell and Hume, September 13, 1847, Lancashire Record Office, QAM 1/33/11. They noted with satisfaction that "about 224 attend divine service in the chapel on Sunday" and that "prayers are also read thrice a week."

85. Lancashire Record Office, QAM 5/1848/6–12. In some districts, "particularly some of the secluded dales formed by the range of hills separating Lancashire from Yorkshire, . . . intermarriage has evidently formed one of the circumstances which have given rise to this degeneracy." But there were many other cases where he felt this cause was clearly not at work. Characteristically, his reaction was to urge that it was "desirable rather to direct attention to the alleviation of the evil, than to devote much time to the investigation of its causes."

86. See the two-part article in *Chambers's Edinburgh Journal*, "Visit to the Bicêtre" and "Education of Idiots at the Bicêtre."

87. Lancashire Record Office, QAM 5/1847/5; also QAM 5/1848/9.

88. This establishment opened in Highgate in 1848. See the brief discussion in Kenneth Day and Joze Jancar, "Mental Handicap and the Royal Medico-Psychological Association: A Historical Association, 1841–1991," in G. E. Berrios and H. Freeman (eds.), *150 Years of British Psychiatry* London: Gaskell, 1991, pp. 268–278.

89. Nestor Roberts, *Cheadle Royal Hospital* Altrincham: Sherratt, 1967, p. 44.

90. On June 19, 1841, William Hitch, the superintendent of the Gloucester Asylum, had circularized eighty-nine of his fellow alienists seeking support for such an association. Gaskell was one of six superintendents who responded to this missive and met at Gloucester to draw up plans. See Minute Book of the Medico-Psychological Association, 1841–1892, now housed at the Royal College of Psychiatrists.

91. Hugh Freeman and Digby Tantam, "Samuel Gaskell," in G. E. Berrios and H. Freeman (eds.), *150 Years of British Psychiatry*, p. 448.

92. As late as 1914, Gaskell's income would have ranked among the top 10 percent of all medical incomes nationally. See the discussion in Peterson, *The Medical Profession*, pp. 214–224.

93. Prichard was appointed in late 1845, after one of the original nominees, Henry Herbert Southey, had resigned to assume the less demanding and more lucrative post of Chancery Visitor in Lunacy. Ashley urged his appointment, notwithstanding his private judgement that "he wants capacity as a Visitor of asylums," simply in virtue of his prior claims as a former Metropolitan Commissioner. Shaftesbury Diaries, August 9, 1845, SHA/PD/4. On Prichard, see generally Leigh, *British Psychiatry*, chap. 3.

94. Prichard and Hume, for instance, continued to attend parties given by Alexander Morison and A. J. Sutherland; Forster was a close friend of Charles Elliot, who owned Munster House; and Lutwidge, the Commission's Secretary, enjoyed a friendly relationship with Forbes Winslow. See the discussion in N. Hervey, "A Slavish Bowing Down," p. 106.

95. "Obituary," *Journal of Mental Science* 32, 1886, p. 236.

96. "Obituary," *British Medical Journal* i, 1886, p. 720.

97. The transformation was further aided by the elevation of the equally meticulous Lutwidge from Secretary to the Commission to fill one of the legal posts.

98. Commissioners in Lunacy, *Further Report*, 1847, p. 132.

99. Compare the complaints voiced by Bryan Procter to his friend John Forster, who would subsequently become Secretary to the Board and later a Lunacy Commissioner himself: "I hear nothing. I see nothing, but tunnels and railroads—madmen and chambermaids. None of these things interest you—and I have no escape . . . I am sick of travelling." Procter to Forster, September 1, 1844, F.48.E.32/5; see also Procter to Forster, July 26, 1861, F.48.F.65/47. Procter, like most of the other Commissioners, nonetheless clung tightly to his well-remunerated position. When a chronic bladder infection became "the torment of my life" in the mid 1850s, he sought sympathy from his friend, John Forster: "When I tell you that I have had serious fears that it would compel me to give up my Commissionership (in which case I must starve almost) you will see that it has distressed me." August 27, 1854, F.48.E.32/37.

100. Commissioners in Lunacy, *Further Report*, p. 135.

101. Ibid., p. 133.

102. Ibid., p. 134.

103. Ibid., p. 6.

104. Despite this, Shaftesbury and the other Commissioners fiercely resisted any growth in their numbers and were particularly opposed to the idea of appointing assistant commissioners. All supervisory power thus remained firmly in the same few hands.

105. In part, this apparent unanimity reflected an unwillingness on all sides to oppose Shaftesbury's views. Notoriously thin-skinned, the chairman was completely intolerant of criticism, which he was always inclined to take as a personal insult. The one occasion where Gaskell did publicly take issue with views Shaftesbury was

known to hold occurred in 1860, when he wrote a piece in the *Journal of Mental Science* advocating a system of voluntary admissions without prior certification. His apostasy was perhaps mitigated by his simultaneous and strong advocacy of asylums for the middle classes, one of Shaftesbury's (and Conolly's) favourite hobby-horses.

106. In a number of respects, this was a somewhat unlikely friendship, given the radical differences between the two men. But as Procter once commented to Forster, "Samuel is always good natured and cheerful and tho' we have no pursuits in common (except our professional ones) and we differ in our likings a good deal—yet he is fond of jokes (with a little mischief in them) and contrives to keep me up now and then when my vivacity—never very great—would give way. Ah, what it is to grow old." Procter to Forster, October 8 [1858], F.48.E.32/86. (Procter, sixty-one when he wrote this letter and a member of the Metropolitan and then the national Lunacy Commissions since 1832, had begun to experience a number of health problems, so it is perhaps unsurprising that his enthusiasm had begun to flag.)

107. Forster served as Secretary to the Commission between 1855 and 1861, before being elevated to Commissioner on the retirement of his close friend Procter. His first tour of inspection, undertaken with Gaskell, served to reinforce their existing friendly relationship. Procter approved: "I was very glad to hear that you and Gaskell have got along so well. He is very good—temperate, accommodating, and unselfish—and I think that you may safely rely on him (as well as on Wilkes) in all matters relating to business." Procter to Forster, April 22, 1861, F.48.E32/103/1. In a subsequent letter to Forster, he acknowledged that "the circuit is sometimes fatiguing—and always wearying. I used to regret that the pursuits of my colleagues differed so much from my own—but I think I was wrong. Our profession should not absorb too much of the thoughts or of the animal spirits [certainly not Gaskell's sentiments!]—when you return from your circuit you will emerge out of insanity into the clear light." August 6 [1861], F.48.E.32/105.

108. Procter and especially Forster were acquaintances and friends of his sister-in-law, Elizabeth, with Forster playing a major role in securing her first publishing contract, for *Mary Barton*, from Chapman and Hall. (See Uglow, *Elizabeth Gaskell*, pp. 182–183, 220, 222–226; Easson, *Elizabeth Gaskell*, pp. 42–43). Forster was also a fellow Unitarian. Wilkes, besides his common background as a county asylum superintendent, also shared both Gaskell's moral earnestness and his enthusiasm for nonrestraint. The four men helped cover for each other on the visitation circuit and dined together in London, along with literary figures like Dickens, Carlyle, and Browning.

109. Cf. Battiscombe, *Shaftesbury*, pp. 217–218; Best, *Shaftesbury* New York: Arco, 1964, pp. 52–72; Hodder, *The Life and Work of the Seventh Earl of Shaftesbury, K.G.* (popular ed.) London: Cassell, 1887, pp. 519–530. On Shaftesbury's attitudes towards Unitarianism, cf. Finlayson, *Shaftesbury*, pp. 118–119, 166, 377 ff. His antipathy is easily understood. Unitarians exemplified the rationalist worldview of the Enlightenment, took the lead in resisting the Evangelical revival, rejected Christ's divinity, dismissed the idea of original sin, and gave no credence to the idea of Hell. Their doctrines were anathema to the seventh Earl. A Methodist hymn neatly captures his feelings: "Stretch out thine arm, thou Triune God! The Unitarian fiend expel, and chase his doctrines back to Hell!"

110. The characterization was offered by the metropolitan madhouse keeper, L. Forbes Winslow, in his memoirs, *Recollections of Forty Years* London: Ouseley, 1910, p. 62.

111. As Shaftesbury later described their routine, "one goes about with a book to see the patients; the other goes about looking into all the rooms and closets, and into the cellars and garrets, and every nook and corner in the place . . . it is absolutely necessary that we should immediately on arriving disperse ourselves into the different parts of the building, where there may be ten thousand things going on, which they would huddle up and conceal, unless we were extremely vigilant; and a great many things have been discovered by the Commissioners arriving on a sudden and unexpectedly, and searching closely through the house." *Select Committee on Lunatics*, 1860, pp. 30–31.

112. See Hervey, "A Slavish Bowing Down," p. 108.

113. Commissioners in Lunacy, *Further Report*, 1847, p. 379.

114. Ibid., p. 369.

115. Ibid., p. 365.

116. Ibid., p. 367.

117. Seeking local support for their resistance to central dictates, the Governors arranged to reprint the whole exchange in a pamphlet they published in 1847. The episode, and the relevant correspondence, are also reviewed in the Commissioners in Lunacy, *Further Report*, 1847, pp. 150–154, and Appendix H, pp. 353 ff.

118. In the eyes of "progressive" alienists, the whole idea of employing visiting physicians to direct treatment was necessarily and inappropriately tied to a now-outmoded antiphlogistic therapeutics, in which the treatment of lunacy could be undertaken by an outsider who periodically visited and prescribed for the patients. Here was surely an anachronistic mode of practice in the era of moral treatment, with its stress on the superintendent as the monarchical ruler of the asylum, the moral governor of all aspects of daily life. See, for example, John Thurnam, *Observations and Essays on the Statistics of Insanity* London: Simpkin Marshall, 1845, p. 79; and [John Charles Bucknill], "Visiting Physicians to County Asylums," *Asylum Journal* No. 3, February 15, 1814, pp. 33–36, esp. p. 34. (One should notice here that one of the unintended side effects of this policy was, of course, to reinforce the isolation of alienists from the rest of the medical profession.)

119. Forster manuscripts, Forster to Procter, October 26, 1858, F.48.E.32/87.

120. Procter to Forster, May 15, 1857, F.48.E.32/74.

121. Procter to Forster, June 1, 1856, F.48.E.32/66; Procter to Forster, April 22, 1861, F.48.32/103/1.

122. For the "reactionary" views of James Mylne on the subject, see Mylne to Shaftesbury, March 16, 1842, PRO/CO7/73; and Mylne to R. Smith M.P., June 2, 1840, PRO/CO54/186; and for J. R. Hume's support of restraint, see Hume to Shaftesbury, March 26, 1842, PRO/CO7/73, all in the Public Record Office. Bucknill actively protested their views. See *Asylum Journal* 1, no. 6, July 1854.

123. Wilkes shared Gaskell's near reverential attitude towards Conollyite dogma. This attitude, and his generally narrow intellectual horizons, made him a rather dull companion on the visitation circuit. Cf. Procter to Forster, August 22, 1856, F.48.E.32/70: "Our talk is solely on asylums. All other things savour of prunella. Wilkes has got Conolly's book with him, which he reads day after day. I recom-

mended him to buy a book or two at the station. He bought *The Younger Son* almost ten days ago. I looked yesterday at the leaf turned down. He is at page 65."

124. Cf. Hervey, "The Lunacy Commission," p. 151. Though initially pleased that two of their number had been elevated to the Commission, even county asylum superintendents began to have second thoughts, resenting the fact that men who had recently been their equals were now in a position to dictate to them about matters they saw as questions of professional judgement. James Huxley, for instance, the superintendent of the Kent Asylum, put up fierce resistance to the Board's attempts to influence his practice. He was particularly scathing about Gaskell's scheme of night-watching for dirty patients, ridiculing the idea by juxtaposing the requirement that patients be roused from their sleep four times a night to another suggestion the Commission had made, that patients be given long, exhausting walks to produce deep sleep.

125. Lancashire Record Office, QAM 5/1848/3.

126. Lancashire Record Office, QAM 5/1847/3–4.

127. For the resultant problems even at Gaskell's old asylum, cf. Walton, "The Treatment of Pauper Lunatics," pp. 183–192.

128. John Conolly, *Select Committee on Lunatics*, 1859, p. 171.

129. See, for example, the very specific guidelines it issued in 1857 on the use of shower baths in asylums. Circular Letters Book No. 1, 1–100, 1845–1863, Circular Number 70, June 8, 1857, PRO MH51/236.

130. Shaftesbury repeatedly and publicly voiced his disdain for the system. Cf. his testimony in 1859: "I feel strongly that the whole system of private asylums is utterly abominable and indefensible." *Select Committee on Lunatics* 1859, p. 14.

131. See the discussions in Hervey, "A Slavish Bowing Down," pp. 113–118; and idem, "The Lunacy Commission," pp. 211–242.

132. However, his and the other medical commissioners' desire to put an end to the licensing of female proprietors (a position strongly supported by Bucknill in the *Journal of Mental Science*) was successfully opposed by Shaftesbury, who objected to driving existing owners out of business.

133. See the Commission's circulars, January 28, 1854, MH50/6; August 27, 1856, October 1, 1856, and April 9, 1857, MH50/8, Public Record Office.

134. See *The Lancet* May 19, 1860, p. 504.

135. There was much resentment of this heightened degree of regulation. Cf. the complaint by the editor of the *Medical Circular* (9, 1856, pp. 8–9), James Yearsley (who was a close friend and former business partner of Forbes Winslow, one of the most prominent metropolitan asylum proprietors) that the Commissioners were engaged in "an attempt by a system of espionage, to ascertain the income of each proprietor and to control the management of private asylums, even to the smallest details."

136. E.g., Daniel Defoe, *A Review of the State of the English Nation* London: Baker, 1706; idem, *Augusta Triumphans* London: Roberts, 1728; Alexander Cruden, *The London Citizen Exceedingly Injured, Or, A British Inquisition Displayed* London: Cooper and Dodd, 1739; and idem, *The Adventures of Alexander the Corrector* London: for the author, 1754.

137. Cf. David Morgan, "Explaining Mental Illness," *European Journal of Sociology* 16, 1975, pp. 262–280, for an elaboration of these points.

138. Cf. McCandless, "Liberty and Lunacy"; and Nicholas Hervey, "Advocacy or Folly? The Alleged Lunatics' Friend Society," *Medical History* 30, 1986, pp. 254–275.

139. E.g., Nottidge v. Ripley, Hall v. Semple, Ruck v. Stillwell, and others.

140. E.g., Georgina Weldon, *The History of My Orphanage; or The Outpourings of an Alleged Lunatic* London: for the author, 1878; Louisa Lowe, *The Bastilles of England; or The Lunacy Laws at Work* London: Crookenden, 1883.

141. House of Commons, *Select Committee on the Lunacy Law* 1877.

142. Reade, *Hard Cash*, pp. v, vi, 332.

143. Ibid., p. 337. The upshot is many more weeks of confinement for Alfred, while his evil relations successfully run rings around the feeble bureaucracy.

144. Nairne was appointed partly to balance the presence of two former county asylum superintendents with a physician who had close ties to the private madhouse sector, but also because his strong Evangelical views recommended him to Shaftesbury. By law, those with a pecuniary interest in a private asylum were debarred from serving as Commissioners (hence Conolly, for instance, was ineligible for an appointment), and Nairne's ties to this sector were purely those of friendship. His appointment was greeted with near fury by the county asylum superintendents, who, after the appointments of Gaskell and Wilkes, had come to see the three medical commissionerships as rightfully theirs.

145. Procter once waspishly informed Forster that "Nairne is still on holiday—an occupation that seems to suit him." September 30, 1857, F.48.E.32/80. Three years later: "I wanted to make some visits with Dr. Nairne, but he says that he is 'going to have a holiday' with his wife, in the Isle of Wight." October 15, 1860, F.48.E.32/102.

146. Her activities may be followed in the Dix correspondence at the Houghton Library, Harvard University. See, for example, Dix to Elizabeth Rathbone, n.d. [Feburary 1855], June 16 [1855]; Dix to Mrs. Torrey, March 8, 1855; Dix to Ann Heath, 18 April, 12 May, 1855; Dix to Lord Shaftesbury, n.d. [March 1855]. The meeting with the Lunacy Commission took place on the afternoon of March 4, 1855.

147. For some of this activity, see James Coxe to Dix, April 11, 1855; Dix to James Moncrieff (Lord Advocate of Scotland), April 1855; Sir George Grey to Dix, April 9, 1855. DPHL.

148. Gaskell to Dix, [April 1855], DPHL.

149. Campbell was a protégé of the Duke of Argyll, a close friend of Dix's friends, the Rathbones of Liverpool, and an early convert to her cause.

150. Coxe's appointment was also engineered by Dix, with the assistance of Sir Walter Trevelyan. See James Coxe to Dix, April 11, 1855, DPHL: "I feel very much obliged by the kind interest you and Sir Walter have taken in getting me included, and my hope now is that I may prove an efficient member."

151. Coxe to Dix, June 12, 1855. For further comments on the halting progress of the inquiry, see Coxe to Dix, April 16, 24, May 14, 21, August 2, 12, 1855; September 10, 1856; June 4, 1857; Sir Walter Trevelyan to Dix, June 29, 1857; Gaskell to Dix, April 7, May 10, August 10, 1855; DPHL.

152. Bucknill had no hesitation in attributing the report to Gaskell, "whose enlightened views and wide knowledge on the subject of insanity, our associates will have no difficulty in recognizing." Cf. "The State of Lunatic Asylums in Scotland,"

Asylum Journal of Mental Science 3, 1856–1857, pp. 548–549. The reaction among Scots was distinctly less positive. Coxe complained privately that "The Scotch Commissioners, I am sorry to say, have not been consulted regarding [the legislation]." He had grave doubts about its wisdom and political prospects. Coxe to Dix, June 20, 1857, DPHL.

153. "The Scottish Lunacy Commission," *North British Review* 22, 1857, p. 58.

154. Ibid., pp. 58, 65. For further discussion of the Scottish reaction to the report, see David Gollaher, *Voice for the Mad: The Life of Dorothea Dix* New York: Free Press, 1995, chap. 13. Dix, too, was dismayed by the report and subsequent legislation. Initially enamoured of the English board, she had later become disenchanted with its failure to shut down all private asylums and eliminate the use of workhouses to confine a portion of the pauper insane. For Scotland to replicate such a flawed system was, in her eyes, a grave mistake: "the Lunacy Commission is next to useless," she complained privately, "indeed it does harm, for the people at large trust in its efficiency, and so abuses lie concealed and perpetuated." As for the Commissioners themselves, she had concluded that they "are too indolent to exert the influence their official station gives to remedy, at least in large measure, what their criminal sufferance makes them participate in maintaining." Dix to Elizabeth Rathbone, March 3, 1860; Dix to William Rathbone, March 18 [1860], DPHL. (Actually, the Commission would gladly have eliminated workhouse provision for the insane and at least theoretically shared her distaste for private asylums; but, practically speaking, it was helpless to implement either policy.)

155. "The Scottish Lunacy Commission," pp. 57–58, 60. See also *Edinburgh Daily Scotsman*, June 1, 22, 1857; *Edinburgh Daily Express*, June 6, 12, 15, 1857.

156. Compare John Conolly: "I more than doubt the propriety of having patients belonging to the higher classes and pauper patients in the [same] asylum." House of Commons, *Select Committee on Lunatics*, 1859, p. 177.

157. The words are Shaftesbury's, in testimony before the 1859 Select Committee (p. 26). The Select Committee's *Report* (1860, p. ix) indicates its own sympathies in the matter: "Insanity under any shape is so fearful a malady, that the desire to withdraw it from the observation of the world is both natural and commendable."

158. See, for instance, the scathing critique of workhouse care for lunatics in the supplement to their *12th Annual Report*, 1858, pp. 37–38. At this time, they estimated that as many as seven thousand pauper lunatics remained in workhouses.

159. On the sources of this increase, see Scull, *The Most Solitary of Afflictions*, chap. 7.

160. Almost the whole of Gaskell's testimony before the Select Committee was taken up with this issue. See *Select Committee on Lunatics*, 1859, pp. 133–148.

161. Nairne's career, too, was ended by a road accident (as, of course, was W.A.F. Browne's). Lutwidge was injured in a similar fashion when he was thrown from a gig but was able to return to work. (Some years later, he was murdered by a patient at Fisherton House, who drove a nail into his skull while he was on a tour of inspection.)

162. Procter to Forster, February 2, 1865, F.48E.32/146.

163. Procter to Forster, September 7, 1865, F.48.E32/154: "I am glad to hear Gaskell has returned—I hope, fit for a little work."

164. Procter to Forster, October 9 [1865], F.48.E.32/157: "Gaskell sent me a

letter from the South of England and another from London. I receive them with pleasure but I can't divine what they mean."

165. "The Late Samuel Gaskell, Esq.," *Journal of Mental Science* 32, 1886, p. 236.

166. Procter to Forster, September 1866, F.48.E.32/187.

167. Procter's prostate condition had finally forced him into retirement in 1861, at the age of seventy-four, after almost thirty years service to the Metropolitan and then the national Lunacy Commission. Much to his dismay, Shaftesbury, who was anxious not to antagonize the Treasury, botched the negotiations over his pension, while obtaining much improved pensions for future retirees (Gaskell among them). See Procter to Forster, July 26, 1861, F.48.F.65/47; July 28, 1861, F.48.F.65/48.

168. Procter to Forster, November 14, 1866. F.48.E.32/192; December 26, 1866, F.48.E.23/194.

169. Procter to Forster, June 25, 1867, F.48.E.32/201.

170. Procter to Forster, June 21, 1868, F.48.E.32/213.

171. Procter to Forster, September 10, 1868, F.48.E.32/216; January 11, 1869, F.48.E.32/220; August 3, 1869, F.48.E.32/224; November 23, 1870, F.48.E.32/236.

172. Procter to Forster, March 9, 1869, F.48.E.32/221; July 19, 1869, F.48.E.32/223.

CHAPTER SEVEN
FROM DISCIPLE TO CRITIC: SIR JOHN CHARLES BUCKNILL (1817–1897)

1. "Valedictory Address," *Journal of Mental Science* 7, 1861, p. 312. See also W. L. Parry-Jones, "The Model of the Geel Lunatic Colony"; and N. Morgan, "Against the Tide at Exmouth: J. C. Bucknill (1817–97)," *South West Psychiatry* 4, 1990, pp. 73–76.

2. John Chandos, *Boys Together: English Public Schools 1800–64* London: Hutchinson, 1984, pp. 248, 252.

3. *The Lancet* ii, 1837–1838, pp. 84–86.

4. *The Lancet* i, 1838–1839, pp. 561–562. For the Elliotson case see W. R. Merrington, *University College Hospital and Its Medical School* London: Heinemann, 1976, p. 24.

5. University College London, college correspondence, AM/22.

6. "Obituary," *Journal of Mental Science* 43, 1897, p. 888.

7. Lt. Col. John Townsend Bucknill; Sir Thomas Townsend Bucknill (1845–1915), who became a judge; and Charles Bucknill (1846–1895).

8. G. E. Langley, "The Devon County Lunatic Asylum, Exminster, 1830–70," *South West Psychiatry* 4, 1990, pp. 65–66.

9. John Charles Bucknill and Daniel Hack Tuke, *A Manual of Psychological Medicine* Philadelphia: Blanchard and Lee, 1858, p. 447.

10. Langley, "The Devon County Lunatic Asylum."

11. Devon County Asylum, *Annual Report*, quoted in J. T. Arlidge, *On the State of Lunacy and the Legal Provision for the Insane* London: Churchill, 1859, p. 96.

12. Commissioners in Lunacy, *Annual Report*, 1853, pp. 125–126.

13. J. C. Bucknill, "Notes on Asylums for the Insane in America," *The Lancet* i, March 18, 1876, p. 418. Bucknill's comments caused great offence among his Amer-

ican counterparts. See, for example, Eugene Grissom, "Mechanical Protection for the Violent Insane," *American Journal of Insanity* 34, 1877–1878, pp. 27–58.

14. He was sternly critical of Conolly for misleading the public on this score. See J. C. B[ucknill], "Review of *The Treatment of the Insane Without Mechanical Restraints* by John Conolly," *Asylum Journal of Mental Science* 3, 1857, pp. 260–261.

15. In 1853 there were 222 instances of seclusion at Devon County Asylum, with its use being more than twice as common in the treatment of female than male patients. Ibid.

16. For discussion, see Tomes, "The Great Restraint Controversy."

17. Commissioners in Lunacy, *Annual Report*, 1857.

18. See, for example, Commissioners in Lunacy, *Annual Report*, 1859, p. 11.

19. N. Tomes, "The Great Restraint Controversy," p. 194.

20. Quoted in John Conolly, "Notice of the Eighth Report of the Commissioners in Lunacy," *Asylum Journal* 1, no. 9, November 15, 1854, p. 135.

21. *Asylum Journal of Mental Science* 1, no. 1, November 15, 1853, p. 4.

22. Ibid., p. 3.

23. *Journal of Mental Science* 6, 1860, p. 22.

24. J. C. Bucknill, "Presidential Address," *Journal of Mental Science* 7, 1860, p. 4. After meeting annually between 1841 and 1844, the Association met only twice more before its 1852 meeting in Oxford, to be discussed below.

25. *Asylum Journal of Mental Science* 1, no. 1, November 15, 1853, p. 4. For a similar assessment, see Forbes Winslow, "The Association of Medical Officers of Asylums and Hospitals for the Insane," *Journal of Psychological Medicine and Mental Pathology* 6, 1853, p. 455.

26. Complaints on this score were understandably muted. As Conolly noted, "it is not always safe to offer opinions of this kind." Dependent as they were on the Commissioners' goodwill, "the proprietors of private asylums" felt particularly exposed and vulnerable. Because of his eminence and his semiretired status, however, Conolly could voice the general resentment among his fellow alienists: "there cannot be a question that a disposition exists to interfere with the medical treatment of our patients, to create an office, not of general commissioners, but of actual extra-superintendents, who, instead of consulting and conferring and making friendly suggestions, will place themselves in the position of detectives, visiting our houses as if we were men of bad character." *Journal of Mental Science* 7, 1861, p. 38.

27. *Asylum Journal* 1, no. 1, November 15, 1853, p. 4.

28. As many as 107 new medical journals were launched between 1801 and 1840, many of them extremely evanescent. For discussions of this phenomenon, see W. R. Lefanu, *British Periodicals of Medicine 1640–1899* Oxford: Wellcome Unit for the History of Medicine, 1984; P.W.J. Bartrip, *Mirror of Medicine: A History of the British Medical Journal* Oxford: Clarendon Press, 1990; W. F. Bynum and R. Porter (eds.), *Medical Journals and Medical Knowledge* London: Routledge, 1992.

29. *British Medical Journal* 29 September 1852, pp. 513–514.

30. *Asylum Journal* 1, no. 1, November 15, 1853, p. 4; no. 11, February 15, 1855, p. 163.

31. Alongside his recognition of the journal's importance for collective and individual advancement, Bucknill's successful completion of his M.D. thesis earlier in 1852 may well have influenced him to assume the job.

32. *Asylum Journal* 1, no. 1, November 15, 1853, p. 4.

33. *Journal of Psychological Medicine and Mental Pathology* 6, 1853, p. 454.

34. *Asylum Journal* 1, no. 11, February 15, 1855, p. 163.

35. Ibid., p. 164.

36. *Journal of Mental Science* 9, 1863, p. 425.

37. One very practical measure of the centrality of the journal to the Association's existence is provided by the fraction of the members' subscription income placed at Bucknill's disposal. Only once during the 1850s did the journal fail to absorb more than 90 percent of the Association's subscription income, and though the percentage fell off somewhat in the ensuing decade, the change was as much a reflection of the fact that "the prosperity of the Journal has been steadily advancing" through the sale of "more numbers than we require for our own members" as of any diminution in the Association's support for the enterprise. (Quotation from *Journal of Mental Science* 7, 1861, p. 37; see also *Asylum Journal of Mental Science* 3, 1856–1857, p. 2; *Journal of Mental Science* 4, 1857–1858, p. 17; 5, 1858–1859, pp. 69; 6, 1859–1860, p. 14; 7, 1860–1862, p. 36; 8, 1862–1863, p. 323.)

38. *Asylum Journal* 1, no. 7, August 15, 1854, p. 88.

39. Thurnam of the Wiltshire County Asylum; Ley (Oxfordshire); Wilkes (Staffordshire); Huxley (Kent); Williams (Gloucestershire); Palmer (Lincolnshire); Boyd (Somerset); Campbell (Essex); Parsey (Warwickshire); Manley (Hampshire); Tyerman (Colney Hatch); and Green (Birmingham Borough Asylum).

40. The private asylum doctors clearly preferred Winslow's journal. The handful who did contribute to the *Asylum Journal* were atypical in other respects of their branch of the profession. Both Thomas Pritchard (of Abingdon Abbey) and Gardiner Hill (of Eastgate House) were strong proponents of nonrestraint, unlike most other alienists outside the public sector, and their contributions were largely concerned with this issue. And John Conolly, now the proprietor of Lawn House, was, of course, the patron saint of the county asylum superintendents and owed his fame to his accomplishments while at Hanwell. (A number of doctors affiliated with the non-profit-making charity asylum sector also wrote for the journal, including Arlidge (St. Luke's); Walsh (Lincoln); Simpson (York Asylum); and D. H. Tuke (York Retreat).) The patterns established in these first years of the journal's existence tended to persist throughout Bucknill's term as editor. Of the three private asylum doctors who contributed to Volume 5, for instance, one was Conolly, another his son-in-law, Harrington Tuke, and the third Conolly's former assistant physician at Hanwell, James Davey; while only a single private asylum doctor contributed a paper to Volumes 2 and 8 (the last volume for which Bucknill was responsible).

41. E.g., *Asylum Journal* 1, no. 10, January 1, 1855, pp. 156–159.

42. See, especially, "On Non-Mechanical Restraint in the Treatment of the Insane," *Journal of Psychological Medicine and Mental Pathology* 7, 1854, pp. 541–572.

43. *Asylum Journal* 1, no. 9, November 15, 1854, p. 129.

44. The *Journal* is now, of course, the *British Journal of Psychiatry*.

45. *Asylum Journal of Mental Science*, 1853–1858, 1–4 passim. Bucknill's essays on Shakespeare and Shakespearean characters were subsequently collected and republished as *The Psychology of Shakespeare* (1859) and *The Medical Knowledge of Shakespeare* (1860). Bucknill recycled much of the prose he published in the *Journal*

d a lowly social rank"—was "a most happy circumstance for mental sufferers"
p. 489); but from the perspective of one committed to the defence of medical
prerogatives, it also constituted a further and still more potent reason for
ng the notion that moral treatment was of primary importance in the treat-
f insanity.

Ibid., pp. 490–491. The usefulness of such claims in mounting a defence of
rracks-asylums that were becoming so prevalent by the late 1850s was fully
ted in short order by one of Bucknill's colleagues, Joseph Lalor: contrary to the
ntional wisdom of an earlier generation of alienists, it now transpired that for
ly these reasons, "large are preferable to small asylums, no less on scientific
les, and from benevolent considerations, than from motives of economy . . .
so far] from producing general turbulence and confusion, . . . the association
e masses of insane people . . . is found to be highly conducive to good order
ietude." Joseph Lalor, "Observations on the Size and Construction of Lunatic
ns," *Journal of Mental Science* 7, 1860, pp. 105–106, 108.

Journal of Mental Science, 4, 1857–1858, p. 317.

Ibid.

Journal of Mental Science 8, 1862, p. 335.

Journal of Mental Science 4, 1857–1858, p. 324.

Commissioners in Lunacy, *Annual Report*, 1858, p. 8.

Journal of Mental Science 4, 1857–1858, pp. 325, 327.

Bucknill, *Care of the Insane*, p. x.

Journal of Mental Science 6, 1860, p. 6.

Journal of Mental Science 8, 1862, p. 333.

"Obituary," *The Lancet* ii, 1897, p. 228.

For his role in *Regina* v. *Huxtable* and *Regina* v. *Handcock*, see *Asylum Journal*
tal Science 2, 1855–1856, pp. 114–120, 245–253. For Bucknill's involvement
ancery inquisitions in lunacy, see, for example, his testimony in the case of
hoebe Ewings, an eighty-year-old spinster of uncertain mental powers (a sep-
y paginated appendix to *Journal of Mental Science* 6, 1859–1860) and for his
retained as a consultant in two other Chancery cases, *Journal of Mental Science*
60–1861, pp. 128–129. For his participation in a Scottish case concerning
entary capacity, see ibid., pp. 414–459. Bucknill also served as the committee
uardian) of a number of Chancery Lunatics during this period.

Journal of Mental Science 4, 1857–1858, pp. 127, 128. He was equally scath-
out the qualifications of two of the Scottish and Irish medical commissioners,
and Hatchell.

Ibid., p. 127.

Asylum Journal of Mental Science 3, 1856–1857, p. 29.

Even the satisfactions associated with editing the *Journal of Mental Science*
ave been beginning to pall. At the annual business meeting of the Association
1860, Harrington Tuke spoke up in favour of Bucknill's request to pay some-
se to prepare the "digest of foreign psychological literature" for each issue, "to
Dr. Bucknill from the absolute drugery attending his editorship." *Journal of*
Science 7, 1860–1861, p. 37.

. "Suicide of Dr. Grahamsley," *Asylum Journal* 1, no. 7, August 15, 1854,
05–106.

of *Mental Science* in this fashion. His portions of *A Manual of Psychological Medicine*, for instance, had previously appeared in draft form in its pages.

46. *Journal of Mental Science* 6, 1860, p. 5. Lockhart Robertson was equally certain of the great strides the journal had made under Bucknill's editorship: see *Journal of Mental Science* 8, 1862–1863, p. 462.

47. *Asylum Journal* 1, no. 9, November 15, 1854, p. 129.

48. E.g., *Journal of Mental Science* 7, 1860–1862, pp. 3, 288–293, 313–314; 8, 1862–1863, p. 446. Bucknill's efforts notwithstanding, it was not until 1909 that the Asylum Officers' Superannuation Act became law, prompting extraordinary celebrations among the profession's leadership and rank and file. Cf. *Journal of Mental Science* 56, 1910, pp. 109–110, 174–183.

49. *Asylum Journal of Mental Science* 2, 1856, p. 14.

50. His ally and protégé, Lockhart Robertson, filled in for him. (The snub, if snub it was, did not prevent Winslow from returning the favour, enthusiastically nominating his erstwhile competitor for reelection as editor of the *Journal of Mental Science*). See *Asylum Journal of Mental Science* 3, 1856–1857, p. 4. In assuming the presidency, Winslow became only the second proprietor of a private asylum (after A. J. Sutherland in 1854) to head the Association, and not till Henry Monro's election in 1864 would there be another.

51. "The Newspaper Attack on Private Lunatic Asylums," *Journal of Mental Science* 5, 1858–1859, pp. 146, 148, 149, 152. The impassioned defence contrasts dramatically, as we shall see, with the stance Bucknill was to adopt towards private asylums at a later stage in his career.

52. "Presidential Address," *Journal of Mental Science* 7, 1860, p. 22. Such pious sentiments collided with the reality that the interests and outlook of the salaried employees of a network of Poor Law institutions were quite sharply divergent from those of the entrepreneurial branch of the profession which catered to the well-to-do and the rich via a loosely articulated group of private asylums; and the divisions within the profession were only further compounded once men like Maudsley, Savage, and Bucknill himself succeeded in carving out consulting practices almost wholly outside any portion of the asylum system.

53. Bedfordshire, for instance, had been one of only three county asylums without a resident medical officer in the early 1840s. Compelled by statute in 1845 to abandon this practice, the magistrates had advertised for a physician offering no more than £100 per annum, though ultimately compelled to pay three times that in order to make an appointment. *Asylum Journal* 1, no. 7, August 15, 1854, p. 102. Here was one of a series of status issues on which Bucknill and Winslow could see eye to eye. Noting that the construction of Colney Hatch had cost the extravagant sum of £280,000, Winslow drew attention to the meagre salary of £200 per annum that the medical men in charge of the male and female divisions were then paid, an indication, he commented with some asperity, of "how carefully the justices guard the public purse, when mind not matter is to be paid for." "Our Pauper Lunatic Asylums," *Journal of Psychological Medicine and Mental Pathology* 6, 1853, p. 405.

54. J. T. Arlidge, "The Middlesex County Lunatic Asylums and Their Reports for 1855–1856," *Asylum Journal of Mental Science* 2, 1856, p. 358; [Winslow], "Our Pauper Lunatic Asylums," p. 416.

55. "Tenth Report of the Commissioners in Lunacy to the Lord Chancellor," *Asylum Journal of Mental Science* 3, 1856–1857, pp. 19–20. He noted with satisfaction, however, that the Lunacy Commissioners were increasingly reluctant to issue licenses to women, so that the "evil . . . is in the process of cure." Beyond the obvious lay-versus-professional issues that surface here, the resentment of women exceeding their station is equally transparent. Such sentiments were still more explicit when Bucknill commented on Dorothea Dix's activities. Though he exempted Dix herself from his strictures, he spoke scathingly of women who meddled in a man's world: "We English certainly do entertain a general aversion to ladies whose mission extends itself beyond the home circle, and who have a propensity to set people to rights; we are apt to ascribe it to restlessness, impatience of control, and other unwomanly motives"; and, in a memorable turn of phrase, he sought to dismiss "the small [Elizabeth?] fry of female philanthropists or philathro-pests as we are tempted to call those whose mental vision is so much occupied with the Borioboola Ghas, that with their bodily eyes they cannot see the buttonless shirts and undarned stockings of husbands and daughters." "Reports of the Irish, Scotch, and American Asylums, 1855," *Asylum Journal of Mental Science* 2, 1856, p. 124. (Bucknill's concluding reference here is to Dickens's portrait of Mrs. Jellyby in *Bleak House*.) Within little more than a decade, as we shall see, Henry Maudsley was to provide a psychiatric-cum-scientific justification for consigning women to domesticity. See Chapter 8 below.

56. "The New Lunacy Bill," *Journal of Mental Science* 8, 1862–1863, p. 156. Bucknill's worries on this score were scarcely idiosyncratic. Cf. Forbes Winslow, *Asylum Journal of Mental Science* 3, 1856–1857, pp. 10–11.

57. *Journal of Mental Science* 5, 1858–1859, p. 149.

58. *Journal of Mental Science* 8, 1862–1863, p. 156.

59. "Quarterly Psychological Review," *Journal of Mental Science* 7, 1861, p. 140.

60. "Presidential Address," p. 20.

61. He had originally refused to publish a paper from James Huxley, superintendent of the Kent County Asylum, that was sarcastically and relentlessly critical of some of Gaskell's initiatives, printing it only when Huxley insisted, with an editorial disclaimer which asserted that the complaints were "not warranted, and we greatly regret that their publication has been imposed upon us." See James Huxley, "On the Dirty Habits of the Insane and Night Nursing," *Journal of Mental Science* 4, 1857–1858, pp. 119–127.

62. *Journal of Mental Science* 5, 1858–1859, p. 154.

63. "Tenth Report of the Commisioners in Lunacy," *Asylum Journal of Mental Science* 3, 1856–1857, pp. 23–24, 28–29. Where the earliest proponents of moral treatment had insisted that appropriate buildings were essential to the success of their schemes, magistrates consistently objected to the expense their designs imposed on ratepayers. Dependent, as were all county asylum superintendents, on the approval of those who employed him, Bucknill had adopted their priorities as his own.

64. *Journal of Mental Science* 4, 1857–1858, p. 119.

65. Bucknill, *An Inquiry into the Proper Classification and Treatment of Criminal Lunatics* London: John Churchill, 1851; idem, *Unsoundness of Mind in Relation to Criminal Acts* London: Samuel Highley, 1854, 2d ed. London: Longman & Co, 1857;

idem, *The Proposed Abandonment of the College Tes* Daniel Hack Tuke, *A Manual of Psychological Med* 1858, further editions same publisher 1862, 1874, a *ogy of Shakespeare* London: Longman & Co, 1859, rei *speare* London: Macmillan & Co, 1867; and idem, *7 speare* London: Longman & Co, 1860.

66. *Asylum Journal* 1, no. 10, 1854, p. 159.

67. *Asylum Journal* 1, no. 11, February 15, 1854,

68. James Cowles Prichard, *A Treatise on Insanity* Mind London: Sherwood, Gilbert and Piper, 1835.

69. Bucknill and Tuke, *Manual*, p. ix.

70. Ibid., p. 269.

71. A review in the *Lancet* praised the book for it same time as it expressed some reservations about B discussion of abstruse and philosophical points. Th only 68 out of a total of 562 pages dealt with treatmer book would have been enhanced if this discussion pense of the history of the treatment of the insane. Tł Such criticisms tended to overlook the ideological val the construction of a geneology and legitimacy for ı dubiously, that a more extended discussion of therap or even practicable.

72. Bucknill and Tuke, *Manual*, p. 444.

73. Ibid., p. 447. The centrality of *medical* forms for his insistence that "the Physician is now the respc and must ever remain so" ("Prospectus," *Asylum Jor* 1853, p. 1), was "demonstrated" in part by arguing th tions, commonly conceived of as forms of moral trea garded as medical intervention: thus his bold claim t intellectual diversion, which are now sought to be obt lishments for the treatment of the insane, are not, str they constitute physiological measures taken to procu ated and diseased organ. . . . Such a rational method physiological." *Manual*, p. 447.

74. Bucknill and Tuke, *Manual*, p. 450.

75. Ibid., p. 455. Remedies like the "bath of surpı as "not manageable remedies, or remedies of the natu reliable knowledge," p. 456.

76. Ibid., pp. 454, 455.

77. Ibid., pp. 457–473.

78. Ibid., p. 501.

79. Ibid., p. 487.

80. Ibid., p. 491.

81. Ibid., p. 486.

82. Conolly, *Treatment of the Insane*, p. 55, quoted

83. Bucknill and Tuke, *Manual*, pp. 488, 490. Th done vicariously by ordinary attendants"—that is, by

101. Bucknill, "Presidential Address," p. 7.

102. Ibid., pp, 6, 7.

103. Bucknill, "Valedictory Address," *Journal of Mental Science* 7, 1860–1861, pp. 310, 314, 316.

104. Bucknill, "Presidential Address," pp. 15–16.

105. Bucknill, "Valedictory Address," p. 314. In reality, asylum superintendents' salaries were quite competitive with the incomes available to general practitioners in this era (cf. Peterson, *Medical Profession*, pp. 207–224; Loudon, *Medical Care*, pp. 256–266), particularly when one takes into account the security such jobs provided. Obviously, though, Bucknill's universe of comparison was the income of the leading metropolitan physicians, to whose ranks he had aspired at the very outset of his career.

106. His testimony is reprinted in House of Commons, *Select Committee on Lunatics*, 1859, pp. 86–101.

107. "A Letter to the Right Hon. Spencer H. Walpole, M.P.," *Journal of Mental Science* 7, 1860–1861, p. 127. Bucknill had explicitly declined to discuss policy towards Chancery lunatics during his oral testimony before the Committee. Perhaps this was because he wanted more time to think through the arguments he wished to present, but one cannot help harbouring some suspicions about his personal motivations in light of subsequent events. Within a few months of stepping down as Chancery Visitor in the mid 1870s, Bucknill changed sides on the issue and himself called for the consolidation of the two inspectorates.

108. Ibid., p. 134.

109. There were three Visitors altogether, two physicians and one lawyer, who collectively had responsibility for inspecting the care and treatment of Chancery cases both in and out of asylums.

110. "The New Lunacy Bill," *Journal of Mental Science* 8, 1862–1863, pp. 156–157.

111. *Journal of Mental Science* 7, 1860–1861, pp. 127–135. Bucknill cited the notorious case of Mrs. Cummings, where "the whole of the lunatic's property was exhausted in the costs of the enquiry."

112. The other appointment made at the same time as Bucknill was of a more traditional character. Although William Charles Hood (1824–1870) had been medical superintendent of the Middlesex County Asylum at Colney Hatch for a brief period, his early career had been in private practice at Fiddington House, and since 1852 he had been the physician to Bethlem Hospital.

113. *The Lancet* ii, 1862, p. 373.

114. LCO 9, 1, 1856–1864, minute book, entries for December 7, 1863, and May 2, 1864.

115. *The Lancet* 1862, ii, p. 373; LCO 11 3, 1876–1941, includes details of Visitors' allowances in 1863.

116. "Obituary," *Journal of Mental Science* 43, 1897, p. 888. On the death of his father-in-law, Thomas Townsend, he also spent part of each year at his wife's family home, Hillmorton Manor, where he assumed the role of a gentleman farmer.

117. He was nominated for "general knowledge" by J. R. Martin, and his sponsors included some of the most illustrious medical men of the age: William Lawrence, W. B. Carpenter, A. Tweedie, and E. Lankester, as well as T. Watson, T. Paget,

E. A. Parkes, G. Busk, R. Quain, T. B. Curling, A. B. Garrod, J. Alderson, F. Sibson, J. Toynbee, and C. H. Hawkins. Bucknill was only the third alienist to achieve this level of eminence (his predecessors being William Battie, who was president of the Royal College of Physicians; and James Cowles Prichard, honoured for his work in anthropology).

118. *Journal of Mental Science* 9, 1863, p. 442.

119. Hood had died of pleurisy on January 4, 1870, aged only forty-five. Robertson, who had succeeded Bucknill as editor of the *Journal of Mental Science* from 1862, also resigned from a long-standing appointment as medical superintendent of a county asylum, at Hayward's Heath in Sussex, to become Lord Chancellor's Visitor. This was scarcely the first occasion on which Robertson was indebted to Bucknill for help in advancing his career. Once the AMOAHI's fortunes had begun to revive in the 1850s, its governance from year to year remained under the tight control of a small cabal who formed its executive committee, Bucknill prominent among them. This self-perpetuating clique presented a single candidate for each office at the year's annual meeting a process that sparked protests at the 1863 annual meeting—which, perhaps significantly, was the first to take place after Bucknill stepped down. (See "Notes and Queries," *Journal of Mental Science* 9, 1863–1864, pp. 431–432.) The committee had appointed Robertson as secretary even when he held no official asylum post, and routinely supported his reelection in subsequent years. Still more important, when he finally stepped down as editor, Bucknill sought to orchestrate his protégé's succession to that post, and through some clever manoeuvering and at the cost of provoking ill-will among some segments of the Association, he succeeded. The news of Bucknill's impending Chancery appointment had obviously leaked out during the summer of 1862, and jockeying immediately began over a successor. Aware that a potential rival of his protégé's had begun campaigning for the job, printing and distributing a prospectus advertising his candidacy, Bucknill sent in his resignation letter on September 16, 1862, and recommended Robertson as his successor. The very next day, the Association's executive committee called a "special general meeting" in London. Attendance was naturally sparse—restricted, with one exception, to Bucknill and his friends, and over the protests of the one outsider (C. M. Burnett, the proprietor of Westbroke House, who urged that "instead of electing a man who represents the superintendents of county asylums, we should this time elect the proprietor of a private asylum"), Robertson's appointment was rammed through. Harrington Tuke, who had obliged Bucknill by describing Burnett's proposal as "monstrous," was rewarded by being elected as Robertson's successor as Secretary; and Robertson himself (with Maudsley seconding the motion) then proposed the motion that Bucknill be elected to honorary membership in the Association. All in all, a rather neat piece of political jobbery. See "Special General Meeting of the AMOAHI," *Journal of Mental Science* 8, 1862–1863, pp. 446–458.

120. "Obituary," *Journal of Mental Science* 43, 1897, p. 887.

121. LCO 9 1 1856–1864, minute book, entries for February 9, 1863, and February 1, 1864.

122. Ibid., entries for March 2, May 4, and November 2, 1863, and March 7, 1864.

123. LCO 9 2 1861–1873, minute book, entries for May 29, 1866, and August 2, 1867.

124. *British Medical Journal* i, 1879, p. 94.

125. Evidence to *Select Committee on the Lunacy Laws*, 1877, pp. 53–55. In support of the claim that career contingencies strongly influenced the views different segments of the profession adopted on the question of the wisdom of extra-institutional care for at least some of the insane, one may note that virtually no English alienist whose career remained tied to the institutional sector gave any credence to such proposals, whereas those who had developed careers outside asylumdom (e.g. Robertson, Maudsley, Mortimer Granville, Arlidge, Wynter) became strong critics of the status quo and were willing to countenance—indeed, actively advocated—alternative policies. The stature of men like Maudsley and Bucknill was only harmed by the embarrassing limitations and failures of the rank-and-file alienists, at whose head they nominally stood. From a sociological standpoint, therefore, it should come as no surprise that such elite figures sought to distance themselves from the beliefs and practices of the mainstream of the profession and from the increasingly stigmatised world of the asylum.

126. Bucknill and Tuke, *A Manual of Psychological Medicine* 3rd ed., pp. 702–707.

127. Other revisions made for this edition removed some of the more extended sections on the history of the insane, as the *Lancet* had recommended in 1858, and added a lengthy new section on the histology of the brain, authored by J. Batty Tuke.

128. *The Lancet* i, 1876, pp. 263–264, 418–419, 455–457, 529–530, 595–596, 701–703, 810–812, 918–921. John Charles Bucknill, *Notes on Asylums for the Insane in America* London: John Churchill, 1876.

129. Bucknill, *Notes on Asylums*, pp. viii–ix.

130. Ibid., pp. ix–x.

131. The first issue appeared in 1878. Bucknill had given one of the famous *conversazione* at Crichton Browne's West Riding Asylum in 1874, on "Responsibility for Homicide," which appears to have been instrumental in bringing him into this segment of the professional world.

132. Cf. Forbes Winslow, "Presidential Address," *Journal of Mental Science* 4, 1857–1858, p. 12; John Conolly speaking at the "Special General Meeting of the Association," *Journal of Mental Science* 8, 1862–1863, pp. 455–456; and Thomas Laycock, "The Objects and Organization of the Medico-Psychological Association," *Journal of Mental Science* 15, 1869, pp. 332–333.

133. "Obituary," *British Medical Journal* July 24, 1897, p. 255; Bucknill to Sir Henry Pitman, May 13, 1885, and Bucknill to Sir Andrew Clark, March 23, 1890, Library of the Royal College of Physicians (London).

134. Bearing in mind that Bucknill had inherited Hillmorton Hall through his marriage and earned £1,500 a year for fourteen years as Lord Chancellor's Visitor, it is worth noting that his final estate was only £48,274—by no means, of course, an inconsiderable sum, but one which does not suggest that he netted a fortune from his years in private practice.

135. Bucknill, *Care of the Insane*, p. 114.

136. Ibid., p. 13.

137. The memorandum, dated April 11, 1877, is reprinted in ibid., pp. 107–109.

138. Quoted in Trevor Turner, "'Not Worth Powder and Shot': The Public Profile of the Medico-Psychological Association, c. 1851–1914," in G. E. Berrios and H. Freeman (eds.), *150 Years of British Psychiatry*, p. 12.

139. John Charles Bucknill, *Habitual Drunkenness and Insane Drunkards* London: Macmillan & Co, 1878, p. xix.

140. Ibid., p. xx.

141. *British Medical Journal* i, 1879, p. 566.

142. *British Medical Journal* i, 1880, p. 220.

143. On the general phenomenon, see P. McCandless, "Liberty and Lunacy"; for discussions of two particularly notorious cases, see Judith R. Walkowitz, *City of Dreadful Delight: Narratives of Sexual Danger in Victorian London* Chicago: University of Chicago Press, 1992 (on the Georgina Weldon case); and Kristine Ottesen Garrigan, *Victorian Scandals: Representations of Gender and Class* Athens: Ohio University Press, 1992 (on the Lady Rosina Bulwer Lytton case).

144. Bucknill, *Care of the Insane*, p. 119–120.

145. *The Lancet* ii, 1880, p. 902.

146. The resentments this behaviour caused could not be completely papered over, even in Bucknill's obituary. "A distinguished alienist physician," asked to contribute to the *British Medical Journal's* notice of Bucknill's death, complained as bitterly as the occasion allowed that "as a controversialist he was of far too extreme views, expressed at times in language overstrained." July 24, 1897, p. 255.

147. J. C. Bucknill, "The Abolition of Proprietary Madhouses," *Nineteenth Century* 17, 1885, pp. 263–279. For rejoinders by two leading private asylum doctors, cf. J. R. Gasquet, "Lunacy Law Reform," *Nineteenth Century* 17, 1885, pp. 857–868; H. Hayes Newington, "Letter to the Editor," *Journal of Mental Science* 31, 1885–1886, pp. 138–147.

148. LCO 1/64, correspondence of Lord Selborne with Lord Shaftesbury, February 18, 19, 1885. At least some patients in private asylums who were aware of these proposals expressed dismay and alarm at the prospect of this change in social policy. Lunacy Commissioners visiting Ticehurst in June 1886, for example, found patients in an uproar: "The bill before parliament for amendment of the Lunacy Laws was on the lips of many, and one lady especially inveighed against the abolition of private asylums, in which she has herself (here and elsewhere) passed many years of her life." Ticehurst Asylum Visitors' Book, 1869–1887, entry for June 1, 1886.

149. LCO 1/66, letter from Bucknill to Lord Selborne, June 8, 1885.

150. Quoted in DNB.

CHAPTER EIGHT
DEGENERATION AND DESPAIR: HENRY MAUDSLEY (1835–1918)

1. In a brief autobiographical essay written some time in 1907, Maudsley records that "the farm was inherited by my father from his elder brother Henry who died unmarried, and had been in the family for several generations." The autograph manuscript of this four-thousand-word document is in the Bethlem Archives, and a transcription, which we rely upon here, appears in Michael Collie, *Henry Maudsley, Victorian Psychiatrist: A Bibliographic Study* Winchester, England: St. Paul's Bibliographies, 1988, pp. 188–194 (hereafter cited as "Autobiographical Sketch").

2. Mary was herself the oldest daughter of a farming family with landholdings in both Lancashire and Yorkshire. Henry's "memories of her are chiefly as a suffering invalid." "Autobiographical Sketch," p. 188.

3. Ibid., pp. 189, 191.

4. Ibid., pp. 188–189.

5. Ibid., p. 191.

6. Ibid., pp. 188, 192.

7. Ibid.

8. Ibid. In his obituary of Maudsley, George Savage recalls that he "felt rather a fraud in winning prizes. . . . He said he had an unusual visual memory, and that if asked a question he seemed to be able to copy the answer from the text-books." "Henry Maudsley, M.D.," *Journal of Mental Science* 64, 1918, p. 118.

9. "Autobiographical Sketch," p. 192. (That is, to falsify the records for him.) Maudsley did, however, somehow acquire a fluent reading knowledge of French and German in these years, an accomplishment that subsequently gave him access to the burgeoning European psychiatric literature and greatly assisted his own professional advancement.

10. Dr. Sharpey, "the distinguished Professor of Physiology," quoted in ibid. The remark was worthy of Maudsley's own waspish pen, and it was one that, however deserved, rankled him for the rest of his days.

11. Ibid.

12. Ibid.

13. Ibid., pp. 192–193. Maudsley, incidentally, never liked the term "psychiatrist," even though it was entering into general usage by the closing years of his career.

14. Collie, *Henry Maudsley*, p. 14.

15. Ibid.

16. Trevor Turner, "Henry Maudsley: Psychiatrist, Philosopher, and Entrepreneur," in Bynum, Porter, and Shepherd (eds.), *The Anatomy of Madness* vol. 3, pp. 154–155.

17. Rev. C. J. Cummings, quoted in Collie, *Henry Maudsley*, p. 15.

18. Henry Maudsley, "The Correlation of Mental and Physical Forces: Or, Man a Part of Nature," and "Edgar Allan Poe," *Journal of Mental Science* 6, pp. 50–78, 328–369.

19. Henry Maudsley, "The Love of Life," *Journal of Mental Science* 7, 1861, pp. 191–210; idem, "The Genesis of Mind," (parts 1 and 2), ibid., 7, 1862, pp. 451–494; and ibid., 8, 1862, pp. 61–102.

20. For evidence of similar disenchantment among other alienists, see Chapters. 4 and 7 above, and Michael Neve and Trevor Turner, "What the Doctor Thought and Did: Sir James Crichton-Browne (1840–1938)," *Medical History* 39, 1995, pp. 399–432

21. Such apparently feckless behaviour brought a stinging rebuke from his normally taciturn father, who described him as "like a woman, belonging to a *varium et mutabile genus*." "Autobiographical Sketch," p. 193.

22. Collie, *Henry Maudsley*, p. 18.

23. *The Lancet* ii, 1865, p. 310.

24. *Journal of Mental Science* 8, 1862, p. 343, quoted in Turner, "Henry Maudsley," p. 157.

25. Ibid., pp. 356–363. Gaskell, too, had also sought to advance this cause. Cf. chapter 6, n.3.

26. Crichton-Browne, "The First Maudsley Lecture," p. 199.

27. "Hamlet," *Westminster Review* 83 o.s., 1865, pp. 65–94. For some suggestive commentary on the possible significance of the literary efforts of men like Maudsley, Conolly, and Bucknill, see Helen Small, " 'In the Guise of Science': Literature and the Rhetoric of 19th-Century English Psychiatry," *History of the Human Sciences* 7, 1994, pp. 27–55.

28. Henry Maudsley, "Delusions," *Journal of Mental Science* 9, 1863, pp. 1–24.

29. The marriage took place in February 1866, only a month before Conolly's death, and was to remain a childless one. At thirty-five, Anne Caroline was four years older than Maudsley, and one has to wonder how far the marriage was a strategic move on his part (though he was to nurse her devotedly in her last years, when she fell victim to senile decay).

30. On the political manoeuvering attending Robertson's succession to the editorship, cf. chapter 7 above, n.119.

31. Bucknill himself had announced at the Association's annual general meeting in July 1862 that the existence of "surplus funds" would allow him "to engage the regular services of a sub-editor" and that he proposed to do so. *Journal of Mental Science* 8, 1862, pp. 327–328.

32. Collie, *Henry Maudsley*, pp. 20–21; Turner, "Henry Maudsley," p. 176. Turner speculates that it may have been his tartness, cynicism, and hypercriticality that cost Maudsley the prize of the Bethlem appointment, which went instead to Rhys Williams.

33. Harrington Tuke, married since 1852 to another of Conolly's daughters, Sophia Jane, had also applied unsuccessfully for the vacant chair at University College London.

34. Curiously, in an earlier incarnation, this establishment had been a boarding school for aristocratic young men, to which Anthony Ashley Cooper, the seventh Earl of Shaftesbury and chairman of the Lunacy Commissioners, had been sent as a young man. In those years, Manor House was, if Shaftesbury's testimony can be believed, a hell on earth: "The place was bad, wicked, filthy; and the treatment was starvation and cruelty." Quoted in Battiscombe, *Shaftesbury*, p. 6.

35. *Medical Directory*, 1866–1869.

36. Henry Maudsley, "Practical Observations on Certain Varieties of Insanity That Are Frequently Confounded," and "Practical Observations on Insanity of Feeling and of Action," *The Lancet* i, 1866, pp. 363–364, 679–680; "On Some of the Causes of Insanity," *Journal of Mental Science* 12, 1867, pp. 488–502; "Recent Contributions to the Pathology of Nervous Diseases," and "Acute Mania and Acute Maniacal Delirium," *Journal of Mental Science* 13, 1867, pp. 44–58, 59–65, respectively.

37. *The Lancet* i, 1867, p. 515; *British Medical Journal* i, 1867, p. 540.

38. Maudsley, *The Physiology and Pathology of Mind*, p. v.

39. H. Maudsley, "Illustrations of a Variety of Insanity," *Journal of Mental Science* 14, 1868, pp. 149–162.

40. Compare, however, his acknowledgement that "the morbid anatomy of insanity would take little room were speculation rigidly excluded and it limited to what is actually seen and known. Nor does that which is seen, it must be confessed, throw much light on the symptoms. . . . The intimate chemical and molecular

changes which are presumably the conditions of mental disorder go on in a domain of nature the subtleties of which far exceed the subtleties of observation." Quoted in Aubrey Lewis, *The State of Psychiatry: Essays and Addresses* London: Routledge and Kegan Paul, 1967, p. 42. Maudsley himself, as Lewis comments, "had no laboratory experience nor any evident taste for experiment."

41. Sir James Crichton-Browne, *The Prevention of Senility and A Sanitary Outlook* London: Macmillan, 1905, p. 74.

42. Maudsley, "An Address on Medical Psychology," *The Lancet* ii, 1872, pp. 185–189. Cf. his insistence that "we may truly say of the theological notion of the relations of mind and body that it has been surpassed by few false doctrines in the evil which it has worked . . . so far as a knowledge of the nature of insanity and of the proper mode of treating it is concerned mankind owe no thanks, but on the contrary, much error and infinite human suffering, to theology and metaphysics."

43. The lunatic, as he memorably phrased it, was an "organic machine automatically impelled by disordered nerve-centres." Maudsley, *The Physiology and Pathology of Mind*, p. 325.

44. See, for example, Burrows, *Commentaries*, pp. 101–102; Combe, *Observations*, p. 91; Thomas Laycock, *A Treatise on the Nervous Diseases of Women* London: Longman, Orme, Brown, Green, and Longmans, 1840, pp. 137–139.

45. B. A. Morel, *Traité des dégénérescences* Paris: Masson, 1857.

46. See the definitive discussion of this development in Michael Clark, "The Rejection of Psychological Approaches to Mental Disorder in Late-Nineteenth-Century British Psychiatry," in Scull (ed.), *Madhouses, Mad-Doctors, and Madmen*, pp. 271–312.

47. H. Maudsley, *Responsibility in Mental Disease* 2d ed., London: Kegan Paul, p. 154; emphasis in the original.

48. Maudsley, *The Physiology and Pathology of Mind*, p. 83.

49. Ibid., pp. 422–423.

50. Ibid., pp. 423–424.

51. H. Maudsley, "Insanity and Its Treatment," *Journal of Mental Science* 17, 1871, pp. 323–324.

52. Ibid., p. 324.

53. Maudsley, *The Physiology and Pathology of Mind*, pp. 204–205.

54. Ibid., p. 423.

55. H. Maudsley, *Body and Will* London: Kegan Paul and Trench, 1883, pp. 240–241; emphasis in the original.

56. Maudsley, *The Physiology and Pathology of Mind*, p. 216. Subsequently, the language he used grew yet more shrill, as he counselled his readers that "new products of an asocial or antisocial kind are formed in the retrograde metamorphosis of the human kind . . . new and degenerate varieties with special repulsive characters . . . ten times more vicious and noxious, and infinitely less capable of improvement, than the savages of primitive barbarism." Idem, *Body and Will*, pp. 241, 321.

57. See Turner, "Henry Maudsley," pp. 151, 175.

58. Henry Maudsley, *Body and Mind* London: Macmillan and Co, 1870.

59. *Journal of Mental Science* 16, 1870, pp. 454–456.

60. Ibid.

61. *Journal of Mental Science* 8, 1863, pp. 326–327.

62. "Insanity and Its Treatment," *Journal of Mental Science* 17, 1871, pp. 311–334.

63. Ibid., p. 313.

64. Ibid., pp. 313, 314, 315, 316.

65. Ibid, p. 319. The hostility this exhibits towards money-grubbing men engaged in "trade" would likely have drawn a warm welcome in aristocratic circles, where nouveaux riches capitalists were widely disdained and despised.

66. Ibid.

67. Ibid., p. 325.

68. Ibid.

69. Ibid., pp. 325–326.

70. Ibid., p. 327.

71. Ibid., p. 330.

72. Ibid., p. 327.

73. His criticisms of asylums should not have come as a complete surprise, for his scepticism about their merits had begun to surface in a sustained fashion in *The Physiology and Pathology of Mind*, whose concluding chapter contained repeated criticisms of the "overgrown and overcrowded asylums to which almost the whole lunatic population of the country has been consigned," and objections to the existing policy "of indiscriminate sequestration—of locking up a person in an asylum simply because he is mad." As early as 1867, he was already comparing confinement in an asylum to "the mighty suffering of a life-long imprisonment" and reminding "those who advocate and defend the present asylum system . . . that there is one point of view from which they who organize, superintend, and act, regard the system, and that there is another point of view from which those who are organized, superintended, and suffer view it."

74. Maudsley, "Insanity and Its Treatment," p. 331.

75. Ibid., p. 332.

76. Ibid., p. 333.

77. Ibid., pp. 332, 333.

78. "Notes and News," *Journal of Mental Science* 17, 1871–1872, p. 456.

79. Ibid., pp. 455–456, 458.

80. Maudsley, "Insanity and Its Treatment," p. 323.

81. James Coxe, "On the Causes of Insanity, and the Means of Checking Its Growth," *Journal of Mental Science* 18, 1872, pp. 311–33.

82. *Journal of Mental Science* 18, 1872, pp. 456–457.

83. *Journal of Mental Science* 19, 1873, p. 472.

84. Henry Maudsley, "Insanity and Its Treatment," pp. 327–328.

85. Dixon had previously served as the matron at Otto House private asylum in Hammersmith.

86. His inaugural address was delivered in August 1872.

87. Henry Maudsley, "The Treatment of the Insane Without Mechanical Restraints," *The Practitioner* 5, 1870, pp. 193–199; "Is Insanity on the Increase," *British Medical Journal* i, 1872, pp. 36–39; "An Address on Medical Psychology," *The Lancet* ii, 1872, pp. 185–189; "Stealing as a Symptom of General Paralysis," *The Lancet* ii,

1875, pp. 693–696; "Introductory Lecture Delivered at University College on October 2, 1876," *The Lancet* ii, 1876, pp. 489–495.

88. Henry Maudsley, "Judges, Juries, and Insanity," *Popular Science Monthly* 1, 1872, pp. 440–445; "Sex in Mind and Education," *Fortnightly Review* n.s. 15, 1874, pp. 466–483.

89. Henry Maudsley, *Body and Mind*; *Responsibility in Mental Disease* London: King, 1874.

90. Many of his fellow alienists must have shuddered, however, to read his boast, in the preface to the 1876 edition of *The Physiology of Mind* (pp. v–vi) that "one is happily more critical, as well as less enthusiastic and confident, at forty than at thirty years of age." Who could look forward with equanimity to a *more* critical Maudsley?

91. What must have been a somewhat scandalous spectacle can be followed in the proceedings, reprinted in *Journal of Mental Science* 23, 1876–1877, pp. 428–433. Perhaps Clouston's insistence that if Maudsley were forced out, he would resign too had something to do with the outcome.

92. Harrington Tuke rose to his feet anyway both to complain that the minutes of the previous year's meeting implied that he had objected to both editors, whereas his criticisms had not been aimed at Clouston, and to make it clear that "he thought it his duty . . . to object to the re-appointment of the former editor, Dr. Maudsley." Once it became clear that the latter's resignation would stand, in seconding the vote of thanks to his brother-in-law for his services as editor, Tuke reiterated that he did so despite differing with him "upon some points of doctrine."

93. Henry Maudsley, "The Physical Conditions of Consciousness," *Mind* 12, 1887, pp. 489–515; "The Double Brain," *Mind* 14, 1889, pp. 161–187; "The Cerebral Cortex and Its Work," *Mind* 16, 1890, pp. 161–90. Review of Henry Maudsley, *Natural Causes and Supernatural Seemings*, London: Kegan Paul, Trench & Co, 1886, in *Mind* 11, 1886, p. 435. (Perhaps Maudsley, too, was the unspoken target of Hughlings Jackson's barbed comment that "it is a great mistake to suppose that those who write books on metaphysics are the most metaphysical. They have, at any rate, the knowledge that they are dealing with metaphysics." *Selected Writings* London: Staples, 1958, vol. 2, p. 342.) Decades later, the first article he published in the *Journal of Mental Science* after his gift to the LCC had been announced was called "The Physical Basis of Consciousness" (*Journal of Mental Science* 55, 1909, pp. 1–22), as though he were intentionally recalling the period of his final split from the Medico-Psychological Association.

94. *Medical Directory*, 1863–1866.

95. Obituaries of Harrington Tuke in *The Lancet* i, 1888, p. 1274; *British Medical Journal* i, 1888, p. 1364.

96. Obituaries of Henry Maudsley in *British Medical Journal* i, 1918, pp. 161–162; *Journal of Mental Science* 64, 1918, pp. 117–129.

97. Maudsley's evidence to the 1877 *Select Committee on Lunacy Laws* (p. 322) on the case of Louisa Lowe particularly revealed his distaste for close domestic association with patients.

98. Alexander Walk, "Medico-psychologists, Maudsley and the Maudsley," *British Journal of Psychiatry* 128, 1976, pp. 19–30.

99. Maudsley, "Insanity and Its Treatment."

100. In 1876 Harrington Tuke's second son, Thomas Seymour, who eventually qualified in medicine and joined him at Manor House, had just completed his second year at Oxford.

101. *British Medical Journal* i, 1877, p. 358.

102. See *Select Committee on the Lunacy Laws*, 1877, pp. 124–126.

103. Ibid., p. 178.

104. In addition to being called to give evidence as an expert witness on April 24, 1877, Maudsley was recalled on June 5, 1877, specifically to give evidence on the case of Louisa Lowe, *Select Committee on Lunacy Laws*, 1877, 320–327.

105. Commissioners in Lunacy, *Annual Report*, 1877, pp. 109–110.

106. *Journal of Mental Science* 23, 1877, pp. 428–433.

107. Thomas Clouston, "The Evidence Given Before the Select Committee of the House of Commons on Lunacy Laws," *Journal of Mental Science* 24, 1878, pp. 457–525.

108. *Select Committee on Lunacy Laws*, 1877, p. 121.

109. Ibid.

110. *Journal of Mental Science* 24, 1878, pp. 494–497.

111. See ibid., pp. 335–343. In his obituary of Clouston, for example, David Yellowlees commented that "he could always differ pleasantly and without shadow of offence" (*Journal of Mental Science* 61, 1915, pp. 494–495)—not an assessment anyone would be likely to offer of Maudsley.

112. *Select Committee on Lunacy Laws*, 1877, p. 545.

113. See, for example, *Journal of Mental Science* 25, 1879, pp. 80–95, 538–547.

114. *Journal of Mental Science* 26, 1880, p. 444; *Journal of Mental Science* 30, 1884, p. 466.

115. *Journal of Mental Science* 34, 1888, p. 311.

116. Henry Maudsley, "Remarks on Crime and Criminals," *Journal of Mental Science* 34, 1888, pp. 150–167; "Criminal Responsiblity in Relation to Insanity," *Journal of Mental Science* 41, 1895, pp. 657–665.

117. Henry Maudsley, "The New Psychology," *Journal of Mental Science* 46, 1900, pp. 411–424.

118. See, for example, Maudsley, "The Treatment of the Insane Without Mechanical Restraints."

119. *Journal of Mental Science* 34, 1888, p. 327.

120. *The Times*, August 16, 1888.

121. *Journal of Mental Science* 35, 1889–1890, p. 399.

122. *Journal of Mental Science* 33, 1887, p. 468.

123. *The Times*, August 16, 1888.

124. *Journal of Mental Science* 44, 1918, p. 119.

125. *The Times*, August 16, 1888.

126. George Henry Savage, "Homicidal Mania," *Fortnightly Review* n.s. 50, 1888, pp. 448–463.

127. Henry Maudsley, "Delusions," p. 2.

128. Maudsley, *The Pathology of Mind* (1879 ed.), p. 88.

129. Maudsley, *Body and Will*, p. 241.

130. Cf. Michael Clark, "'The Data of Alienism': Evolutionary Neurology, Physio-

logical Psychology, and the Reconstruction of British Psychiatric Theory, c. 1850—
c. 1900," D. Phil. thesis, Oxford University, 1985.

131. Maudsley, *The Pathology of Mind* (1895 ed.), pp. 78, 82.

132. Ibid., p. 30.

133. Maudsley, *Body and Mind*, p. 53.

134. See *Journal of Mental Science* 25, 1879, pp. 230–238, 538–547.

135. *Journal of Mental Science* 30–31, 1885, pp. 597–603. The review of the 1895 edition of *The Pathology of Mind* was equally harsh, denouncing his philosophy as "frequently unsound, his psychology prohibitive of truth, and his sociology repulsive and unsuited to average humanity." *Journal of Mental Science* 42, 1896, pp. 186–190.

136. *Brain* 6, 1884, pp. 531–538. Much of Mercier's review consisted of lengthy quotations of Maudsley's own words, followed by commentary that mocked him mercilessly.

137. Maudsley, *Body and Mind*, p. 61.

138. Cf. Janet Oppenheim's conclusion that "Victorian psychiatrists welcomed a theory that held out the promise of rescue from impending professional disgrace." *"Shattered Nerves"*, p. 286.

139. Dr. Major, superintendent of the Wakefield County Asylum, quoted in R. Greene, "Hospitals for the Insane and Clinical Instruction in Asylums," in H. C. Burdett, *Hospitals and Asylums of the World* London: Churchill, 1891, vol. 2, p. 250.

140. R. Greene, "The Care and Cure of the Insane," *Universal Review* July 1889, p. 503.

141. For discussions of the broad influence of degenerationist ideas in late Victorian psychological medicine, see Clark, "'The Data of Alienism,'"; idem, "The Rejection of Psychological Approaches"; Showalter, *The Female Malady*, esp. chaps. 4 and 5; Oppenheim, *"Shattered Nerves"*, chap. 8; Scull, *The Most Solitary of Afflictions*, pp. 315–333.

142. Showalter, *The Female Malady*, p. 116.

143. Maudsley, "Memoir," p. 173.

144. Maudsley, "Autobiographical Sketch," p. 188.

145. Ibid., pp. 188–189.

146. Ibid., p. 189.

147. Ibid., p. 193.

148. Maudsley, "Sex in Mind and Education." For discussion, see Joan Burstyn, "Education and Sex: The Medical Case Against Higher Education for Women in England, 1870–1900," *Proceedings of the American Philosophical Association* 117, 1973, pp. 79–89; idem, *Victorian Education and the Ideal of Womanhood* London: Croom Helm, 1980, pp. 84–98; Anne Digby, "Women's Biological Straitjacket," in Susan Mendus and Jane Rendall (eds.), *Sexuality and Subordination: Inter-disciplinary Studies of Gender in the Nineteenth Century* London and New York: Routledge, 1989, pp. 192–220; and Showalter, *The Female Malady*, pp. 123–125.

149. J. Burstyn, "Education and Sex," p. 8.

150. St. Mary's Hospital, where Maudsley had been lecturer in insanity since 1868, had been intimately involved in the controversy over women's entry into the medical profession. Sophia Jex Blake, Mary Edith Pechey, and Isabel Thorne had all

applied for admission in 1869 and had been refused. In subsequent years, several doctors on the staff had provided private tuition for them, assuming (incorrectly) that this would force the examining bodies to allow them to sit their qualifying examinations. The internal tensions this gave rise to at the hospital were exacerbated in the months before and after Maudsley's article appeared, and Michael Collie (*Henry Maudsley*, pp. 49–50) plausibly suggests that the piece may have been intended, in part, as an intervention in this internal debate.

151. Maudsley, "Sex in Mind and Education," p. 466.

152. Ibid., pp. 481–482.

153. Ibid.

154. Ibid., p. 466.

155. Ibid., pp. 468, 479.

156. Ibid., p. 466.

157. Ibid., p. 475.

158. Ibid., pp. 475–476.

159. Ibid., pp. 466, 467.

160. Ibid., p. 477.

161. Cf. Burstyn, "Education and Sex," pp. 80, 88–89. The University of London finally abandoned the regulations that prohibited women taking degrees in 1878, but women were not accepted as graduates at Oxford or Cambridge until the twentieth century.

162. "Sex in Mind and Education: A Reply," *Fortnightly Review* n.s. 15, 1874, p. 582. Maudsley was also sternly rebuked for leaving "nothing to the imagination" by Herbert Cowell, "Sex in Mind and Education: A Commentary," *Blackwoods* 115, 1874, pp. 736–749.

163. Ibid., p. 585.

164. Ibid., p. 590.

165. Ibid.

166. See, for example, Burstyn, "Sex and Education," p. 81; Oppenheim, *"Shattered Nerves"*, p. 197.

167. See, for example, Robert Lawson Tait, *The Pathology and Treatment of the Ovaries* 4th ed. Birmingham: Cornish, 1883; John Thorburn, *Female Education From a Physiological Point of View* Manchester: Cornish, 1884; William Withers Moore, "Presidential Address to the British Medical Association," *The Lancet* ii, 1886, p. 315; T. S. Clouston, *Female Education From a Medical Point of View* Edinburgh: Macniven and Wallace, 1882; idem, *Clinical Lectures on Mental Diseases* 2d ed., London: Churchill, 1887, esp. pp. 40–42.

168. E.g., Arabella Keneally, "Woman as an Athlete," *Nineteenth Century* 45, April 1899, pp. 636–645; Mary Scharlieb, "Adolescent Girlhood Under Modern Conditions, With Special Reference to Motherhood," *Eugenics Review* 1, 1909–1910, pp. 174–183.

169. For a wide-ranging analysis of the predominance of this perspective in the Victorian era, cf. Brian Harrison, *Separate Spheres: The Opposition to Women's Suffrage in Britain* London: Croom Helm, 1978, esp. chap. 4.

170. "Women at Oxford and Cambridge," *Quarterly Review* 186, 1897, p. 543. In the end, Burstyn suggests ("Sex in Education," p. 89), it was not scientific arguments

of Mental Science in this fashion. His portions of *A Manual of Psychological Medicine*, for instance, had previously appeared in draft form in its pages.

46. *Journal of Mental Science* 6, 1860, p. 5. Lockhart Robertson was equally certain of the great strides the journal had made under Bucknill's editorship: see *Journal of Mental Science* 8, 1862–1863, p. 462.

47. *Asylum Journal* 1, no. 9, November 15, 1854, p. 129.

48. E.g., *Journal of Mental Science* 7, 1860–1862, pp. 3, 288–293, 313–314; 8, 1862–1863, p. 446. Bucknill's efforts notwithstanding, it was not until 1909 that the Asylum Officers' Superannuation Act became law, prompting extraordinary celebrations among the profession's leadership and rank and file. Cf. *Journal of Mental Science* 56, 1910, pp. 109–110, 174–183.

49. *Asylum Journal of Mental Science* 2, 1856, p. 14.

50. His ally and protégé, Lockhart Robertson, filled in for him. (The snub, if snub it was, did not prevent Winslow from returning the favour, enthusiastically nominating his erstwhile competitor for reelection as editor of the *Journal of Mental Science*). See *Asylum Journal of Mental Science* 3, 1856–1857, p. 4. In assuming the presidency, Winslow became only the second proprietor of a private asylum (after A. J. Sutherland in 1854) to head the Association, and not till Henry Monro's election in 1864 would there be another.

51. "The Newspaper Attack on Private Lunatic Asylums," *Journal of Mental Science* 5, 1858–1859, pp. 146, 148, 149, 152. The impassioned defence contrasts dramatically, as we shall see, with the stance Bucknill was to adopt towards private asylums at a later stage in his career.

52. "Presidential Address," *Journal of Mental Science* 7, 1860, p. 22. Such pious sentiments collided with the reality that the interests and outlook of the salaried employees of a network of Poor Law institutions were quite sharply divergent from those of the entrepreneurial branch of the profession which catered to the well-to-do and the rich via a loosely articulated group of private asylums; and the divisions within the profession were only further compounded once men like Maudsley, Savage, and Bucknill himself succeeded in carving out consulting practices almost wholly outside any portion of the asylum system.

53. Bedfordshire, for instance, had been one of only three county asylums without a resident medical officer in the early 1840s. Compelled by statute in 1845 to abandon this practice, the magistrates had advertised for a physician offering no more than £100 per annum, though ultimately compelled to pay three times that in order to make an appointment. *Asylum Journal* 1, no. 7, August 15, 1854, p. 102. Here was one of a series of status issues on which Bucknill and Winslow could see eye to eye. Noting that the construction of Colney Hatch had cost the extravagant sum of £280,000, Winslow drew attention to the meagre salary of £200 per annum that the medical men in charge of the male and female divisions were then paid, an indication, he commented with some asperity, of "how carefully the justices guard the public purse, when mind not matter is to be paid for." "Our Pauper Lunatic Asylums," *Journal of Psychological Medicine and Mental Pathology* 6, 1853, p. 405.

54. J. T. Arlidge, "The Middlesex County Lunatic Asylums and Their Reports for 1855–1856," *Asylum Journal of Mental Science* 2, 1856, p. 358; [Winslow], "Our Pauper Lunatic Asylums," p. 416.

55. "Tenth Report of the Commissioners in Lunacy to the Lord Chancellor," *Asylum Journal of Mental Science* 3, 1856–1857, pp. 19–20. He noted with satisfaction, however, that the Lunacy Commissioners were increasingly reluctant to issue licenses to women, so that the "evil . . . is in the process of cure." Beyond the obvious lay-versus-professional issues that surface here, the resentment of women exceeding their station is equally transparent. Such sentiments were still more explicit when Bucknill commented on Dorothea Dix's activities. Though he exempted Dix herself from his strictures, he spoke scathingly of women who meddled in a man's world: "We English certainly do entertain a general aversion to ladies whose mission extends itself beyond the home circle, and who have a propensity to set people to rights; we are apt to ascribe it to restlessness, impatience of control, and other unwomanly motives"; and, in a memorable turn of phrase, he sought to dismiss "the small [Elizabeth?] fry of female philanthropists or philathro-pests as we are tempted to call those whose mental vision is so much occupied with the Borioboola Ghas, that with their bodily eyes they cannot see the buttonless shirts and undarned stockings of husbands and daughters." "Reports of the Irish, Scotch, and American Asylums, 1855," *Asylum Journal of Mental Science* 2, 1856, p. 124. (Bucknill's concluding reference here is to Dickens's portrait of Mrs. Jellyby in *Bleak House*.) Within little more than a decade, as we shall see, Henry Maudsley was to provide a psychiatric-cum-scientific justification for consigning women to domesticity. See Chapter 8 below.

56. "The New Lunacy Bill," *Journal of Mental Science* 8, 1862–1863, p. 156. Bucknill's worries on this score were scarcely idiosyncratic. Cf. Forbes Winslow, *Asylum Journal of Mental Science* 3, 1856–1857, pp. 10–11.

57. *Journal of Mental Science* 5, 1858–1859, p. 149.

58. *Journal of Mental Science* 8, 1862–1863, p. 156.

59. "Quarterly Psychological Review," *Journal of Mental Science* 7, 1861, p. 140.

60. "Presidential Address," p. 20.

61. He had originally refused to publish a paper from James Huxley, superintendent of the Kent County Asylum, that was sarcastically and relentlessly critical of some of Gaskell's initiatives, printing it only when Huxley insisted, with an editorial disclaimer which asserted that the complaints were "not warranted, and we greatly regret that their publication has been imposed upon us." See James Huxley, "On the Dirty Habits of the Insane and Night Nursing," *Journal of Mental Science* 4, 1857–1858, pp. 119–127.

62. *Journal of Mental Science* 5, 1858–1859, p. 154.

63. "Tenth Report of the Commisioners in Lunacy," *Asylum Journal of Mental Science* 3, 1856–1857, pp. 23–24, 28–29. Where the earliest proponents of moral treatment had insisted that appropriate buildings were essential to the success of their schemes, magistrates consistently objected to the expense their designs imposed on ratepayers. Dependent, as were all county asylum superintendents, on the approval of those who employed him, Bucknill had adopted their priorities as his own.

64. *Journal of Mental Science* 4, 1857–1858, p. 119.

65. Bucknill, *An Inquiry into the Proper Classification and Treatment of Criminal Lunatics* London: John Churchill, 1851; idem, *Unsoundness of Mind in Relation to Criminal Acts* London: Samuel Highley, 1854, 2d ed. London: Longman & Co, 1857;

idem, *The Proposed Abandonment of the College Test* Exeter, 1857; Bucknill with Daniel Hack Tuke, *A Manual of Psychological Medicine* London: John Churchill, 1858, further editions same publisher 1862, 1874, and 1879; Bucknill, *The Psychology of Shakespeare* London: Longman & Co, 1859, reissued as *The Mad Folk of Shakespeare* London: Macmillan & Co, 1867; and idem, *The Medical Knowledge of Shakespeare* London: Longman & Co, 1860.

66. *Asylum Journal* 1, no. 10, 1854, p. 159.

67. *Asylum Journal* 1, no. 11, February 15, 1854, p. 176.

68. James Cowles Prichard, *A Treatise on Insanity and Other Disorders Affecting the Mind* London: Sherwood, Gilbert and Piper, 1835.

69. Bucknill and Tuke, *Manual*, p. ix.

70. Ibid., p. 269.

71. A review in the *Lancet* praised the book for its clarity and practicality, at the same time as it expressed some reservations about Bucknill's tendency to stray into discussion of abstruse and philosophical points. There were complaints, too, that only 68 out of a total of 562 pages dealt with treatment, and it was suggested that the book would have been enhanced if this discussion had been expanded at the expense of the history of the treatment of the insane. *The Lancet* i, 1858, pp. 505–506. Such criticisms tended to overlook the ideological value of the historical materials in the construction of a geneology and legitimacy for the profession; and to assume, dubiously, that a more extended discussion of therapeutics would have been useful or even practicable.

72. Bucknill and Tuke, *Manual*, p. 444.

73. Ibid., p. 447. The centrality of *medical* forms of treatment, an essential prop for his insistence that "the Physician is now the responsible guardian of the lunatic, and must ever remain so" ("Prospectus," *Asylum Journal* 1, no. 1, November 15, 1853, p. 1), was "demonstrated" in part by arguing that certain therapeutic interventions, commonly conceived of as forms of moral treatment, were more properly regarded as medical intervention: thus his bold claim that "the emotional repose, the intellectual diversion, which are now sought to be obtained in well-conducted establishments for the treatment of the insane, are not, strictly speaking, moral agencies; they constitute physiological measures taken to procure functional repose for a vitiated and diseased organ. . . . Such a rational method of proceeding is not moral but physiological." *Manual*, p. 447.

74. Bucknill and Tuke, *Manual*, p. 450.

75. Ibid., p. 455. Remedies like the "bath of surprise" were dismissed, however, as "not manageable remedies, or remedies of the nature of whose operation we have reliable knowledge," p. 456.

76. Ibid., pp. 454, 455.

77. Ibid., pp. 457–473.

78. Ibid., p. 501.

79. Ibid., p. 487.

80. Ibid., p. 491.

81. Ibid., p. 486.

82. Conolly, *Treatment of the Insane*, p. 55, quoted in ibid.

83. Bucknill and Tuke, *Manual*, pp. 488, 490. That "so much of it may be . . . done vicariously by ordinary attendants"—that is, by those "with a defective educa-

tion and a lowly social rank"—was "a most happy circumstance for mental sufferers" (ibid., p. 489); but from the perspective of one committed to the defence of medical men's prerogatives, it also constituted a further and still more potent reason for resisting the notion that moral treatment was of primary importance in the treatment of insanity.

84. Ibid., pp. 490–491. The usefulness of such claims in mounting a defence of the barracks-asylums that were becoming so prevalent by the late 1850s was fully exploited in short order by one of Bucknill's colleagues, Joseph Lalor: contrary to the conventional wisdom of an earlier generation of alienists, it now transpired that for precisely these reasons, "large are preferable to small asylums, no less on scientific principles, and from benevolent considerations, than from motives of economy . . . [since, so far] from producing general turbulence and confusion, . . . the association of large masses of insane people . . . is found to be highly conducive to good order and quietude." Joseph Lalor, "Observations on the Size and Construction of Lunatic Asylums," *Journal of Mental Science* 7, 1860, pp. 105–106, 108.

85. *Journal of Mental Science*, 4, 1857–1858, p. 317.

86. Ibid.

87. *Journal of Mental Science* 8, 1862, p. 335.

88. *Journal of Mental Science* 4, 1857–1858, p. 324.

89. Commissioners in Lunacy, *Annual Report*, 1858, p. 8.

90. *Journal of Mental Science* 4, 1857–1858, pp. 325, 327.

91. Bucknill, *Care of the Insane*, p. x.

92. *Journal of Mental Science* 6, 1860, p. 6.

93. *Journal of Mental Science* 8, 1862, p. 333.

94. "Obituary," *The Lancet* ii, 1897, p. 228.

95. For his role in *Regina v. Huxtable* and *Regina v. Handcock*, see *Asylum Journal of Mental Science* 2, 1855–1856, pp. 114–120, 245–253. For Bucknill's involvement in Chancery inquisitions in lunacy, see, for example, his testimony in the case of Miss Phoebe Ewings, an eighty-year-old spinster of uncertain mental powers (a separately paginated appendix to *Journal of Mental Science* 6, 1859–1860) and for his being retained as a consultant in two other Chancery cases, *Journal of Mental Science* 7, 1860–1861, pp. 128–129. For his participation in a Scottish case concerning testimentary capacity, see ibid., pp. 414–459. Bucknill also served as the committee (i.e., guardian) of a number of Chancery Lunatics during this period.

96. *Journal of Mental Science* 4, 1857–1858, pp. 127, 128. He was equally scathing about the qualifications of two of the Scottish and Irish medical commissioners, Coxe and Hatchell.

97. Ibid., p. 127.

98. *Asylum Journal of Mental Science* 3, 1856–1857, p. 29.

99. Even the satisfactions associated with editing the *Journal of Mental Science* may have been beginning to pall. At the annual business meeting of the Association in July 1860, Harrington Tuke spoke up in favour of Bucknill's request to pay someone else to prepare the "digest of foreign psychological literature" for each issue, "to release Dr. Bucknill from the absolute drugery attending his editorship." *Journal of Mental Science* 7, 1860–1861, p. 37.

100. "Suicide of Dr. Grahamsley," *Asylum Journal* 1, no. 7, August 15, 1854, pp. 105–106.

but changes in social arrangements that broke down these prejudices: "When a growing number of middle-class women found it necessary to join their lower-class sisters in earning a living, the ideal had to be changed so that unmarried women, at least, could enter occupations that did not demean their families."

171. *British Medical Journal* i, 1872, pp. 36–39.

172. *Popular Science Monthly* 1, 1872, pp. 440–445.

173. *The Lancet* ii, 1875, pp. 695–696.

174. *Fortnightly Review* n.s. 24, 1878, pp. 370–386.

175. As Roger Smith documents, in his *Trial by Medicine* (p. 14), medical men with an interest in the issues raised by the insanity defence were, with scarcely an exception, "enraged by the criminal law. . . . It appeared to many that existing law, with its variable verdicts, embodied a *lack* of science; it other words it epitomised social reaction and unreason."

176. Maudsley, "Judges, Juries, and Insanity," p. 441.

177. Ibid., pp. 440, 442. The medical profession as a whole had reason to welcome this spirited defence of its prerogatives. Characteristically, however, Maudsley could not resist a remark that must have deeply offended most of his fellow alienists, claiming that "the prospect of being confined in a lunatic asylum . . . is one which excites as much horror and antipathy in the minds of both sane and insane persons as can well be imagined." Ibid., p. 443.

178. For useful discussions, cf. Gareth Stedman-Jones, *Outcast London: A Study of the Relationship Between Classes in Victorian Society* New York: Pantheon, 1984; and Oppenheim, *"Shattered Nerves"*, chap. 8.

179. Clark, "'The Data of Alienism,'" p. 161.

180. On the slow process by which Lamarckian theories of evolution fell into disrepute, and the tenacious fashion in which most alienists held on to the notion of the inheritance of acquired characteristics, cf. Clark, "'The Data of Alienism,'" esp. chap. 7; Oppenheim, *"Shattered Nerves"*, pp. 290–292. As Oppenheim notes, "the Lamarckian perspective was not definitively discredited until the 1940s."

181. Maudsley, *Responsibility in Mental Disease*, pp. 278–280; *The Pathology of Mind* (1895 ed.), pp. 90, 542.

182. Clark, "'The Data of Alienism,'" p. 304. The preceeding paragraph is considerably indebted to Clark's penetrating analysis of these developments.

183. It remains unclear just how lucrative the business at Lawn House was, though Maudsley's testimony to the Select Committee (*Report*, p. 322) revealed that the payments for Louisa Lowe, just one of his half dozen patients, considerably exceeded £400 on an annual basis.

184. Maudsley, "Autobiographical Sketch," p. 193.

185. Ibid., p. 175.

186. T. Turner, "Henry Maudsley," p. 175. Among these eight patients were a countess and the heir to a dukedom.

187. M. E. Broadbent, *Life of Sir William Broadbent* London: Murray, 1909, p. 118.

188. *The Lancet* ii, 1889, pp. 33–34.

189. Christopher Lawrence, "Incommunicable Knowledge: Science, Technology, and the Clinical Art in Britain 1850–1914," *Journal of Contemporary History* 20, 1985, p. 503.

190. Sir George Savage, "Henry Maudsley, M.D.," p. 118.

191. Ibid., p. 118. Compare Lawrence ("Incommunicable Knowledge," p. 510): "Clinical medicine embodied science, but more than that it needed the ineffable wisdom and experience that came only with advanced years, a classical education, and the bearing of a gentleman."

192. See Aubrey Lewis, "Edward Mapother and the Making of the Maudsley Hospital," *British Journal of Psychiatry* 115, 1969, pp. 1344–1366.

193. Quoted in Turner, "Henry Maudsley," p. 178.

194. The Contemporary Medical Archives at the Wellcome Institute for the History of Medicine in London contain a letter from one such (female) patient, dated August 27, 1905.

195. Savage, "Henry Maudsley, M.D.," p. 118.

196. Frederick Mott, "The Second Maudsley Lecture," *Journal of Mental Science* 67, 1921, pp. 319–320. Mott had been appointed as the first pathologist to the LCC asylums and directed the "central" laboratory at the Claybury Asylum in Essex. Part of his motivation in promoting the scheme seems to have been his own desire to move his laboratory to a site in London.

197. Brudenell Carter, who had been elected to the LCC in 1888, was an opthalmic surgeon who had written extensively on hysteria and the prevention of nervous diseases earlier in his career, when he was a general practitioner. His committee's conclusions, *Report of the Committee of the London County Council on a Hospital for the Insane*, are reprinted in H. C. Burdett, *Hospitals and Asylums of the World* vol. 2, pp. 159–247.

198. For the organized campaign, cf. Richard Greene, "Hospitals for the Insane and Clinical Instruction in Asylums," reprinted in ibid., pp. 248–264; for Yellowlees's address, cf. *Journal of Mental Science* 36, 1890, pp. 473–489, and the discussion by the profession at large in ibid., pp. 583–587.

199. Early on in the negotiations, he had written to the Council that he was of the "opinion that the presence of students would bring to the hospital an atmosphere of sanity as compared with the atmosphere of insanity in the County Asylums"—a remark that would scarcely have endeared him to those running such places (and one which the Asylums Committee would quote, attributing it to him, on several later occasions). Maudsley's formal letter offering his donation, dated February 14, 1908, further records his determination "to break down the unfortunate isolation from general medical knowledge and research in which the study of insanity remains"—precisely the burden of Carter's earlier critique.

200. Maudsley, "Autobiographical Sketch," p. 194. Construction of the hospital did not begin until 1913, and when it was completed in 1916, the structure was promptly requisitioned by the Royal Army Medical Corps and temporarily renamed the Maudsley Neurological Clearing Centre, treating the victims of shell shock. The Hospital's Visitors' Book reveals that Maudsley himself toured the facility on August 30, 1916, but it was not until 1923 that it finally opened as a hospital for voluntary patients only, under the auspices of the LCC.

201. *Archives of Neurology* 4, 1909, pp. 1–12.

202. *Journal of Mental Science* 57, 1911, pp. 512–513, 697–698; 58, 1912, pp. 328, 702–703.

203. Henry Maudsley, "Optimism and Pessimism," *Journal of Mental Science* 63,

1917, pp. 1–16; "Materialism and Spiritualism," *Journal of Mental Science* 63, 1917, pp. 494–506; Walk, "Medico-Psychologists, Maudsley, and the Maudsley," p. 25.

204. Henry Maudsley, *Pathology of Mind* (1895 ed.), p. 563.

CHAPTER NINE
CONCLUSION

1. Forbes Winslow, "Presidential Address," *Journal of Mental Science* 4, 1857–1858, p. 6.

2. Ibid., pp. 8, 16.

3. L. Forbes Winslow, *Recollections of Forty Years* London: Ouseley, [1910], pp. 26–27.

4. "Report of the Committee Concerning the Status of British Psychiatry and of Medical Officers," *Journal of Mental Science* 60, 1914, pp. 667, 675.

5. Ibid., pp. 667–669, 670. A year later, in a similar pessimistic assessment of the situation, Hubert Bond would refer to psychiatry as "the Cinderella of medicine." "The Position of Psychiatry," *Journal of Mental Science* 61, 1915, pp. 1–17.

6. Charles Mercier, *Lunatic Asylums: Their Organization and Management* London: Griffin, 1894, p. 246.

7. Protests about this situation were met by resistance and ridicule. One superintendent, for instance, commented that "marriage meant to a medical officer, a diminution of his value to the service for a time; in some it amounted to an observable post-nuptial inertia or dementia, a condition whose course was about twelve months. 700 pounds a year would have a tendency, he feared, to make this condition chronic." *Journal of Mental Science* 12, 1914, p. 689.

8. "Report of the Committee Concerning the Status of British Psychiatry," pp. 667–694.

9. Drs. Dodd, Strahan, and Greenlees, "Assistant Medical Officers in Asylums: Their Status in the Specialty," *Journal of Mental Science* 36, 1890, pp. 43–50.

10. J. Conolly, "On the Prospects of Physicians Engaged in Practice in Cases of Insanity," *Journal of Mental Science* 7, 1861, pp. 181, 185, 192. Compare Forbes Winslow's protest against the public's continued use of "the odious, offensive, and repulsive designation of 'mad-doctor'" and his lament about "how often we see asylums and their unhappy inmates brought in the market and offered for sale, like a flock of sheep, to the highest bidder, in a manner calculated to destroy all public confidence and trust, in the honesty, integrity, and even common respectability of those connected with similar institutions." "Presidential Address," pp. 9–10.

11. Indeed, an editorial in the *Journal of Mental Science* ("The Disabilities of Alienist Physicians," 51, 1905, pp. 144–146) spoke bitterly of the "contumely and insult" the public continued to heap upon the specialty, men it persisted in treating as disreputable and dishonest.

12. Most notably, as Trevor Turner suggests, these included "physical and social damage limitation." "Henry Maudsley," p. 176.

13. "The prejudice against asylums," Sir George Savage lamented, "may be said to be organic." "Presidential Address," *Journal of Mental Science* 59, 1913, p. 19. Cf. Sir James Crichton-Browne's comment about "the odium of having been in an asylum." "The First Maudsley Lecture," p. 203.

14. Cf. L. A. Weatherly's acknowledgement that "this disease . . . is not looked upon by the general public at all in the same light as other diseases; . . . it is considered to be something to be ashamed of, something to be kept a profound secret as long as possible." "Can We Install Rational Ideas Regarding Insanity into the Public Mind?" *British Medical Journal* ii, 1899, pp. 709–710.

15. "The Disabilities of Alienist Physicians," p. 144; emphasis in the original.

16. Ibid.

17. J. Oppenheim, *"Shattered Nerves"*, p. 295.

18. Protesting that such views were "unjust and ill-informed," Crichton-Browne nevertheless acknowledged how tattered psychiatry's reputation had become. "We are, it appears, [in the eyes of one recent and widely read critic,] backward and negligent to a shocking degree. The ignorance of our asylum officers . . . is deplorable. Research is non-existent, our text-books are contemptible, our system of treatment does not conduce to recovery." "The First Maudsley Lecture," p. 201.

19. Crichton-Browne ruefully granted as much when he delivered the first Maudsley lecture; he lamented the "gross misconceptions of our status and performances [which] are prevalent in some quarters" and conceded in the next breath that these were "misconceptions to which we have ourselves in some measure contributed by our proclamation of grievances and calls for reforms." "The First Maudsley Lecture," p. 201.

20. J. Oppenheim, *"Shattered Nerves"*, p. 303; see also M. Clark, "The Rejection of Psychological Approaches to Mental Disorder"; and A. Scull, *The Most Solitary of Afflictions*, pp. 384–388.

21. On this development, see, for example, Martin Stone, "Shellshock and the Psychologists," in W. F. Bynum, R. Porter, and M. Shepherd (eds.), *The Anatomy of Madness* vol. 2, pp. 242–271; and E. Showalter, *The Female Malady*, chap. 7.

22. N. G. Hale, Jr., *Freud and the Americans* New York: Oxford University Press, 1971, p. 48.

23. Ibid.

24. James Jackson Putnam, "Discussion of Edward Wyllys Taylor," *Journal of Nervous and Mental Diseases* 35, 1908, p. 411. In the United States, these advantages allowed psychoanalysts to become increasingly prominent and ultimately the dominant force in the psychiatric profession, a dominance which would persist until the late 1960s or early 1970s. On their failure for the most part to make similar inroads in Britain, cf. the discussion in A. Scull, *The Most Solitary of Afflictions*, pp. 385–388, on which we have drawn here.

25. For a subtle analysis of this "psychiatric dilemma," see J. Oppenheim, *"Shattered Nerves"*, chap. 9.

26. Charles Mercier was particularly vociferous in his opposition to "Freudism" and its followers (cf., for example, *A Textbook of Insanity and Other Mental Diseases* 2d ed., London: Allen and Unwin, 1914); and even after the Great War, Crichton-Browne continued to object to an approach that rested upon the deliberate "ferreting out [of] verminous reminiscences" (*What the Doctor Thought* London: Benn, 1930, p. 228). Such attitudes were widely shared in the medical profession at large, as was demonstrated most vividly in 1911, when David Eder and Ernest Jones addressed the British Medical Association on psychoanalysis. Before their papers could be discussed, the entire audience expressed their outrage by walking out of the room.

INDEX

Abercrombie, J., 139
Ackerknecht, E., 87
Adams, Serjeant, 150, 151, 152
Addington, Anthony, 279n.31
Alexander, Disney, 98
Alexander, Henry, 92
alienists. *See* psychiatry
Alleged Lunatics' Friend Society, 182, 203
Anderson, Elizabeth Garrett, 258–259
antiphlogistic medicine, 26, 326n.118
aphasia, 263
apothecaries, 20
Apothecaries Act (1815), 97
Archives of Neurology, 265
Arlidge, J. T., 200, 332n.40
Arnold, Thomas, 13, 21, 22, 91
Association of Medical Officers of Asylums
  and Hospitals for the Insane, 68, 140, 153,
  156, 175, 194, 203, 210, 211, 217, 232,
  307n.170; and *Journal of Mental Science*,
  188, 194, 196, 197–198, 332n.37,
  338n.119. *See also* Medico-Psychological
  Association
Asylum Journal. See *Journal of Mental Science*
Asylum Journal of Mental Science. See *Journal of
  Mental Science*
asylums: as antitherapeutic, 53–55, 80, 117,
  212–213, 224, 240, 242; architecture of,
  107; attitudes of families towards, 114,
  145–148, 159, 185, 195, 208; costs of,
  168; effects of, on superintendents, 212–
  213, 268; as means of cure, 107, 108–109,
  195; and nonrestraint, 167; overcrowding
  of, 116–117, 166–167, 170, 193, 208; patient attitudes towards, 168–169; pauper,
  7, 105, 170, 172, 307n.167; private, 7, 79–
  80, 154, 178–179, 180–181, 185, 250,
  270–271, 307n.167; regimentation in,
  173, 180; as warehouses, 159, 185, 214,
  268–269, 336n.84. *See also* madhouses
asylum superintendents: role of, 107, 108,
  109, 113, 153, 155–156, 159, 168–169,
  178, 194–195, 201, 214, 224, 269–270,
  303n.111; and Lunacy Commissioners,
  177–180; and nonrestraint, 193
Atheneum, 217
attendants, 167, 180, 193, 240, 248, 335n.83
Auckland, Lord, 58

Bagster, Miss, 41
Baillie, Matthew, 132, 137, 143
Bakewell, Thomas, 65, 278n.28, 281n.68
Barts. *See* St. Bartholomew's Hospital
bath of surprise, 335n.75
Battie, William, 21, 27, 278n.31
Beddoes, Thomas, 12
Bedfordshire County Asylum, 165,
  333n.53
Bedlam. *See* Bethlem
Belle Grove Asylum, 21
Bellot, H. H., 60
Bennett, J. R., 59
Bentham, Jeremy, 28
Bethlehem Hospital. *See* Bethlem
Bethlem, 8, 12, 15, 17, 25, 26, 28, 41, 45, 89,
  138; and Lunacy Commissioners, 154–
  156; and Morison, 149, 151–152, 153;
  physical condition of, 18–20, 30; pictures
  of, 16, 154; and restraint, 150–152, 251;
  and Savage, 251–252; site of third hospital,
  20, 36; treatment of patients in, 30–33,
  155–156; visit to, by reformers in 1814,
  29–31; and Wakefield, 28–29, 33
Bethlem Governors, 15, 16, 18–19, 29, 150,
  154–155, 217, 284n.104; attitudes of, to
  Haslam and Monro, 32–33, 36; and James
  Norris, 32, 35, 106; responses of, to criticism, 31–32, 36
Bicêtre, 133
biography, 4
Birkbeck, George, 25
Blandford, George Fielding, 224, 250, 271
bleeding, 26, 33, 93, 106, 137, 170, 206
boarding out system, 188
bourgeoisie, 5
Boyd, Robert, 242
Brain, 188, 220, 224, 244, 339n.131
brain: appearances of, in insanity, 26, 101
Brewer, John, 11
Bright, John, 216
Brislington House Asylum, 145
British Medical Association, 221, 234, 243,
  352n.26. *See also* Provincial Medical and
  Surgical Association
British Medical Journal, 196, 223, 234, 248
Broadbent, William, 262–263, 266
bromides, 241

Thornhill, John, 136
Thorpe, Robert, 162
Thurnham, John, 197
Ticehurst House Asylum, 145, 262, 313n.83,
340n.148
Tierney, Sir Matthew, 137, 143
Times, 31, 36, 65, 66, 68, 251, 252
Todd, Eli, 101
Tomes, Nancy, 194
Townsend, Maryanne. *See* Bucknill, Lady
Maryanne
Townsend, Thomas, 190
trade in lunacy, 6, 13, 17, 20–22, 43, 55, 77–
78, 85, 93–95, 105–106, 180–181
Trimmer, Rev. H.S., 151, 315n.101
Trollope, Anthony, 50
Trotter, Thomas, 91
trust, 6, 275n.10, 351n.10
Tuileries, 18
Tuke, Daniel Hack, 188, 250, 251, 261,
332n.40
Tuke, Samuel, 27–28, 29, 33, 92, 134, 203,
204; his praise of Haslam, 28, 30; on re-
straint, 66, 68
Tuke, Thomas Harrington, 210, 234, 238,
242, 243, 244, 246–249, 250, 251,
336n.99, 338n.119, 345n.92
Tuke, William, 10, 27, 33, 37, 66, 91, 92, 97,
159, 169, 173, 203, 204, 303n.97
Turner, Thomas, 172, 178, 181, 183
Turner, Trevor, 262
Tuthill, Sir George, 149
typhus, 192

Unitarians, 162, 163, 165, 177, 318n.10; and
social reform, 164, 320n.25
University College Hospital, 190, 229
University College London. *See* University of
London
University of London, 52, 56–61, 62, 64,
142, 150, 190, 229, 234, 237, 250, 264
Ure, Andrew, 59
Uwins, David, 98

Visiting Physicians, 156, 164, 178, 261,
316n.118, 317n.121, 326n.118
vomiting: as treatment, 25, 26, 33

Wakefield Asylum. *See* West Riding Asylum
Wakefield, Edward: and medical profession,
37–38, 92–93; and Select Committee on
Madhouses, 33, 34, 36, 38; visits of, to
Bethlem, 28–31
Wakley, Thomas: and Conolly, 55,
290n.25, 292n.80, 294n.140; and
Haslam, 287nn.153 and 162; and
Morison, 136; and nonrestraint, 67–
68, 71
Walk, Alexander, 266
Wallett, George, 37
Walpole, Spencer, 215, 216
Warburton, Thomas, 279n.31
Warrington, 161, 162
Warwick, 62
Western, Charles Callis, 29
Westminster Hospital, 127
West Riding Asylum, 134, 141, 165, 230,
320n.31, 339n.131
whips, 29, 66
Wilkes, James, 176, 179, 180, 181, 202,
326n.123
Williams, Rhys, 243
Willis, Francis, 23, 24, 278n.27
Willis, Francis, Jr., 96
Wiltshire County Asylum, 197
Wimpole Street, 188, 217
Winslow, Forbes Benignus, 98, 197, 199,
200, 268, 333nn.50 and 53
Winslow, Lionel Forbes, 268
women: in asylums, 106
Wood, Alexander, 126, 308n.9
Wood, George, 126
Wood, William, 241
Wood End Asylum, 245
Woodhouse, John, 15
Worcester County Asylum, 212
work. *See* employment of patients
workhouses, 120, 214; and lunatics, 173,
176, 185, 200
working class. *See* proletariat
Working Man's Companion, 64
Wright, Edward, 138, 140–141
wrongful confinement: public fear of, 40, 74–
77, 181–183, 223

Yellowlees, David, 264
York Asylum, 230
York Retreat, 27, 28, 37, 66, 91, 92, 134,
203, 320n.26
Young, Grace, 158

ABOUT THE AUTHORS

Andrew Scull is Professor of Sociology and Science Studies at the University of California, San Diego. His many publications in the history of psychiatry include *Museums of Madness*; *Social Order/Mental Disorder: Anglo-American Psychiatry in Historical Perspective*; and *The Most Solitary of Afflictions: Madness and Society in Britian, 1700–1900*. Charlotte MacKenzie is Inspector for the Higher Education Funding Council for England. Nicholas Hervey is Principal Care Manager for Mental Health Services for the London Borough of Southwark.